AF292464

EDITED BY TINA PANG

HONG KONG VISUAL CULTURE: THE M+ GUIDE

Over 200 illustrations in colour

Thames &Hudson

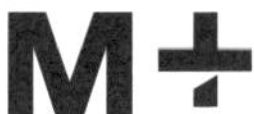

First published in the United Kingdom in 2021 by
Thames & Hudson Ltd, 181A High Holborn, London WC1V 7QX,
in collaboration with M+, West Kowloon Cultural District,
38 Museum Drive, Kowloon, Hong Kong

Editor: Tina Pang
Editorial supervision: Pauline J. Yao
Assistant editor: Chloe Chow
Project management: Kary Woo
English editing: Andrew Goodhouse
Chinese editing: Lam Lap Wai, Zhong Yuling
English to Chinese translations: Tong Wai Ho
Chinese to English translations: Sonja Ng
Design: Julia Studio
Publishing manager: Dustin Cosentino
Publishing coordinator: Sylvia Chow
Image rights and reproductions: Tom Morgan, Jacqueline Chan
Image researcher: Rebecca Moldenhauer

British Library Cataloguing-in-Publication Data
A catalogue record for this book is available from
the British Library

ISBN 978-0-500-02496-6

Printed and bound in Thailand by Cyberprint Group Co. Ltd

FOREWORD

Choose Your Own Adventure
Suhanya Raffel

That the visual culture of Hong Kong informs M+'s ambition, voice, and activities has been clear since the institution's inception. To work in the context of this city is to allow it to guide one's position, to look along the perspectives it defines, and to gain from the opportunities it offers. For M+, this positioning offers a rich opportunity to uncover relationships, follow histories, and propose new lines of research, collaboration, and conversation that lead in many directions. Hong Kong's historic mix of the local and the international has been a core assumption that M+ has used to develop a range of projects about the city and its connections far beyond. Hong Kong is intrinsic to M+, no matter what we do. Rather than simply celebrating our home, we recognise the myriad realities of belonging that are woven deeply into the city's fabric, allowing them to define our approach to researching and collecting visual culture. This book brings to readers some of the relationships we have formed and the questions we are posing. It uses the M+ Collections as a lens to introduce the scope and scale of the museum's engagement with visual culture in Hong Kong and to suggest directions for future projects and for other stories.

This guide presents Hong Kong visual culture from the M+ Collections according to three categories: things, places, and perspectives. The idea of a guide implies an itinerary, a companion for the reader on their journey through the material. The structure of this book is simple, and the texts are short and easy to digest. But the paths that it charts branch in many directions, leading to a density and a complexity that are characteristic of Hong Kong's visual histories and realities. The project records of the Hong Kong Hilton offer a rich example. The hotel was designed by the architect James H. Kinoshita of the renowned firm Palmer & Turner, and it became a symbol of Hong Kong's position as an international centre of commerce upon its completion in 1963. The hotel commissioned its branding from Henry Steiner—whose graphic-design work pervades the modern history of the city—and invited prominent artists such as Douglas Bland, Cheung Yee, and David Lam to create work for its interiors. During the civil unrest that swept

Hong Kong in 1967, the hotel served as a refuge. It saw its heyday in the 1970s, with its club the Den, a fixture of the city's nightlife, and its introduction of the in-room minibar in 1974, a simple yet inspired innovation that fundamentally altered the hotel industry worldwide. The Hilton was demolished in 1995, and today its site is occupied by the Cheung Kong Center office tower. The bare facts of the three decades of the Hilton's life hint at the multiple directions and varied possibilities that a study of its design history, social history, and cultural legacy could take. This is what is offered in *Hong Kong Visual Culture: The M+ Guide*: a fascinating collection of stories and signposts related to the cultural spaces of Hong Kong.

Here, the reader is presented with choices, in an invitation to explore and to encounter Hong Kong visual culture. Through a strategy of collecting, exhibitions, programmes, and publications, M+ continues to engage with Hong Kong, to learn from it, and to contribute to it. In this spirit, with this book as a guide, I say: have a safe journey, have a pleasant stay, and welcome home.

INTRODUCTION

Dear Reader
Tina Pang

In this book, you will find works of art, design objects, and architectural projects from M+'s collection of Hong Kong visual culture. By bringing together grand narratives, intimate histories, and nuanced interpretations, it embraces openness and multiplicity and is a reflection of M+'s cross-disciplinary approach to research and collecting. This is a guide to reading the city through its images and things.

The guide is divided into three chapters: 'Things', 'Places', and 'Perspectives'. The objects and ideas in each are connected by individual and collective histories, patterns of consumption, and global relationships of circulation. The first chapter of the book, titled 'Things', looks at the material culture that has shaped the history of Hong Kong. Beginning in the early twentieth century, Hong Kong produced a vast range of things for both local and global markets. The city benefited from the skills and capital that accompanied migrants in the aftermath of the Chinese Civil War and from access to international markets thanks to its strategic geographic location and its status as a British colony. As a global centre of finance and logistics and a Special Administrative Region of China, Hong Kong found a new place on the international landscape. The material presented here shows some of the ways in which the city has engaged with the world, and how everyday materials have inspired artistic and design practices.

Hong Kong is among the most recognisable cities in the world, largely as a result of its representation in film. Some may recall the pastiche set of the Repulse Bay Hotel in Ann Hui's 1984 adaptation of Eileen Chang's novel *Love in a Fallen City*, published in 1943, or Faye Wong's languorous journey up the Central–Mid-levels Escalator in Wong Kar-wai's postmodern romance *Chungking Express* (1994). But it is the unique skyline of the central business district, which sits between the harbourfront and Victoria Peak—the backdrop to so many Hong Kong films—that unmistakably defines the city. The second chapter, 'Places', addresses some of Hong Kong's most important architectural projects and examines how the city has been a creative catalyst.

The third chapter, 'Perspectives', views Hong Kong through the practices of artists who offer personal, introspective, and inevitably political interpretations of their lived experiences. The nature of artistic practice resists being identified as culturally specific, speaking as it does with a timbre beyond language or location. The works included in this section are presented to express personal as well as shared sentiments about Hong Kong.

This book is M+'s most comprehensive statement yet on Hong Kong visual culture, but it is part of a much larger discussion on the city's histories, cultures, and individual creative practices. The works that we have selected during the process of building M+'s collection of Hong Kong visual culture have led us to investigate new lines of enquiry. There are many more areas to be uncovered. For example, the Cantonese language plays a quiet but central role in the visual culture of the city. Like Hong Kong itself, it collapses the distinction between local and global. For years the language of Chinatowns around the world when patterns of migration from China were limited, Cantonese was disseminated through Hong Kong film and Cantopop. The reader of this guide could keep this question in mind in order to look for aspects of another story, one that is not addressed directly here but which is nonetheless at the heart of the historical narratives and contemporary experiences of Hong Kong. This guide is meant as a point of departure, and we include a map illustrated by Don Mak to introduce another way of navigating the interconnected stories of things, places, and perspectives in Hong Kong. It is in this spirit of possibility and open-endedness that we look forward to continuing the exploration with you.

ACKNOWLEDGEMENTS

Putting together this guide to the visual culture of Hong Kong would not have been possible without the support of Suhanya Raffel, Museum Director, M+, who leads the museum in placing Hong Kong at the centre of our work; the guidance and support of Doryun Chong, Deputy Director, Curatorial, and Chief Curator, who defined the direction of the book from its earliest beginnings; and the work of Pauline J. Yao, Lead Curator, Visual Art, who provided key advice through its development and production.

At my side have been Chloe Chow, former Associate Curator, Hong Kong Visual Culture, whose commitment and energy have been instrumental in shaping the content of this book, and Andrew Goodhouse, Editor, whose critical eye has endowed the multiple histories and ideas presented here with a consistent editorial tone. Kary Woo, Curatorial Assistant, has overseen the project with mastery and skill, corralling resources across the museum and elsewhere to ensure the project stayed on track. I am also highly indebted to Lam Lap Wai, Senior Editor, and Zhong Yuling, Editor, with whom we have worked closely to shape the editorial voice of the Chinese edition. Fei Tse, Curatorial Assistant, has worked tirelessly to support the team throughout, ably assisted by curatorial interns Eunice Cheung and Yannis Lo. No publication on visual culture can effectively communicate without images, and Tom Morgan, Senior Manager, Rights and Reproductions, and Jacqueline Chan, Copyright and Licensing Officer, have supported us in clearing rights, assisted by Rebecca Moldenhauer.

The multiple perspectives contained here represent the research and insight of many writers and colleagues. I thank Blues Wong and Sylvia Chan for their generous contributions, and extend my gratitude to Shirley Surya, Curator, Design and Architecture, and Jennifer Wong, former Assistant Curator, Design and Architecture.

I thank Li Cheuk-to, Curator, Hong Kong Film and Media, and Chanel Kong, Associate Curator, Moving Image, for lending their expertise to the moving image texts. Special thanks go to John Carroll for his invaluable comments on the English manuscript, and to Chow Yiu Fai for his close reading of the Chinese manuscript. Vivian Poon ensured the accuracy of much of the content. Any factual discrepancies or errors are entirely my own.

A publication such as this is not possible without accurate information about the collections, and for this we have been magnanimously supported by the Conservation team led by Jo-Fan Huang, Senior Conservator; the Collections Registration team, led by Keri Towler, Senior Registrar; Hester Chan, Curator, Collections; and Fion Wong, Curatorial Assistant, all of whom worked closely with us to verify the details of works. Kevin Forkan, former Head, Archives and Library, and Rebecca Yiu, Assistant Archivist, supported us with new research and information on the many archival works represented here. Lok Cheng, Manager, Photo Studio; Dan Leung, Picture Editor; and Davis Leung, Copyright and Images Officer, were generous in photographing parts of the collection where new images were needed.

I thank Julia Studio for their design and reading of the material. Dustin Cosentino, Senior Manager, Museum Publishing, and Sylvia Chow, Publishing Coordinator, shepherded the book through the production process and gave expert guidance. I thank them and our publishing partner, Thames & Hudson, in particular Lucas Dietrich, Editorial Director, for ensuring a wider readership for the unique story of Hong Kong's visual culture. I also thank Jonathan Earl, who played an important role in facilitating early discussions on M+'s nascent publishing programme.

Lars Nittve, inaugural Executive Director, M+, established many of the defining characteristics of M+ and I will be forever indebted to him for giving me the opportunity to play a part in shaping the Hong Kong Visual Culture collections. I owe much to former Managing Curator, Tobias Berger, and former Associate Curator, Yung Ma, for their foundational work in this area and for their generous support during the museum's formative years.

Conversations with many friends, scholars, and writers have contributed to the content contained in this book. Thanks go to Cynthia Tongson and John Young for helping us build a fuller picture of the plastics industry in Hong Kong, to Henry Steiner and Kan Tai-keung for their accounts of Hong Kong's design histories, and to M+ Design Trust fellows Daniel Cooper and Julianna Kei, whose research on Hong Kong's participation at Expo '70 has enriched our ability to interpret this history. Conversations with John Warner and Rose Lam have added to our knowledge of aspects of institutional and artistic histories of the 1960s and 1970s. I would also like to thank Helen Ting and Alice Tam for entrusting M+ with the Lui Shou-kwan Archive, which will yield many further lines of research in years to come.

Finally, my thanks go to Don Mak for his clever, playful interpretation of Hong Kong visual culture and his elegant sensitivity, and to all the artists, architects, designers, and filmmakers included in the M+ Collections, whose works inspire and motivate us in equal measure.

Tina Pang
Curator, Hong Kong Visual Culture, M+

NOTE TO THE READER

Cantonese has no standardised romanisation system. The names in this book follow the preferences of individual artists, designers, and architects, or received use.

Texts by:
Sylvia Chan (SC)
Chloe Chow (CC)
Tina Pang (TP)
Shirley Surya (SS)
Fei Tse (FT)
Blues Wong (BW)
Jennifer Wong (JW)
Kary Woo (KW)

Unless otherwise noted in the captions, all works are in the collections of M+, Hong Kong.

TIMELINE

Key social, historical, and economic events

1800s

1842: The Treaty of Nanking extends the terms of foreign trade with China, ends the First Opium War, and cedes Hong Kong Island to the British. Hong Kong becomes a Crown colony of the United Kingdom.

1860: The First Convention of Peking brings the Second Opium War to a close and cedes the Kowloon Peninsula to the British.

1865: The Hongkong Bank establishes its head office in Hong Kong.

1868–1904: The Praya Reclamation Scheme extends the land into Victoria Harbour by approximately twenty-four hectares.

1869–1933: Hong Kong's first city hall is built on Queen's Road.

1888: The Peak Tram, running between Central district and Victoria Peak, begins operating. It is considered a triumph of engineering.

1894: An outbreak of bubonic plague in Hong Kong kills thousands. The city is at the centre of an epidemiological race to find a vaccine. Control measures imposed by the colonial government, including the practise of Western medicine and the removal of the dead for burial elsewhere, generate disquiet among the Chinese population. The heart of the epidemic in Tai Ping Shan is razed and an epidemiological centre is established nearby (today's Museum of Medical Sciences).

1898: With the Second Convention of Peking, the New Territories are leased to the British from the Qing Empire for ninety-nine years. A Chinese walled garrison is excluded from the terms of the convention and later becomes the Kowloon Walled City.

1898: The Kowloon Ferry Company is sold to the Hongkong and Kowloon Wharf and Godown Company. It is renamed the Star Ferry Company that same year.

1900–1930s

1904: The first trams begin operating on Hong Kong Island, from Kennedy Town in the west to Causeway Bay in the east.

1911: The Republican revolution ends dynastic rule in China.

1912: Establishment of the Republic of China.

1912: The University of Hong Kong opens, offering an English-language university education.

1916: The southern terminus of the Kowloon–Canton Railway opens in Tsim Sha Tsui.

1925: An airport is developed at Kai Tak. Located in urban Kowloon, it becomes known as one of the most difficult airports in the world for landings.

1933: The old city hall is demolished to make way for a new, larger Hongkong Bank building.

1937: Japan invades China, beginning the Second Sino-Japanese War.

1940s

1941–1945: Japan occupies Hong Kong.

1946: Cathay Pacific Airways is established.

1947–1949: Chinese Civil War.

1949: The People's Republic of China is established. Shanghai companies relocate to Hong Kong, and around one million people leave mainland China for the city, bringing the population to 2.5 million by the mid-1950s.

Late 1940s: Chinese-language cinema grows in popularity across Southeast Asia.

1949: The New Asia College is established by scholars from mainland China. In 1963, the college is incorporated into the Chinese University of Hong Kong.

1950s

1950–1972: Trade restrictions are imposed on China by the United States and the United Nations after the establishment of the People's Republic in 1949 and the beginning of the Korean War in 1950. With access to China off limits, Hong Kong industrialists turn from trade to manufacturing.

1953: A massive fire in Shek Kip Mei destroys squatter areas, leaving 58,000 people homeless. The disaster accelerates a resettlement programme for migrants and a government-led public housing initiative.

1953: The Fung Ping Shan Library for Chinese-language books established in 1932 at the University of Hong Kong becomes a museum of Chinese art and archaeology.

1957: New Star Ferry piers are built on reclaimed land in Central on Hong Kong Island and in Tsim Sha Tsui in Kowloon.

1959: Textiles, clothing, rattan ware, enamel, and plastic toys and flowers make up 70 per cent of all goods exported from Hong Kong. This represents an increase of 40 per cent in six years.

1960s

1961: Run Run Shaw establishes Shaw Brothers Studios in Clear Water Bay.

1962: City Hall opens with the City Museum and Art Gallery, a library, a theatre, and a concert hall.

1966: A peaceful hunger strike against a proposed 25 per cent fare increase on the Star Ferry leads to Hong Kong's first large-scale civil unrest, and three days of rioting.

1967: TVB television station is founded, offering the first free-to-air broadcasts.

1967: Influenced by the Cultural Revolution in China, labour strikes at a plastic-flower factory in Kowloon spark six months of anti-colonial riots across Hong Kong.

1969: The first Festival of Hong Kong takes place.

1970s

1970: Hong Kong participates in the World Exposition in Osaka, the first time an international exposition has been held in Asia.

1972: Opening of the first cross-harbour tunnel.

1972: Radio Television Hong Kong's *Below the Lion Rock* television series begins.

1973: The government begins to develop 'new town' projects in the New Territories to relieve population density in Hong Kong Island and Kowloon.

1973: Robert Clouse's film *Enter the Dragon*, starring Bruce Lee, is a turning point in martial-arts filmmaking, leading to greater international awareness of Hong Kong action cinema.

Mid-1970s–1990s: Cantopop becomes a phenomenon.

1975: Building of the Mass Transit Railway (MTR) begins. It is completed in the late 1980s. The City Museum and Art Gallery is divided into separate art and history museums.

1975: The southern terminus of the Kowloon–Canton Railway is relocated from Tsim Sha Tsui to a larger site on newly reclaimed land in Hung Hom. The station's clocktower is preserved in its original location.

1975: The first group of Vietnamese refugees fleeing the aftermath of the United States–Vietnam War arrives in Hong Kong.

1979: Hong Kong is declared a 'port of first asylum'.

1979: Directors who come to be known as the Hong Kong New Wave emerge, continuing the success of the city's film industry.

1980s

1982: The establishment of the Shenzhen Special Economic Zone sees manufacturing move to China, and Hong Kong shift towards becoming a finance- and service-based economy. China's economic reforms from the late 1970s onwards encourage Hong Kong investment in Guangdong. By the mid-1990s, around 90 per cent of Hong Kong's factories have relocated to Shenzhen.

1984: The signing of the Sino-British Joint Declaration by Prime Minister Margaret Thatcher of the United Kingdom and Premier Zhao Ziyang of China settles the terms of Hong Kong's return to Chinese sovereignty when the lease of the New Territories expires in 1997.

1985: Norman Foster's design for the fourth HSBC building is completed. It is the most expensive building in the world at the time.

1988: Hong Kong introduces the Comprehensive Plan of Action, which changes the refugee status of boat people arriving from Vietnam to asylum seekers who can be repatriated.

1989: More than one million people march in Hong Kong, in solidarity with student demonstrators in Beijing's Tiananmen Square.

1990s

1990: The Bank of China opens its Hong Kong headquarters. I. M. Pei is the architect of the seventy-storey building in the central business district.

1993: The Central–Mid-levels Escalator opens. At eight hundred metres, it is the longest escalator system in the world. Work begins on the first phase of the Central and Wanchai Reclamation project. Public opposition to the project, including from the Society for the Protection of the Harbour, limits the amount of land reclaimed.

1995: The Kowloon Walled City is razed and the site is transformed into a public park.

1997: On 1 July, Hong Kong reverts to Chinese sovereignty as a special administrative region. The Basic Law of the Hong Kong Special Administrative Region of the People's Republic of China comes into effect. Under this law, Hong Kong retains a high degree of autonomy under the 'one country, two systems' principle, to remain effective until at least 2047.

1997: Outbreak of H5N1 avian influenza.

1997–1999: The Asian financial crisis affects East and Southeast Asia.

1998: The Hong Kong International Airport at Chek Lap Kok, designed by Norman Foster, replaces Kai Tak as the city's airport. Tung Chee-hwa, the first chief executive of the Hong Kong Special Administrative Region, proposes the establishment of the West Kowloon Cultural District to develop Hong Kong as an Asian cultural hub.

2000s

2000: The Hong Kong Heritage Museum opens in Sha Tin, focusing on the art, history, and culture of Hong Kong.

2001: Hong Kong's first official participation in the Venice Biennale.

2003: An outbreak of severe acute respiratory syndrome (SARS) in Hong Kong kills nearly three hundred people.

2003: The second IFC tower (Two IFC) opens as the then-tallest building in Hong Kong, at 88 storeys and 415 metres. It is home to the Hong Kong Monetary Authority.

2003: Cantopop and film icons Leslie Cheung and Anita Mui die within nine months of each other.

2003: A bill to enact national security legislation (Article 23 of the Basic Law) is withdrawn due to widespread opposition.

2005: Shaw Studios opens at a new site in Tseung Kwan O with extensive digital, social media, and streaming production facilities.

2006: The Central Star Ferry Pier, with its historic clocktower, is demolished as part of the Central and Wanchai Reclamation project. It is relocated further west to Central Ferry Piers 7 and 8 on newly reclaimed land.

2010s

2011: The International Commerce Centre tower opens at West Kowloon. At 118 storeys and 484 metres, it is the tallest building in Hong Kong.

2011: The Legislative Council and Central Government Complex, designed by Rocco Yim, opens on a newly reclaimed site on the Central waterfront.

2011: Foster + Partners' City Park is selected from three proposals as the masterplan for the West Kowloon Cultural District.

2013: Herzog & de Meuron win an international architectural competition to design the M+ building.

2014: The Standing Committee of the National People's Congress proposes changes to the Hong Kong electoral system. These changes would allow a nominating committee to pre-screen candidates for the position of chief executive of Hong Kong. Demonstrations are held in opposition to the proposals, sparking a seventy-nine-day occupation of parts of central Hong Kong. Known as the Umbrella Movement, the occupation brings the city to a standstill.

2018: The Hong Kong phase of the Guangzhou–Shenzhen–Hong Kong Express Rail Link opens at West Kowloon.

2019: Widespread opposition to the proposed introduction of a bill allowing the extradition of fugitives to places without extradition arrangements with Hong Kong, including mainland China, Taiwan, and Macau, leads to months of protests.

2019: COVID-19, an acute respiratory illness caused by a coronavirus, is first detected in Wuhan. By March 2020, its global spread has been declared a pandemic by the World Health Organization.

2020s

2020: The Standing Committee of the National People's Congress introduces the National Security Law in Hong Kong.

2021: The M+ building opens.

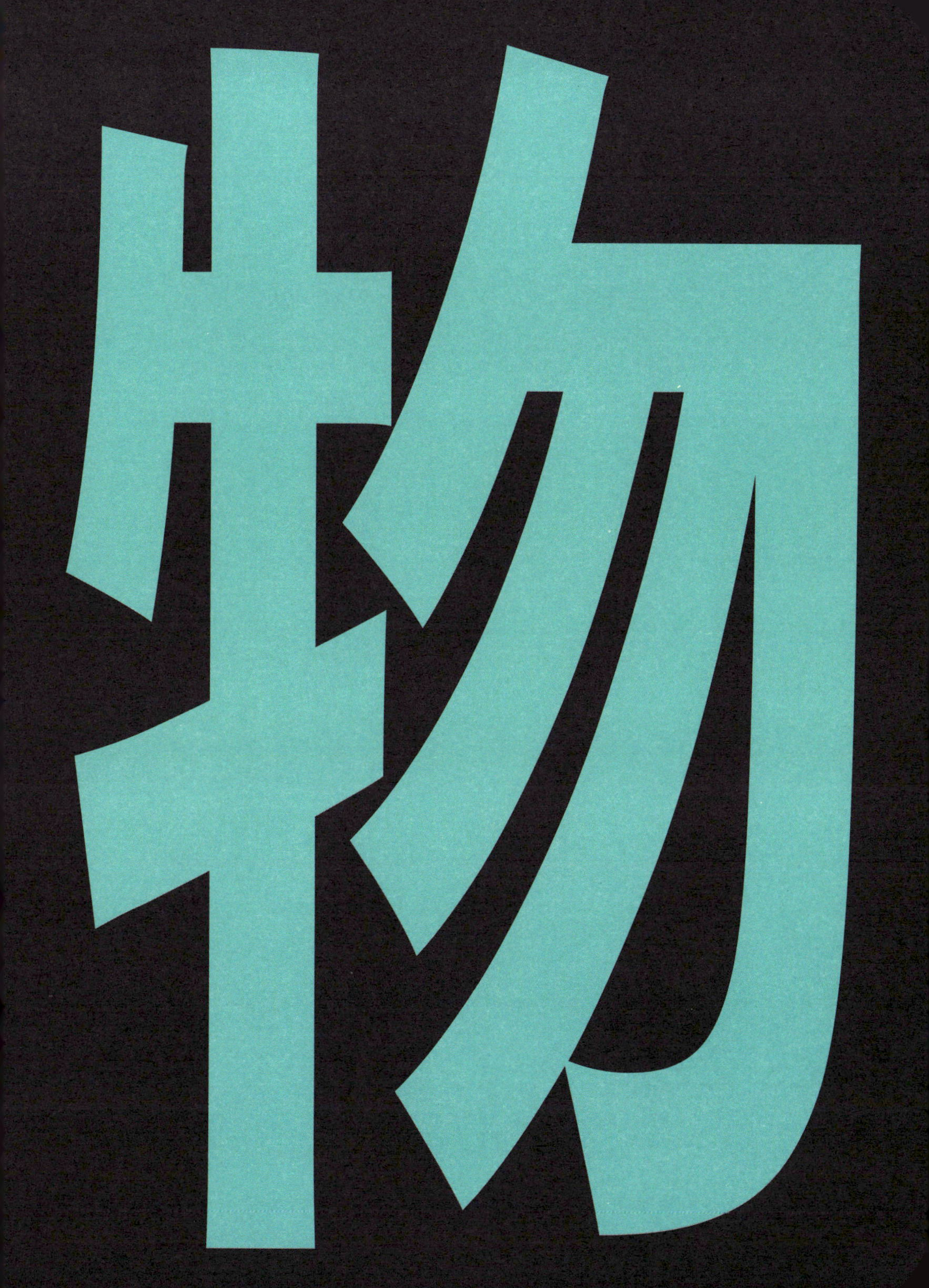

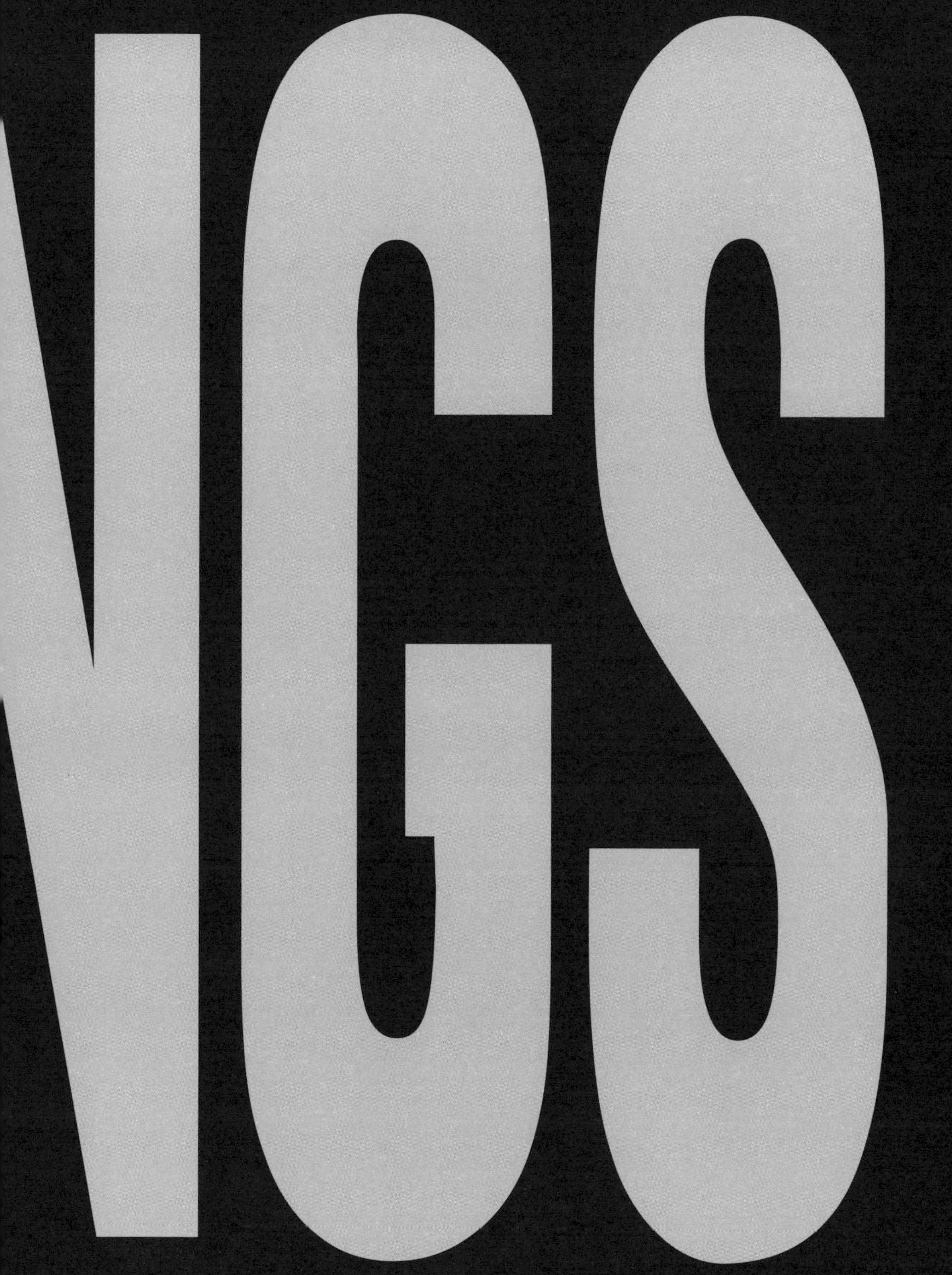

In 1970, when Hong Kong took part in the World Exposition in Osaka, the city's status as a British colony turned out to be an inadvertent publicity coup. The press reported on the one dependent territory among the seventy-six nations participating. At Expo '70, memories of Hong Kong's anti-colonial riots of 1967 were still fresh, and the Hong Kong Pavilion was defined as a means to promote the city as a cosmopolitan hub of manufacturing. Central to this positioning were internationally recognised 'made in Hong Kong' products such as cameras, clothing, watches, and plastic consumer goods.

The set of materials presented in this chapter weaves between the realities of Hong Kong's manufacturing past and present, and interpretations of how materials, ideas, and practices have developed. The story that emerges is one that pays equal attention to everyday and exceptional things, grouped into three sections. The first, 'Made in Hong Kong', addresses objects that were produced in Hong Kong and widely circulated. The second section, 'Leap the Stage', examines how artists and designers moved into the spotlight with new visual languages informed in equal measure by adaptation of and innovation with a wide range of imagery. The third section, 'Are You Crazy?', considers the deep, lasting impact of histories and popular culture on creative practices.

The objects included in the first section all demonstrate pragmatism, ingenuity, and a keen awareness of for whom and for what purpose they were made. Many were designed with unpretentious materials and in practical forms. But the histories here are not straightforward, as illustrated by the *Diana* camera, which was initially intended to be given away as a toy, and which has found an audience decades later among a global revival of lo-fi photographic culture.

Alan Chan's airbrushed design for the cover of *Leap the Stage*, the 1984 album by Cantopop diva Anita Mui, provides a lens through which to view the second group of materials, which examines how artists and designers have expanded the boundaries of image-making. Chan's design illustrates Cantopop's position in a global landscape as it references Japanese artist Yamaguchi Harumi's depictions of powerful, sexy female figures and the postmodern designs of the Milan-based Memphis group. Given that Cantopop artists moved seamlessly between music, television, and film, it comes as no surprise that their creativity was supported by intensive collaborations with artists, photographers, and art directors.

Tsang Tsou-choi's iconic calligraphic mark-making across the Kowloon peninsula is a subversive adaptation of Chinese writing conventions, announcing his claim to be the 'King of Kowloon'. Other artists in this section adapt familiar forms in unfamiliar ways, such as Stanley Wong in his influential publicity campaign for Hong Kong's Mass Transit Railway (MTR).

The archival collection of Lambert Yam and Ruby Yang offers unprecedented insight into the consumption of Hong Kong cinema by diasporic communities in North America. The archival material from the Phoenix Cine Club and Lo Yuk-ying, on the other hand, speaks to the circulation of international films among a tight-knit community of artists and critics in Hong Kong. Out of this environment emerged pioneering and experimental works in video in the 1980s and 1990s.

Taking as a prompt part of the title of Chow Chun Fai's satirical homage to Stephen Chow's 1990 film *All for the Winner*, 'Are you crazy?', the third group brings together works that use vernacular ideas and materials in surprising new ways. Michael Young transforms paper-folding into furniture, while Tsang Kin-Wah subverts the decorative conventions of printed wallpaper designs in his irreverent works. This section ends with Sara Wong and Leung Chi Wo's *Museum of the Lost*, which offers a critique of the role of archives in preserving the historical record. The project can also be seen as a comment on the malleability of materials, whose meanings change with each new context.

MADE IN HONG KONG

The wide range of designs and consumer goods produccd
in this global centre of industry and trade

Made in Hong Kong in the 1960s as a giveaway toy, the *Diana* camera has since become part of a global photographic culture. It was first produced by the Great Wall Plastics Factory but was never patented. Other manufacturers quickly produced their own versions, resulting in market saturation. Alongside the falling prices of professional equipment, there was a drop in demand for cheap handheld cameras, and it became unprofitable to continue producing the *Diana* in the 1970s. Nevertheless, the distinctive visual qualities of photographs taken by the camera, which include unpredictable colour discrepancies and a granular texture—a result of light leaking into the plastic body—are admired by professional and amateur photographers alike.

In 2007, the Vienna-based camera manufacturer Lomography, a promoter of experimental film and photography, redesigned the camera and reintroduced it to the market, transforming it into a distinctive cult object for enthusiasts. The *Diana* camera's return has introduced a new generation of photographers around the world to this Hong Kong design.   FT

Great Wall Plastics Factory (established 1955)
***Diana* camera, model no. 151**
1960s–1970s
Plastic
8.9 × 13 × 7.5 cm
2019.339

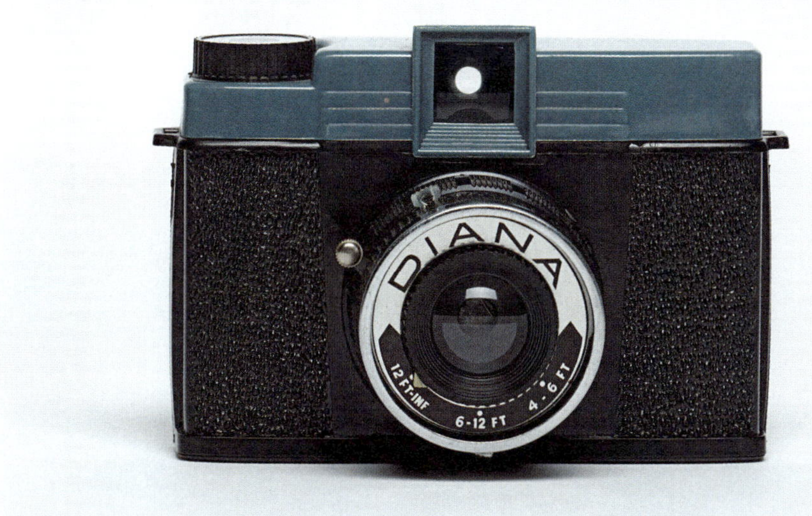

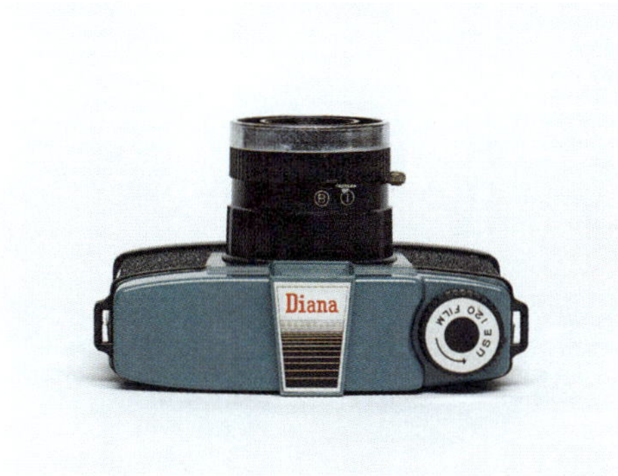

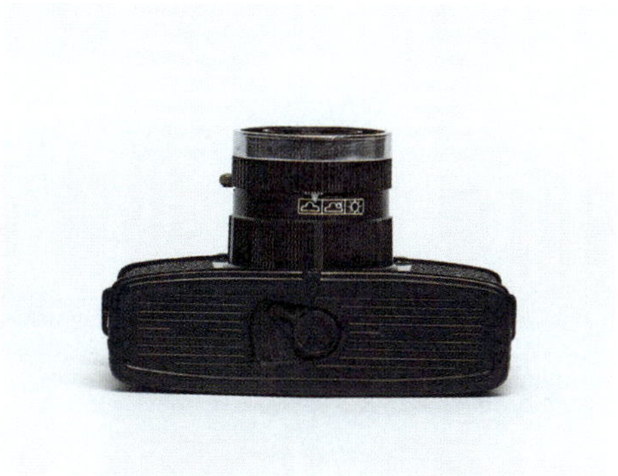

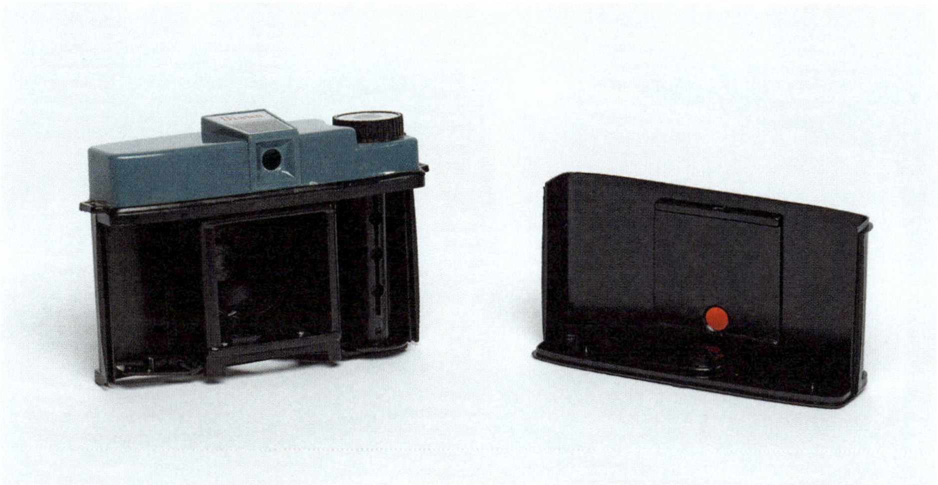

Affordable, high-quality objects made out of imported rattan from Southeast Asia were produced in Hong Kong for both local consumption and export. This child-sized chair, a mid-1950s design attributed to Chan Kin-fai of the Kowloon Rattan Ware Company, is a marked departure from the conventional practice of using rattan to imitate traditional Chinese and Victorian furniture styles. The durability of the material made it an economical and popular choice for those wanting beautiful and practical furniture for everyday use.

Chan's design is an adaptation of three-legged chairs with concave seats commonly used in the Philippines. His version was more durable and could appeal to overseas, specifically American, markets. The success of this design strategy also lay in Chan's adaptation of an extrusion method used to make electrical cables, which allowed the rattan to be coated in PVC. This innovation facilitated cleaning and made it possible to introduce a wider range of colours and patterns. The chair became a fixture in Hong Kong photo studios, featuring in many children's portraits, as its oval, concave seat was thought to keep young models perfectly still during a shoot.

The rattan industry waned in the 1970s as manufacturing moved north to mainland China. As Hong Kong consumers became more affluent, preferences shifted towards larger, upholstered furniture modelled after the latest Euro-American fashions. Changing aspirations eventually led to rattan being replaced by furniture made in wood, leather, metal, and synthetic materials.   JW

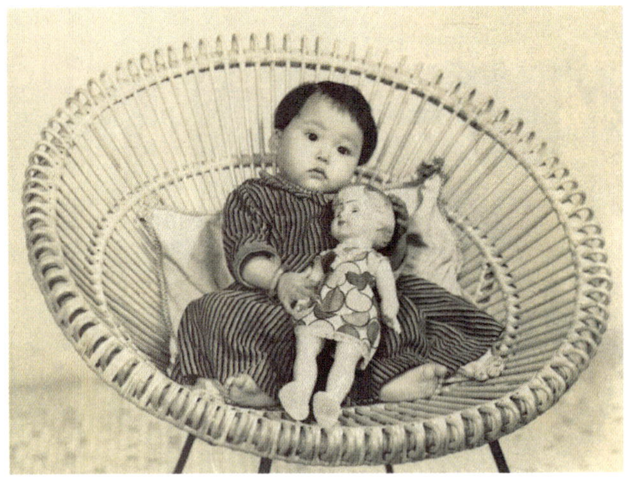

Rattan chair and child during a photo shoot, ca. 1960

Attributed to Kowloon Rattan Ware Company (1925–2003)
Rattan chair
Designed ca. 1954, made 1950s–1960s
Rattan, plastic, iron, and rubber
51 × 52 × 46 cm
2016.373

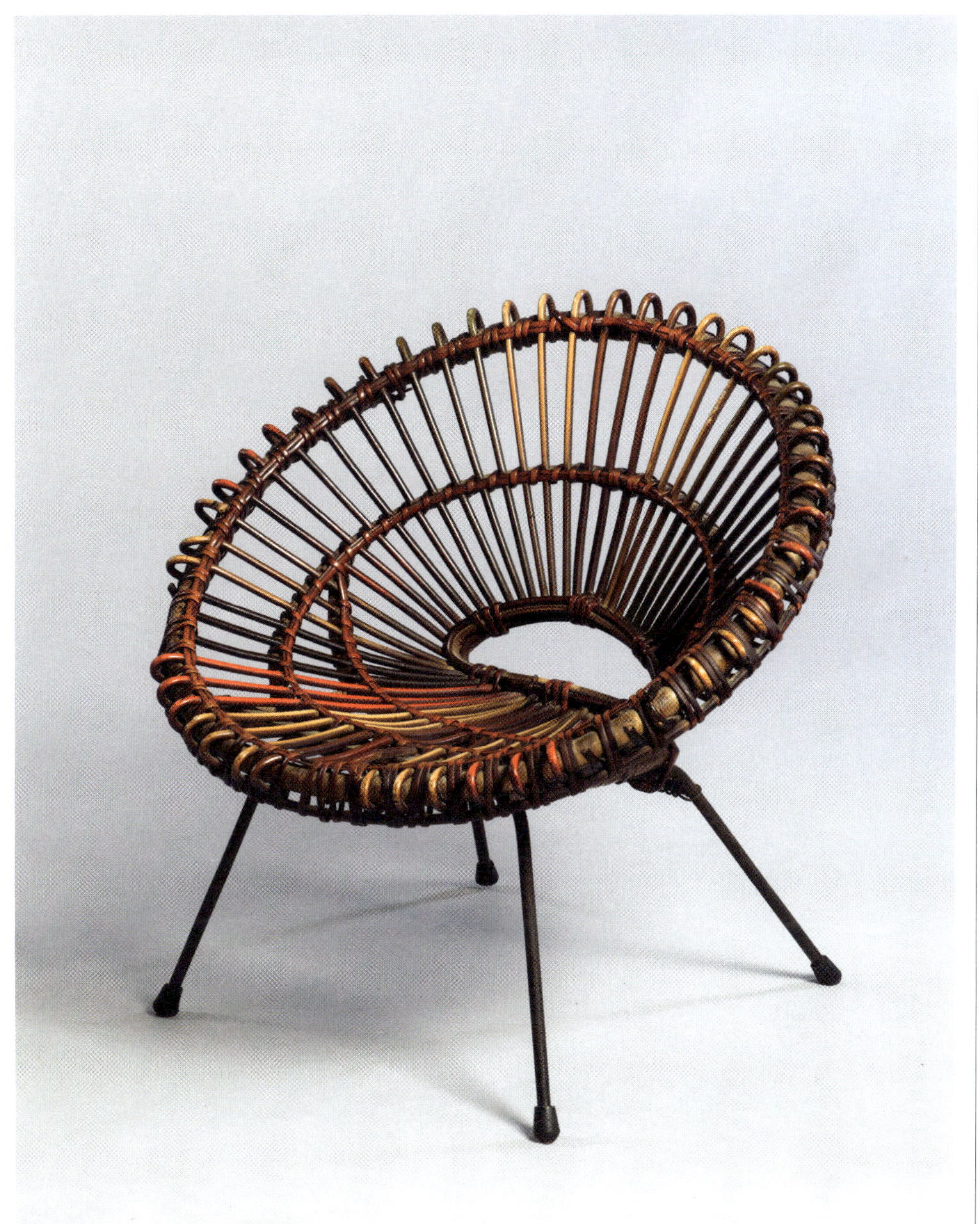

Introduced in the 1970s, this clock became a fixture of offices, banks, hotels, and theatres for its functionality, accuracy, and clean design. The Auto-20 is one of the first clocks to bring together time-keeping and calendar functions in a single, elegant interface. Its success, then and now, lies to a great extent in an ingenious customisable design that allows for either single-language or bilingual Chinese and English dates to be displayed. Inspired by earlier Swiss and Italian designs of the 1960s, the Auto-20 represented an important new shift for its manufacturer, Tai Wah Electrical Manufacturing Company (later TWEMCO Industries), towards a more design- and market-driven mode of manufacturing.

Originally a maker of electrical fans, Tai Wah identified a way to apply its technical know-how to new consumer products. The calendar flip mechanism of the Auto-20 required a complex technical process; Tai Wah were able to simplify and patent this process, thereby keeping costs low and achieving considerable success both in and outside of Hong Kong.   KW

Tai Wah Electrical Manufacturing Company (established 1960)
TWEMCO calendar clock, model Auto-20
1970
Aluminium, iron, acrylic, plastic, and electronic components
53.5 × 51.5 × 10.7 cm
Gift of Twemco Industries Ltd, 2019
2019.345

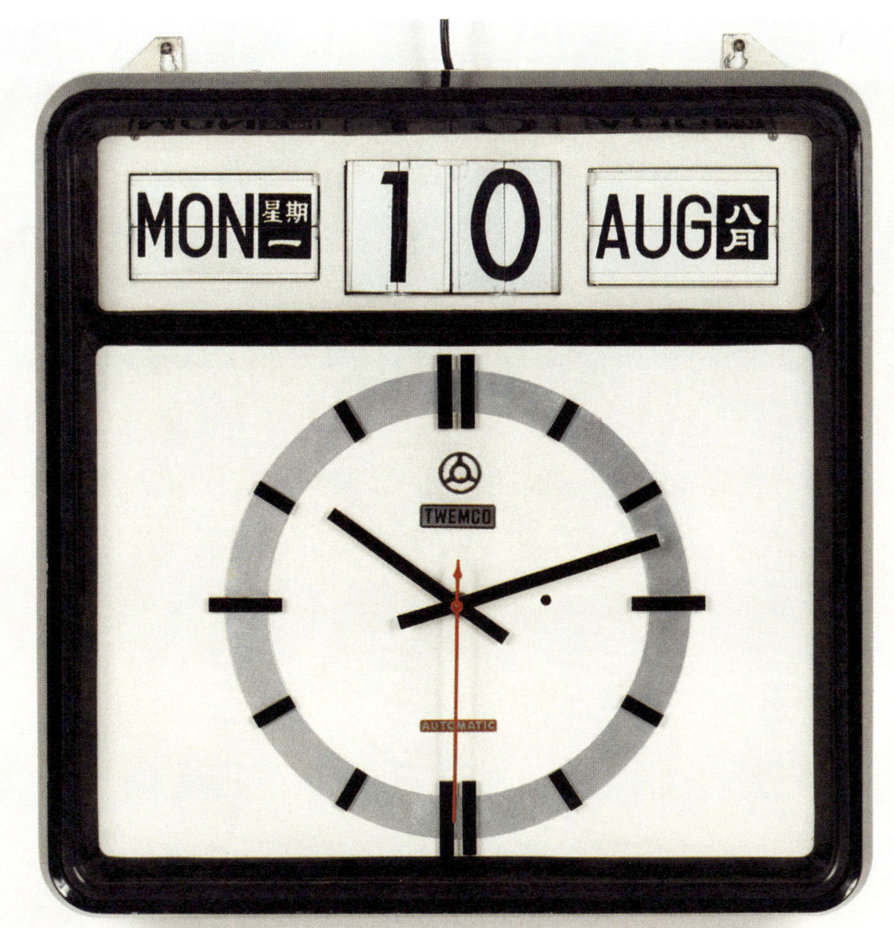
MON 星期一
10
AUG 八月
TWEMCO
AUTOMATIC

In 1962, the Eastern Enamelware Factory moved from Hong Kong to Port Harcourt, Nigeria. The government of Nigeria, which had gained independence from British colonial rule just two years earlier, offered tax credits and land incentives to attract foreign investment, and the Eastern Enamelware Factory responded to a high demand for durable, affordable household goods on the local market. The firm initially used the same moulds it had developed to produce vessels in Hong Kong and replaced the traditional Chinese decorative motifs with representations of local fauna including fish, antelopes, and leopards. Over time, the company created new wares tailored to regional eating conventions. This ability to adapt demonstrates the entrepreneurial spirit and flexibility that drove the Eastern Enamelware Factory's success in Nigeria and, more broadly, the success of Hong Kong manufacturing around the world.   TP

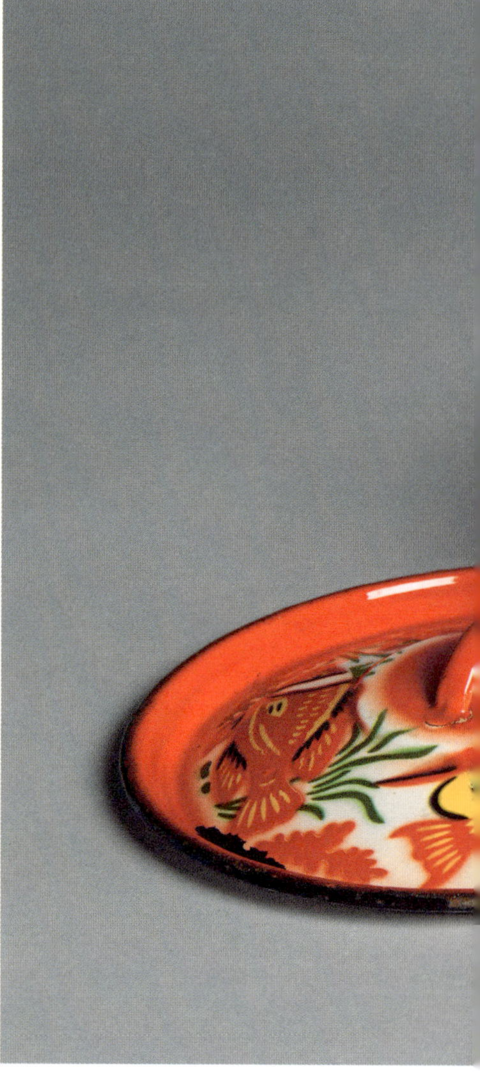

Eastern Enamelware Factory (established 1962)
Footed bowl with cover
Designed ca. 1971, made ca. 1972–early 1980s
Steel and porcelain enamel
14.2 × 22 × 22 cm
Gift of Eastern Enamelware Factory Ltd, 2017
2017.343

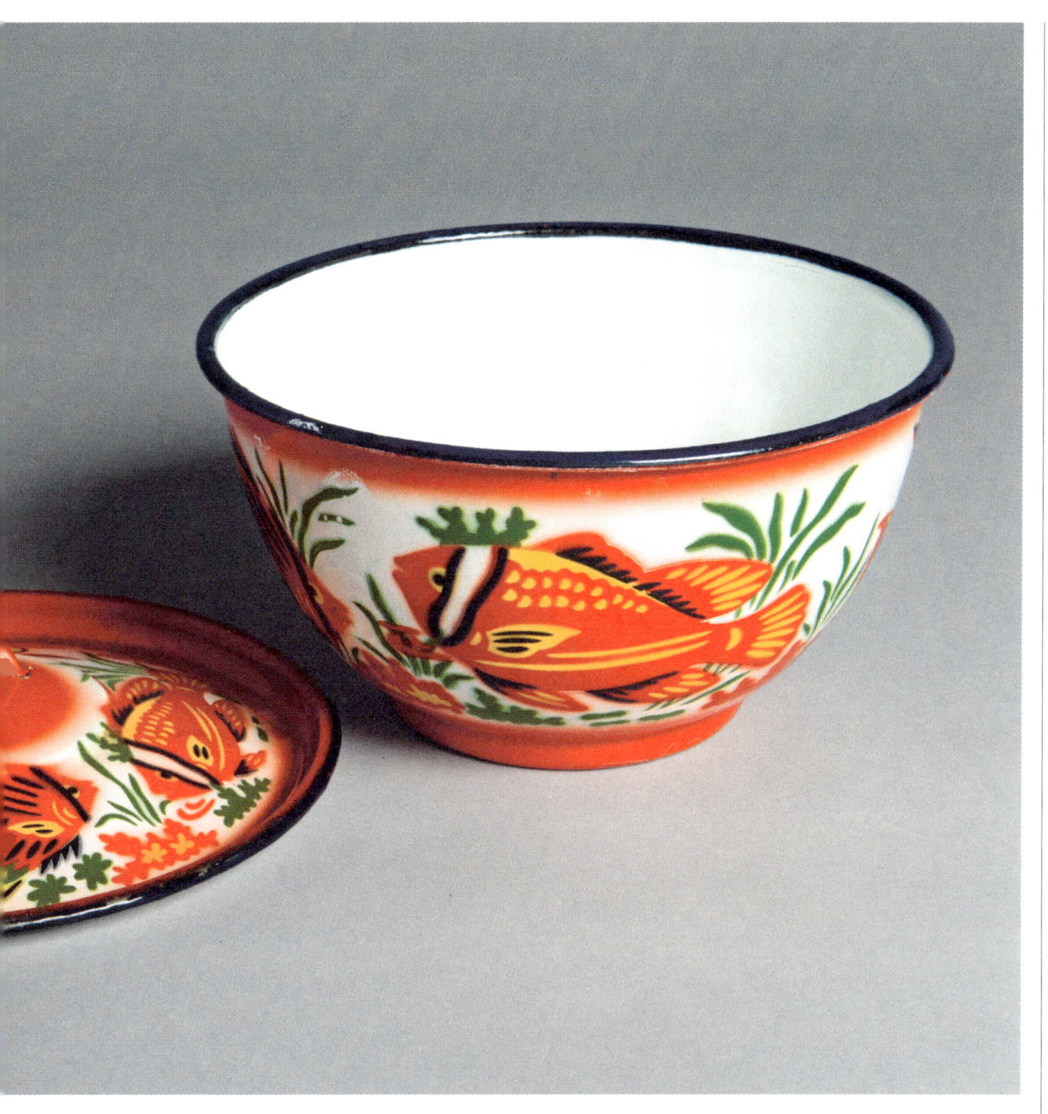

Established in 1956 by a group of seven businessmen in Hong Kong, Tai Ping, whose name means 'great peace', originally made hand-knotted carpets in its small atelier in Castle Peak in the western New Territories. From the start, the company's founders had international ambitions, drawing on their experience in textile exportation and branding products for the American market. Tai Ping pioneered and patented the use of a manually operated tufting gun, which allowed it to produce intricate designs at a large scale quickly. The company soon moved to a larger factory in Tai Po, to the east, in part prompted by an early commission—in 1958—to produce a carpet for the foyer of Grauman's Chinese Theatre in Los Angeles.

Since then, the House of Tai Ping has been a leading manufacturer of luxury carpets worldwide. Its approach to design, mediating Chinese and Asian iconographies, presents a high-end, Chinese-inflected sophistication but also embraces influences from around the world. Tai Ping is distinctively a product of mid-twentieth-century Hong Kong, a leveraging of the city's position as a centre of international commerce and engineering innovation and a meeting point of commercially minded individuals from around the world.   JW

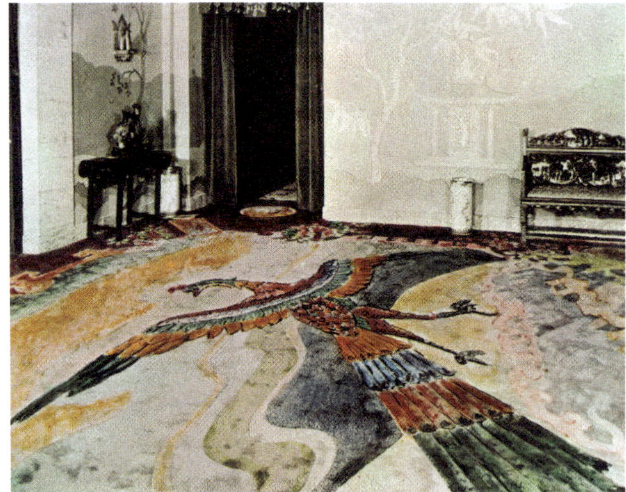

Carpet for the lobby of Grauman's Chinese Theatre, Los Angeles, 1970

House of Tai Ping (established 1956)
Sketch for Chinese-style carpet design
ca. 1970s–1980s
Print, graphite, ink, and colour on paper
38 × 29.2 cm
Gift of House of Tai Ping, 2019
CA61

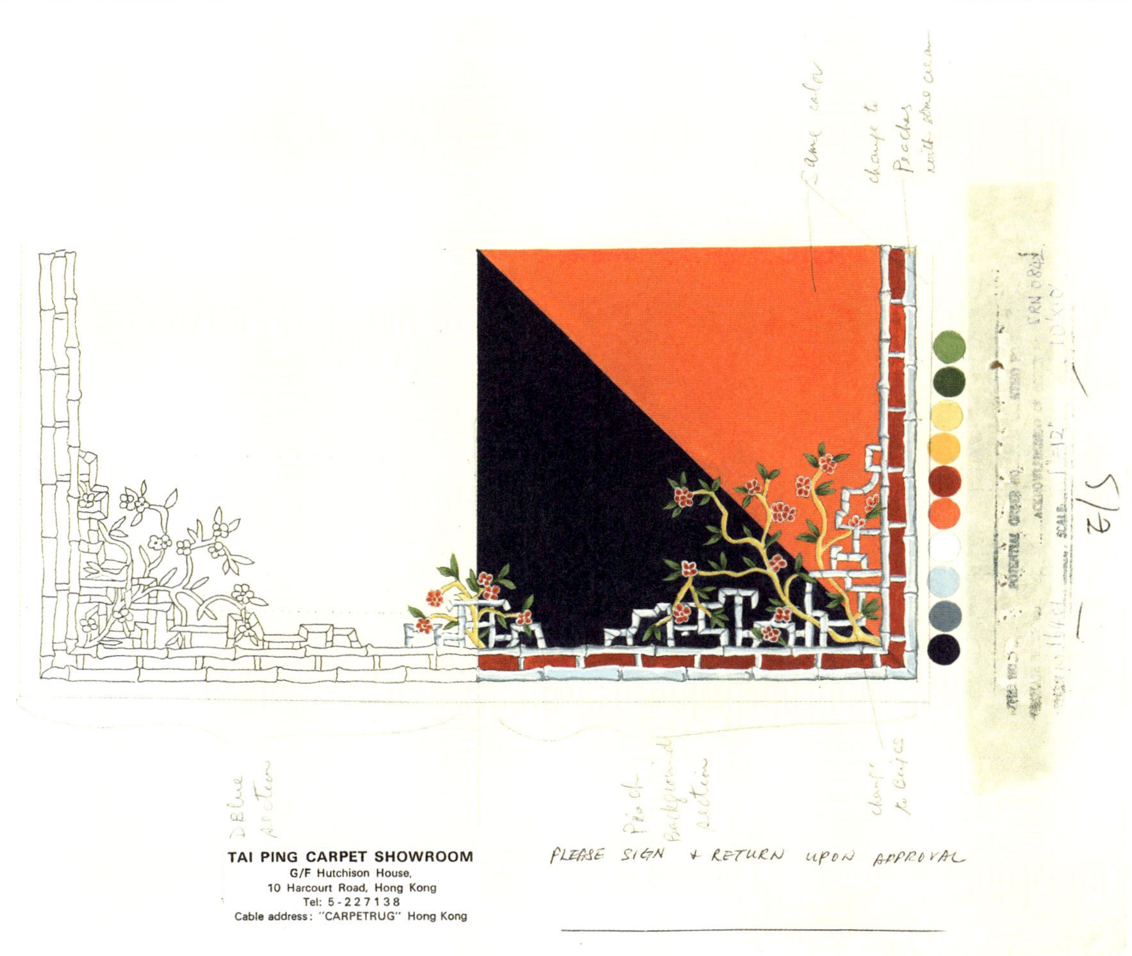

Same color
change to Peaches with some cream
POTENTIAL ORDER NO.
SIGNED BY
ACKNOWLEDGEMENT OF ORDER
ERN 0845
SCALE 1"=12"
10'X10'
S/E
D.Blue section
Peach Background section
change to Bricks
TAI PING CARPET SHOWROOM
G/F Hutchison House,
10 Harcourt Road, Hong Kong
Tel: 5-227138
Cable address: "CARPETRUG" Hong Kong
PLEASE SIGN + RETURN UPON APPROVAL

Plastics are synonymous with post-war Hong Kong, defining the city as a centre of manufacturing at a time of economic expansion. While the concept of 'made in Hong Kong' soon became associated with cheap, disposable goods, this belies the complexity of the history and evolution of the plastics industry. The story is one in which political and economic migration meets global and colonial business interests to produce one of the leading industries in Hong Kong.

The industry coalesced in the mid-1940s, when Hong Kong became a refuge for migrants fleeing the Chinese Civil War. Among them were industrialists and entrepreneurs who brought their capital and technical know-how to the city. Within a decade, plastics had become one of the city's largest industries, aided by its ready access to imported raw materials. Hong Kong quickly emerged as a major hub of trade in Asia thanks to its advantageous geographic location and its status as a Crown colony, enmeshing plastics manufacturers in an extensive global network.

Founded by Norman Young Sze-kuen and his wife, Annie Lam Young, in the 1940s, Yuen Hing Hong & Company was among the earliest suppliers of raw materials to the plastics industry in the city. In the 1930s, Young had worked for the Hong Kong office of the British chemical company ICI, which claimed to have coined the term 'plastic' in the late 1920s. Pioneering companies such as Kader Industrial, founded by the Ting family, and Star Industrial, founded by the Leung family, originally from Shanghai, developed product lines for a growing domestic market.

Social changes in the 1950s, most significantly the development of public housing, established the conditions for social stability and mobility. Plastics came to represent the purchasing power of a population with greater disposable income. Household goods remain among the most significant product lines for the plastics industry today. Popular items such as rice bowls and chopsticks were also sought after by Chinese émigré communities, for whom these objects helped sustain a familiar way of life in their adopted homelands. Export products also included a wide range of household goods, toys, and artificial flowers. The success of Hong Kong's plastics industry resulted from an ability to anticipate the needs of markets across Asia, the Middle East, Africa, Europe, and North America.

The catalogues of Star Industrial's Red A line include hundreds of products and variations, behind which was a commitment to local market research. The malleable nature of plastic facilitated the imitation of other materials and offered a range of colours and styles. Manufacturers took inspiration from crystal chandeliers, paper lanterns, ceramic dining ware, glass tumblers, and leather suitcases. Inexpensive, durable, and ubiquitous designs became inadvertent ambassadors of Hong Kong on the world stage and inseparable from global consumer culture.

With the rising costs of land and labour in Hong Kong and Chinese economic liberalisation in the 1980s, the production of plastic goods gradually moved to mainland China. Today, Star Industrial is one of the few plastics manufacturers to maintain production in Hong Kong. While environmental concerns have affected perceptions of plastics, these products remain ingrained in Hong Kong's visual and material culture and its histories.   JW

Star Industrial Company (established 1949)
Red A plastic goods
ca. 1960s–1980s
Plastic and various materials
Dimensions variable

Kader Industrial Company (established 1948)
OK plastic goods
ca. 1960s–1970s
Plastic and various materials
Dimensions variable

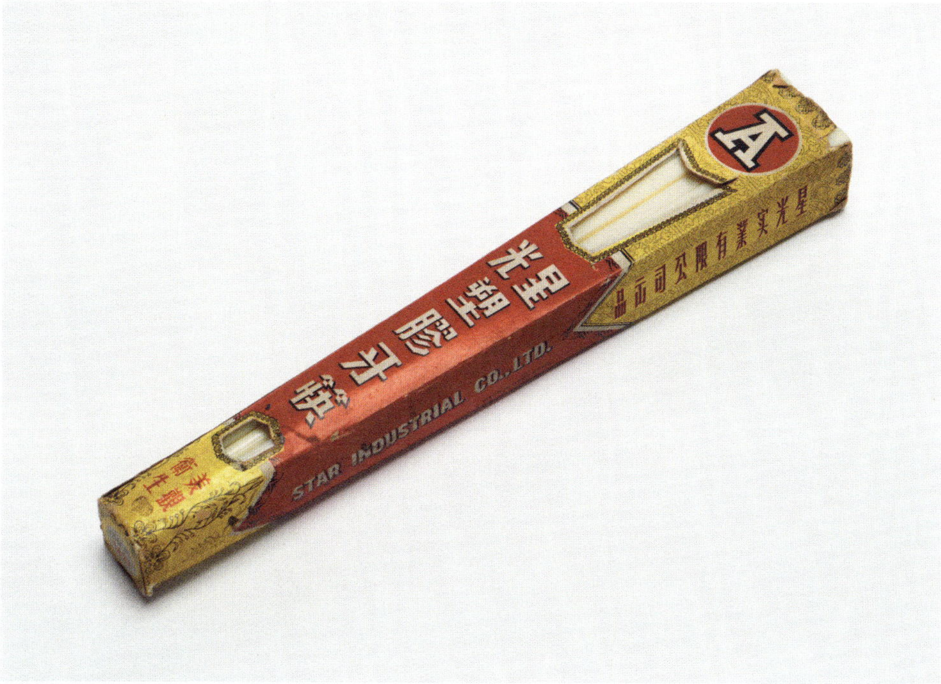

Red A chopsticks, no. 1491. 2016.122

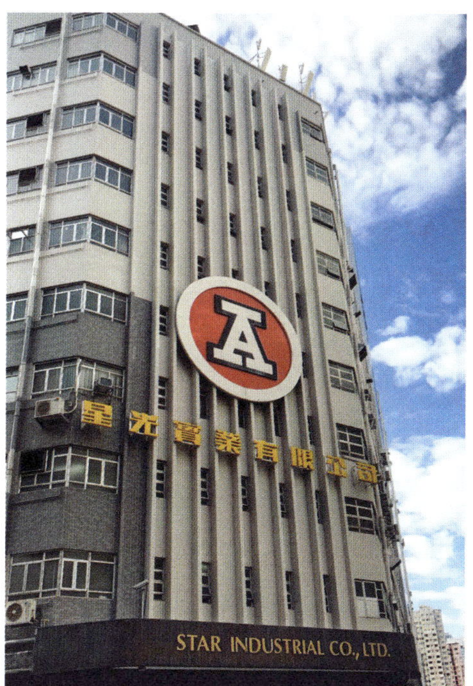

Star Industrial factory, San Po Kong

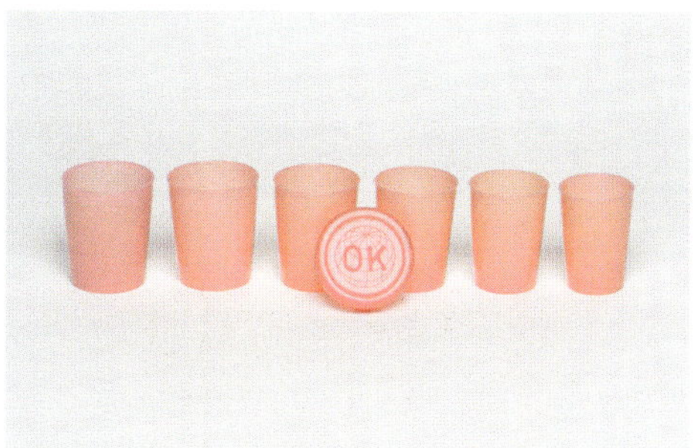

OK tumbler set with cover, model no. 2551/6A.
2019.335

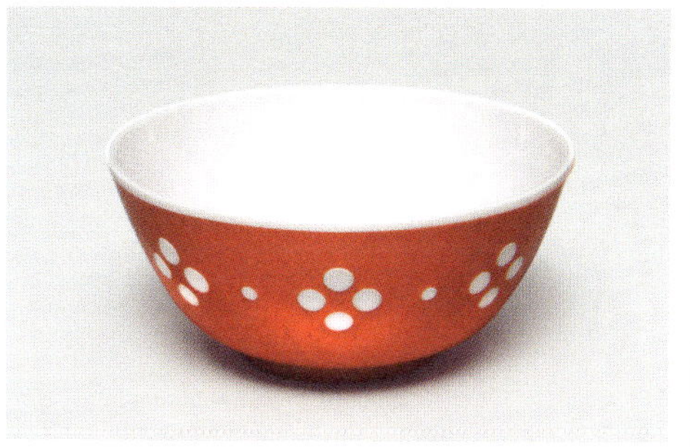

Red A plastic bowls, no. 866. 2016.368

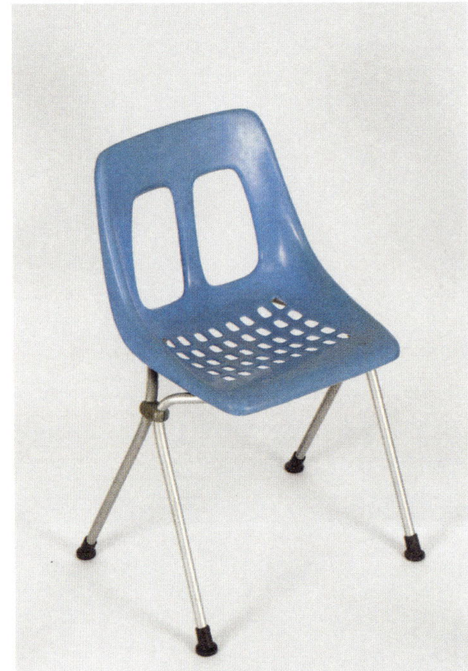

OK *Best-Line* chair, model no. 902A (1973). 2019.362

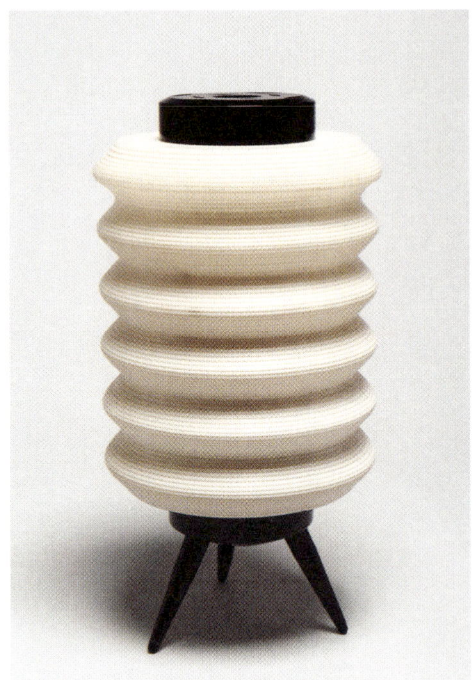

Red A *Artistic Plastic Lamp*, no. 113. 2016.372

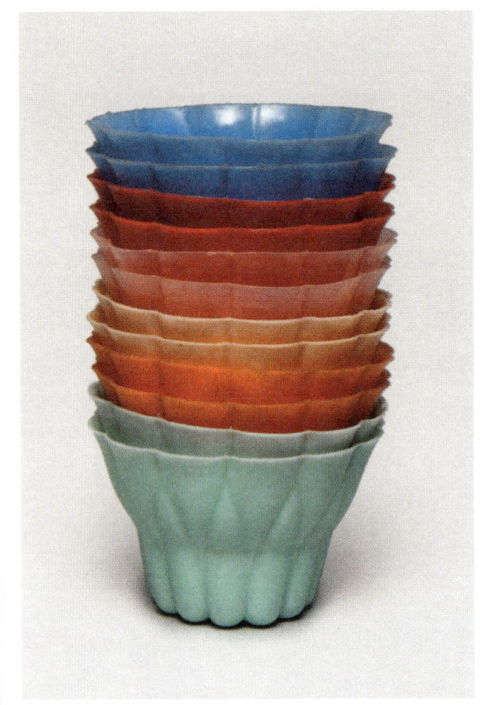

Red A jelly moulds, no. 303. 2016.139

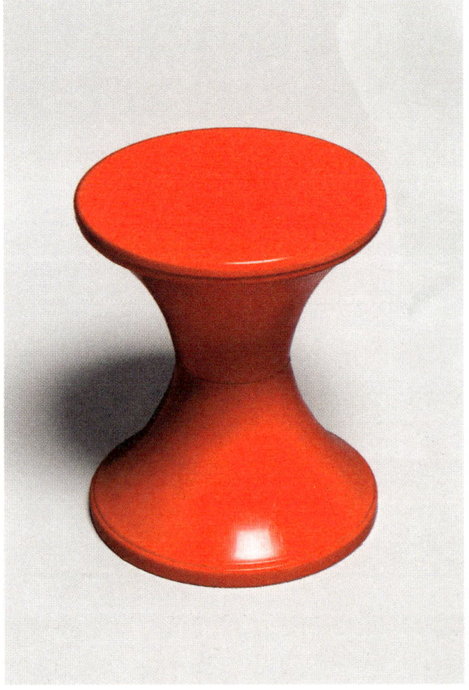

Red A stool, no. 366. 2019.350

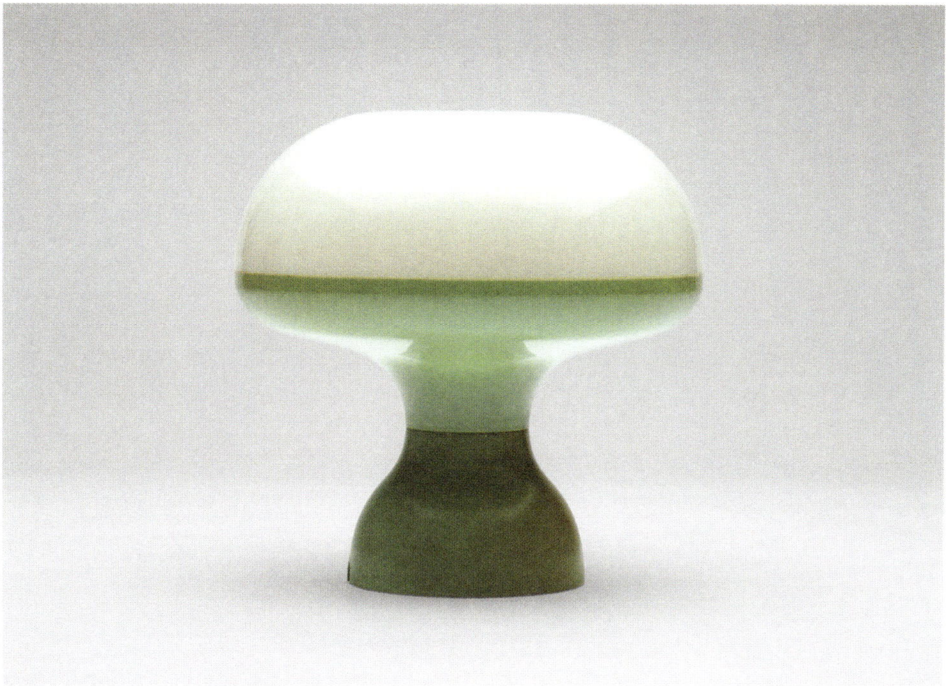

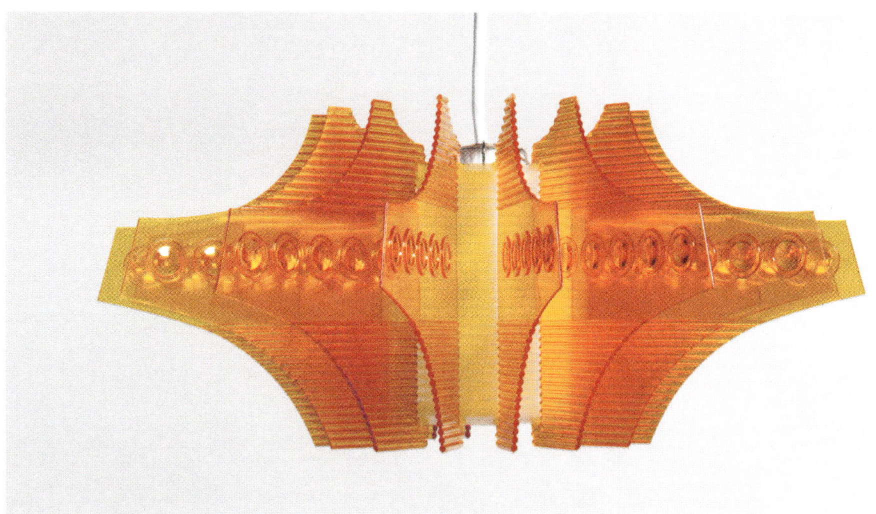

Red A table lamp, no. 1619/1619A. 2016.518

Red A *Plastic Crystal* lamp fixture, no. 1616. 2016.106

This product—known as the watermelon ball—was one of the most popular plastic toys in twentieth-century Hong Kong. Lightweight and affordably priced, it was loved by generations of children, particularly from the 1960s to the 1980s. Its purported inventor, Chiang Chen, an engineer, arrived in Hong Kong from mainland China in the 1940s. Chiang established the Chen Hsong Machinery Company and developed a machine for extrusion blow-moulding in two colours, allowing melted plastic to be shaped while preserving the distinction between the colours. The ball was a prototype developed to demonstrate this innovation, with a design said to be inspired by Chiang's memory of the Yangtze River meeting its tributary the Jialing River at Chongqing, where the rapid current kept the Yangtze's murky water from blending with the Jialing's clear flow. The ball quickly became a success and entered mass production. Chiang did not file a patent for his machine, allowing other manufacturers to adopt the technology to produce their own versions of the watermelon ball—often with distinctive patterns and colours in addition to the classic red-and-white stripes—as well as other small plastic goods. Made of a thin layer of hard plastic that breaks easily, the ball had a limited bounce, rendering it ideal for play in the small apartments and public spaces of Hong Kong. Its breakable nature, combined with the complexity of the ball's design history, makes it difficult to identify the earliest versions. Nevertheless, it has become a symbol not only of twentieth-century Hong Kong childhood, but also of the city's manufacturing heyday.   CC

Watermelon ball
Designed ca. 1959, made ca. 1970s–1980s
Plastic
Diameter: 18 cm
Gift of Vincent Au Yeung, 2016
2016.764

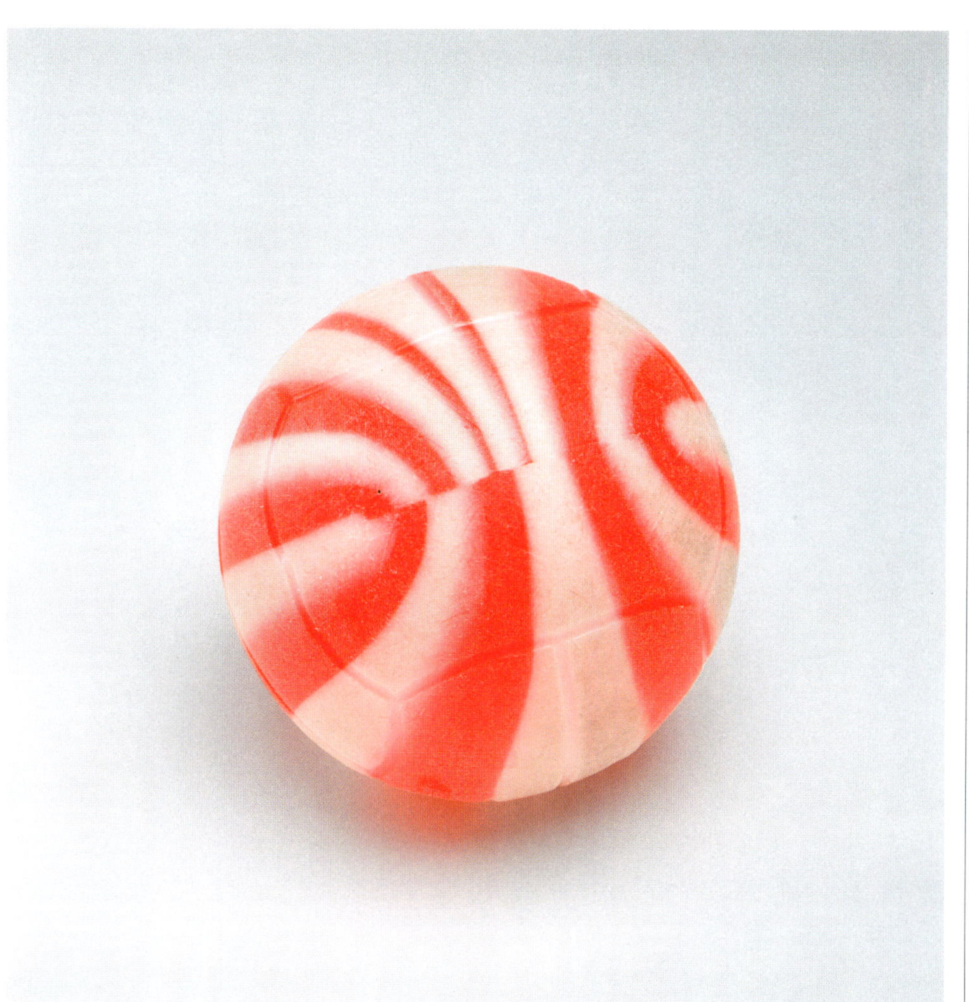

Before the advent of electric kettles, vacuum flasks that keep water hot could be found in every household. After the Second World War, Hong Kong's two leading vacuum flask brands were Gold Coin, manufactured by the Freezinhot Bottle Company, and Camel, produced by the Wei Yit Vacuum Flask Manufactory. Both were known for their durable, high-quality products, and both developed signature flask designs.

The classic Gold Coin flask features the company's logo on the body incorporated into an ancient Chinese coin, a symbol of good fortune. Gold Coin's designs commonly used bright colours and traditional Chinese motifs as decorative elements.

Camel's *Pion* baby feeder exemplifies the company's emphasis on practical innovations in their product designs. The distinctive bullet-shaped form of this flask has a fluted body, a feature designed to improve grip and prevent dents that was first adopted in 1947. The *Pion* was introduced onto the baby-care market in 1951 and became one of Camel's most successful products.   KW

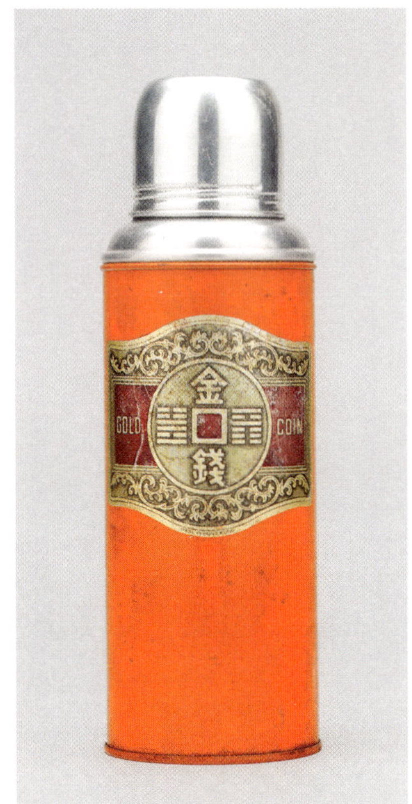

Freezinhot Bottle Company (established 1940)
Gold Coin vacuum flask
1960s
Aluminium, glass, silver, rubber, and cork
24.9 × 8.3 × 8.3 cm
Gift of Wong Pui Kai, 2018
2018.399

Wei Yit Vacuum Flask Manufactory (established 1940)
Camel *Pion* baby feeder
1950s–1960s
Metal, glass, and rubber
23 × 7.5 × 7.5 cm
2016.383

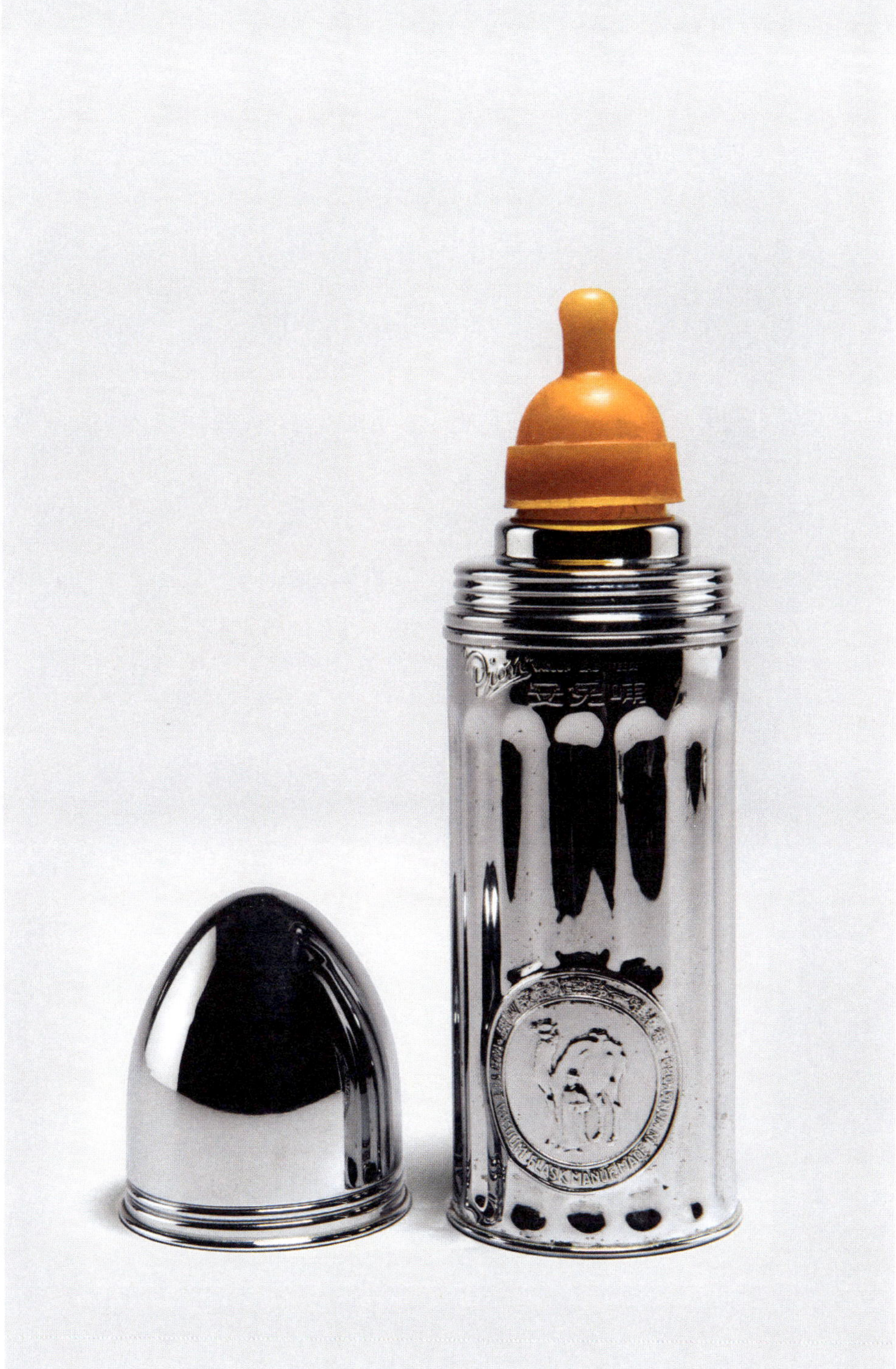

Created for Cathay Pacific Airways by Milk Design, this set of in-flight tableware recalls the translucent rice-grain patterns of delicate Ming- and Qing-era *linglong* porcelain vessels. The design brings together two aspects of the material culture of everyday life in Hong Kong. It is based on porcelain rice bowls commonly found in homes and restaurants; and it is made in plastic, a material that is integral to the story of the city's development. The designers collaborated with Dutch manufacturer deSter to use a double-injection process to mould the plastic and introduce the pattern as a semi-perforated element on the bowls. The pattern is applied as a decorative element on the surface of the cups. The tableware is a practical response to the conditions of air travel, namely limited space and occasional turbulence. As a contemporary interpretation of a centuries-old design, this tableware aligns with Cathay Pacific's position as a Hong Kong–based international airline and the company's projection of an image of 'Oriental' cosmopolitanism on the world stage.   FT

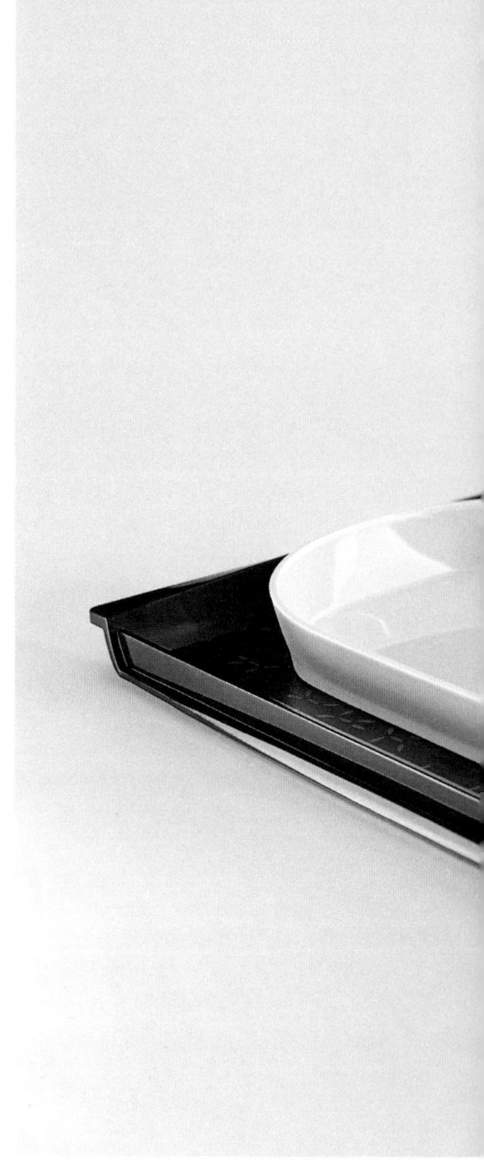

Milk Design (established 1998)
Cathay Pacific in-flight tableware
2007
Plastic
Dimensions variable
Gift of Milk Design, 2021
2021.66

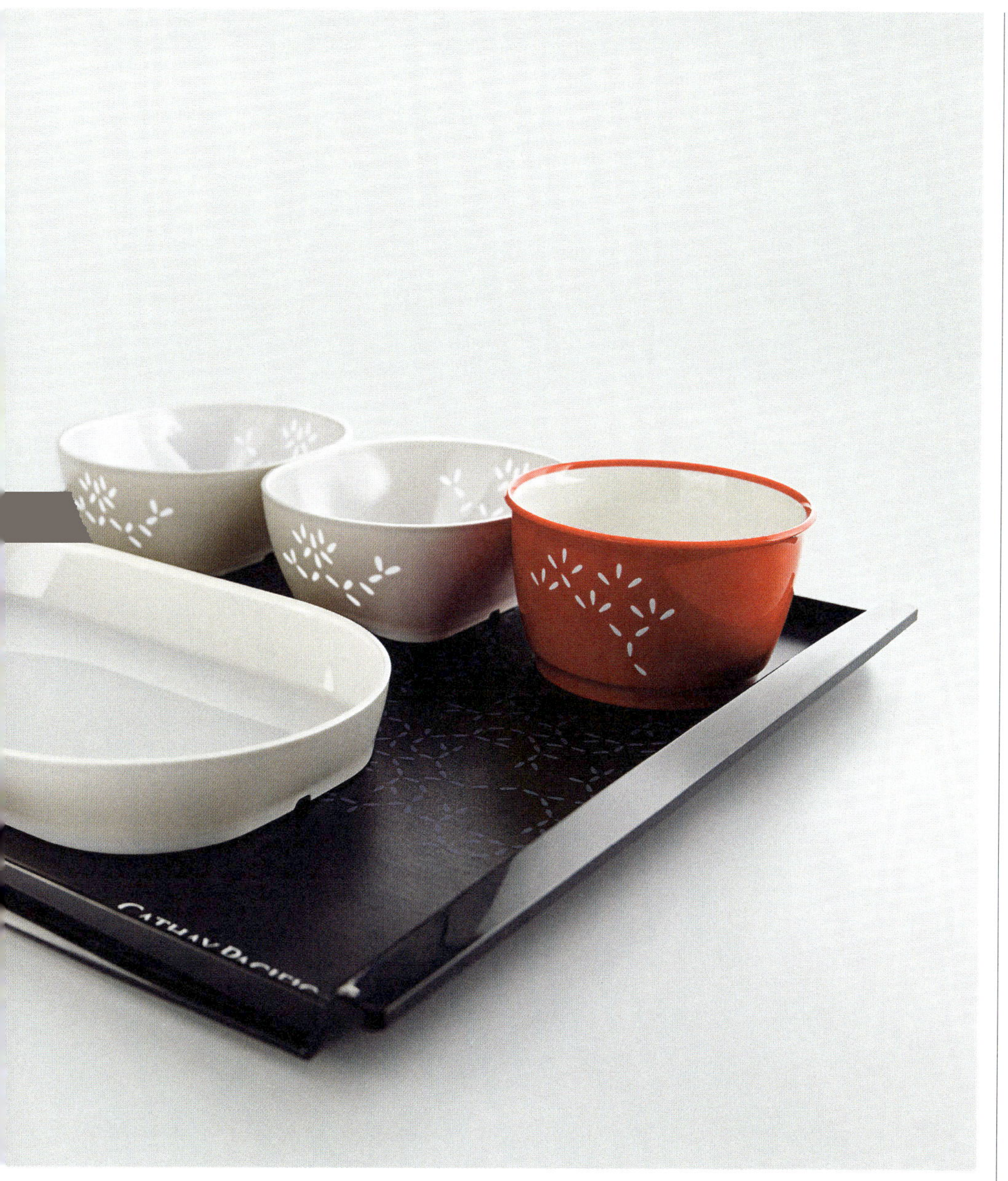

This design reveals the often invisible spatial intelligence required to respond to Hong Kong's physical and regulatory constraints. Architect Andrew Lee King Fun pioneered the use of the scissor stair when designing a twelve-storey residential building in Wan Chai in 1963. This design has been widely adopted in high-rise architecture across the city. Consisting of two interlocking staircases entered from opposite ends of the building, scissor stairs maximise spatial efficiency and comply with building and fire codes that mandate at least two exit routes on each floor.

Lee produced this model of his 1963 staircase for the exhibition *Tall Storeys: Evolution in Hong Kong Architecture, 1965–2014*, held at the Royal Institute of British Architects in London in 2014. The inclusion of Lee's design in the exhibition points to the growing international recognition of design solutions developed in Hong Kong to the limitations of the city's built environment.   SS

Andrew Lee King Fun & Associates Architects (established 1962)
Model of scissor stairs
2014
Acrylic
53.2 × 61.4 × 41.5 cm
Gift of Andrew Lee King Fun, 2019
2019.561

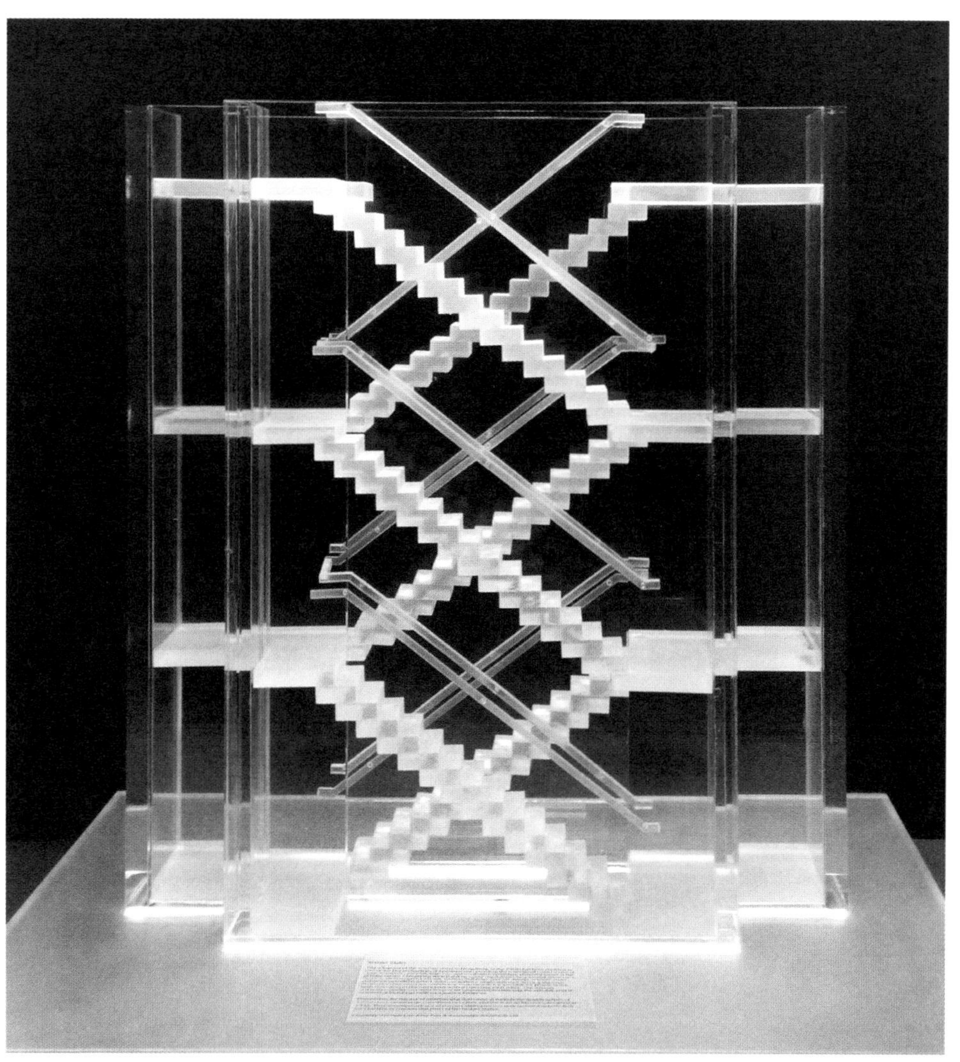

First presented at the 1910 Salon de l'automobile et du cycle, a motor show in Paris, neon signs were introduced to Hong Kong in the 1930s and over the following decades became a defining feature of the city's visual culture. The image of Hong Kong as a neon city was propagated in large part by depictions of neon-saturated scenes in popular cinema. In addition to giving shape to the city's dense urban space, neon signs have charted the blossoming and decay of manufacturing and commerce.

Designs feature a wide range of typographic styles, often reflecting the businesses for which they are commissioned. Many neon signs in Hong Kong feature bilingual type designs. Early designs were typically composed of simple patterns and lines. For example, the typography for 'Very Good Tailor' adopts bold geometric forms, with the water radical in the third Chinese character, *yeung*—part of the word compound meaning Western-style clothing—replaced by three circles and slanted lines, a reflection of the influence of 1920s Shanghai Art Deco. Similarly, the two 'O's in the English word 'good' are replaced with buttons to visually communicate the nature of the shop.

Alongside the growth of the advertising industry in the 1970s, text-based designs were gradually replaced by image-based ones. Among the most recognised was the large Angus bull hanging outside Sammy's Kitchen restaurant on a narrow stretch of Queen's Road West in Sai Ying Pun. A local icon, the sign incorporates the restaurant's name in the owner's own handwriting across the bull's profile. Over the years, many neon signs have become structurally unsound and are often required to be taken down in accordance with government regulations.

In addition to its widespread use in commercial advertising, neon has become a popular medium for contemporary artists. Hong Kong artist Lam Tung Pang's 2008 work *Shaking China*, consisting of three neon signs reading 'Made in UK', 'Made in China', and 'Made in Hong Kong', is a commentary on a unique political relationship centred around Hong Kong. Lam produced a sign in each of the three locations with the same budget for each, and the difference in size of the signs reflects the difference in cost of production and the economic disparities between the three places. His use of neon illustrates its central position in the material culture of Hong Kong.   CC

Sammy Yip (born 1930, Hong Kong)
Fu Wah Neon Engineering Company (established 1969)
Neon sign for Sammy's Kitchen
ca. 1978
Exhausted glass tubes, neon gas, zinc, steel, and paint
450 × 360 × 40 cm
Gift of Sammy's Kitchen, 2013
2015.304

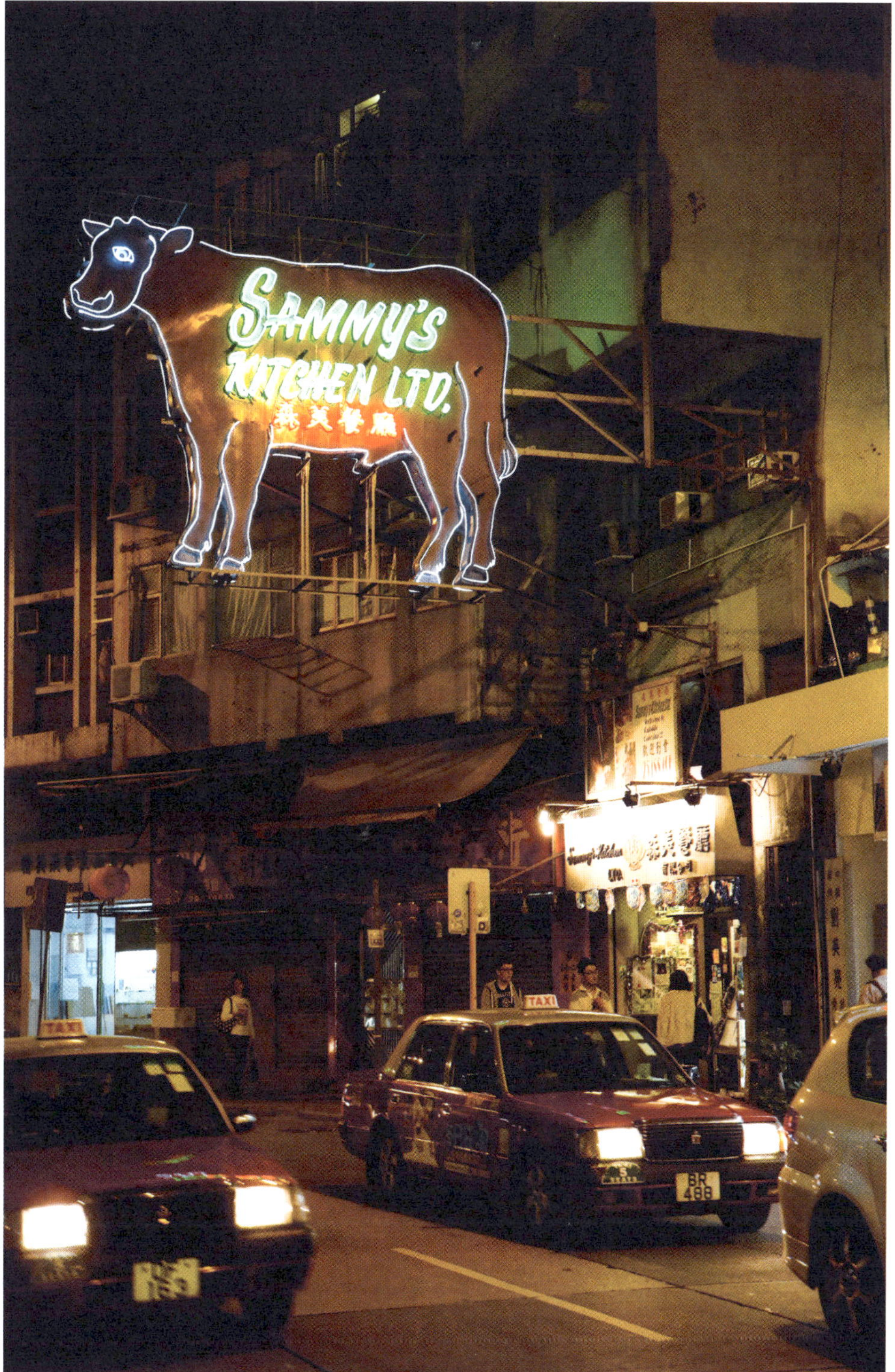

SAMMY'S
KITCHEN LTD.
森美餐廳
TAXI
BR 488

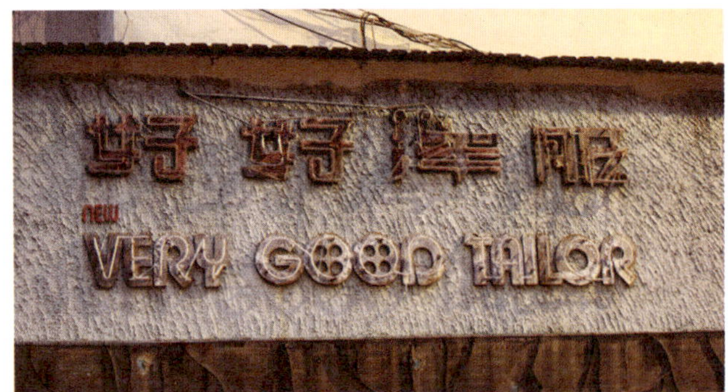

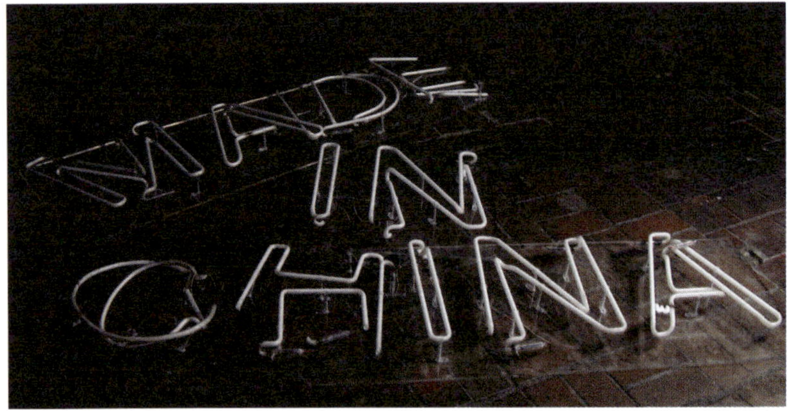

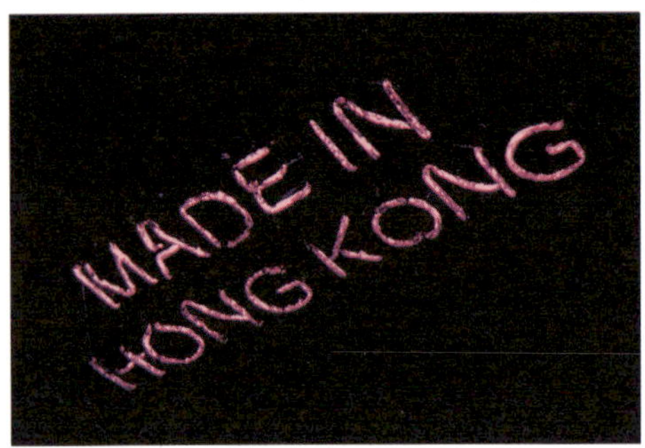

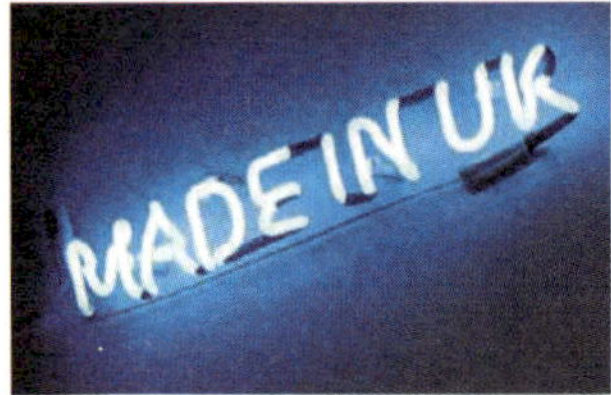

Neon sign for Very Good Tailor
1963
Exhausted glass tubes, neon gas, zinc, steel,
and paint
101 × 348 × 5 cm
2016.475

Lam Tung Pang (born 1978, Hong Kong)
Shaking China
2008
Exhausted glass tubes, metal, neon gas, acrylic,
and transformer
Dimensions variable
2012.1633

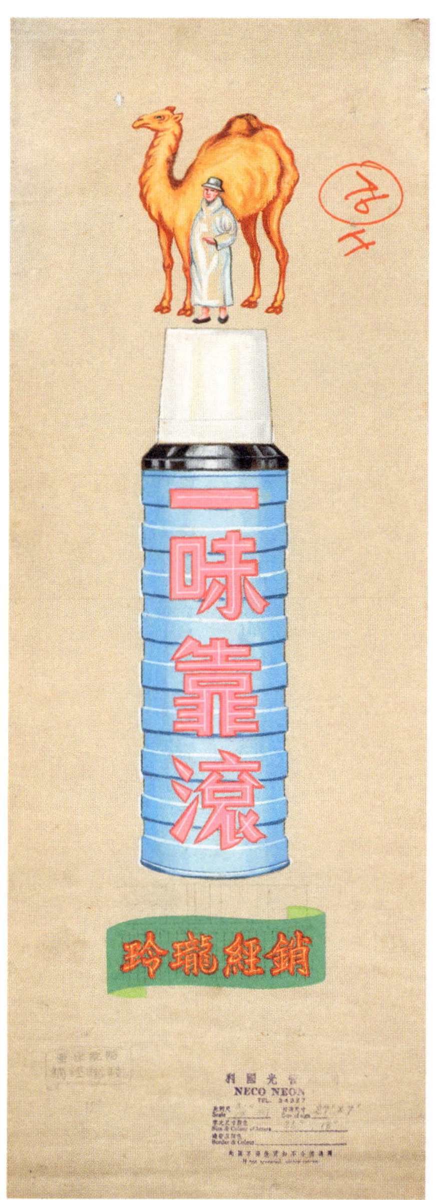

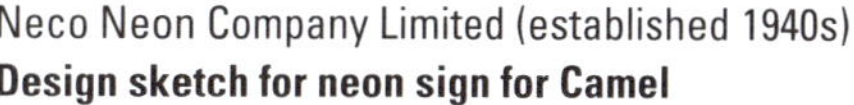

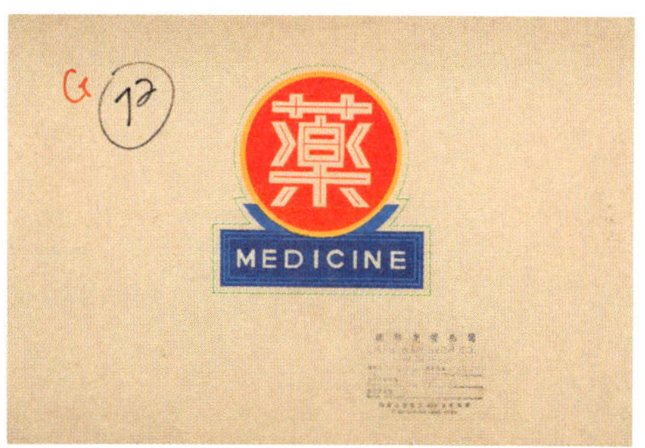

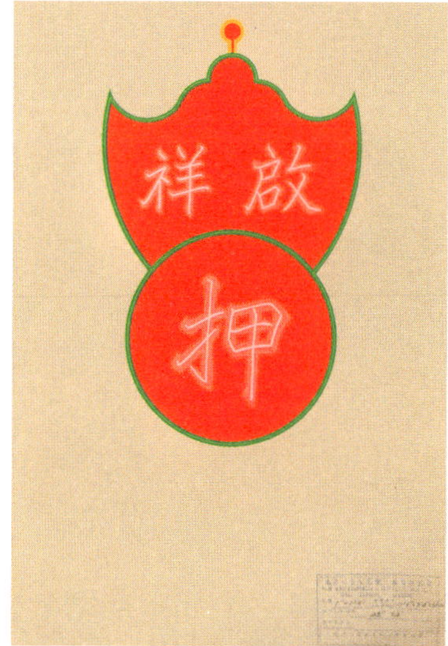

Nam Wah Neon Co. (established 1953)
Design sketch for 'Medicine' neon sign
ca. 1963–ca. 1968
Paint and ink on paper
29 × 43 cm
Gift of Nam Wah Neonlight & Electrical Mfy, Ltd.,
2015
CA13/1/47

Nam Wah Neonlight & Electrical Manufactory
(established 1953)
**Design sketch for neon sign for Kai Yeung
Pawn Shop**
ca. 1968–1980s
Paint and ink on paper
57.5 × 31 cm
Gift of Nam Wah Neonlight & Electrical Mfy, Ltd.,
2015
CA13/1/92

Neco Neon Company Limited (established 1940s)
**Design sketch for neon sign for Camel
vacuum flasks**
1950s–1960s
Paint, ink, and graphite on paper
71.7 × 25.5 cm
Gift of Nam Wah Neonlight & Electrical Mfy, Ltd., 2015
CA13/6/14

LEAP THE STAGE

Artists and designers put the city, its pop music, and its cinema in the global spotlight

For close to fifty years, beginning in the 1950s, Tsang Tsou-choi adopted the moniker 'King of Kowloon' in distinctive calligraphic works painted on highly visible surfaces in public spaces, including walls, postboxes, pillars, and utility housings. He was viewed as a nuisance, an eccentric, and even a vandal, and his calligraphy was often painted over, but he would repeatedly return to the same locations to reapply it. Broadly based on the formal conventions of Chinese genealogies and printed advertisements, Tsang's writings do not adhere to any lineage or school and are entirely his own creative expressions. Tsang expressed his 'ownership' of much of the Kowloon peninsula, a claim that he insisted was documented in his ancestral records. Through his act of writing across the urban landscape, he asserted his sovereignty.

This work, written on a map of Kowloon, is an example of Tsang's idiosyncratic calligraphic compositions. The two largest characters, reading *sai zo*, mean 'ancestor'. The four lines beneath, read vertically from right to left, give the names and 'kingdoms' of four of his family members. At the top Tsang uses a combination of Chinese characters and Arabic numerals to depict the five numbers from five to nine. From the 1990s onwards Tsang's calligraphic practice was recognised as an important manifestation of an artistic vernacular often compared to Western graffiti and street art. Although many of his original works in public spaces have not survived, his writings can now be seen in museum collections and—in a handful of situations—in the city itself.   CC

Tsang Tsou-choi (King of Kowloon) (born 1921, Guangdong; died 2007, Hong Kong)
Map of Kowloon
ca. 1994–1997
Ink on printed paper
88 × 32.2 cm
2013.34

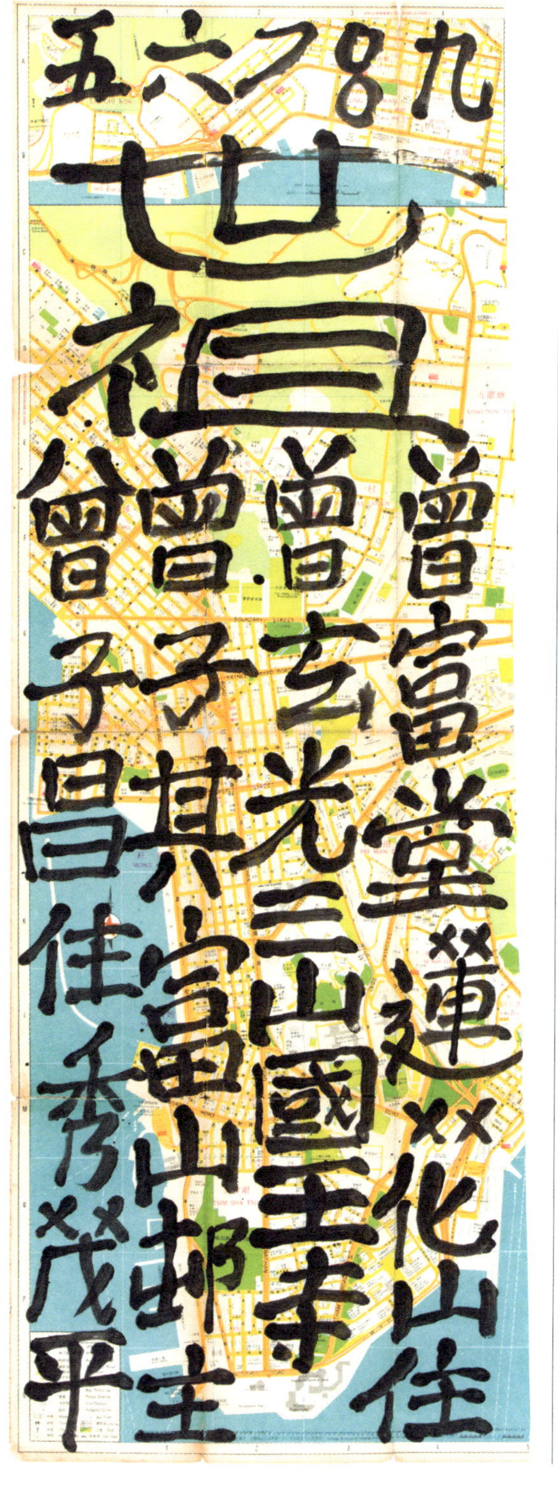

A founding member of the avant-garde Circle Art Group in the 1960s, Cheung Yee was a key figure among a small group of pioneers in Hong Kong who established the foundations of a distinctive artistic identity. He is known for his imposing sculptural works in bronze, wood, and stone that draw on both contemporary modernist sculpture and Chinese history, philosophy, and iconographies. An important part of his practice was his work in relief. Whether cast in bronze, carved in wood, or cast in paper, Cheung's reliefs may be considered a hybrid form of sculpture in two dimensions. His paper casting used individually carved blocks that could be applied interchangeably, allowing him to retain an element of spontaneity and chance in his works.

Trained in seal carving and Chinese painting, Cheung appropriated forms from ancient China, specifically symbols of power and fecundity in works that, regardless of size, possess a striking monumentality. *Purple Four* presents four views of a form inspired by ancient Chinese oracle bones. In Shang-dynasty China, turtle plastrons and ox scapulae were used in elite divination rituals aimed at predicting and controlling future outcomes. The circular holes seen in Cheung's work correspond with circular depressions in the bone or plastron, into which in ancient times a hot poker was inserted. The resulting cracks, also replicated in Cheung's work, were then 'read' by a shaman or diviner. Cheung's oeuvre negotiates between a distant cultural past and a global modern present.   TP

Cheung Yee (born 1936, Guangdong; died 2019, United States)
Purple Four
1977
Cast paper print mounted on wooden board
59 × 43 × 1.2 cm
2016.138

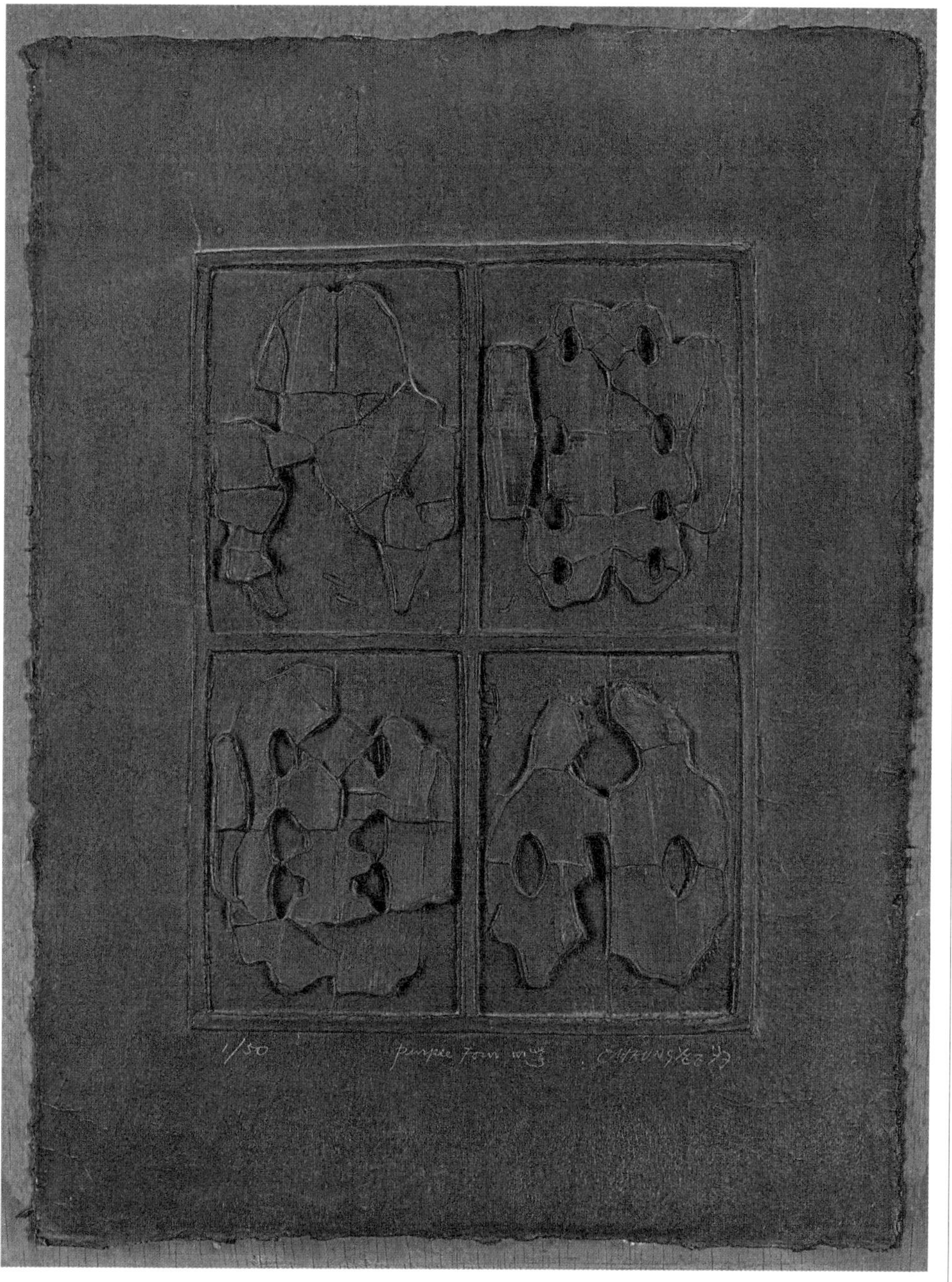
1/50
purple form
CHEUNG/83

Artist, designer, photographer, and filmmaker Stanley Wong, who uses the moniker anothermountainman for his art projects, pioneered the appropriation of everyday materials into works spanning the fields of art and design. Some of his best-known works involve the distinctive red-white-and-blue woven plastic fabric commonly seen across the urban landscape.

Originally manufactured in Japan, the fabric was imported to Hong Kong in the 1950s through the 1970s via Taiwan. Versions have subsequently been produced locally, later moving into the mainland along with other manufacturing sectors. The material was widely used on construction scaffolding, and from the 1970s onwards large holdalls made from this fabric became popular with cross-border traders.

This work is composed of five panels, each cut from different variations of the fabric design. It is printed with statements in formats commonly used on construction hoardings. Prominent among these are the dates 1997–2047, representing the fifty-year period that safeguarded Hong Kong's high degree of autonomy following the transfer of sovereignty from the United Kingdom to China. The work subverts the conventional use of the material and the vernacular communication with which it is associated.   FT

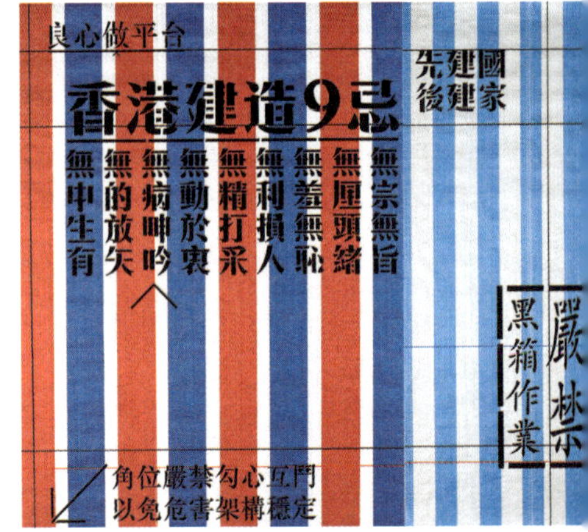

anothermountainman (Stanley Wong) (born 1960, Hong Kong)
building hong kong 03 / redwhiteblue
2002
Screen print on plastic woven fabric
119 × 89 cm (each, set of five)
Gift of anothermountainman (Stanley Wong), 2017
2017.149

左180° 向右180°
請勿關閉此門
疊保自由出入
筆直向上避東歪西斜
加闊氣量
19°97-20°47
不移不變
倒下來
要立刻
壞牆
不好的
建造的第一步
先行出第一步
建築香港 2021 沙圖 03

良心做平台
香港建造9忌
無宗無旨
無厘頭緒
無羞無恥
無利損人
無精打采
無動於衷
無病呻吟
無的放矢
無中生有
角位嚴禁勾心互鬥
以免危害架構穩定

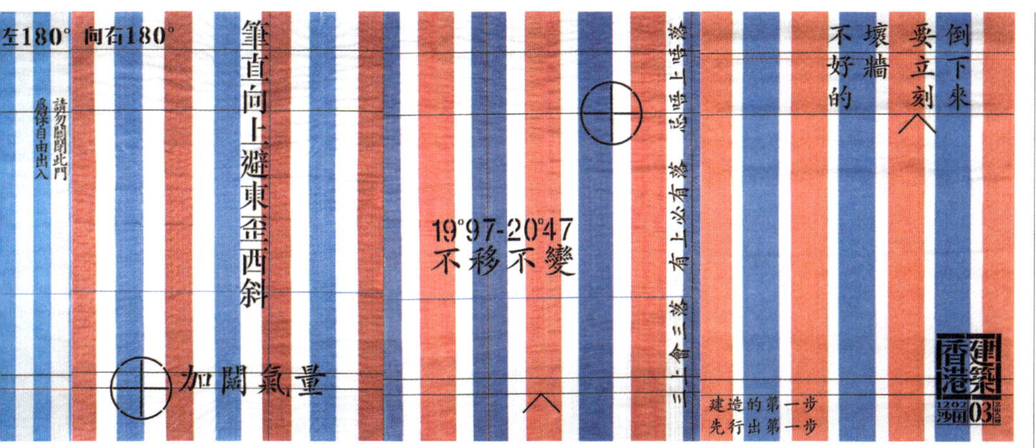

Detail view

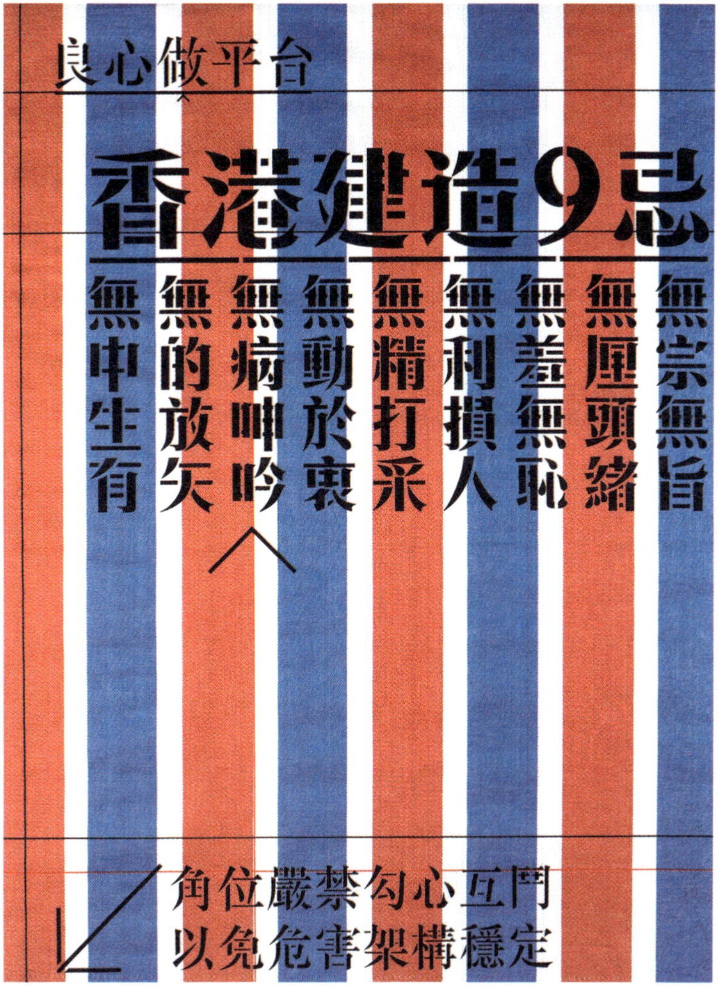

Conceived by Stanley Wong, these posters are part of an innovative campaign produced in the 1990s by the J. Walter Thompson advertising agency for Hong Kong's Mass Transit Railway (MTR) system. The campaign used an oblique yet visually arresting approach based on the lifestyle aspirations of the MTR's users. Integrated seamlessly across multiple mediums, including print, radio, and television, the campaign reached large audiences. Using the form of word puzzles commonly found in newspapers, these advertisements playfully deliver a message of how travelling by MTR can improve your daily life.

The first poster is in the form of a crossword puzzle, within which clues at the bottom refer to popular local food. The second poster is a partially completed word search puzzle, in which the words circled are phrases referring to everyday items. In both, embedded in the bottom right is a tagline stating that, no matter what you want to eat or buy, taking the MTR makes your journey easier. This campaign catalysed the career of creative director and designer Stanley Wong, for whom a vernacular-inspired approach has been a mainstay of his later artistic and design practices.   JW

Stanley Wong (born 1960, Hong Kong)
J. Walter Thompson Company (established 1979)
***No Matter What You're Looking for . . . Take MTR*, poster printing proofs for Mass Transit Railway Corporation**
1992
Offset lithograph
Top: 32.9 × 65.9 cm
Bottom: 34.1 × 66.1 cm
Gift of anothermountainman (Stanley Wong), 2017
2017.143
2017.511

橫直提示: [1-10] 凍冰冰夏日妙品係乜? [21-30] 生猛鮮美好味道係乜? [38-44] 唔使筷子嘅大餐係乜? [59-65] 清清淡淡益腸胃係乜?
[11-20] 暖笠笠地道風味係乜? [31-37] 每逢知己份外啱係乜? [45-58] 香香滑滑凍甜品係乜? [66-70] 無論想食乜,搭＿就得!

影	磁	飛	鏢	古	鑽	朱	義	盛	耳	環	迴	立	體	聲	音	響	明	非
不	碟	鐵	的	玉	石	盆	景	高	爾	夫	球	棒	儲	乂	打	清	比	洲
求	甲	機	確	電	戒	磨	泰	腳	室	內	無	線	電	話	字	古	堅	海
人	蔘	皮	涼	動	指	耳	藍	凳	毛	黑	龍	論	池	畫	機	董	尼	底
茸	雲	鞋	匹	牙	簽	筒	瓷	牛	公	色	眞	鬚	想	筆	座	金	泳	泥
指	南	針	頭	刷	線	收	碗	墨	仔	皮	波	板	糖	買	魚	撈	衣	面
甲	白	底	印	花	恤	音	樂	盒	手	褲	斯	鞋	浴	缸	乜	車	譜	膜
箍	菥	材	章	蜜	飛	機	恤	袋	招	財	貓	手	巾	仔	搭	米	就	得

In the aftermath of the Chinese Civil War, among the migrants who sought refuge in Hong Kong were movie producers and actors who brought with them cinematic techniques and narrative conventions from Shanghai and other metropolitan centres. This influx met with the British and American cultural influences already prevalent in Hong Kong and contributed to the blossoming of the Hong Kong film industry during the 1950s and 1960s. The city was beginning to project an international allure through films such as *The World of Suzie Wong* (1960) starring William Holden and Nancy Kwan.

In 1963, when the government introduced a requirement for films to include English subtitles as part of the ratings process, Hong Kong films found new audiences across Southeast Asia, Europe, and North America. These posters for Cantonese-language films were used to advertise screenings in Chinatowns across North America and represent four popular genres: traditional opera (*Fun on Polygamous Marriage*); the Hollywood-style musical (*A Maiden's Love*); the Chinese historical drama (*Humanity*); and the modern martial-arts film (*Sky Dragon Castle*). Often inspired by wuxia martial arts novels by writers such as Jin Yong and Liang Yusheng, these films represent an approach to storytelling that is unique to the Hong Kong film industry.   CC

Mid-twentieth-century Chinese-language film posters from the Lambert Yam and Ruby Yang Archive
Offset lithograph
Dimensions variable
Gift of Lambert Yam & Ruby Yang, 2018
CA64

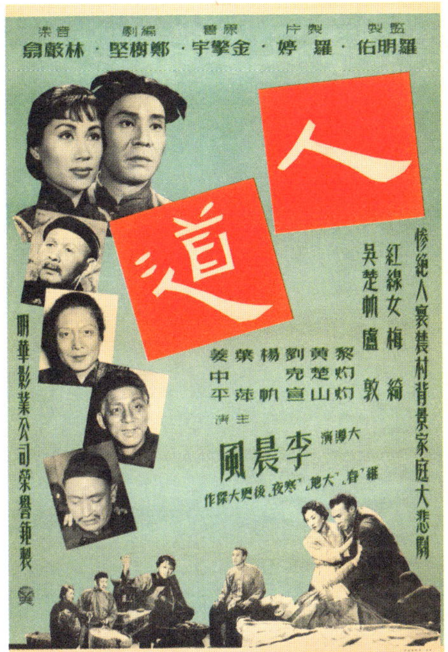

Grandview Film Company, *Humanity* (1955)

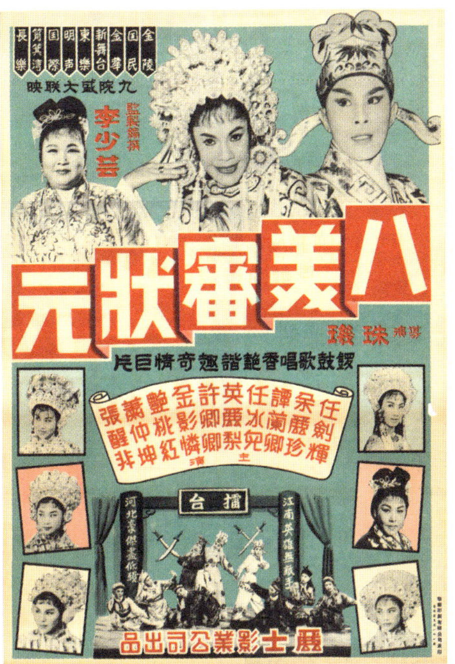

Lux Film Company, *Fun on Polygamous Marriage* (1961)

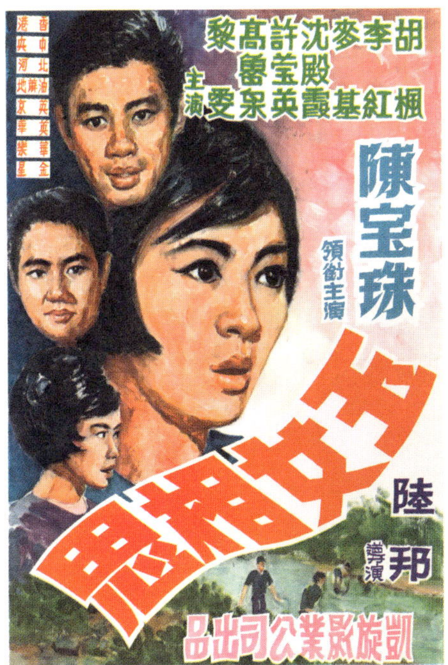

Triumph Motion Picture Company, *A Maiden's Love* (1967)

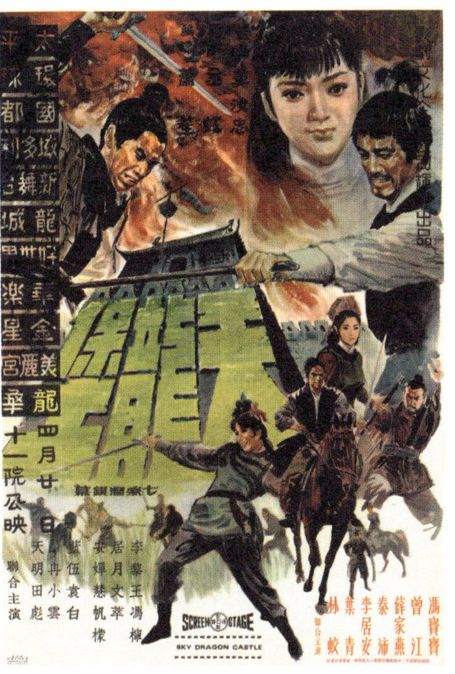

Screen & Stage Cultural Enterprise Company, *Sky Dragon Castle* (1969)

The 1970s and 1980s were decades of unprecedented economic growth in Hong Kong, and saw a concomitant growth in a distinctive local popular culture. It was film in particular that had the greatest global influence and reach. While commercial studios such as the Shaw Brothers Studios were producing films that captured local and international audiences, an alternative film culture was blossoming among artistic circles.

The Phoenix Cine Club, active from the mid-1970s until 1988, was an important platform for promoting film viewing and criticism in Hong Kong. The club organised exhibitions to showcase members' work, with an emphasis on the experimental use of new tools and techniques. It held independent film festivals as well as screening programmes of experimental films and world classics, organised in collaboration with the Hong Kong Urban Council. The club's magazine published film criticism and interviews with filmmakers, with a commitment to intellectual exchange around cinema. Across its activities, the Phoenix Cine Club introduced audiences to independent films and nurtured budding film practitioners, many of whom subsequently took up roles in Hong Kong cinema and also became pioneers of video art.   FT

Phoenix Cine Club (established 1973)
Phoenix Cine Club ephemera
ca. 1975–1988
Offset lithograph
Dimensions variable
Gift of Lo Yuk Ying, 2020
CA65

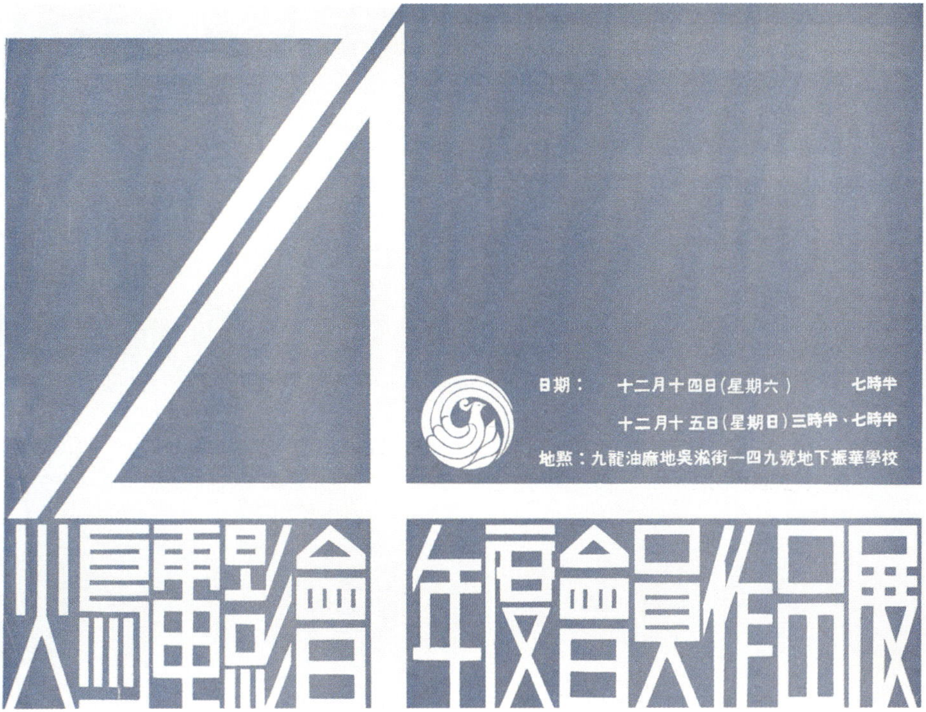

Poster for 'Phoenix Cine Club Member Film Show' (1974–1976)

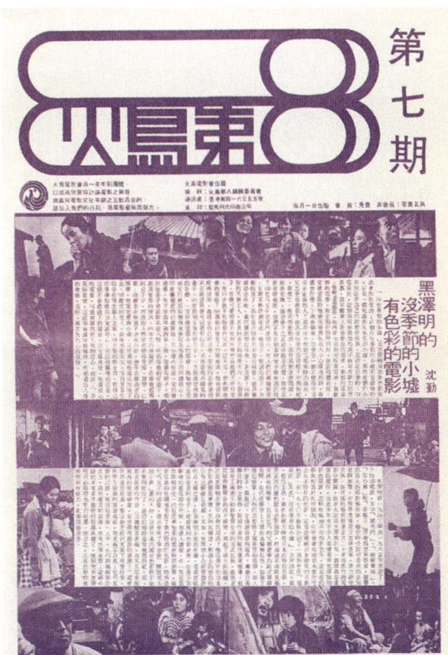

Huo niao di ba newsletter, issue 7 (1976)

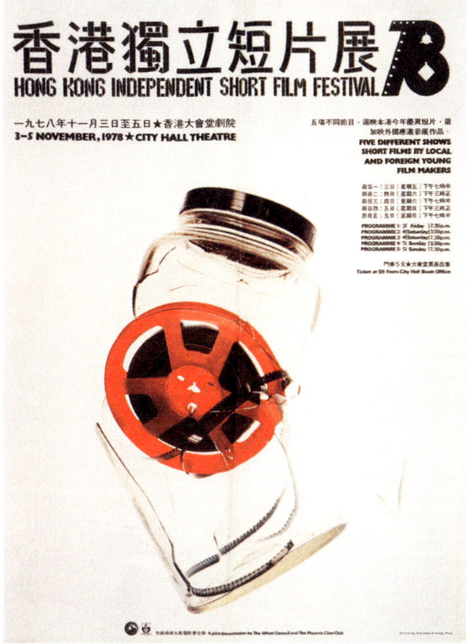

Poster for Hong Kong Independent Short Film Festival (1978)

The Hong Kong New Wave transformed the city's film industry in the 1970s and 1980s. Young filmmakers who had trained in North America and Europe returned to Hong Kong after completing their studies, bringing with them new approaches, themes, and styles. Photographer Lo Yuk-ying captured this moment of change in a series of intimate portraits of filmmakers and actors commissioned by *Film Biweekly*, reflecting a growing consciousness in terms of the construction of images and the presentation of identities and sensibilities within the film system. She depicts the directors Tsui Hark and King Hu in candid portraits in their offices, action filmmaker John Woo smoking a cigarette during a break on-set, and Jackie Chan, pioneer of the comedic form of kung fu cinema, in a moment of repose. Through penetrating portrayals of faces and gestures, Lo offers intimate insights into the leading figures and rising stars of Hong Kong cinema during an era of intense creativity.   BW

Lo Yuk-ying (born ca. 1950, Hong Kong)
Photographs for *Film Biweekly*
Gelatin silver print
Dimensions variable
Gift of Lo Yuk Ying, 2020
CA66

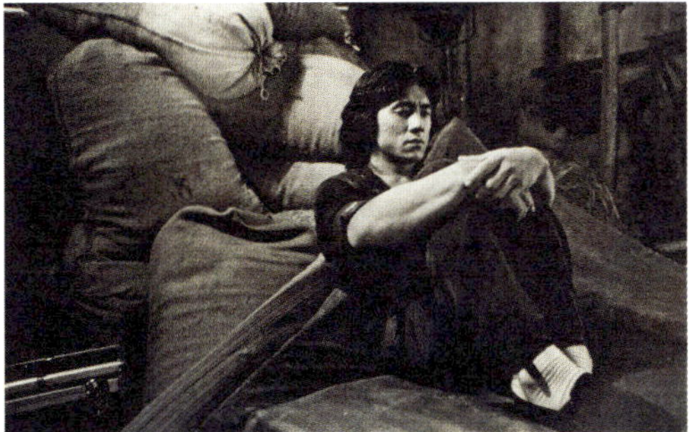

Jackie Chan (director, actor), 1981

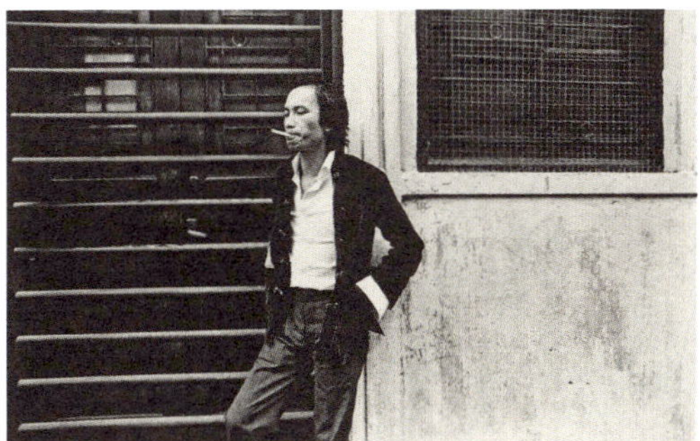

John Woo (director, producer), 1979

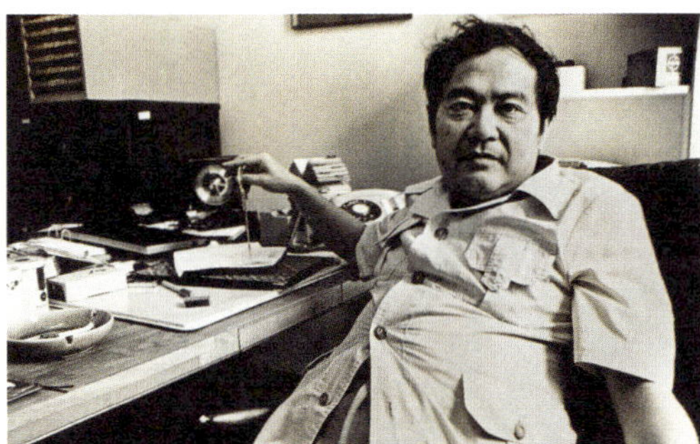

King Hu (director), 1980

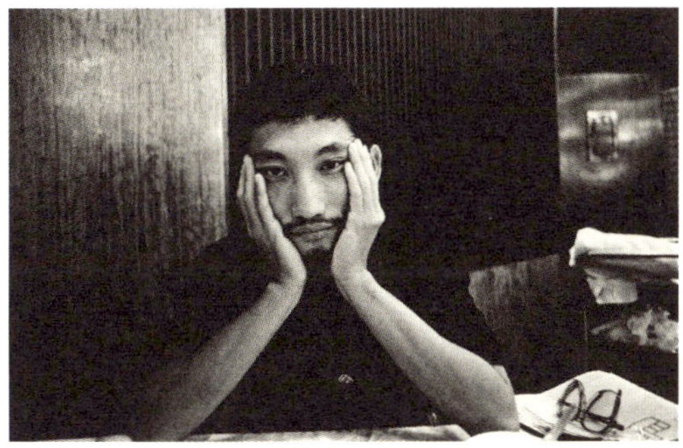

Tsui Hark (director, producer), 1980

Founded in 1976 by writer Chan Koon-chung, Peter Dunn, and Henry U, the monthly *City Magazine* is notable for its emphasis on the visual. With its focus on contemporary culture, lifestyle, and trends, the magazine champions a cosmopolitan perspective that reflects Hong Kong's creative milieu. It was founded as a fundamentally collaborative project and its artistic style was shaped by practitioners from a range of disciplines. In 1982, the cultural entrepreneur Alan Zie Yongder was appointed as publishing consultant and transformed the magazine's aesthetic. This included enlarging the format and logotype and featuring a portrait on the cover of each issue. The first issue published after this re-design was art directed by William Chang Suk-ping, with Raymond Suen as photographer and Tina Liu as stylist. The dark colour palette and arrangement of the model's profile with a calla lily convey a refined elegance and a spatial sensibility. The publication of the magazine each month was eagerly awaited by the city's style-conscious set, with the cover being a particular subject of conversation.   CC

City Magazine (established 1976)
William Chang Suk-ping (born 1953)
No. 68, April 1982
Print on paper
43.5 × 28 cm
M+ Library Special Collection

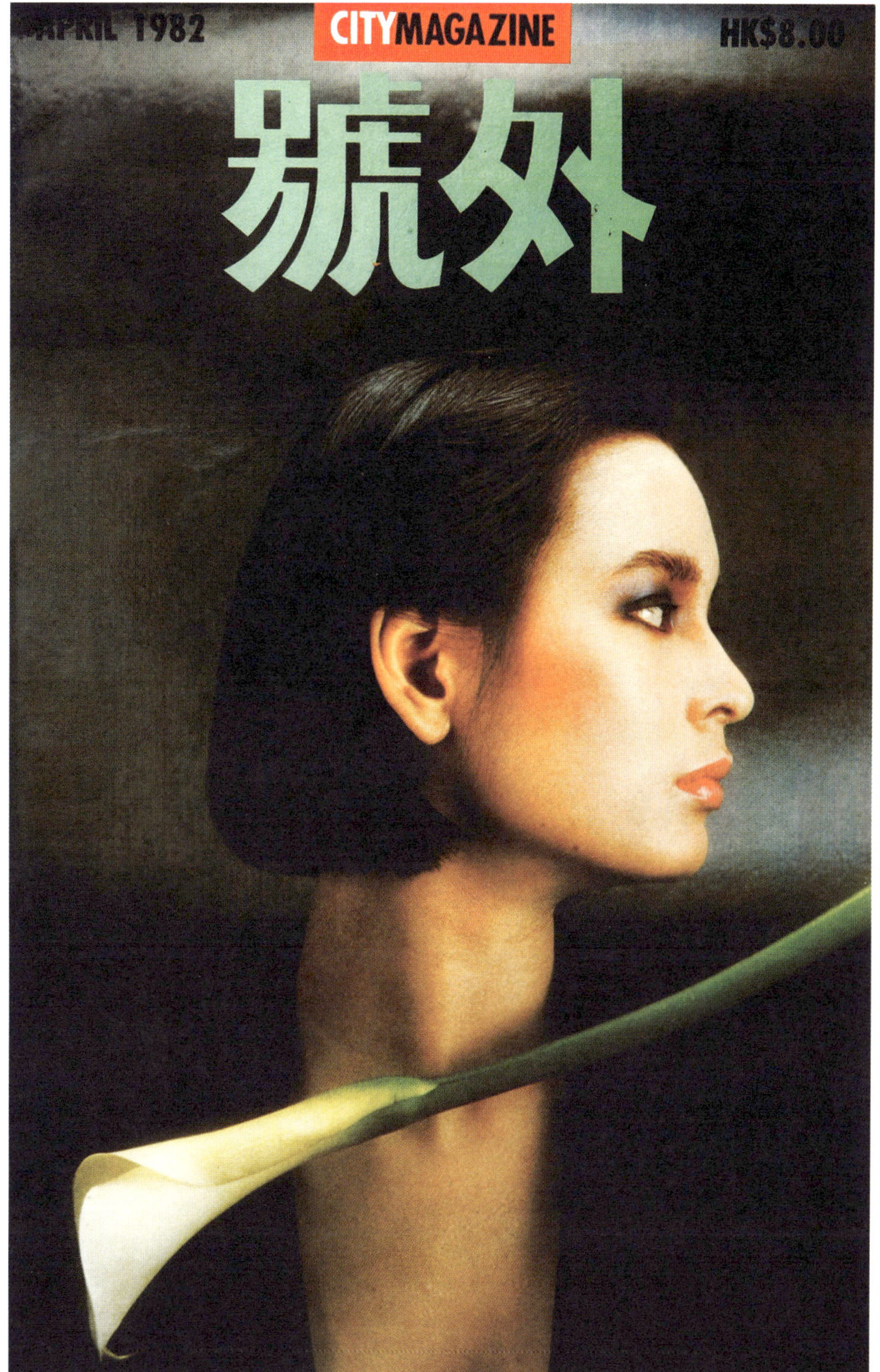

APRIL 1982
CITYMAGAZINE
HK$8.00
號外

Cantopop came to occupy a central position in the city's collective identity in the mid-1970s. Its growth over the following decades was inextricably linked with developments in television, film, and graphic design. Cantopop received extensive radio airplay throughout the 1980s and 1990s, but the genre's popularity was also a consequence of its prominence in films and television series for which artists were commissioned to write theme songs and soundtracks. Many Cantopop performers, including Leslie Cheung and Anita Mui, were also well-known actors. Alongside the success of Cantopop domestically, the growth of diasporic communities and the visibility of Hong Kong cinema and music celebrities spread the genre globally.

In the 1980s, Cantopop defined Hong Kong popular culture at its most diverse and experimental. This was an era of visual inventiveness, in which fashion editors, designers, filmmakers, illustrators, and photographers collaborated across disciplines. Cantopop's success provided them with an expanded role in crafting the imagery of popular music and led to a fluidity in the application of new approaches and visual paradigms. Design and music became important forces in developing a widely exported transcultural image of Hong Kong.

The atmosphere in which designers operated maintained porous boundaries between disciplines and between the professional and the amateur. Advertising guru Alan Chan, photographer and former art director of Atlantic Records Basil Pao, production and costume designer William Chang Suk-ping, and image stylist Tina Liu captured Cantopop's energy and performativity through album art embodying individual performers' identities and musical styles. Liu, a founding member of the editorial team of the highly influential *City Magazine*, applied her approach to fashion styling to her design for the covers of Deanie Ip's albums. On the cover of Anita Mui's 1984 album *Leap the Stage*, designed by Alan Chan, Mui is rendered in a dazzling airbrush technique, a choice inspired by Yamaguchi Harumi's depictions of women for Tokyo's PARCO department store in the 1980s. For George Lam's *Love Fever* of 1984, Basil Pao combined a photograph of Lam with a background of flames depicted in oil and chalk against a blue sky. These examples demonstrate how packaging design contributes to the consumer's aesthetic engagement with the music and the personas of the performers. Reflecting Cantopop's close relationship with television, Chan's cover design for the soundtrack album of the hit drama series *Legend of the Condor Heroes* uses video stills of its stars, Roman Tam and Jenny Tseng. Designs produced during the heyday of Cantopop remain deeply woven into the fabric of Hong Kong's collective memory today.   SS

Alan Chan (born 1950, Hong Kong)
Album cover for Anita Mui: *Leap the Stage*
1984
Offset lithograph
31.5 × 32 × 0.5 cm
2017.203

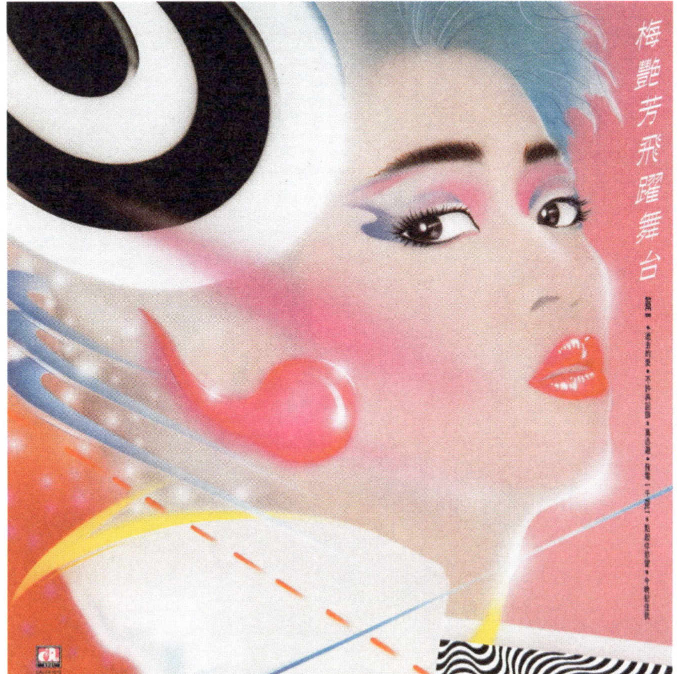

Front

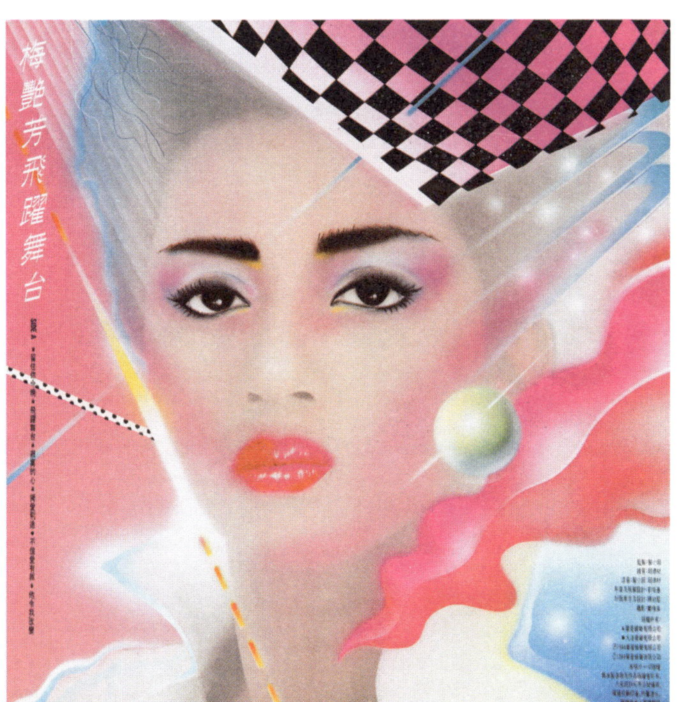

Back

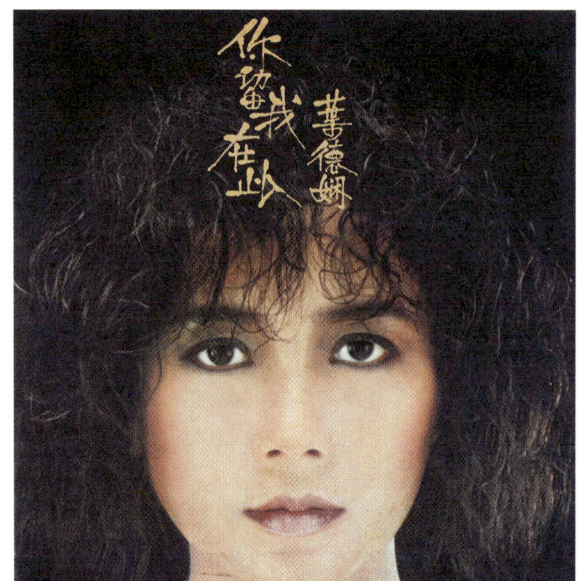

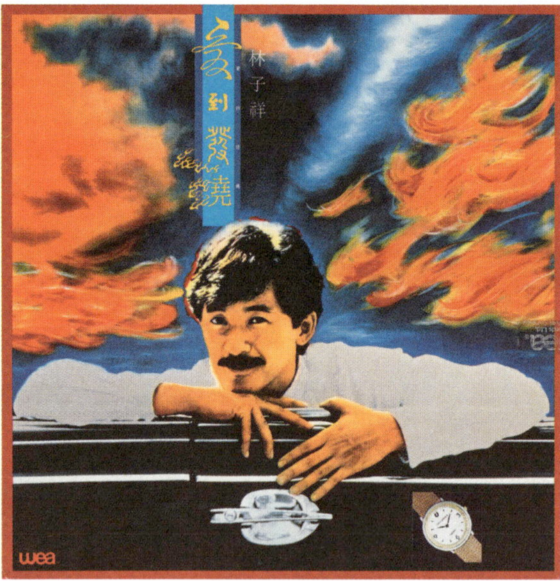

Tina Liu (born 1957, Hong Kong)
Album cover for Deanie Ip: *You Left Me Here*
1984
Offset lithograph
31.3 × 31.2 × 0.5 cm
2019.160

Basil Pao (born 1955, Hong Kong)
Album cover for George Lam: *Love Fever*
1984
Offset lithograph
31 × 31.5 × 0.2 cm
2017.204

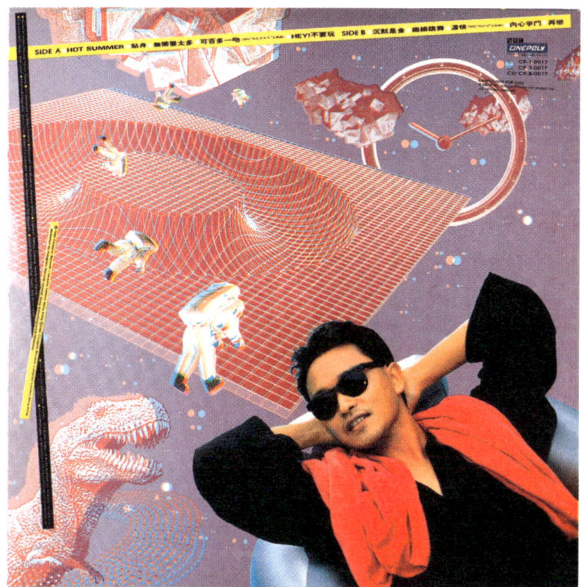

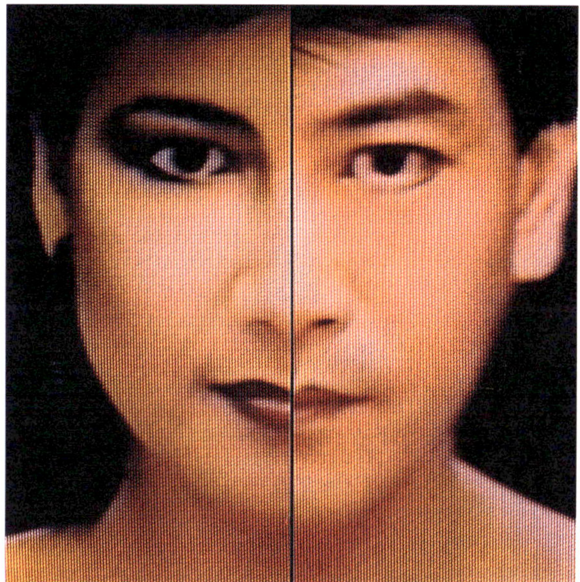

Alan Chan (born 1950, Hong Kong)
Album cover for Leslie Cheung: *Hot Summer*
1988
Offset lithograph
31 × 31 cm
Gift of Alan Chan, 2019
2020.325

Alan Chan (born 1950, Hong Kong)
Album cover for Roman Tam and Jenny Tseng: *Legend of the Condor Heroes*
1983
Offset lithograph
31 × 31 cm
Gift of Alan Chan, 2019
2020.322

The growth in the popularity of Cantopop from the mid-1970s was in large part due to the role of radio stations. In the early 1990s, the newly established Metro Radio organised the Hit Awards to capitalise on Cantopop's appeal and connect with listeners. Designer Tommy Li created this poster for the Second Annual Hit Awards, of 1992–1993. The design is a play on the Cantonese term *ging baau*, meaning 'powerful', in the title of the awards. In the style of American comic books, the image of a fist smashing a stone wall is accompanied by exclamatory text in a speech bubble. The retro–comic-book aesthetic was adopted for the album art of many American punk rock bands in the 1990s, suggesting a transnational context. Li is one of the most prominent graphic designers in Hong Kong, and this poster illustrates the humour and sensitivity to branding that characterise his practice.   KW

Tommy Li (born 1960, Hong Kong)
Tommy Li Design Workshop (established 1990)
Poster for Metro Radio Hit Awards '92–'93
1992
Offset lithograph
76 × 51 cm
2020.162

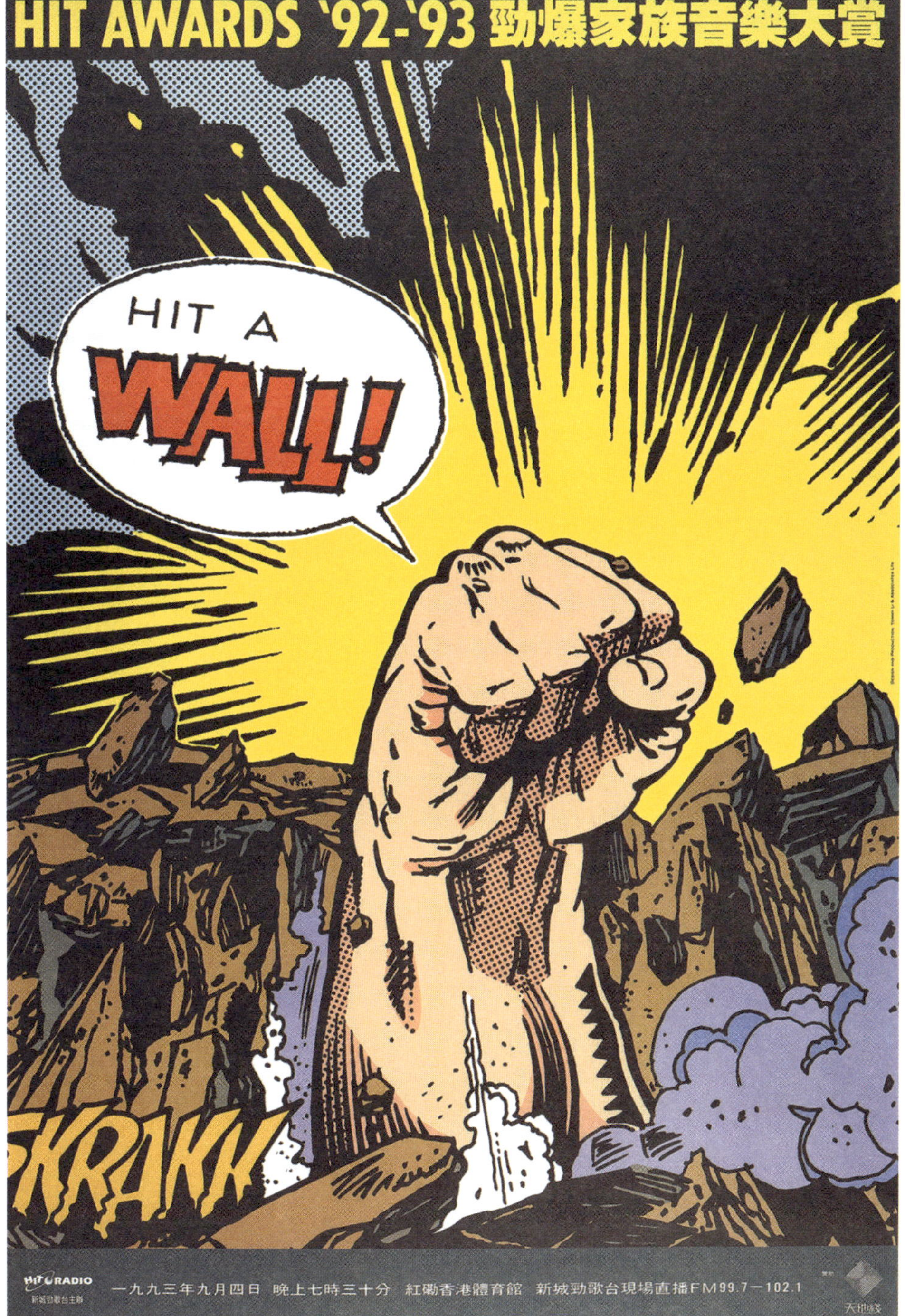
HIT AWARDS '92-'93 勁爆家族音樂大賞
HIT A WALL!
SKRAKK
HIT RADIO
新城勁歌台主辦
一九九三年九月四日　晚上七時三十分　紅磡香港體育館　新城勁歌台現場直播FM99.7－102.1
大地唱文

In the 1980s, Hong Kong's clubs and discos offered spaces for hedonistic celebration, personal distinction, and collective creative awakening. While quite different from one another in nature, both the I Club and Canton Discotheque were platforms for the avant-garde in art, design, interiors, and music. Their visual identities, developed by two of the city's leading designers, communicated their distinctive definitions of a night out.

Located in the Bank of America Tower in Central, the short-lived I Club was founded in 1982 as a private club for the city's elite. Highly aspirational, the design and culture of the I Club reflected the world of its cosmopolitan patrons. The lavish interiors displayed works by artists such as Andy Warhol—who attended the club's opening—and Roy Lichtenstein. The interiors were designed by New York–based designer Joseph D'Urso and included rooms themed around the iconic work of designers like Josef Hoffmann and Charles Rennie Mackintosh. Hong Kong designer Henry Steiner conceived the club's name and its visual identity, which is defined by the letter 'I' in various permutations to reflect the dynamic individuality of the 'me generation'. The graphic identity was articulated in coasters, invitation cards, and matchboxes, as well as full-page advertisements in magazines, a reflection of Steiner's total design approach to defining a cultural space that was both adaptable and immediately identifiable. Although the club operated for only a year owing to a dramatic change in financial sentiment in the run-up to Hong Kong's handover, it signalled an important moment of 1980s cultural and material ambition.

Canton Discotheque, located in Tsim Sha Tsui's Canton Road, offered a more glamorous vision of nightlife, hosting acts from Hong Kong and elsewhere—including New Order, Tat Ming Pair, and Kylie Minogue—as well as club nights that drew from Hong Kong's musical and cultural milieux. Operating between 1985 and 1991, it was shaped in equal part by international club culture and the city's long tradition of a commingling of local and global. Alan Chan's graphic identity for the club features the motif of a swimming man appropriated from cigarette cards from 1930s Shanghai, a design that emphasises the club's playfully subversive invitation to 'plunge in at the deep end'. Chan rendered the club's name in retro-futuristic lettering and extended the typographic and visual character across coasters and other accoutrements—even designing swizzle sticks that echoed the logotype and complemented the interior, which was saturated with neon tubes. The visual identity represents Chan's larger interest in combining imagery from China's cosmopolitan past with a postmodern graphic sensibility that relies on the quoting of visual references. Beyond its significance on the city's nightlife, Canton Discotheque cultivated a generation of tastemakers, extending its influence into fashion, music, and design.   SS

Henry Steiner (born 1934, Austria)
The I Club (1982)
1982
Print on paper
Various dimensions
2020.114
CA31

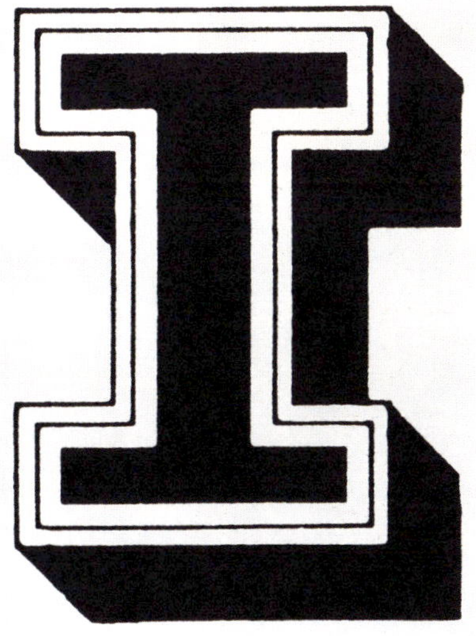

Magazine advertisement

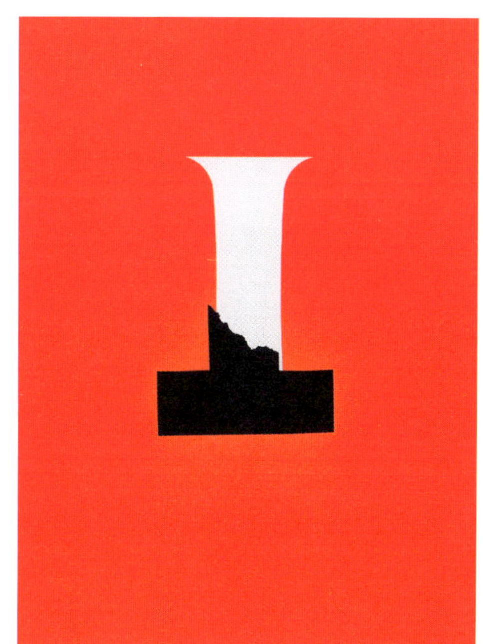

Brochure

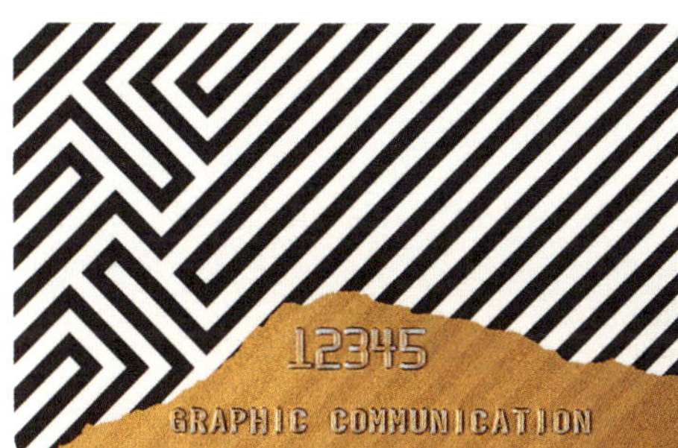

Membership card

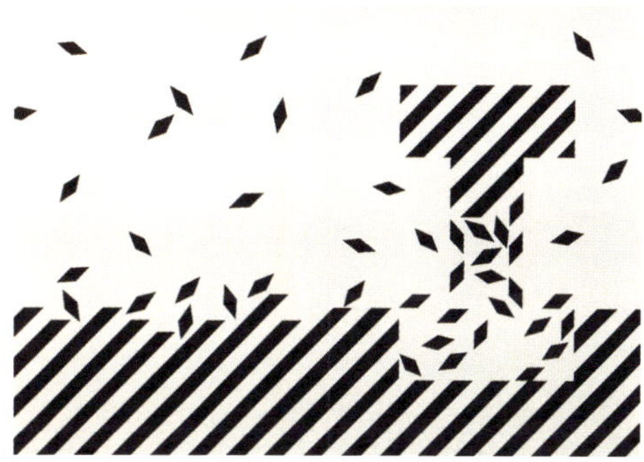

Menu

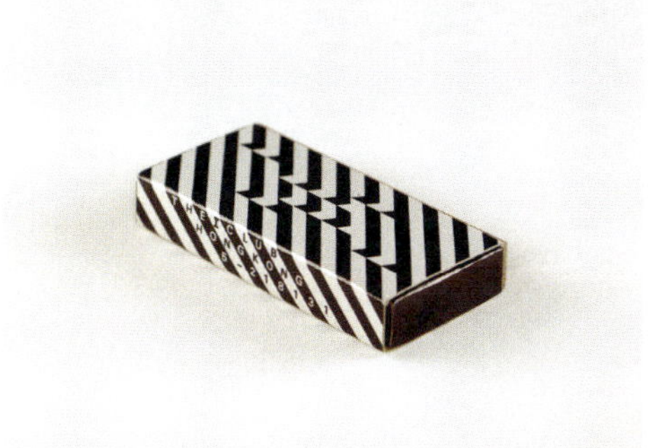

Matchbox

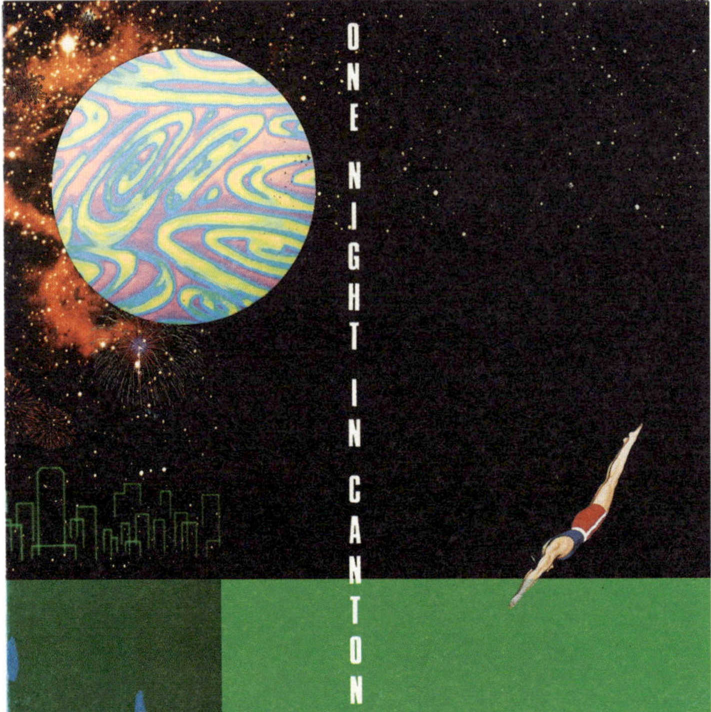

One Night in Canton, album cover

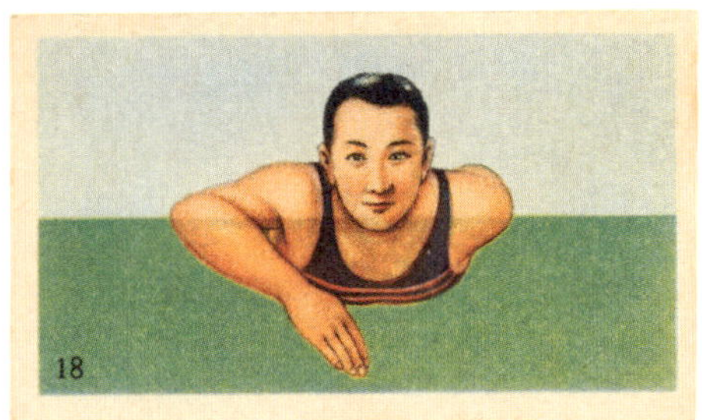
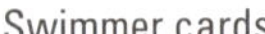
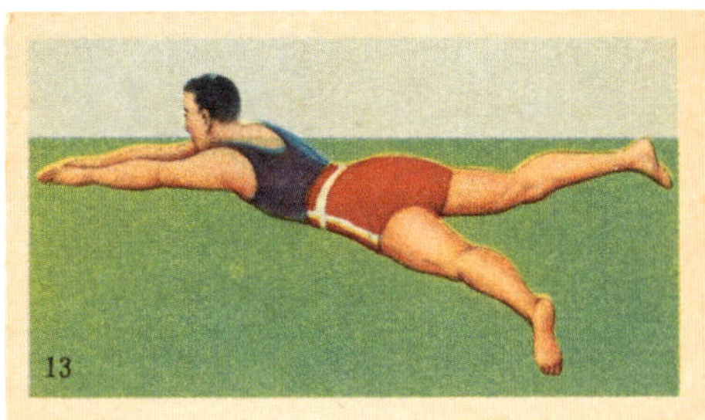

Swimmer cards

Alan Chan (born 1950, Hong Kong)
Canton Discotheque (1985–1991)
1984
Print on paper, plastic
Various dimensions
2020.326
2020.346–2020.349
2020.350–2020.357
CA70

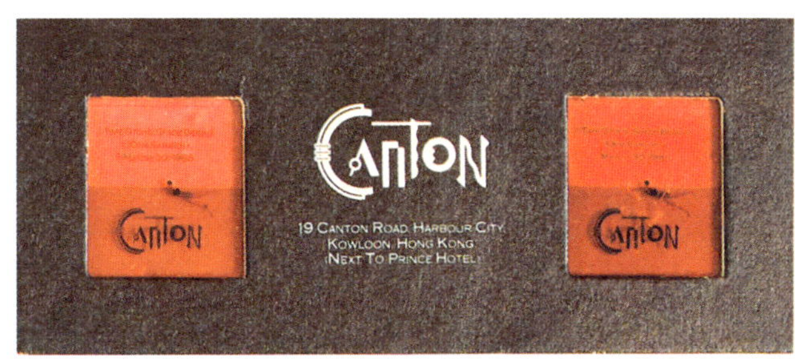

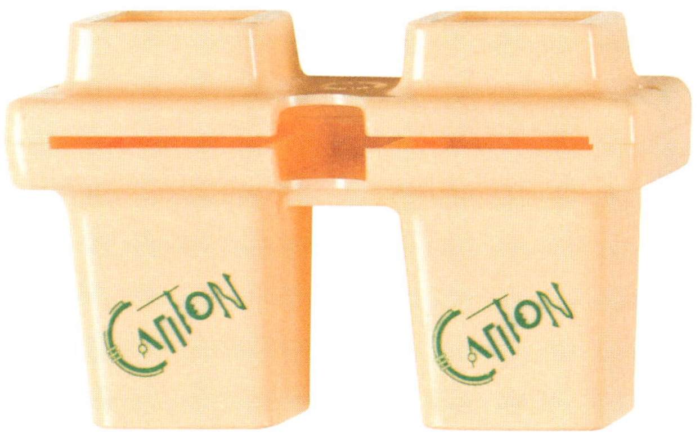

Invitation in the form of a slide viewer and slide

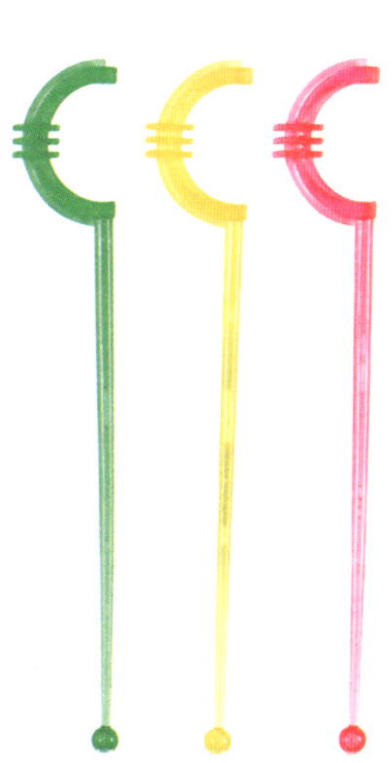

Round-tip stirrers

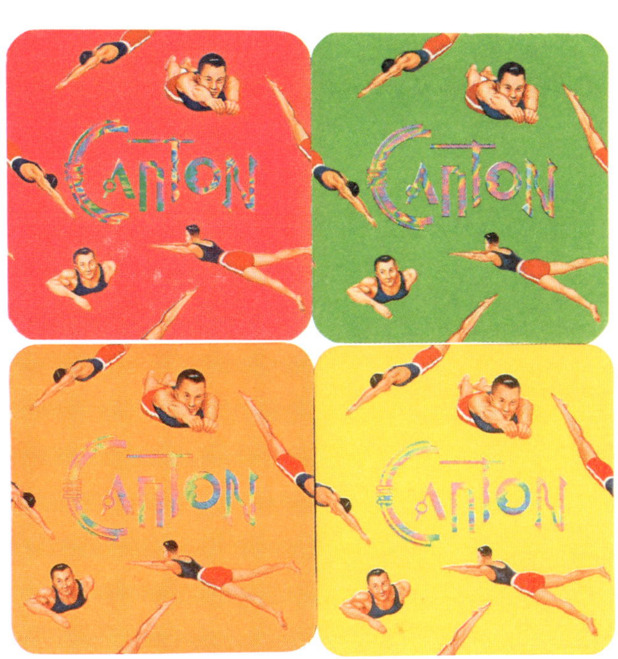

Coasters

ARE YOU CRAZY?

Everyday objects and experiences inspire creative expressions that are distinctly Hong Kong

Pak Sheung Chuen examines everyday interactions and experiences, including words, objects, behaviours, and social norms. This work originates in an observation that he made while taking the MTR one day. He noticed a fellow passenger studying a supermarket receipt. Reading the receipt upside down, Pak became intrigued by the potential meanings lying hidden and unrecognised in this mundane record of daily life.

Part performance, part installation, this work is named for the sum total of Pak's own supermarket purchase. *The Miracle of $132.30* consists of the eight items that he bought, and the accompanying receipt. When read from top to bottom, the receipt contains a hidden message; together the second Chinese character of each item listed recreates the Bible verse 'Whosoever believeth in him should [not perish, but] have eternal life'. As with Pak's artistic practice as whole, this work draws attention to the potential for wonder in simple everyday actions and banal routines.　CC

Pak Sheung Chuen (born 1977, Fujian)
The Miracle of $132.30
2009
Thermal paper receipt, supermarket goods, and plastic bag
Dimensions variable
M+ Sigg Collection, Hong Kong. By donation
2012.769

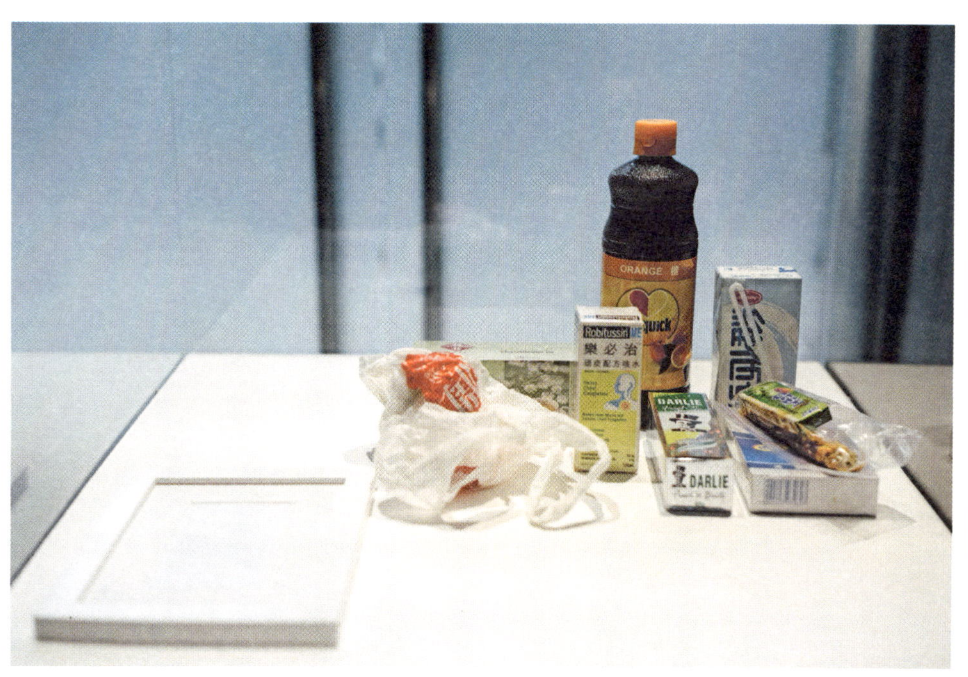

```
          C R C 超 市 (0017)
          欢   谢   光   临


   德宝菊花 25s        *10.50        7.50  A
   维他奶 375 毫升                   4.20  A
 新的橙汁840ml                      35.90  A
 黑人美白牙膏90g                    10.90  A
   乐必拍顽疾配方咪=   *45.50       39.90  A
   能得利黑加仑子糖    *5.80         5.80  A
   真永青苹果糖 33g                  4.20  A
   强生防水褙霉胶布    *39.80       23.90  A
              Subtotal            132.30
TOTAL                     132.30
CASH -THANK YOU -                 200.00
Change                             67.70
```

13-11-2003 12:46:24 R#2 C:360 T#21323

Designer Lee Chi-wing's ethos of appropriating familiar materials and forms in new objects is exemplified in *Repair – floor lamp*. He repurposes a plastic butcher's pendant lampshade, commonly seen in Hong Kong's wet markets and grocery stores, as a floor lamp. The lampshade is produced by leading plastics manufacturer Star Industrial Company as part of their Red A line. Lee's use of wood for the tripod base establishes a contrast between organic and synthetic materials. The development of light industry in Hong Kong balanced aesthetics with practicality and cost as major considerations in the design process. However, technological advances and greater disposable income with a corresponding increase in quality of life saw the emergence of a culture of consumption and convenience. To propose an alternative to this lifestyle, Lee develops products that amplify the original character of his materials, inspiring the public to recognise the enduring value of vernacular design.   KW

Milk Design (established 1998)
Repair – floor lamp
Designed 2010, made 2019
Plastic and wood
123.2 × 43.6 × 38.7 cm
2019.557

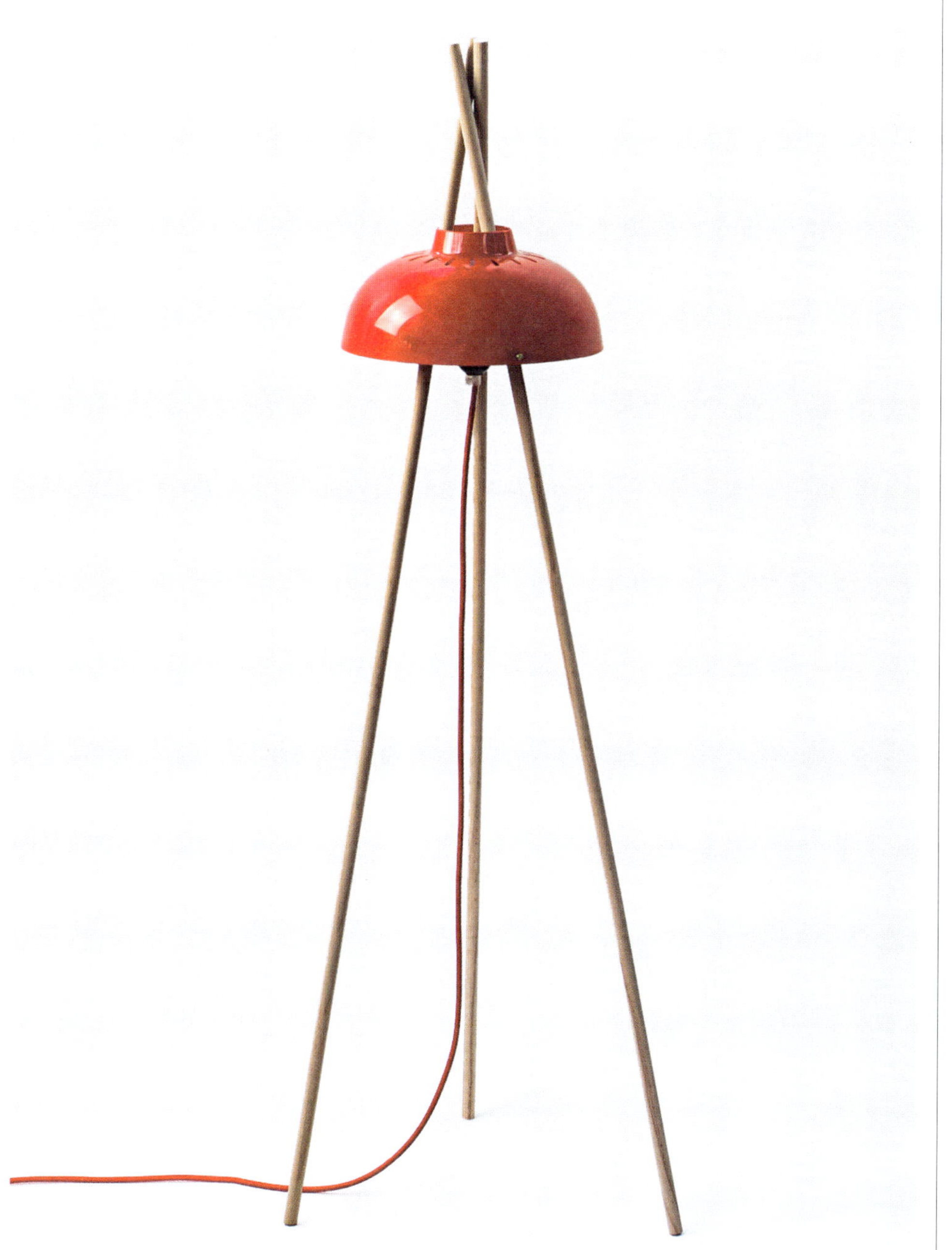

When British designer Michael Young moved to Hong Kong in 2006, he was struck by the folded paper toys he saw for sale in outdoor markets in Sheung Wan and began to incorporate elements of paper-folding—*zipzi* in Cantonese—into his product designs. *Folded Newspaper Zipzi* is a table composed of a round glass top and a cone-shaped metal stand covered in a structure formed by interlocking triangles of folded newspaper. Young began the *Zipzi* series in 2007, and this example incorporates local newspapers as source material, bringing the series back to its point of inspiration. The vibrant, varied colours of the paper create an intricate motif when arranged together, and the process translates craft into high-end design. The *Zipzi* series extends Young's interest in texture and materials, which he articulates with flexible and functional designs for furniture, lighting, and other products.   KW

Michael Young (born 1966, United Kingdom)
Folded Newspaper Zipzi
2009
Paper, metal, and glass
42 × 30 × 30 cm
Gift of Michael Young, 2014
2015.124

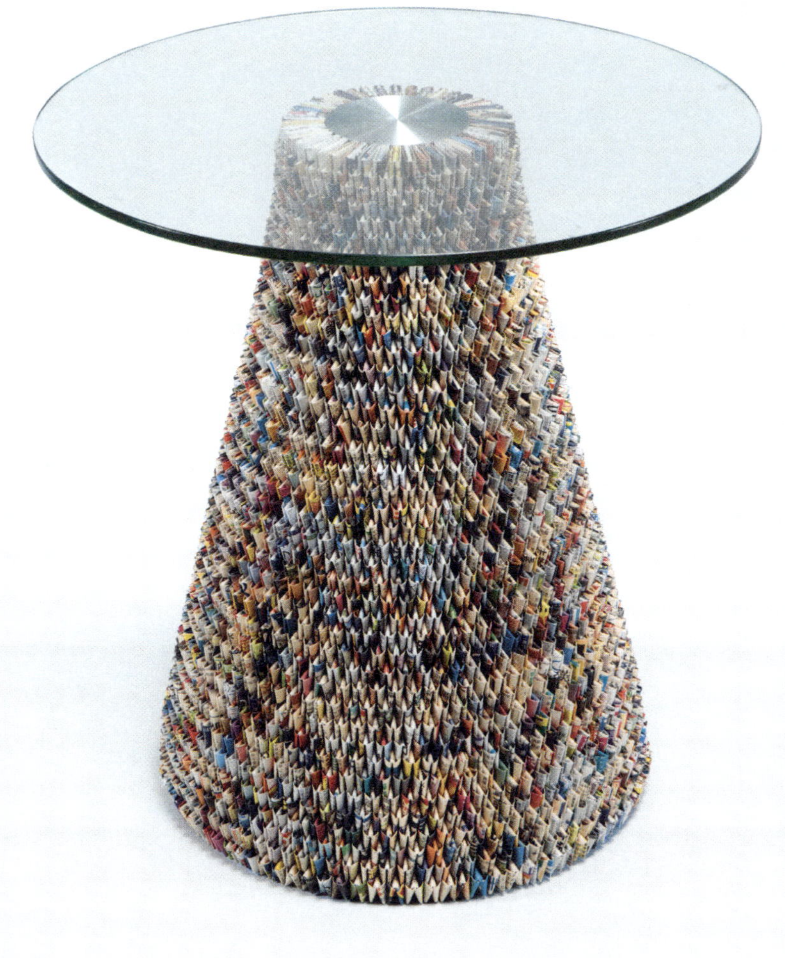

The global upcycling movement advocates the transformation of used objects, usually intended for landfill, into new materials and products. Upcycling has been widely adopted by designers and engineers, with applications identified across diverse fields. Designer Kevin Cheung believes the practice can inform a design strategy that extends the typically short lifespan of consumer products. *Boombottle* is made from a discarded plastic container and speaker components. The container's cap is repurposed to become the speaker's volume switch, and an LED inside the translucent plastic body allows it to glow in the dark. Recycled felt is used to line the speaker, contain a battery unit, and make a pouch that can hold a mobile phone or other media player. Created in collaboration with NGOs that offer employment opportunities to the disadvantaged, *Boombottle* uses the airtight and lightweight quality of plastic in a product that can meet market demand, reduce waste, and protect the environment.   FT

Kevin Cheung (born 1987, Hong Kong)
Boombottle
2014
Plastic, felt, electronic components, and metal
30.1 × 21.3 × 14.5 cm
2019.202

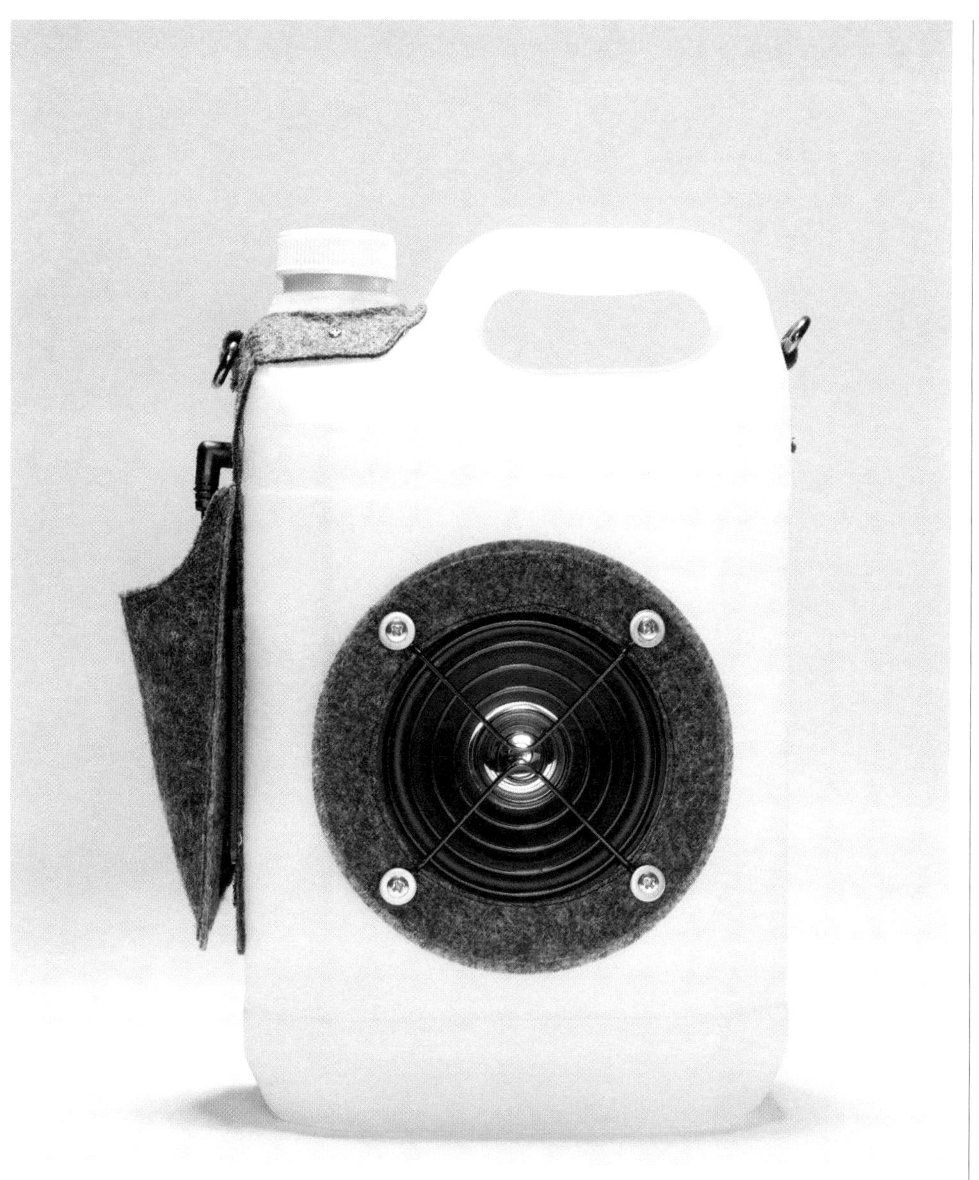

Fashion designer Vivienne Tam's *Mao* collection adopts an irreverent attitude towards a key image in Chinese communist iconography. This skirt and fitted Zhongshan suit jacket—a garment that became inseparable from the public image of Mao Zedong—are cut from a fabric with a design of alternating positive and negative portraits of the chairman created by Zhang Hongtu, a Chinese artist based in the United States. The image of Mao was used extensively by the Chinese government in its propaganda, particularly during the Cultural Revolution. Since then, it has been appropriated by artists and designers as a contemporary icon. Zhang's design references Andy Warhol's screen-printed portraits of the chairman and other celebrities. Tam's collaboration with Zhang reflects a moment in the mid-1990s marked by China's entry onto the world stage, prompted by Deng Xiaoping's economic reforms. International audiences began to encounter the visual culture of the People's Republic through its incorporation into works of art as well as consumer products. Tam applied the image of Mao to a range of clothing, an appropriation that signals its total absorption into contemporary popular culture.   FT

Vivienne Tam (born 1957, Guangdong)
Mao suit from *Mao* collection, Spring/Summer 1995
1995
Woven polyester
100 × 96.3 cm
Gift of Vivienne Tam, 2020
2020.112

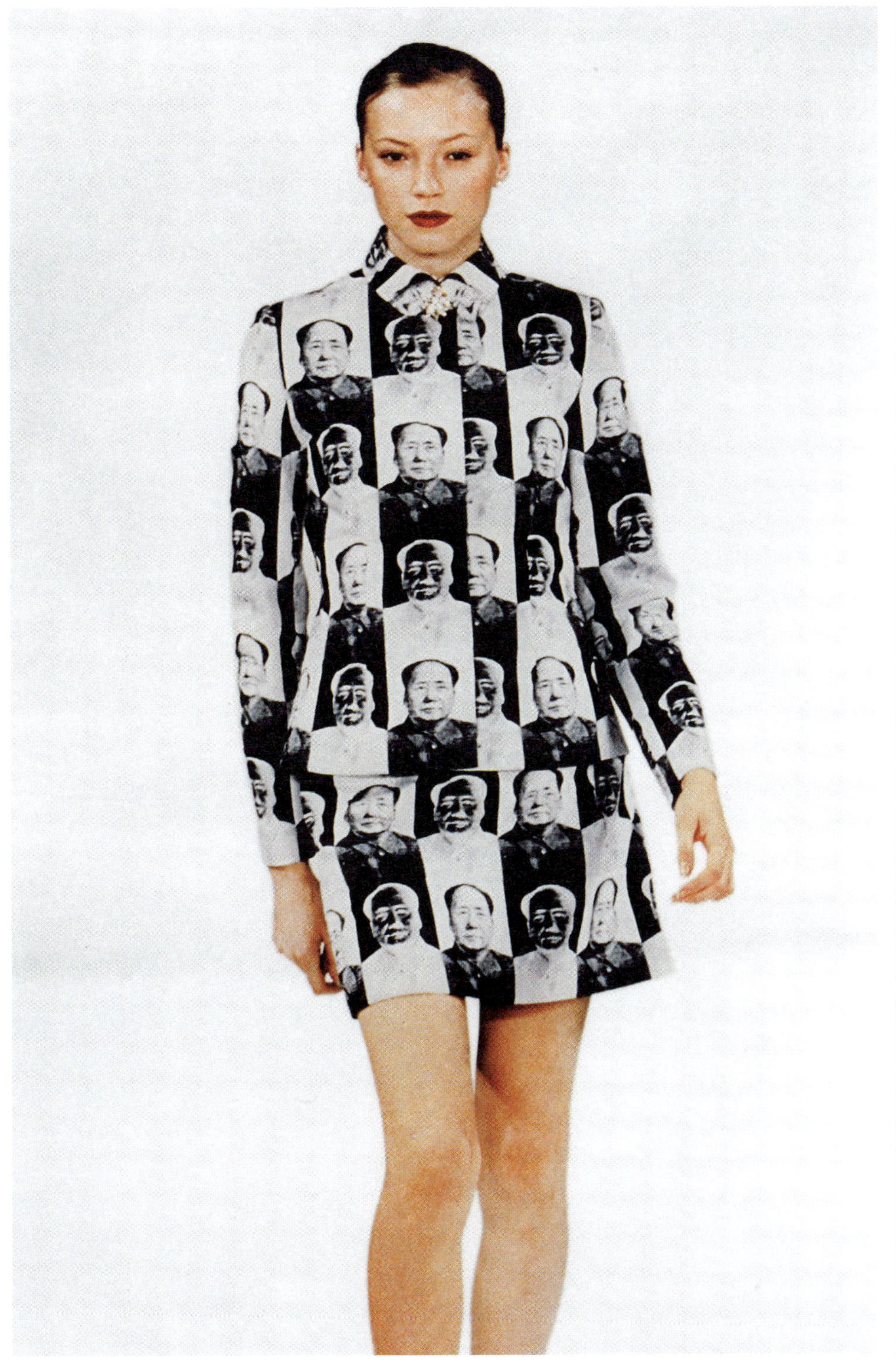

Jerry Kwan was a member of the first generation of artists from Hong Kong to study overseas. Following studies in Columbus, Ohio, Kwan became a part of the New York–based Epoxy Art Group in the late 1980s, made up largely of artists from Hong Kong. After his return to Hong Kong in the late 1990s, he expanded his practice in abstract painting to more playful works. He began the *Pseudo-Folk Art* series of collage works in 2000, taking inspiration from his childhood memories of traditional forms of Chinese folk art such as opera, paper-cutting, and kite-making. Kwan applies a collage technique to found objects such as newspaper, cardboard, and hemp rope to depict Chinese opera figures. These two characters represent a warrior and a scholar, with the mosaic backdrop enhancing their three-dimensional, sculptural quality. In traditional opera, the colour, pattern, and imagery on performers' masks and costumes denote specific meanings, but Kwan replaces these conventional forms with abstract patterns and newspaper fragments to propose a more relevant cultural context. Through his examination of traditional forms, Kwan expands the interpretation of folk art, recasting it as a contemporary practice.   KW

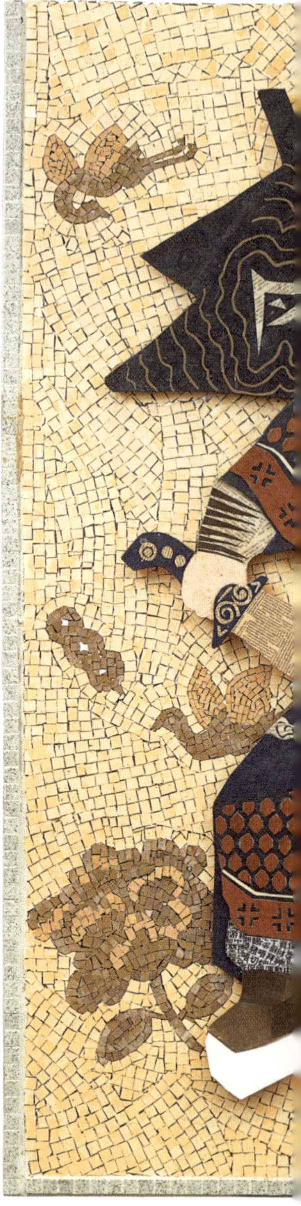

Jerry Kwan (born 1934, Guangdong; died 2008, Hong Kong)
Opera Figures
2007
Mixed media on wood
147.6 × 177 × 11 cm
Gift of an anonymous donor, 2015
2016.400

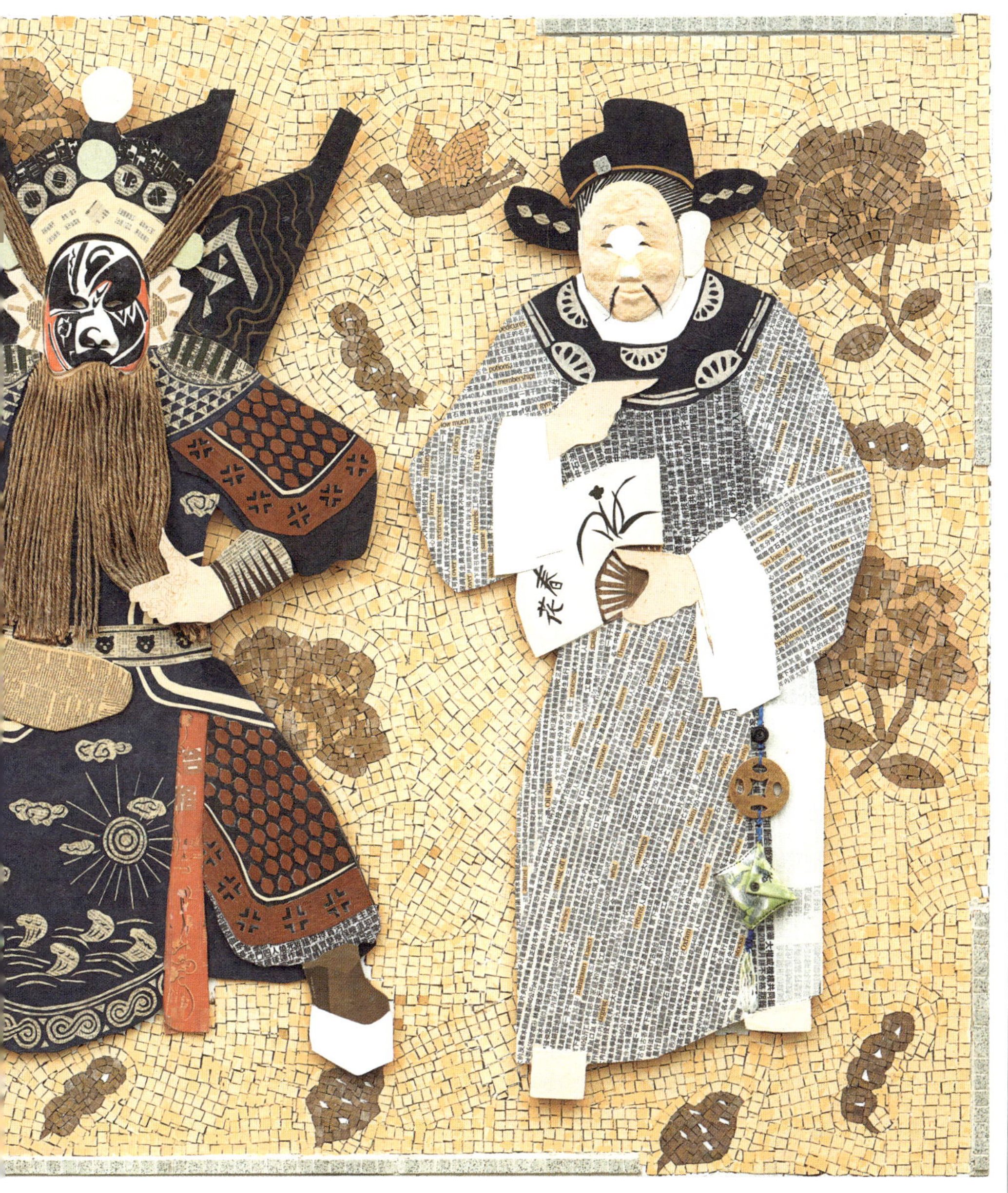

Tsang Kin-Wah investigates the tensions between individual psychology, societal norms, and the history of ideas. He is known for his cerebral, immersive digital projections as well as his earlier hand-crafted 'wallpapers'. *Untitled – Hong Kong* is a site-specific room-sized installation lined with Tsang's printed wallpaper. This work's decorative language was inspired by the patterns created by William Morris, a leading member of the nineteenth-century British Arts and Crafts movement, as well as by the surface decorations of Ming- and Qing-era blue-and-white porcelain. The decorative impact is upset when the pattern is viewed close up. This reveals how the design is in fact made up of profanities in English and colloquial Cantonese. The disjunction between the elegant aesthetic and the abrasive bilingual content crystallises feelings of malaise and rage and investigates the role of language in postcolonial societies.   KW

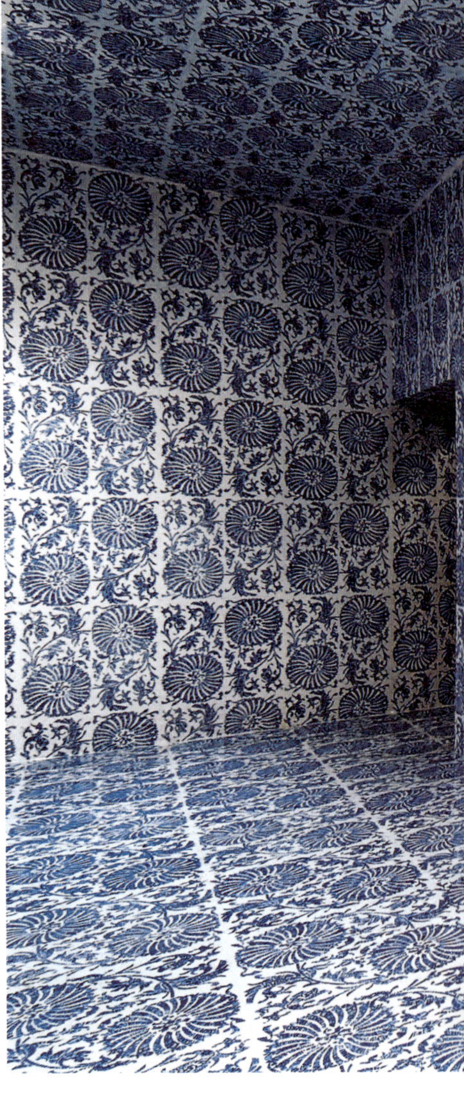

Tsang Kin-Wah (born 1976, Guangdong)
Untitled – Hong Kong
2003–2004
Screen print and acrylic on paper
Dimensions variable
2017.239

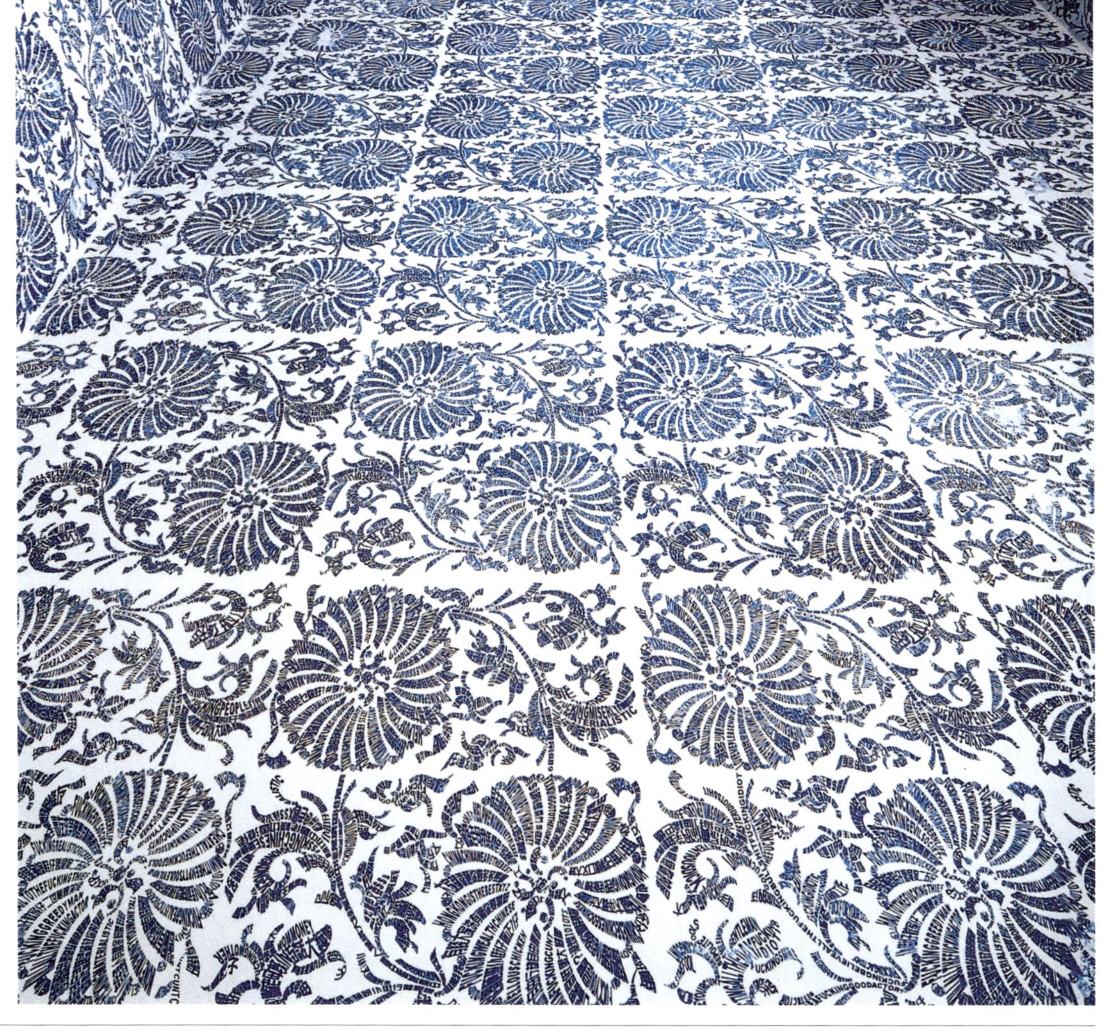

Game designer and technologist Alan Kwan's practice transforms the videogame environment into an experimental artistic medium. His works tap into deep-seated aspects of human psychology. *The Hallway* is a single-player joystick-controlled game inspired by Kwan's childhood experience of being shut out of the house by his father. The player, in the role of a child trapped in the carpeted hallway of a Hong Kong apartment building, is able to move through the corridors—populated with discarded furniture and everyday objects—and through a series of doorways. Every door, however, leads back to the same corridor. The game's design creates an atmosphere of anxiety, even panic, at the futility of action. Kwan turns a personal memory into a collective experience using the virtual realm, generating a very human psychological response.   KW

Alan Kwan (born 1990, Hong Kong)
The Hallway
2016
Videogame
2020.96

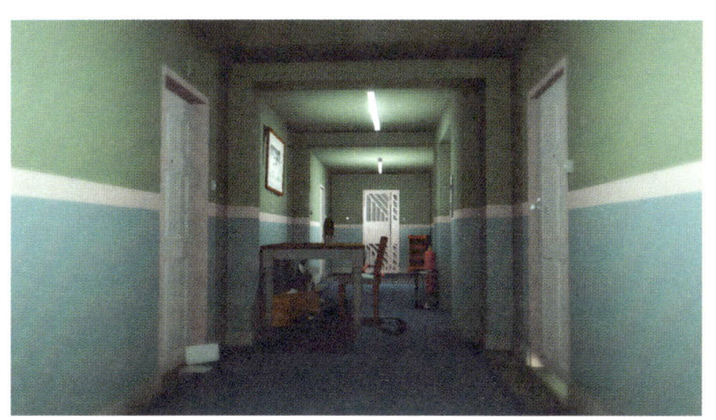

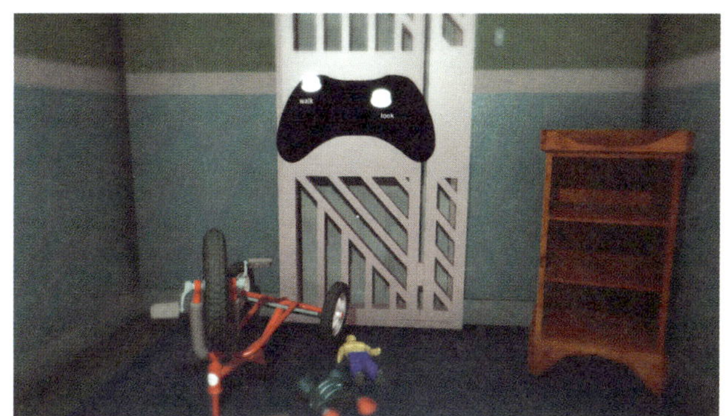

walk
look

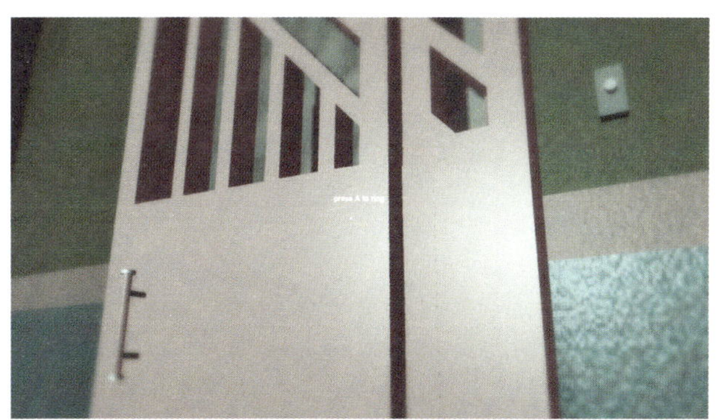

press A to open

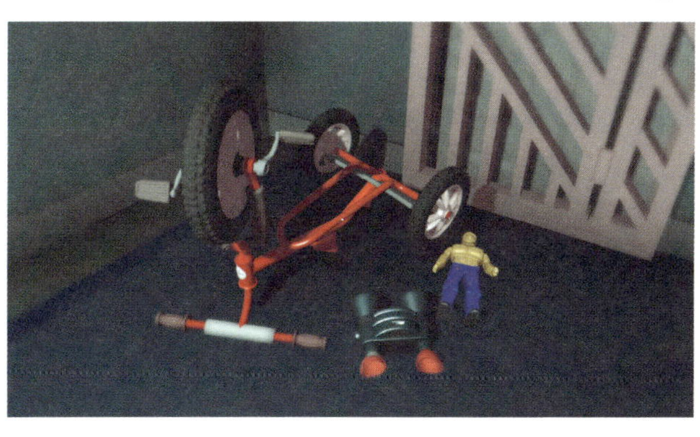

Inspired by the programming of the Hong Kong International Film Festival, Ho Sin Tung created the imaginary *Hong Kong Inter-vivos Film Festival*, a set of thirty-five drawings, videos, and installations that resemble film posters, stills, and trailers. Founded in the 1970s, the Hong Kong International Film Festival played a central role in bringing Asian and world cinema to the city and fostering a vibrant film culture. Ho's body of work relates to twenty-eight fictional movies, some of which are adapted from literature. For example, her *Voyage au bout de la nuit* (Journey to the End of Night) is based on the novel of that name by the French writer Céline, a semi-autobiographical journey through wartime devastation, colonial exploitation, and urban poverty. Ho identifies Céline's work as an influence on her practice, taking it as a point of departure for a possible cinematic narrative. By turning the framework of a commercial film festival into source material for art-making, Ho reinterprets the cultural and artistic references that have shaped her work.   KW

Ho Sin Tung (born 1986, Hong Kong)
Voyage au bout de la nuit
2012
Ink and coloured pencil on paper
104 × 70 cm
2013.522

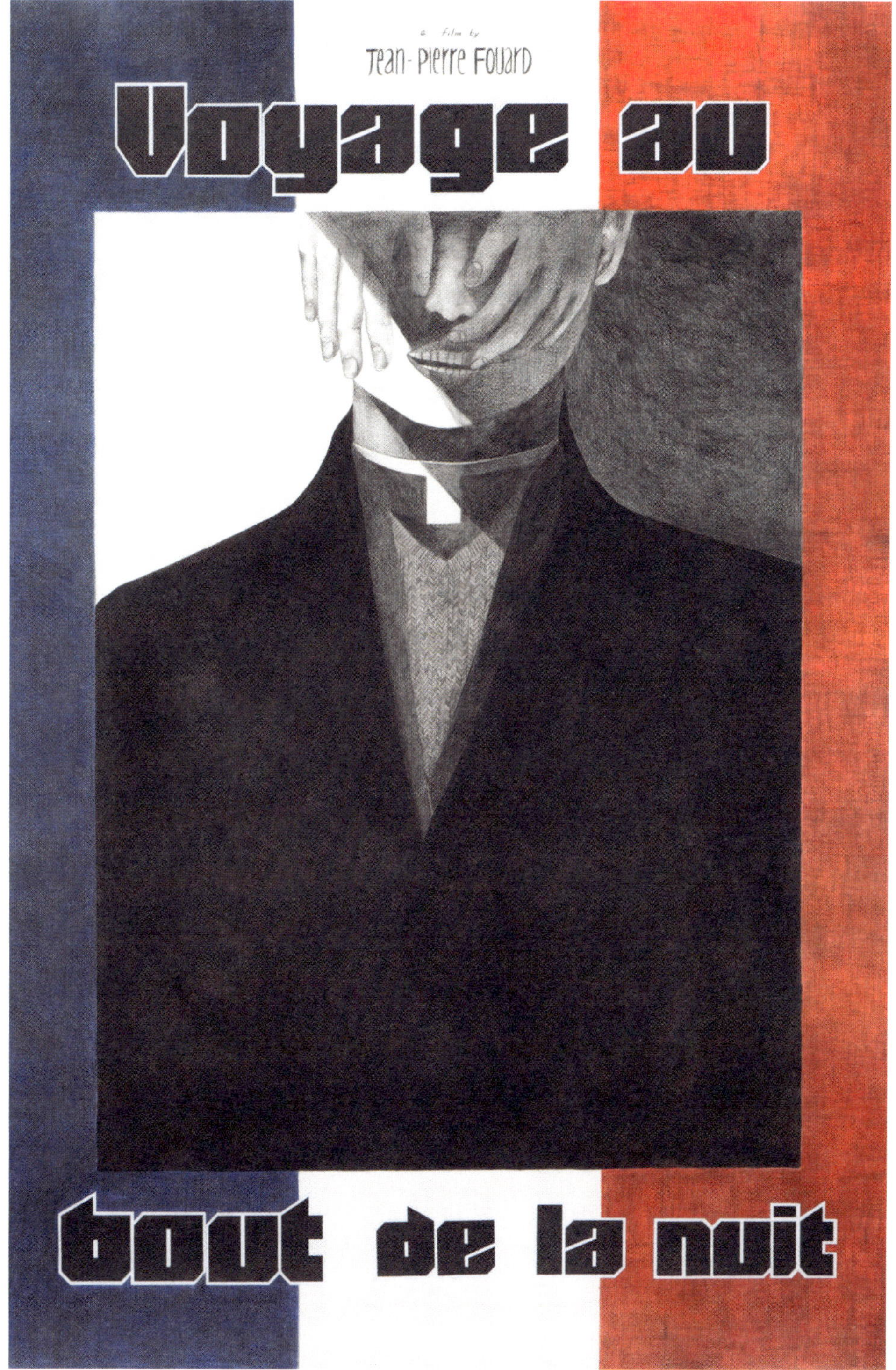

a film by
Jean-Pierre Fouard
Voyage au
bout de la nuit

Museum of the Lost is an archive of news clippings, postcards, and vintage photographs selected by artist duo Sara Wong and Leung Chi Wo. Through the process of building and researching their 'collection', the artists interrogate the histories within each image, reinterpreting them through the perspective of the peripheral figures in the images. Each record is accompanied by a fictional narrative presented in the form of an exhibition label, including personal or subjective details. The labels prompt viewers to imagine the hidden or lost histories in the images that we consume every day. In their related series of nearly life-size photographic portraits, *he was lost yesterday and we found him today*, Wong and Leung assume the identities of the new protagonists of their archival images. Meticulously reproducing personal characteristics and details of costume and gesture, they photograph themselves re-enacting each image in a studio setting, stripped of the context of the original photograph. The imaginative excavation of the lives and motivations of the figures proposes a new way of reading history between fact and fiction.

Among other subjects, Wong and Leung focus on an American naval officer in Hong Kong from a photograph by Yau Leung, a British woman waiting to depart from the port of Yokohama during the Second World War, and a relief worker responding to the 2011 Fukushima nuclear disaster. The artists conjure their stories and motivations, adding a fictional dimension to the historical significance of the subjects.

Taken together, *Museum of the Lost* and *he was lost yesterday and we found him today* uncover the limitations of the role of photographic images as records of the past. Through a process of research and reconstruction, Wong and Leung highlight how visual documentation can isolate certain events and individuals in the writing of history.   KW

Leung Chi Wo + Sara Wong (established 1992)
Museum of the Lost
2013–2015
Set of sixty archival objects
Dimensions variable
2019.479

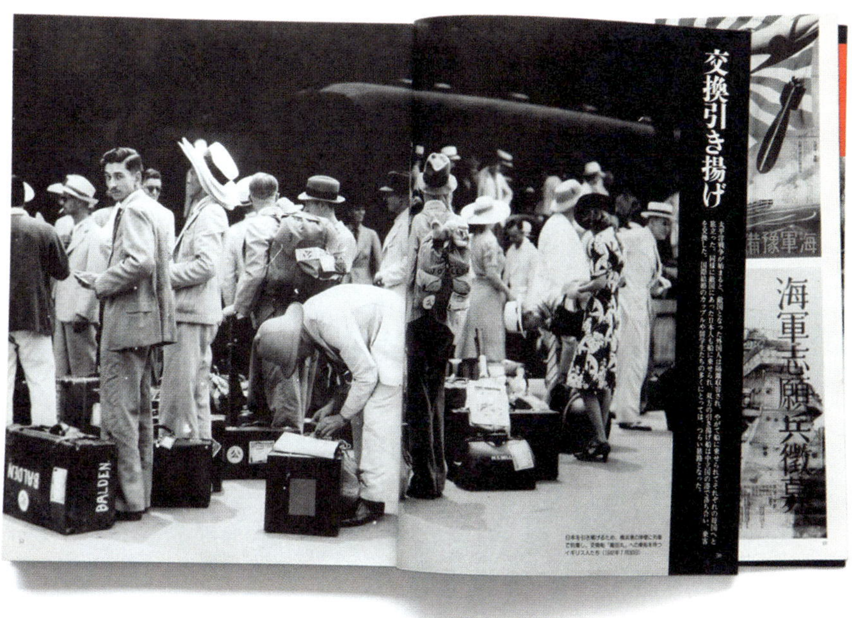

War and People, 1940–49, volume 2, published
by Asahi Shimbun, Tokyo, 1995, 27.5 × 21cm

In pages 50–51 is the scene when the British
diplomats and nationals alight from the train
and are waiting to board IJN Tatsuta Maru on
July 30, 1942 at Yokohama Port for repatriation
as the beginning of exchange for Japanese
nationals living in the enemy states. Here most
are plainly dressed except the lady on the
right. Matched with handbag, hat and gloves
especially for this departure, she wears a
dress with Japanese floral pattern. Young in
her twenties and fashionable, she could be
from a well-off family, perhaps of a senior
consul or wealthy businessman.

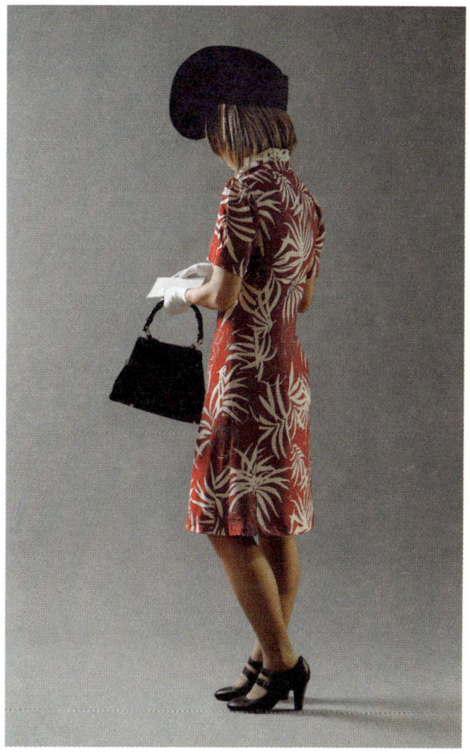

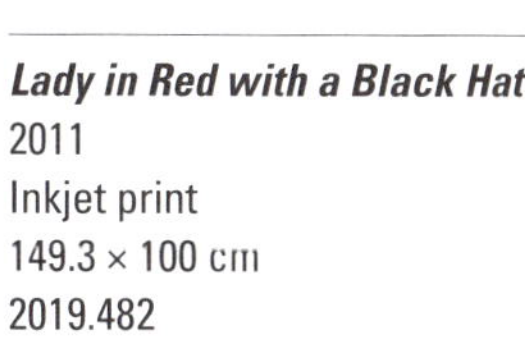

Lady in Red with a Black Hat
2011
Inkjet print
149.3 × 100 cm
2019.482

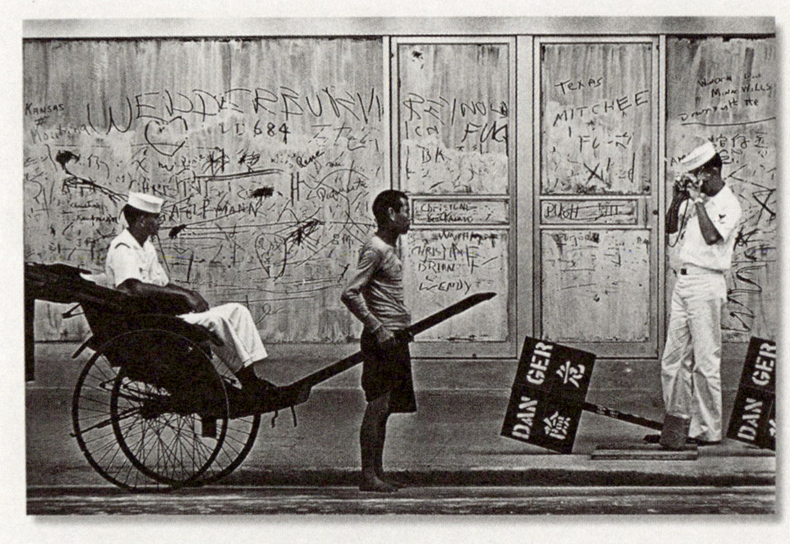

邱良・拉車 (1964) YAU Leung • Rickshaw

Rickshaw, 1964, by Yau Leung, postcard, published by Hong Kong Heritage Museum, 2001, 11 × 15.5 cm

Hong Kong photographer Yau Leung has documented different facets of the city extensively in the 1960s and 1970s. This picture shows during the visit of USS Constellation in the summer of 1962 that two American navy men enjoying the sightseeing. On the right is a 3rd Class Petty Officer taking a photo – with flowers in his hand – probably having been warmly welcomed by bargirls in Wan Chai.

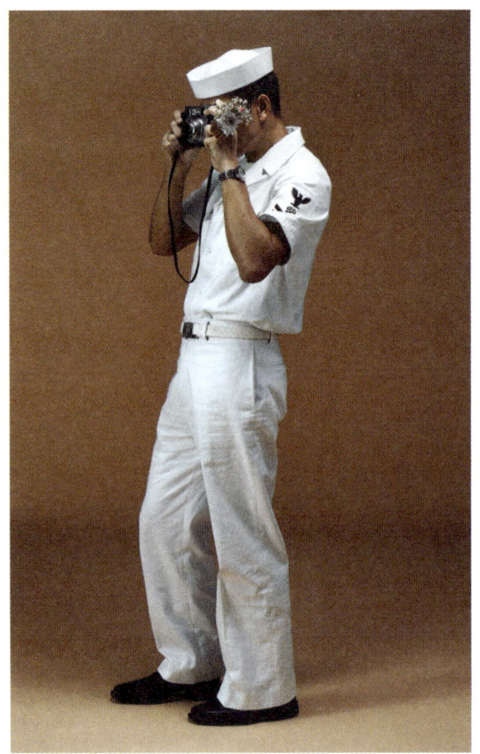

US Navy Man Shooting with His Camera
2014
Inkjet print
149.4 × 100 cm
2019.485

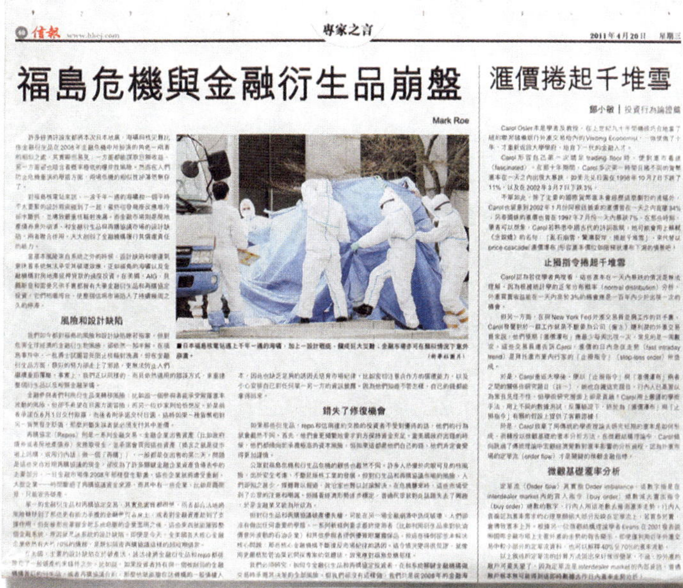

Hong Kong Economic Journal, April 20, 2011,
29 × 35.5 cm

This photograph in page 40 was taken after earthquake at Richter magnitude-9 shook northeastern Japan and unleashed a savage tsunami to destroy the Fukushima nuclear plants on March 11, 2011. In the picture, a team in highly protective suit is working to contain the nuclear disaster. They are exposed to highly radioactive contamination and are regarded as martyrs by the media. The second man from the right may think differently. He was previously unemployed but was recruited after the disaster happened. Although extremely tired and even unable to stand firmly, he is happy with what he is earning which is 20 times more than what he earned before.

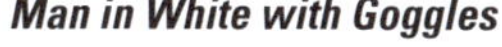

Man in White with Goggles
2013
Inkjet print
149.8 × 100 cm
2019.484

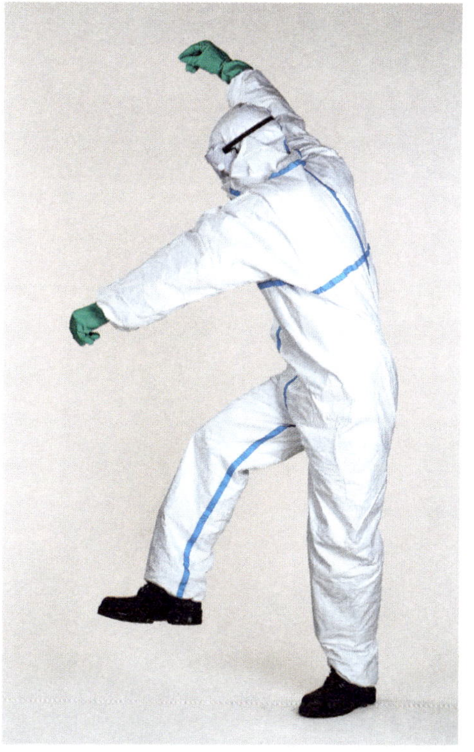

This painting captures a scene from the film *All for the Winner*, which was the highest-grossing film of 1990 in Hong Kong when it was released and transformed the career of 'King of Comedy' Stephen Chow. In this scene, the Guangzhou-born protagonist, played by Chow, is reprimanded by a police officer as he tries to use renminbi to purchase a beverage from a vending machine in Hong Kong. The interaction, alongside the Chinese and English subtitles, points to issues surrounding mainland China–Hong Kong identities, cultural differences, and social conflicts in the years before the handover. The work is part of Chow Chun Fai's *Painting on Movie* series, in which the artist appropriates subtitled movie scenes in order to create new meanings. By referencing the popular consciousness embedded in specific films, Chow Chun Fai transforms scenes and dialogue excerpts into social metaphors, offering a reading of moments from the recent past that can resonate with contemporary viewers.   KW

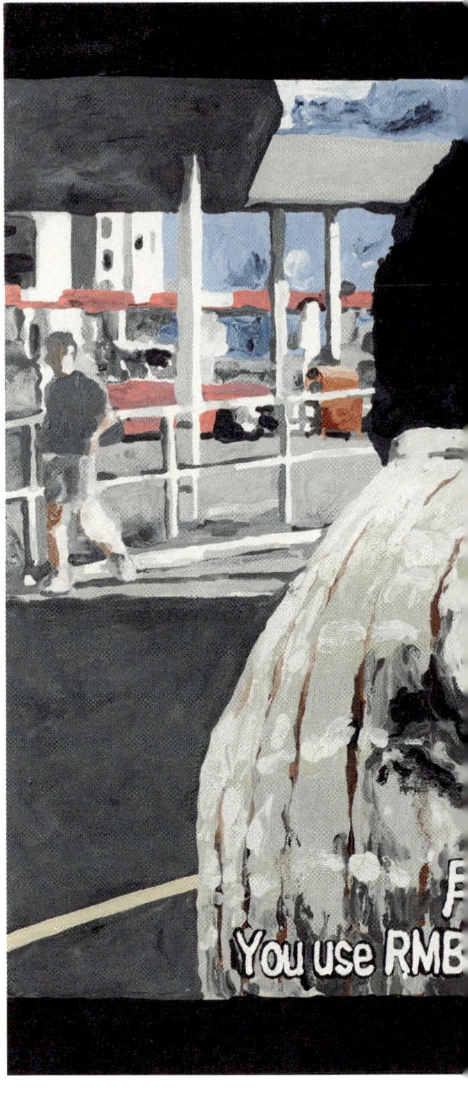

Chow Chun Fai (born 1980, Hong Kong)
All for the Winner, "You use RMB in a vending machine in Hong Kong? Are you crazy?"
2008
Enamel paint on canvas
100 × 149.8 cm
2016.817

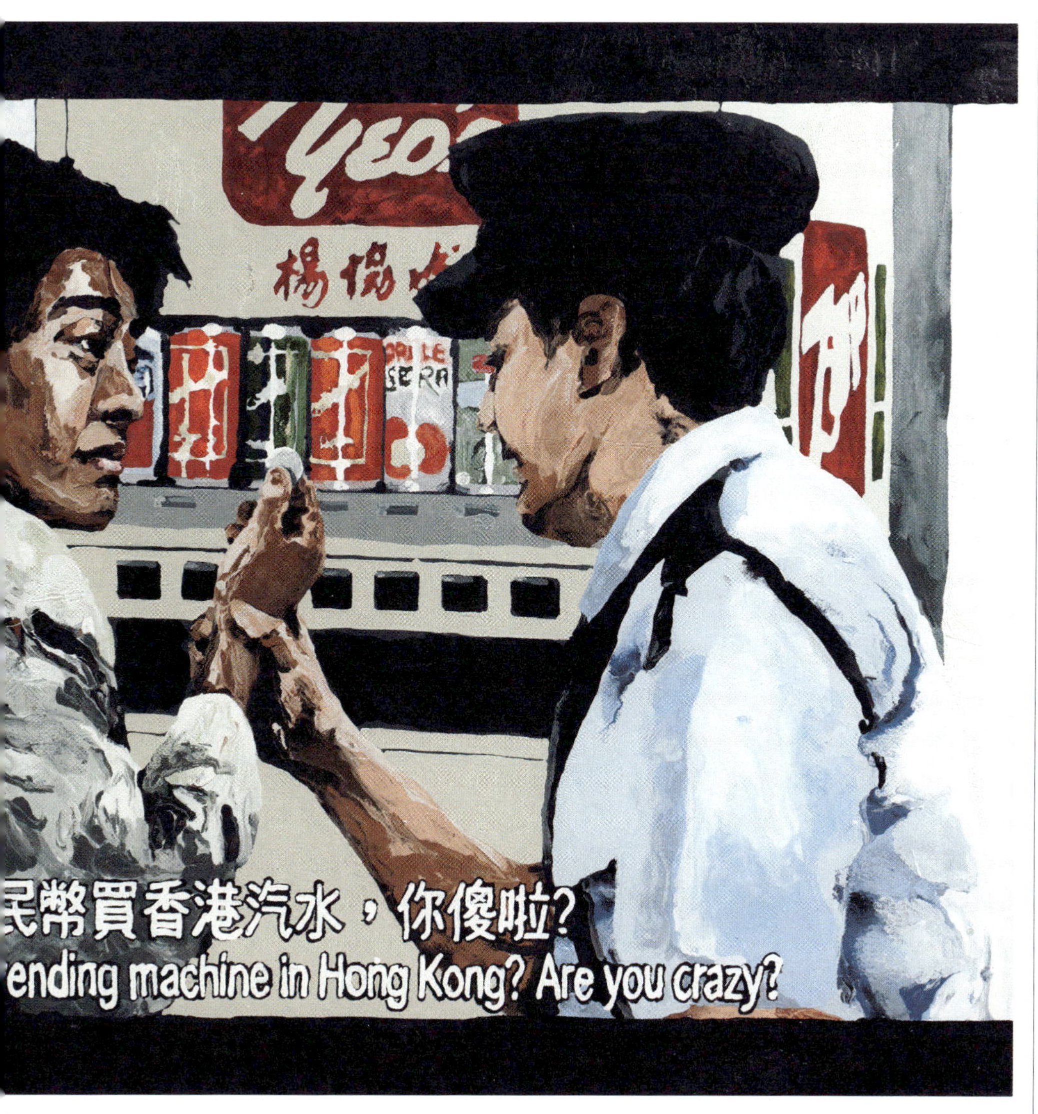
YEO'S
楊楊城
民幣買香港汽水，你傻啦?
ending machine in Hong Kong? Are you crazy?

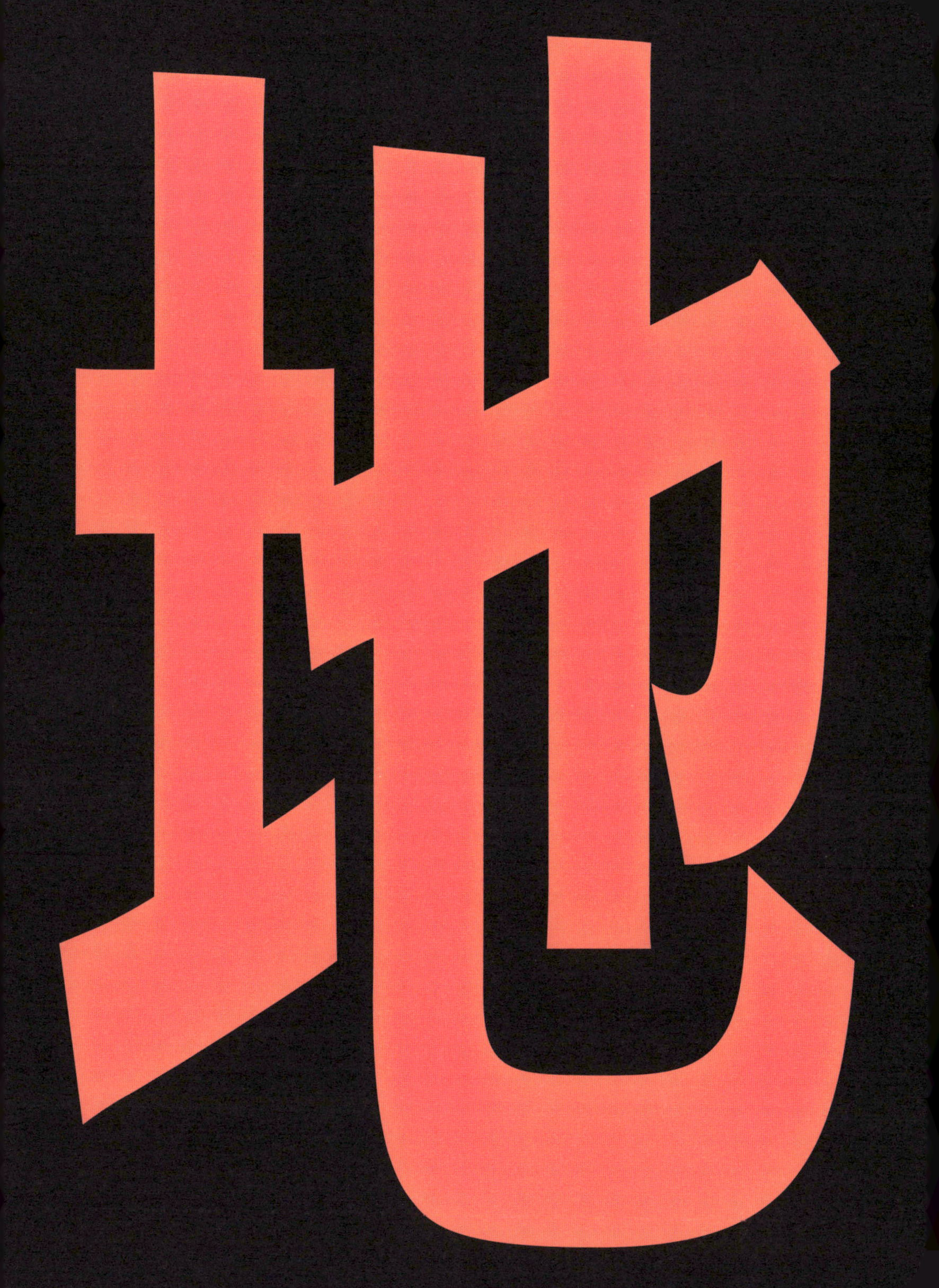

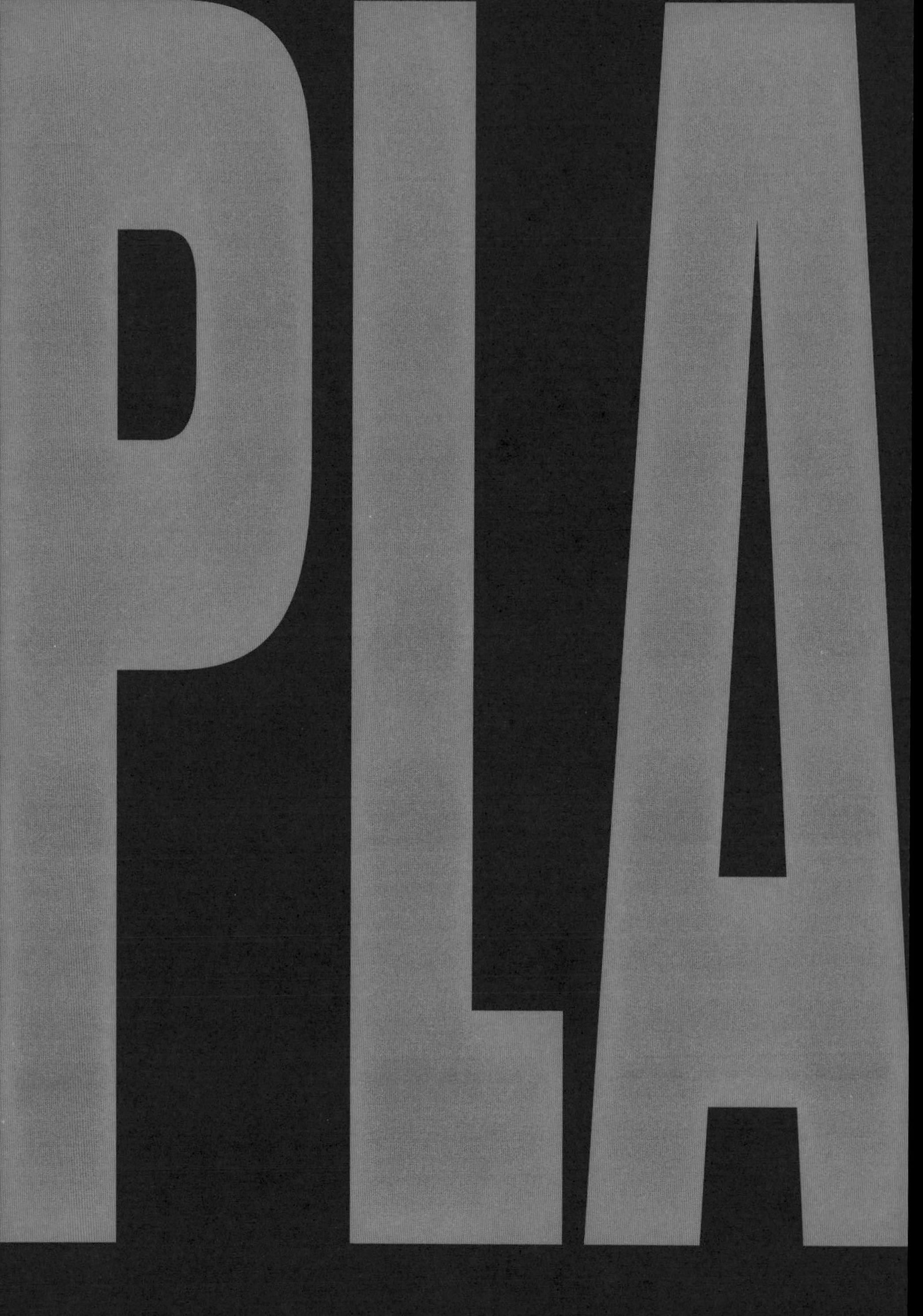

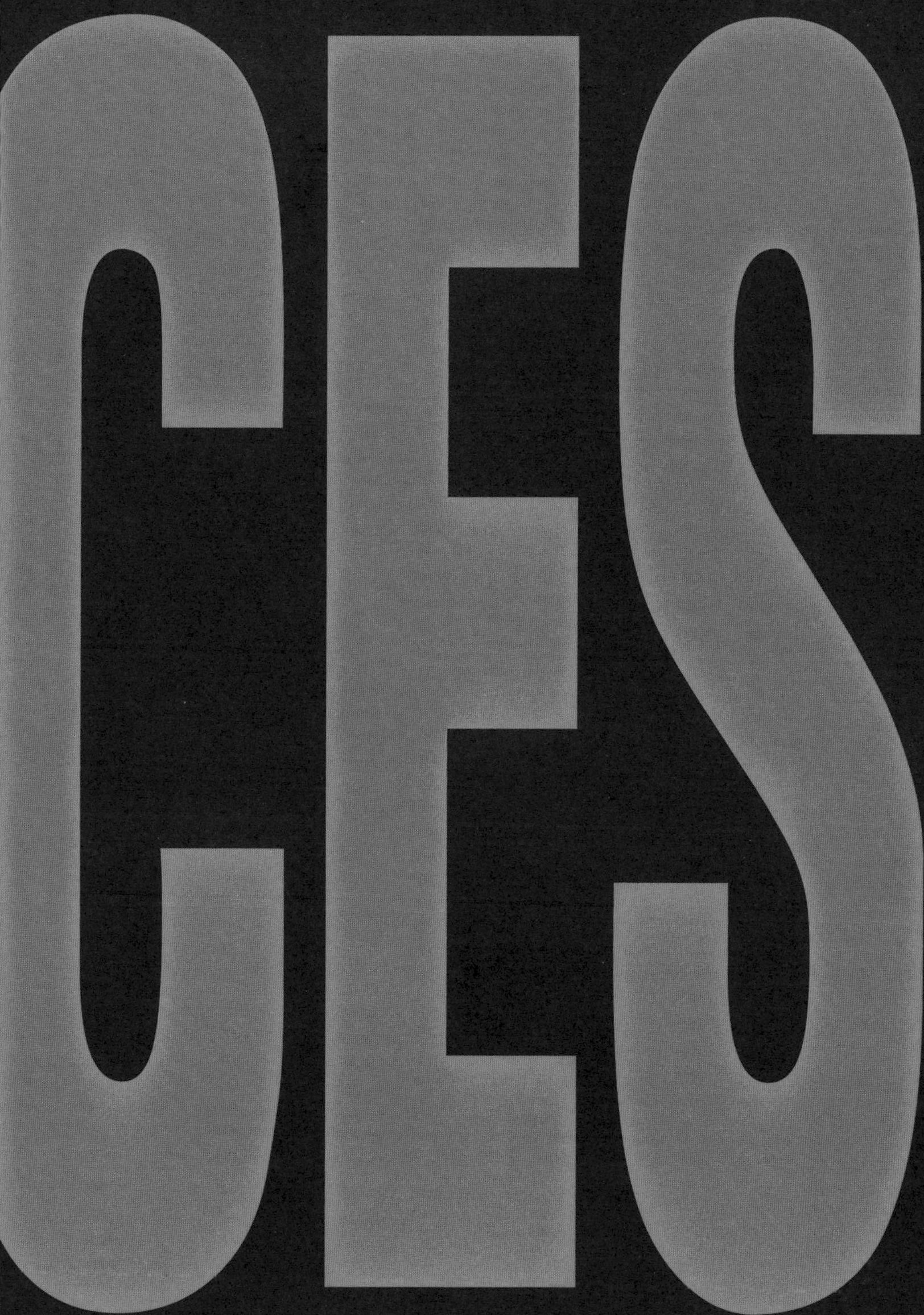

This chapter examines Hong Kong as a site, a place, and an idea, through the work of architects, developers, and designers who have played a role in shaping the way the city looks and feels. In Hong Kong's central business district, skyscrapers connected by elevated walkways and bridges are set against lush, mountainous terrain overlooking the harbour. This dramatic and photogenic image resulted from one of Hong Kong's defining features: only 24 per cent of the city's 1,111 square kilometres has been developed. A scarcity of available land and challenging topography have led property developers and architects to devise innovative approaches to maximising profits and creating efficient use of space. The urban landscape is defined by permeability and individual buildings that fit together seamlessly as an improbable whole. The first section of this chapter, 'A Man-Made Polished Granite Mountain', focuses on key architectural projects that have defined Hong Kong's built environment. The second, 'Give Us a Call, We Have Lots to Talk About', looks at images of the city that have been crafted to express specific agendas. The third section, 'Tides of Time', encompasses artistic responses to changing conditions in Hong Kong and the perspectives that result from living and working in this city.

Very little of Hong Kong's early architecture has survived the drive to maximise limited land supply, and while there will always be some regret about losing historic buildings, this has made way for architects from Hong Kong and elsewhere to venture in often unexpected directions. Projects for public housing and commercial developments both respond to and intensify Hong Kong's constantly changing urban character, inadvertently creating a position for the city in a global history of architecture.

Zaha Hadid described her design for a luxury club and residential complex on Victoria Peak as a 'man-made polished granite mountain'. Responding to the challenging conditions of the steep site, Hadid proposed a set of horizontal volumes that appear to float, overlooking the urban density below. Although the project was never built, it exemplifies the meeting of architectural ambition and visionary property development that has shaped the city—the focus of the first section.

Whether working for tourism, corporate identities, or civic messaging, designers perpetuated certain ideas about Hong Kong. This is the subject of the second section. Henry

Steiner moved to the city in the 1960s to set up the headquarters of *The Asia Magazine*. His flirtatious invitation to potential advertisers, 'Give us a call, we have lots to talk about', illustrates his image-driven approach to communication, which he infused into his art direction of the magazine. Many of his branding strategies for prominent clients have become synonymous with the city. In architecture, projects such as Hong Kong's pavilion for the 1970 World Exposition in Osaka and the Peak Tower speak to the branding of a city in an age of global tourism.

Named for Annie Wan's video work *Tides of Time*, the third section captures a sentiment in which modernity and progress are in dynamic tension with ideas of disappearance. This tension is often portrayed in photography. Lui Shou-kwan was passionate about ensuring that ink painting remain a relevant medium amid developments in abstraction in Euro-American art worlds, but depicting the city as he saw it, not as an idealised landscape of the mind, was also a crucial part of his practice. Photographer Yau Leung captured urban scenes with a documentarian's eye, whereas Fan Ho used precise staging and darkroom manipulation to create his striking images of a modern Hong Kong.

The idea of a city in transition shared by questions of history, politics, and identity characterises a range of contemporary artistic engagements with Hong Kong. Luke Ching's ghostly portrait of Pok Fu Lam Village captures a disappearing way of life, while Sara Tse's melancholy homage to her mother in delicate porcelain pieces offers a more personal perspective. The photographer Michael Wolf is best known for his dramatic portraits of the city's architecture, but his series *100x100* captures residents of a public housing estate in Shek Kip Mei before it was demolished. The series comments on loss and casts an uncomfortable light on social disparities within the urban fabric of one of the wealthiest cities in the world.

A
MAN-MADE
POLISHED
GRANITE
MOUNTAIN

Architects and property developers respond to Hong Kong's unique
natural landscape, creating another landscape altogether

When it was completed, City Hall was a modernist landmark representing a new era in civic and colonial architecture. Comprised of a low and a high block, the complex houses spaces for a wide range of civic functions and cultural activities including a theatre, a concert hall, a museum, and a public library. It was for many years Hong Kong's only venue for prominent international and local cultural events. Designed by British architects Alan Fitch and Ron Phillips for the Public Works Department, the building was a clear departure from its neoclassical predecessor in its Bauhaus-influenced geometric forms, use of concrete and glass, and application of principles of efficient circulation. The project was in direct dialogue with post-war modernism in Europe and the United States and also maintained a relationship with the local context in its dense layering of functions.   SC

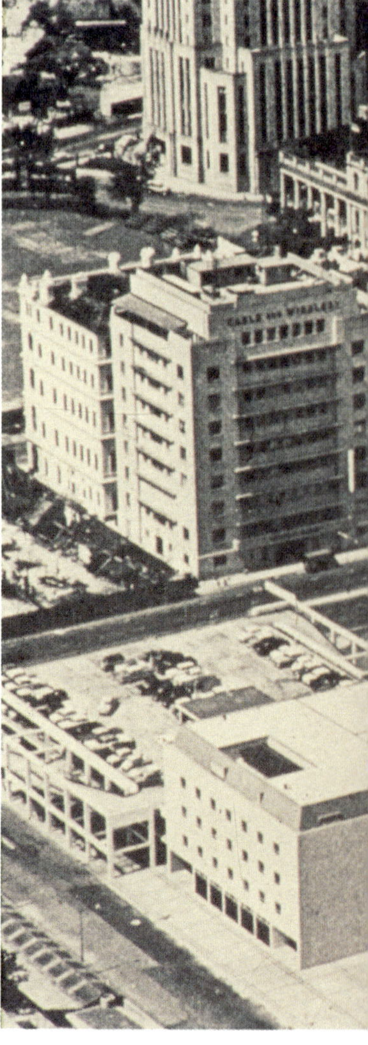

Alan Fitch (born 1921, United Kingdom;
died 1986, France)
Ron Philips (born 1928, United Kingdom)
Hong Kong Government Public Works
Department (1871–1986)
Aerial view of City Hall (1956–1962)
1962
Black-and-white slide
5 × 5 cm
Gift of Chung Wah Nan Architects Limited, 2014
CA10/2/3

**Interior view of concert hall main auditorium,
City Hall (1956–1962)**
1962
Digital print
35.5 × 25.5 cm
Gift of Family of Alan Fitch, 2014
CA35/1/2

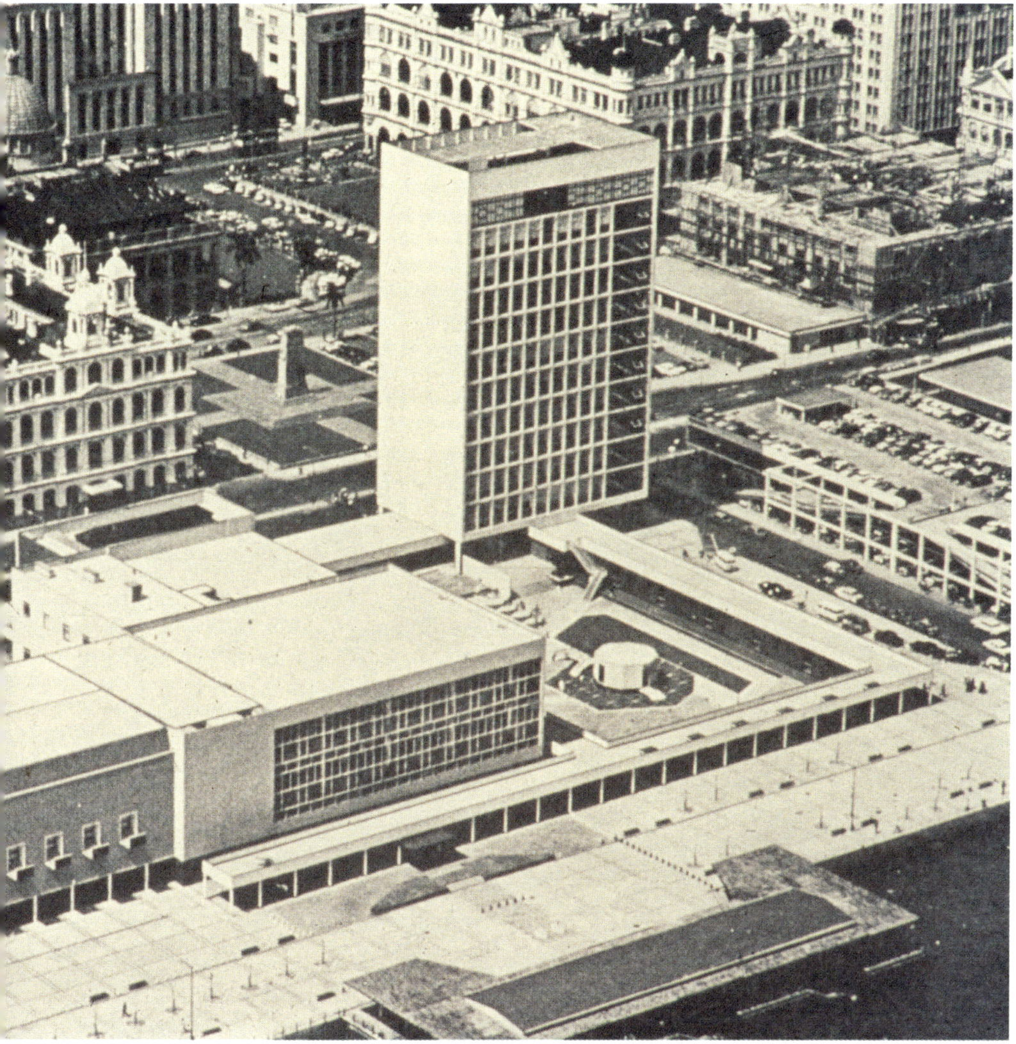

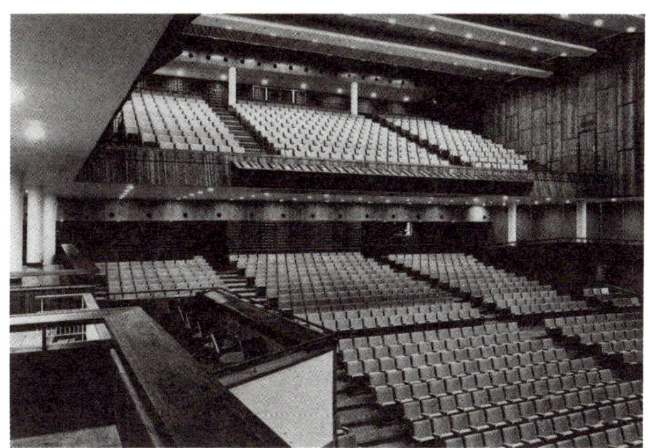

Statue Square was originally created in 1897 along Victoria Harbour as a site for statues of British monarchs and dignitaries. Wardley Street, which connected the second-generation Hongkong and Shanghai Bank building to the old Queen's Pier, formed its central axis. After the Second World War, the square was home to a single statue—of Thomas Jackson, an influential manager of the bank from its earliest days in Hong Kong—and in the 1950s it was briefly converted into a car park. In 1965, HSBC and the Public Works Department commissioned Alan Fitch, working for the firm W. Szeto & Partners, to redesign the square as a civic space. Now connected to the reclaimed waterfront via a pedestrian tunnel, the square created links between Central's business district and the then-new Queen's Pier and City Hall. Fitch's design introduces a visual rhythm on the rectilinear site through planting beds and pools placed asymmetrically and paths of varying widths to guide pedestrian circulation. Seating areas are sheltered by pitched roofs with irregularly placed openings for ventilation and light. Since the 1980s, it has been a popular gathering place for foreign domestic workers and a site of political demonstrations.   SC

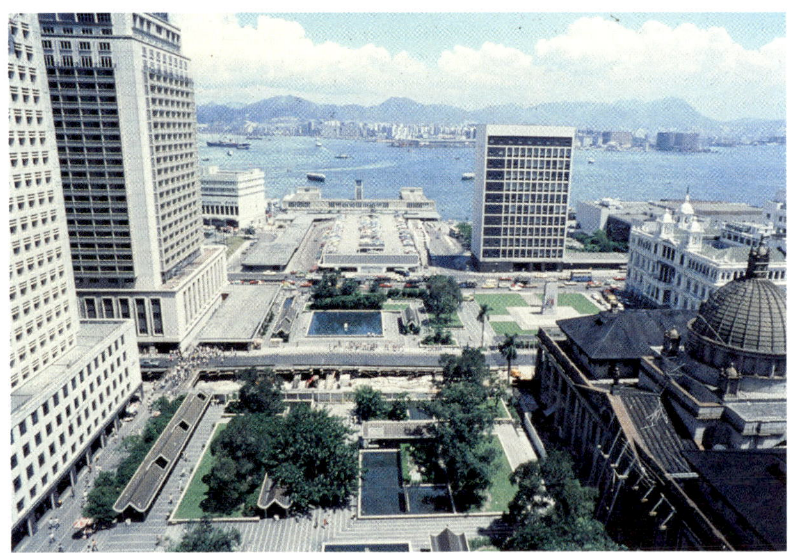

Alan Fitch (born 1921, United Kingdom;
died 1986, France)
W. Szeto & Partners (1948–1998)
Aerial view of Statue Square (1965–1966)
1966
Colour slide
5 × 5 cm
Gift of Chung Wah Nan Architects Limited, 2014
CA10/2/4

Site plan for Statue Square (1965–1966)
1966
Ink on paperboard
21.1 × 30.4 cm
Gift of Family of Alan Fitch, 2014
CA35/2/1

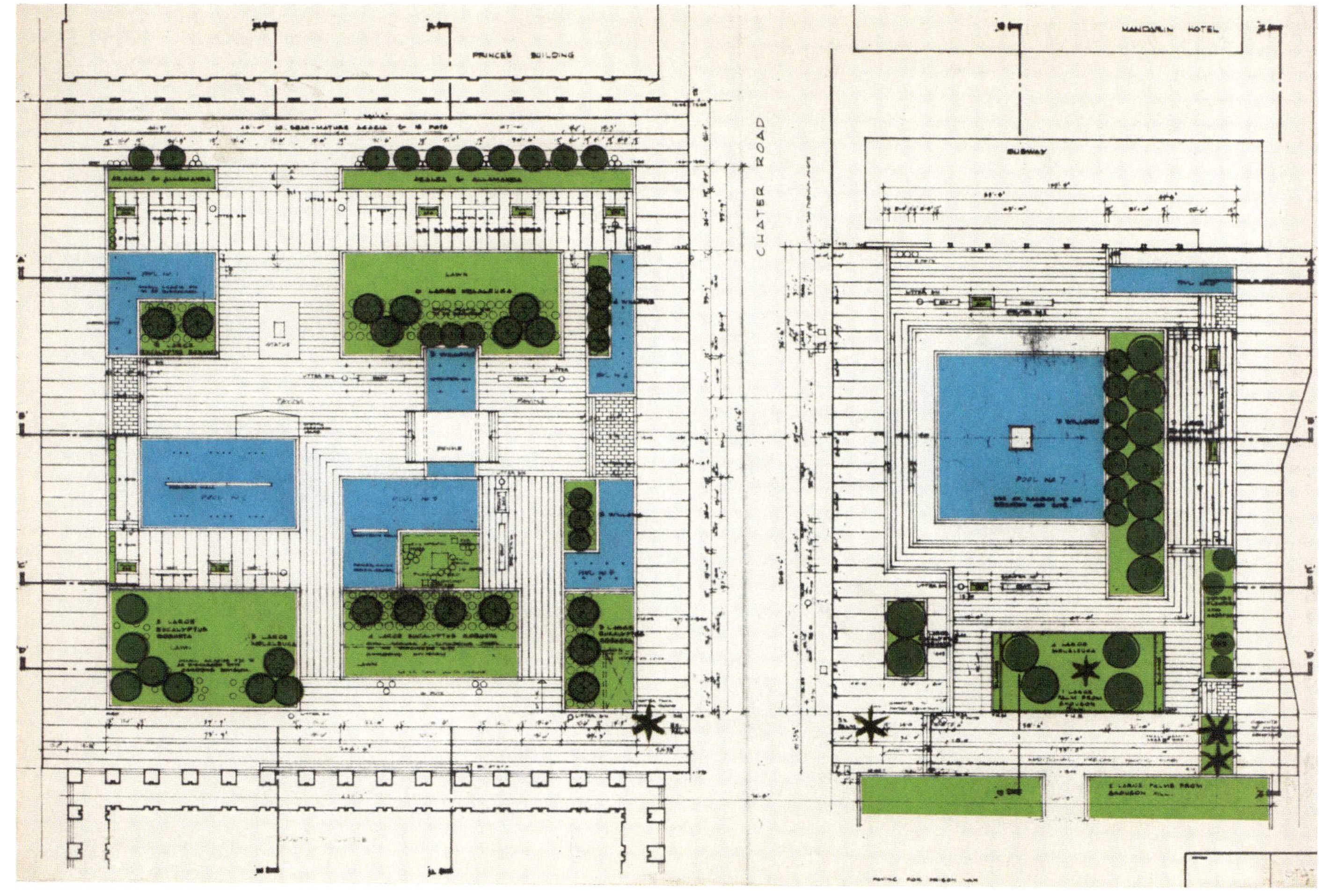

PRINCES BUILDING
MANDARIN HOTEL
CHATER ROAD
SUBWAY
POOL No 7

Built on reclaimed land, the Connaught Centre (now Jardine House) was, at the time of its completion, the city's tallest building, and was instrumental in defining the elevated, high-density character of Central. Under the leadership of James H. Kinoshita, architects Palmer & Turner created a sophisticated synthesis of structure and design. The project was the result of a method of light and efficient construction, with its distinctive circular windows distributing the stress around the external wall instead of concentrating it on the corners. This structural solution also allowed for column-free office spaces, an attractive proposition for prospective tenants. Palmer & Turner's proposal to design an overhead pedestrian link from the tower into Central led to the development of a network of elevated walkways, which spread quickly throughout Hong Kong's central business district. The building was an instant landmark, fronted by reflecting pools and commanding views of both the city and the waterfront. Hongkong Land, the developer of the site, commissioned Henry Steiner to design the branding for the building, and the graphic system for its lobby. Steiner integrated the architectural form into his designs, taking direct inspiration from the signature circular windows.   SC

James H. Kinoshita (born 1933, Canada)
Palmer & Turner (established 1868)
Exterior view of Connaught Centre (1970–1972)
ca. 1973
26 × 20.3 cm
Gelatin silver print
CA31

**Plan, elevation, and section for basement and podium
of Connaught Centre (1970–1972)**
1972
70.8 × 99.2 cm
Graphite and ink on paper
Gift of P&T Group (formerly known as Palmer and Turner), 2020
CA71

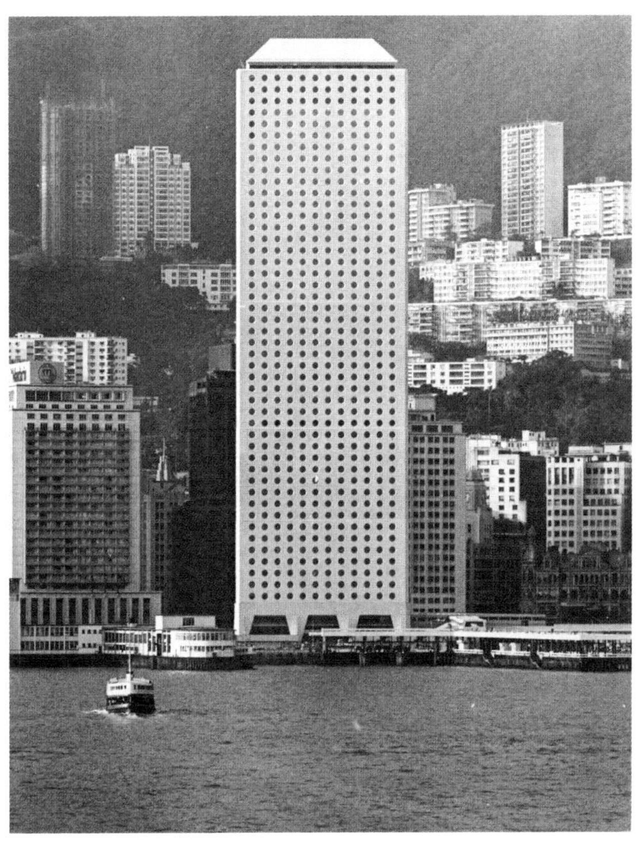

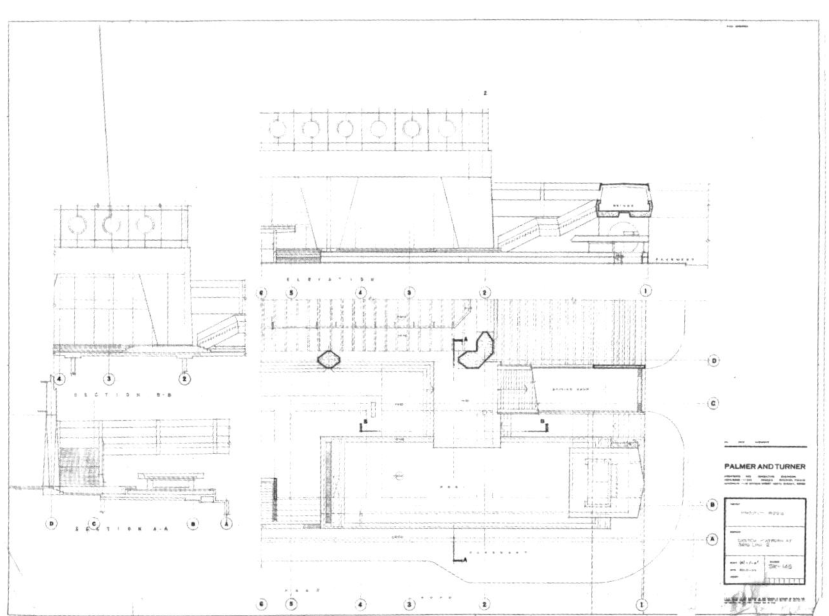

The completion of Exchange Square was a watershed moment for Hong Kong's position as a global centre of financial services. Including an office tower and home for the Stock Exchange of Hong Kong—a new body that brought together four independent stock exchanges—the project was built on a prominent site on the waterfront. Developed by Hongkong Land, it achieved an unprecedented 94 per cent occupancy rate before its opening. In the context of Hong Kong's changing financial landscape and greater market regulation, as well as the political anxieties surrounding the Sino-British Joint Declaration of 1984, the ambitious development testified to Hongkong Land's confidence in the city's future.

The developer engaged prolific Hong Kong–based architects Palmer & Turner to design the project. The complex consists of two adjacent towers linked to a third, smaller tower across an elevated plaza that features sculptural commissions by artists including Elisabeth Frink, Ju Ming, and Henry Moore. Connecting with the extensive network of elevated walkways in Central, Exchange Square became a hub of vehicular and pedestrian circulation. Principal architect Remo Riva defined a columnar grid for the design that is derived from the plan of the bus station below the complex. He positioned the two taller towers as open hands, an auspicious gesture meant to capture the flow from Victoria Harbour. The sketches and paintings he created during the design process vividly express a postmodern sensibility and articulate the symmetry, striated facades, and geometric elements that define the built form.   SS

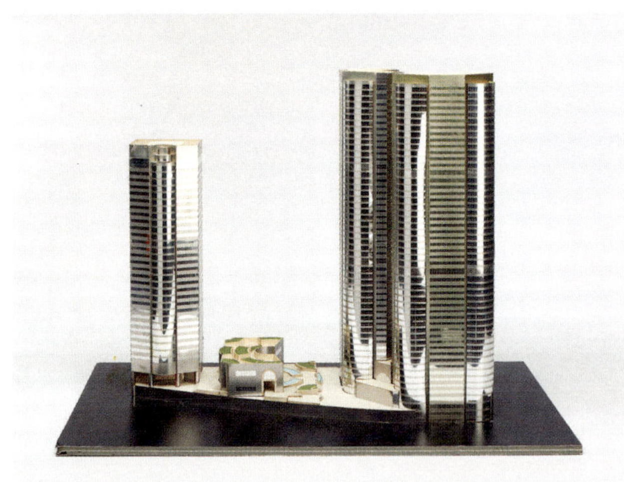

Remo Riva (born 1946, Switzerland)
Palmer & Turner (established 1868)
Model for Exchange Square (1983–1988)
ca. 1983–1985
Various materials
46.5 × 67.2 × 36.5 cm
Gift of Remo Riva, 2013
2013.144

Axonometric drawing for Exchange Square (1983–1988)
1983
Ink and coloured pencil on paper
29.7 × 21 cm
Gift of Remo Riva, 2013
CA12/2/2

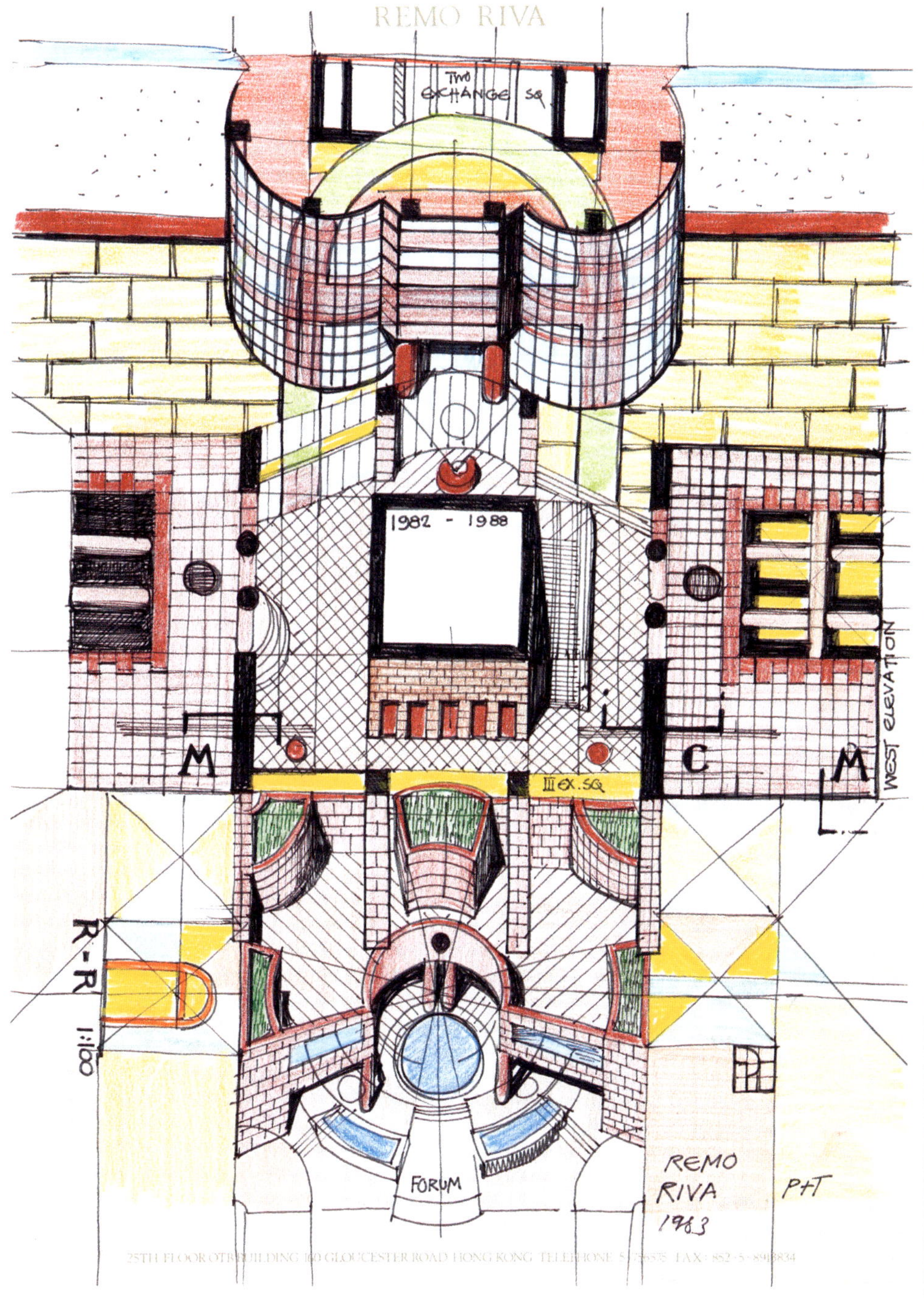

REMO RIVA
TWO EXCHANGE SQ.
1982 - 1988
III EX. SQ.
M
C
M
WEST ELEVATION
R-R 1:100
FORUM
REMO RIVA 1963
P+T
25TH FLOOR OTB BUILDING 160 GLOUCESTER ROAD HONG KONG TELEPHONE 5-8938635 FAX: 852-5-8943834

Established in 1846 as a meeting place for the heads of *hongs*—foreign-owned trading companies—the Hong Kong Club became the ultimate seat of power in the British colony. In 1897, the club moved to its current site on Jackson Road, adjacent to Statue Square in Central. The move was part of the first phase of the Praya Reclamation Scheme, completed in 1873, which extended the central business district into Victoria Harbour. The Victorian Italianate building was one of the last of its kind in the city, but its prime location and the opportunity to generate greater revenue prompted the club to demolish it and commission a high-rise design for an office tower.

Harry Seidler, the leading proponent of architectural modernism in Australia, designed the new tower. The building's undulating facade features flared corners that provide structural support and a pediment wall at the top turned inward. The project manifests Seidler's interest in expressing structural solutions through the marriage of concave and convex curves and column-free interiors. Seidler collaborated with renowned engineer Pier Luigi Nervi to develop the club's traverse beams and concave supports. In his drawing of an exterior view, Helmut Jacoby depicts not only the building's distinctive curvilinear facade, but also the monumental Cenotaph and the pool in Statue Square, emphasising the tower's stately presence on its prominent site. A drawing of the interior embodies the club's formal sophistication and its significant location with a backdrop of the central business district and Victoria Harbour.   SS

Harry Seidler (born 1923, Austria; died 2006, Australia)
Helmut Jacoby (1926–2005, Germany)
Rendering of exterior for the Hong Kong Club building (1980–1984)
(original in colour)
1981
Ink, coloured pencil, and airbrush on paper
85.5 × 52.1 cm
Gift of Penelope Seidler, 2020, in memory of Harry Seidler
CA69/1

Rendering of interior for the Hong Kong Club building (1980–1984)
(original in colour)
1981
Ink, coloured pencil, and airbrush on paper
42.8 × 65.1 cm
Gift of Penelope Seidler, 2020, in memory of Harry Seidler
CA69/2

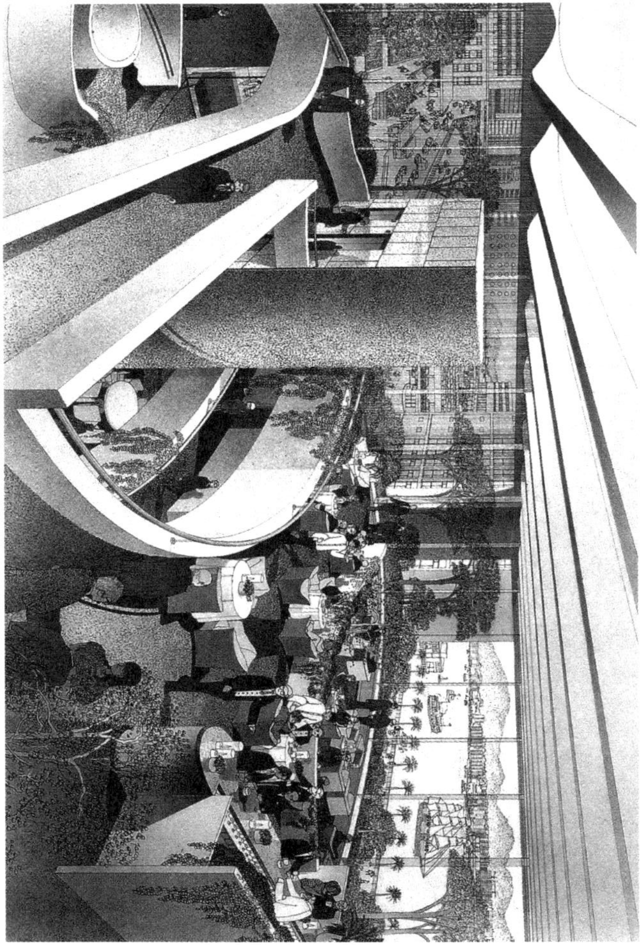

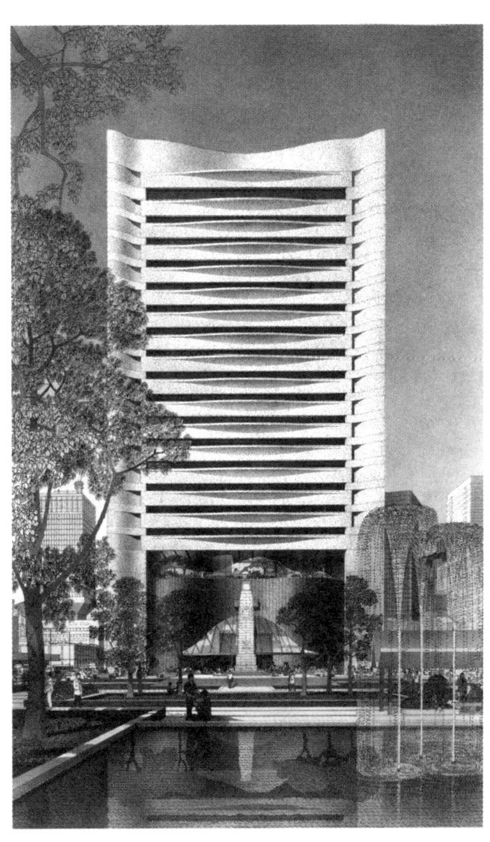

From the 1960s to the 1980s, Hong Kong underwent rapid development through both private and public infrastructure projects to meet the needs of a growing population and to serve an expanding economy. The new building types that emerged were designed to be functional sites of manufacturing and logistics, and they embody the aspirations of a modern city.

The Pacific Trade Centre at Kowloon Bay, completed in 1990, is a multi-use factory building meant to accommodate both industrial and commercial programmes. Designed by Andrew Lee King Fun & Associates Architects, the fifteen-storey building is an early example of the factory-office typology that was widely adopted in Hong Kong in subsequent years. It includes a lobby and passenger lifts for workers in the office floors above in addition to cargo lifts serving the lower floors. As Hong Kong transitioned from manufacturing centre to service economy, the building shifted principally to office use.

By the 1980s, Hong Kong had become one of the busiest ports in the world. Built between 1979 and 1994, the ATL Container Freight Station (now known as ATL Logistics Centre) was the world's largest multi-level industrial building when it opened at the Kwai Chung Container Terminal in Kowloon. The design by Dennis Lau of Ng Chun Man & Associates, Architects & Engineers comprises two vast rectangular buildings tailored to the expanded needs of the logistics industry. It drew from Lau's earlier design for the Aberdeen Market Complex (1979–1983), a civic commission that introduced multiple uses across the levels of a stacked structure. With warehouses, offices, and support facilities situated over 800,000 square metres of floor space, the ATL Container Freight Station features an integrated vehicular circulation network of ramps, parking bays, internal roadways, and a loading zone to accommodate container trucks. This network enables seamless movement of vehicles between levels and the rapid loading and unloading of cargo, alleviating congestion at the port. The design is an intelligent, efficient response to Hong Kong's dense urban condition.   SC

Andrew Lee King Fun (born 1933, Hong Kong)
Andrew Lee King Fun & Associates Architects (established 1962)
North-east elevation for Pacific Trade Centre
1988, revised 1989
Carbon and graphite on transparent paper
59.5 × 84 cm
Gift of Andrew Lee King Fun & Associates Architects Limited, 2013
CA9/4/5

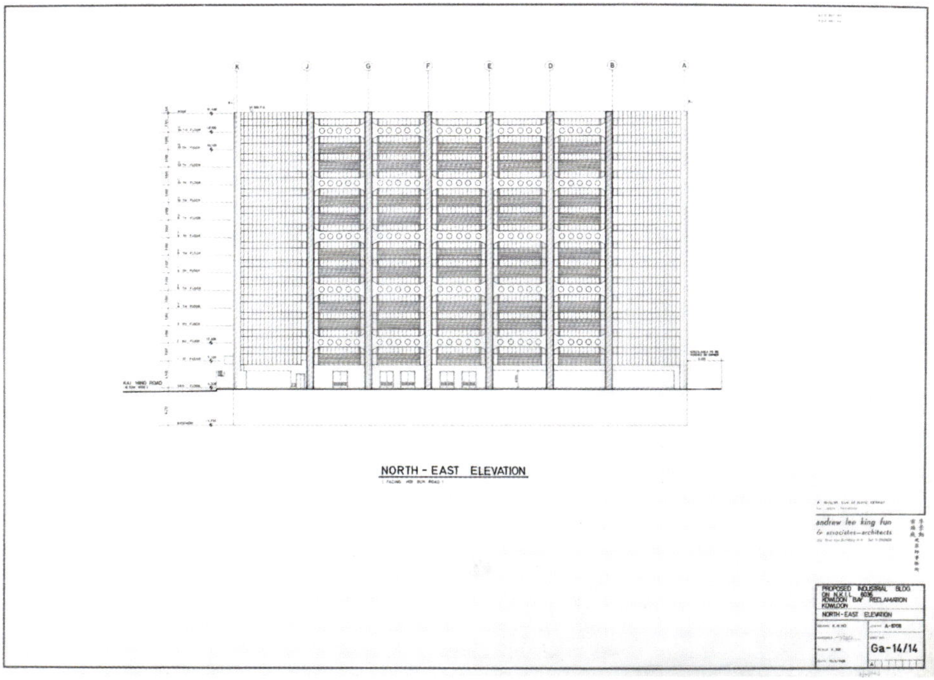

NORTH – EAST ELEVATION

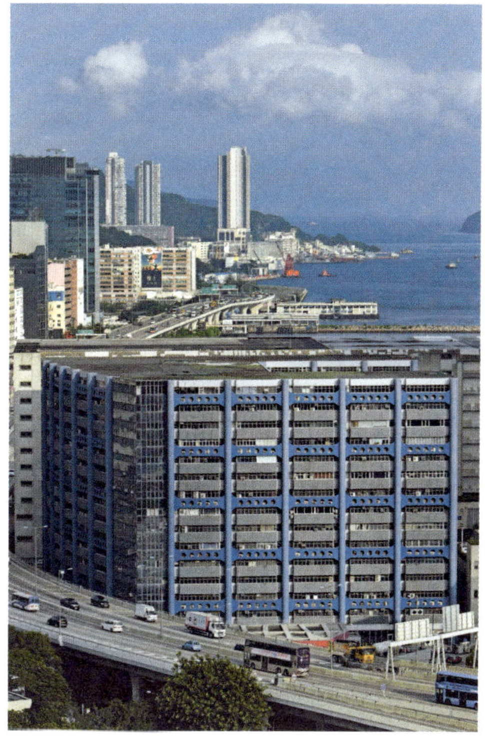

View of the Pacific Trade Centre

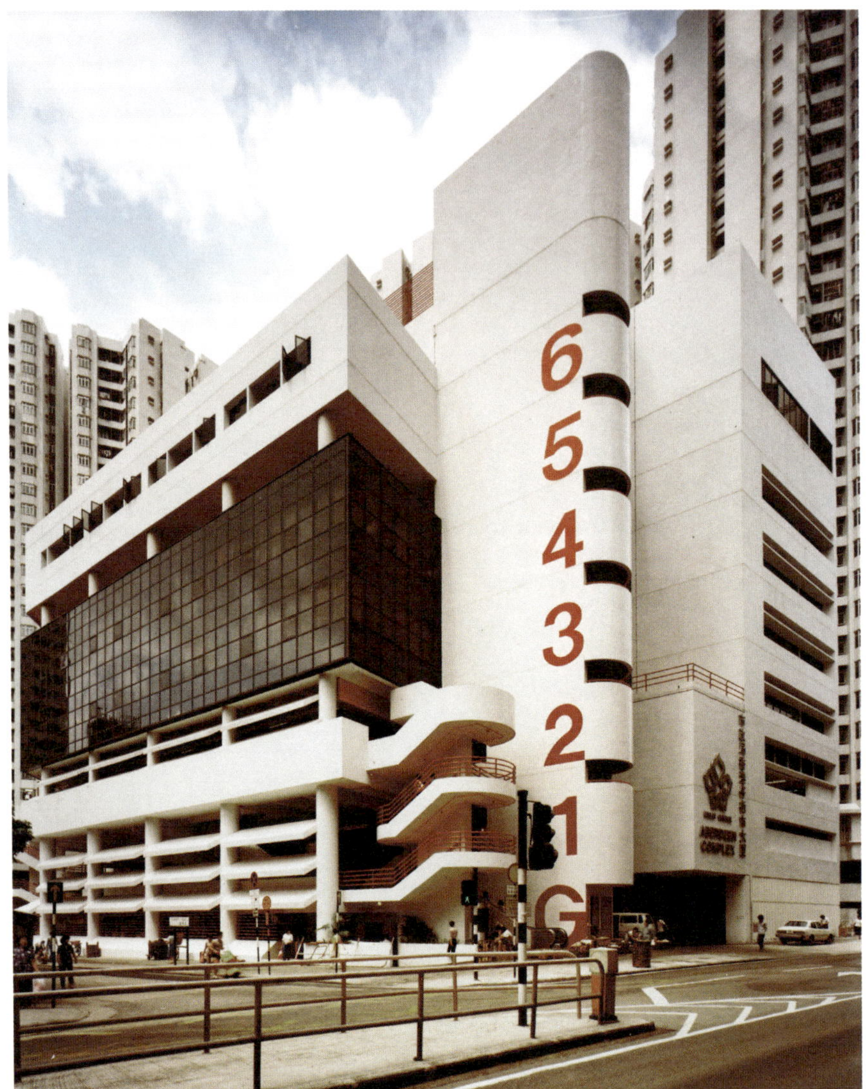

Dennis Lau (born 1941, Hong Kong)
Ng Chun Man & Associates, Architects & Engineers (HK) (established 1972)
Exterior photograph for Urban Council Aberdeen Market Complex (ca. 1979–1983)
ca. 1983
Chromogenic print
25.4 × 20.3 cm
Gift of Dennis Lau & Ng Chun Man Architects & Engineers (HK) Limited, 2013
CA11/5/2

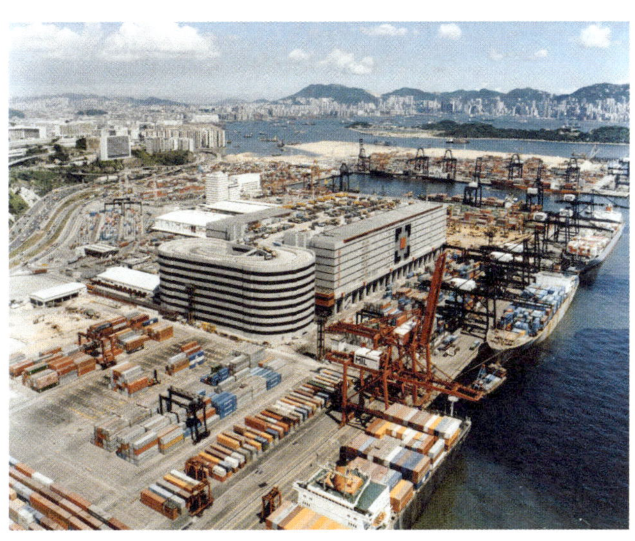

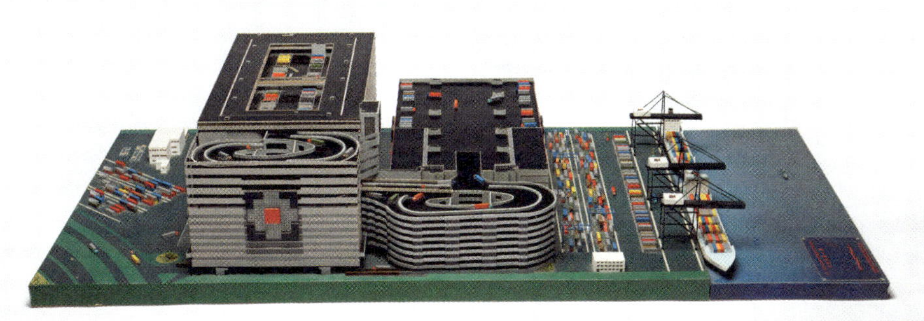

Dennis Lau (born 1941, Hong Kong)
Ng Chun Man & Associates, Architects
& Engineers (HK) (established 1972)
**Aerial view of ATL Container Freight Station
(1979–1994), Phase 1 and Phase 2**
ca. 1988
Chromogenic print
20.4 × 25.5 cm
Gift of Dennis Lau & Ng Chun Man Architects
& Engineers (HK) Limited, 2013
CA11/8/2

Model for ATL Container Freight Station (1979–1994)
1987
Acrylic, cardboard, and wood
43 × 136 × 66.8 cm
Gift of Dennis Lau & Ng Chun Man Architects
& Engineers (HK) Limited, 2013
2013.135

In 2005, the members of MAP Office—Laurent Gutierrez and Valérie Portefaix—boarded the French-registered cargo ship *Baudelaire* in the port of Yantian in Shenzhen and travelled with it to the container terminal at Kwai Chung, Hong Kong. The voyage was possible only after a year-long process of negotiation with the shipping company. MAP Office's project offers unusual insight into the economic activities of the Pearl River Delta through the apparently innocuous movements of dock cranes hoisting containers before dawn and the hours of sailing across the tranquil sea. The photographs they produced signal the enormous movement of goods shipped from mainland China to Hong Kong, illustrating Guangdong's role as a centre of manufacturing, and Hong Kong as a free port and international logistics hub. Gutierrez and Portefaix locate Hong Kong within the commercial constellation of southern China. Less than ten years after the transfer of sovereignty over Hong Kong, the city is presented as a node in the Pearl River Delta network, following a trajectory of economic assimilation and political integration. *Back Home with Baudelaire* simultaneously traces the specificity of the economic and urban phenomena taking place in the region and alludes to the complex forces that define any global chain of commodities.

MAP Office developed the work as part of a research project into the dynamics, territories, and relationships within the Pearl River Delta, which they titled *My PRD Stories*. Other parts of the *My PRD Stories* project address urbanisation, the idea of the family, property development, manufacturing, and the environment, offering a multifaceted portrait of a region undergoing transformation.   FT

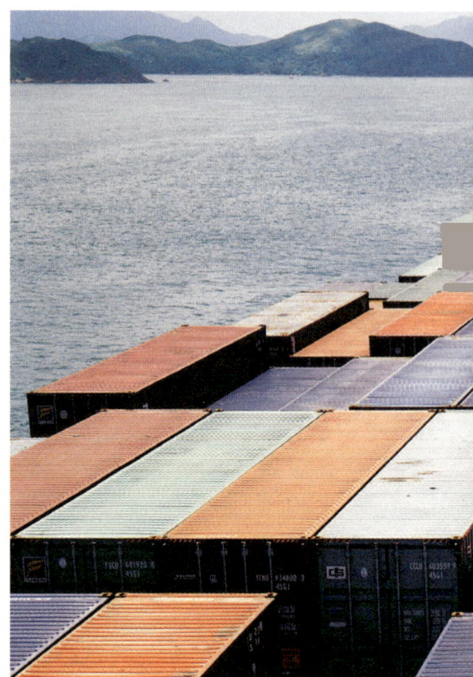

MAP Office (established 1996)
Back Home with Baudelaire (No.5)
2005
Chromogenic print
100.2 × 200 cm
2013.254

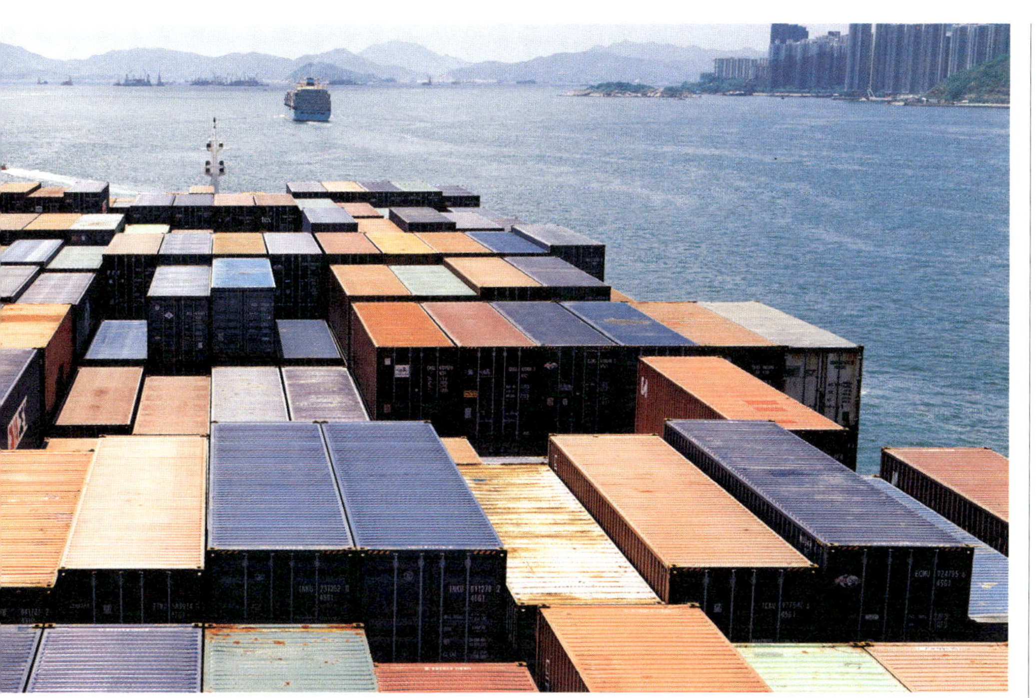

The Hong Kong Academy for Performing Arts (HKAPA) complex was conceived in an era of major infrastructure-building in the arts in Hong Kong. The ambitious project to establish an institution dedicated to the performing arts was originally put forward by the Royal Hong Kong Jockey Club in 1981, but began to take shape only when a site was identified adjacent to the Hong Kong Arts Centre, which had been completed in 1977 in Wan Chai. In an international competition, six firms were invited to submit entries to design the HKAPA. The winning entry, by Simon Kwan, proposed a dramatic ensemble of triangular volumes. The triangular form also became the unifying motif of the building, found in the multi-level windows of the dance studios and the space-frame structure of the upper floors. The building is linked to the city via an elevated pedestrian walkway that crosses Gloucester Road. Home since 1985 to Hong Kong's first and only school dedicated to the performing arts, the HKAPA has educated countless classical musicians, popular entertainers, and avant-garde performers.   SS

Simon Kwan (born 1941, Hong Kong)
Simon Kwan & Associates (established 1973)
Model for Hong Kong Academy for Performing Arts (1981–1985)
ca. 1981
Acrylic and cardboard
33 × 98.5 × 83 cm
Gift of Hong Kong Academy for Performing Arts, 2013
2013.158

Rendering for Hong Kong Academy for Performing Arts (1981–1985)
ca. 1980
Gouache on paperboard
51.3 × 72.6 cm
Gift of Simon Kwan & Associates Limited, 2014
CA15/2/1

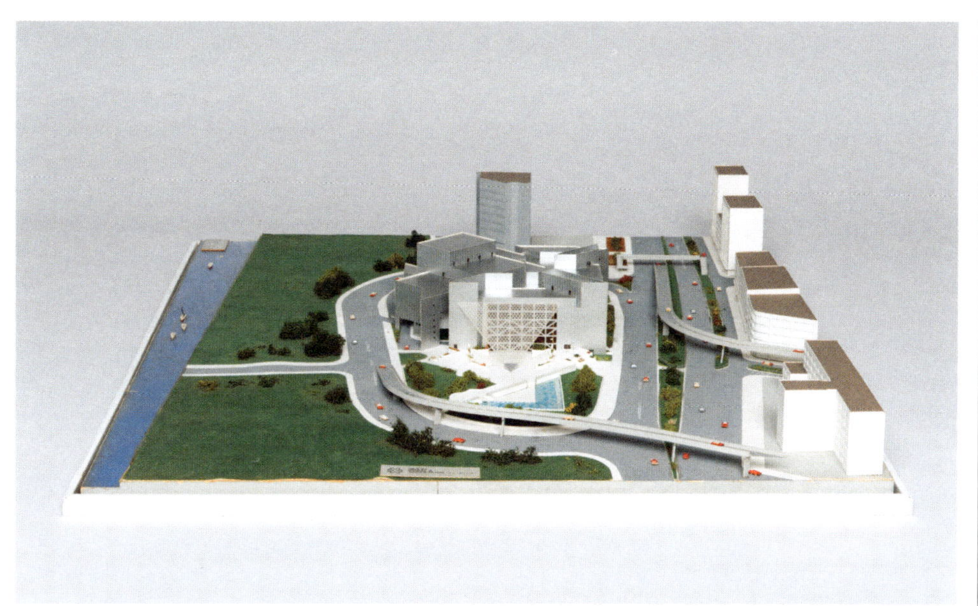

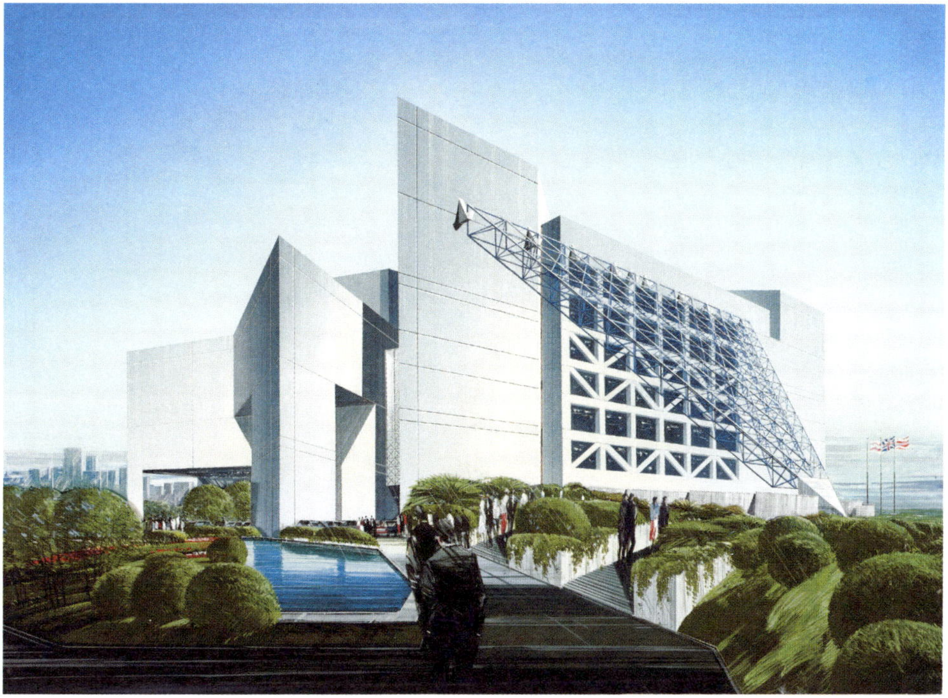

Commissioned by the Far Eastern Division of the General Conference of Seventh-Day Adventists, the Hong Kong Adventist Hospital is a distinctive circular structure perched on a hilly site along Stubbs Road. The project was developed as part of the international humanitarian mission of the Seventh-Day Adventist Church. The church engaged architects Wong, Ng, Ouyang and Associates, a practice that was originally established in 1957 as Wong, Ng and Associates by Jackson Wong and Ng Chun Man, who were among the earliest graduates of the University of Hong Kong Department of Architecture. The firm was instrumental in the urban development of post-war Hong Kong and introduced new typologies and approaches to materials.

The design was inspired by the panopticon, an approach to organising space that allows for the observation and control of behaviour in institutional settings, first developed by Jeremy Bentham in eighteenth-century Britain. Each floor of the hospital features a central nurses' station surrounded by wards, allowing for direct lines of sight between healthcare workers and patients. This spatial organisation reduces the need for service corridors, providing more space for clinics and chapels. The hospital's facade, now painted pink, was originally finished in fair-faced exposed concrete, which was an unusual choice for a tropical climate but one the architects favoured for its egalitarian associations with Brutalist civic structures in Britain.   SC

Wong, Ng, Ouyang and Associates (established 1964)
Exterior view of Hong Kong Adventist Hospital (1971)
ca. 1973
Digital file
Gift of Wong & Ouyang (HK) Ltd., 2017
CA16/3/18

First-floor plan for Hong Kong Adventist Hospital (1971)
1968
Diazotype (copy) and ink on paper
53.5 × 76.5 cm
Gift of Wong & Ouyang (HK) Ltd., 2017
CA16/3/4

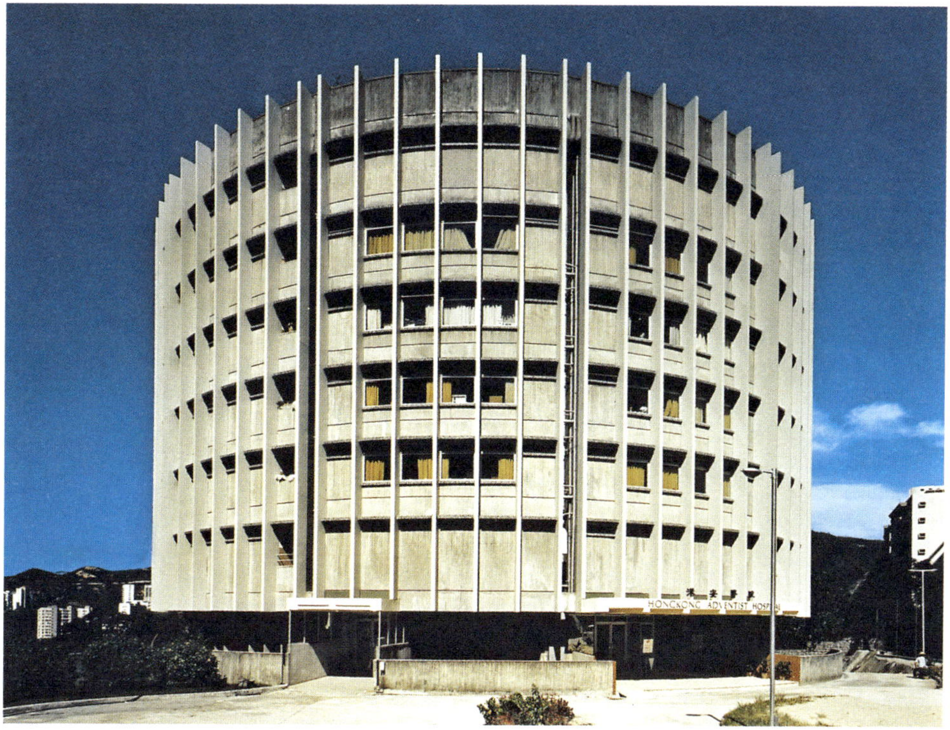

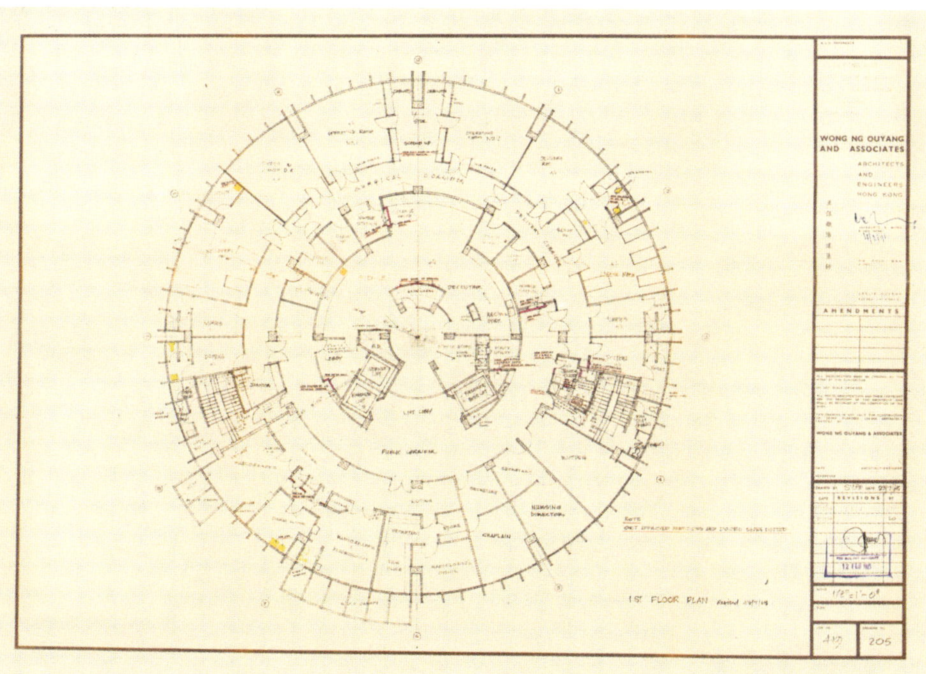

Taikoo Shing was a project to repurpose and develop the disused Taikoo Dockyard in eastern Hong Kong Island. The development owed much to humanistic public housing design of the 1960s, specifically Donald Liao Poo-huai's design for the Wah Fu Estate in Pok Fu Lam, and Wong Tung & Partners' Mei Foo Sun Chuen in Lai Chi Kok. Wah Fu was built as a new town with integrated facilities for fifty thousand people, while Mei Foo Sun Chuen, developed on the site of a disused Mobil petroleum storage facility, was planned as a self-sufficient residential and commercial complex.

For Wong Tung & Partners, the project was an evolution of the innovations they had introduced at Mei Foo Sun Chuen. The sixty-one cruciform and diamond-shaped residential blocks, each between twenty-two and thirty storeys in height, are linked by a rhizomic podium, with large, open landscaped areas creating natural communal zones. At the centre of the development is the Cityplaza commercial and entertainment complex, which connects the residential blocks with an office tower and recreational and transportation facilities via sky-bridges and sheltered walkways at different levels.   SC

Wong Tung & Partners (established 1963)
Comprehensive plan for Taikoo Shing (1977–1988)
1973, revised 1974
Diazotype on paper
99.6 × 103.8 cm
Gift of Wong Tung & Partners Limited, 2013
CA25/3/1

Trend Publishing (1976–2002)
Building Journal Hong Kong
August 1976
Print on paper
28.3 × 21.4 cm
Gift of Wong Tung & Partners Limited, 2013
CA25/3/18

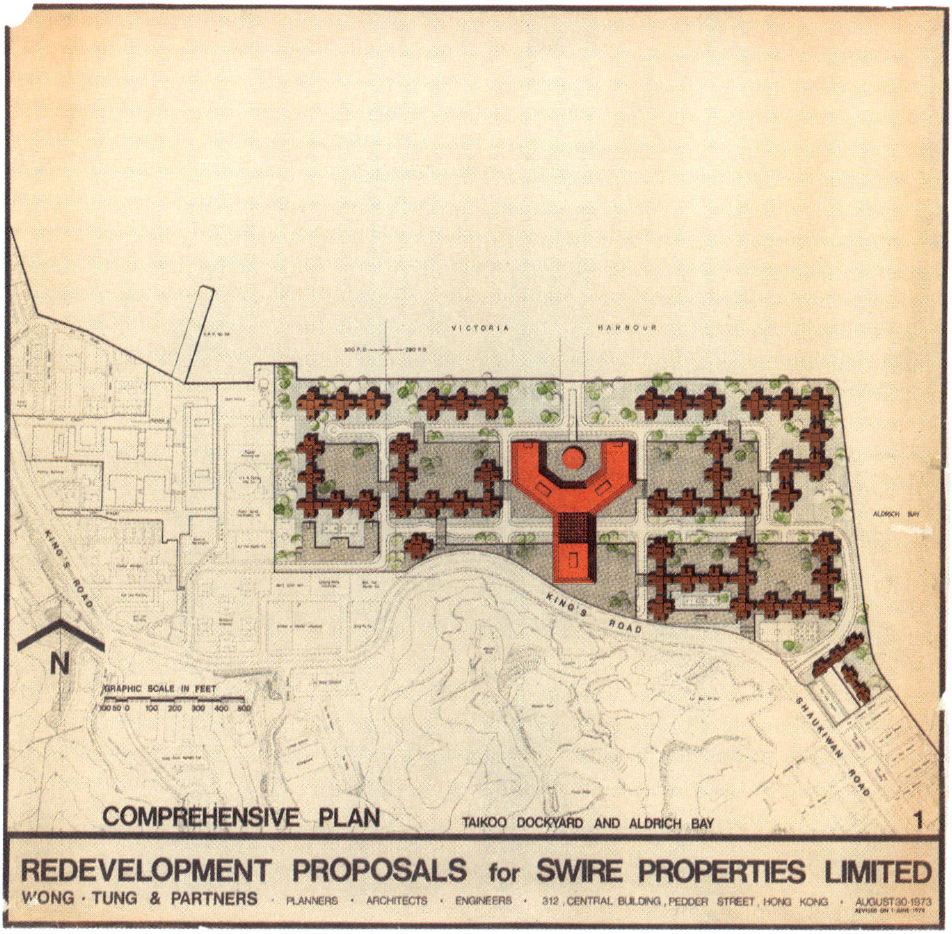

COMPREHENSIVE PLAN

TAIKOO DOCKYARD AND ALDRICH BAY

1

REDEVELOPMENT PROPOSALS for SWIRE PROPERTIES LIMITED

WONG · TUNG & PARTNERS · PLANNERS · ARCHITECTS · ENGINEERS · 312, CENTRAL BUILDING, PEDDER STREET, HONG KONG · AUGUST 30 1973
REVISED ON 1 JUNE 1978

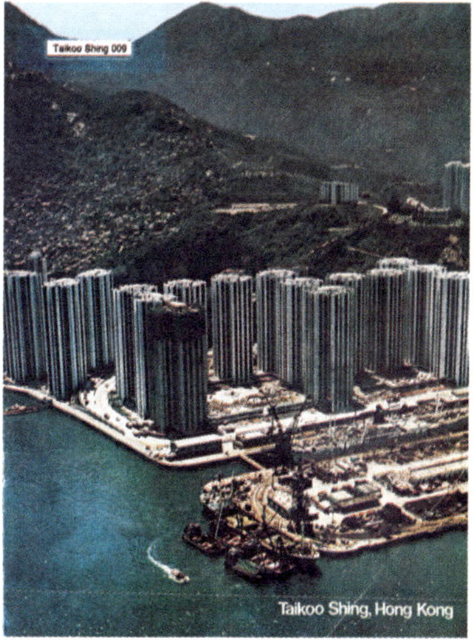

Taikoo Shing, Hong Kong

From the 1920s onwards, refugees fleeing civil unrest in mainland China began to cross into Hong Kong, settling in makeshift accommodation. In 1949, the colonial government under Alexander Grantham began to devise a housing policy intended for those living in shanty towns in different parts of the city. However, the policy was not implemented until after a catastrophic fire destroyed many squatter homes in Shek Kip Mei in December 1953.

Completed between 1962 and 1964, Choi Hung Estate was among the earliest public estates. Housing almost 7,500 flats in eleven seven-storey blocks, it was also the largest in its day. The design by Palmer & Turner raised standards of living by introducing private kitchen and toilet facilities for each unit and natural lighting and ventilation across the buildings. The blocks enclose two large open areas that connect to schools, shops, a post office, gardens, and play areas, a layout that fostered a strong sense of community. The introduction of public housing in Hong Kong with Choi Hung and other projects contributed to social mobility, but a continuing lack of affordable housing means that almost half of the population live in subsidised public housing today.

In his *Architecture of Density* series, Michael Wolf was inspired by the beauty of Hong Kong's urban landscape. His large-format photographs of high-rise residential and industrial buildings draw out abstract form and repetition, reflecting his unique perspective on the city's urban infrastructure and social histories. Wolf's images of Choi Hung are among his most recognisable. His depiction of the estate's distinctive rainbow-coloured facade reveals his sensitive journalistic commitment to documenting the lives of those who live there.   SC

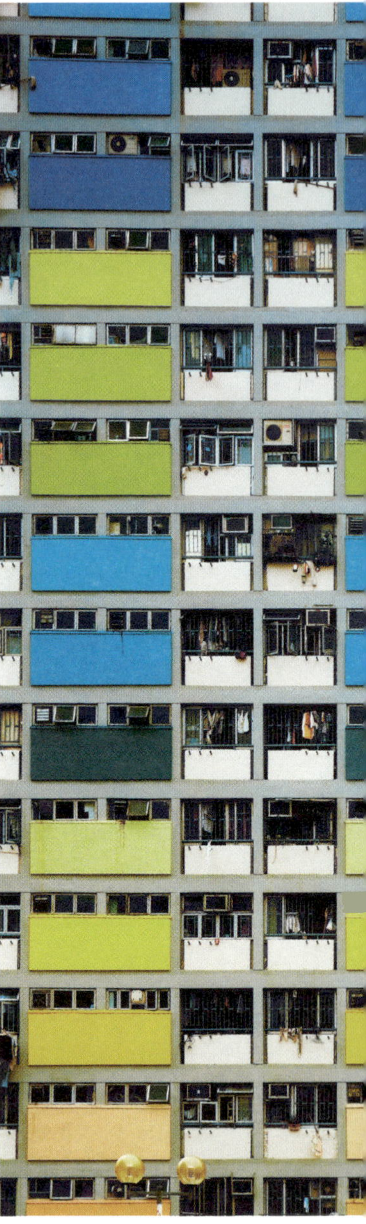

Michael Wolf (born 1954, West Germany (now Germany); died 2019, Hong Kong)
Architecture of Density #8b
2005
Chromogenic print
122.1 × 152.5 cm
2015.724

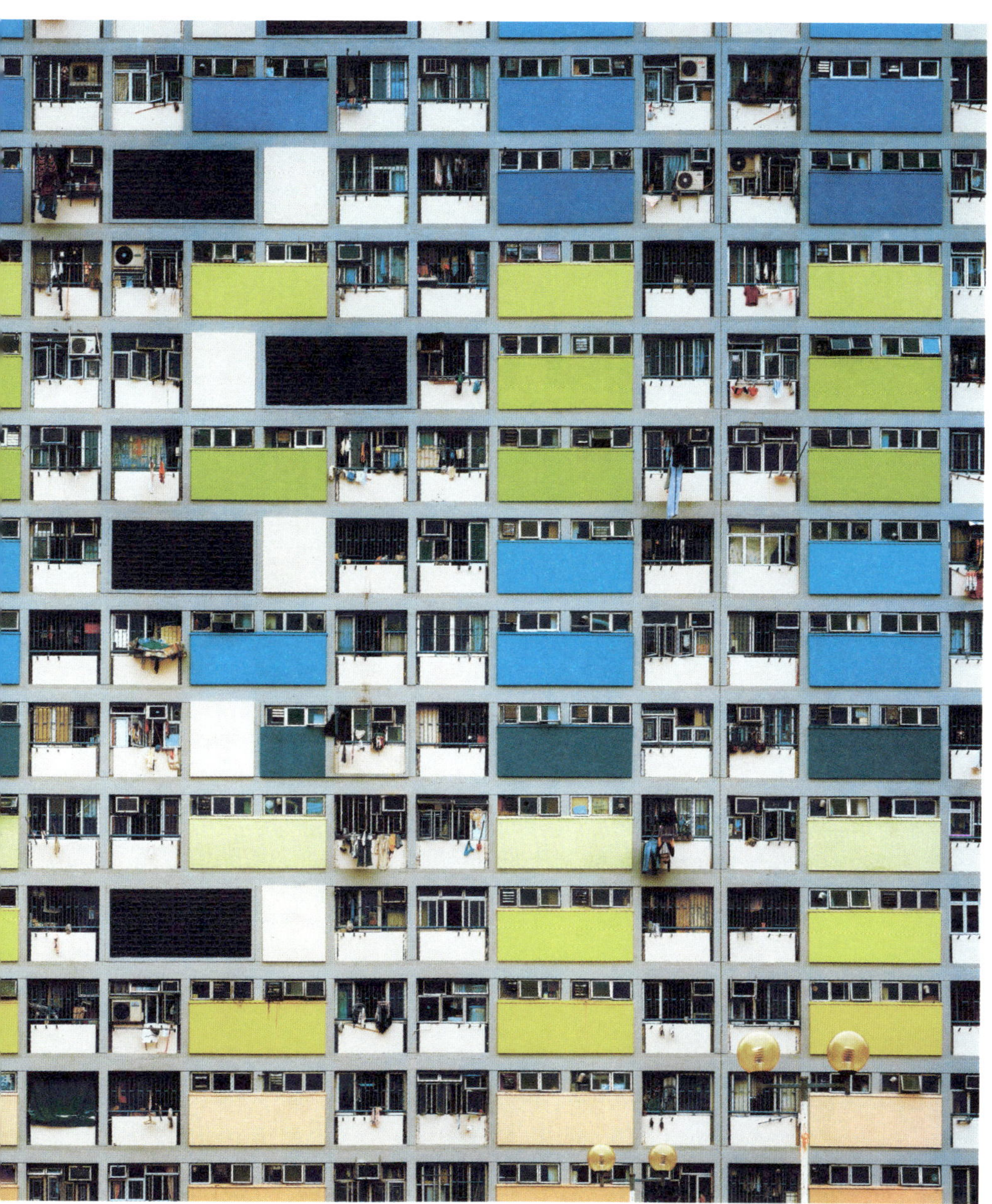

Architects Team 3 designed this house for Singaporean shipping executive and developer Robin Loh, a friend of the firm's co-founder, Lim Chong Keat. Perched on a hillside overlooking Happy Valley, it is nestled within the site's dense vegetation and steep topography. The elevated form is comprised of overlapping trapezoids supported by six large circular columns. The two uppermost volumes are clad in sloping glass, framing dramatic views while contrasting with the heavy concrete structure. These volumes seem to hover over a shaded outdoor zone like a futuristic spaceship; two of the columns touch down into a semicircular pool. Heightening the design's air of dropped-in luxury and leisure, the roof accommodates a putting green enclosed by a clear glass wall. To build the cantilevered form on the steep site, Loh was required to purchase air rights from the Lands Department. A curved driveway delivers cars around the trees into a parking area west of the house. The building is one of two projects Architects Team 3 has completed outside of Malaysia and Singapore, and it was realised in collaboration with the prolific Hong Kong–based firm Palmer & Turner.   SS

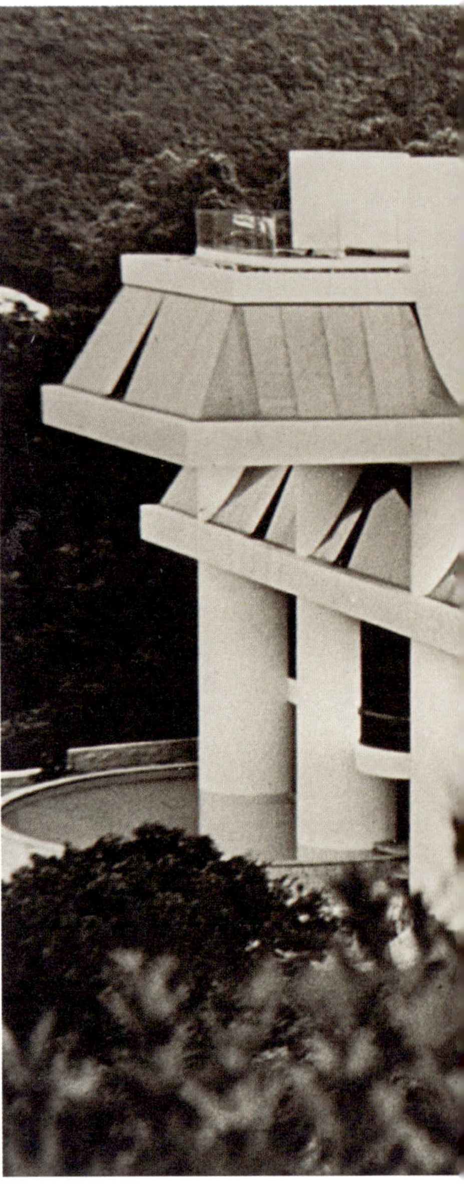

Lim Chong Keat (born 1930, British Malaya (now Malaysia))
Architects Team 3 (established 1967)
Exterior view of house for Robin Loh (1973)
ca. 1973
Gelatin silver print
21 × 29.7 cm
Gift of Architects Team 3, 2015
CA29/2/8

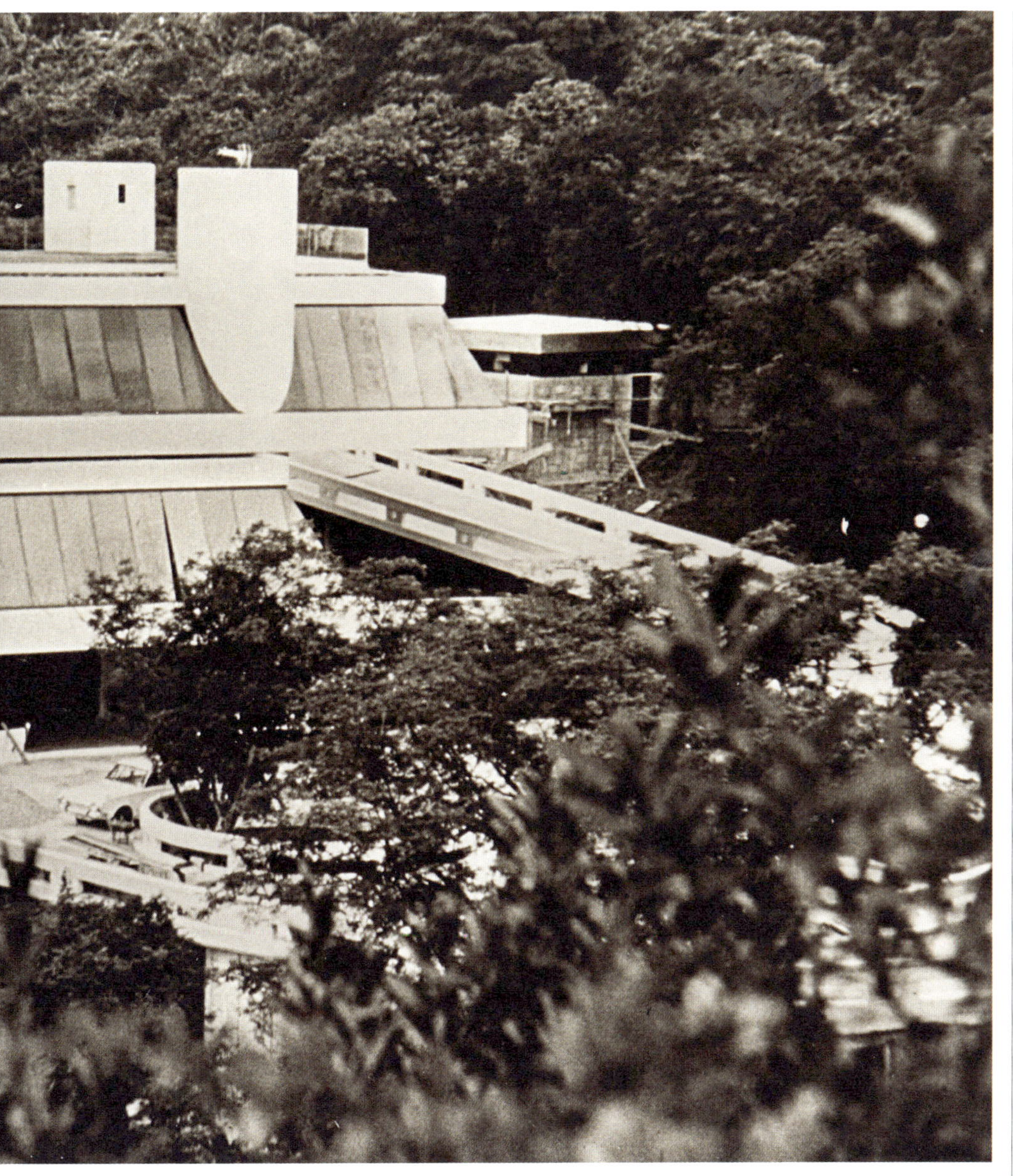

Situated on a hill in Pok Fu Lam with a view of the sea, these twelve three-storey private houses are characterised by double-height spaces, rooftop gardens, and a dialogue between interior and exterior, recalling Le Corbusier's modernist designs for houses of the 1920s. Remo Riva's axonometric drawing conveys the geometric composition of the project, which is anchored on a modernist grid, while also expressing a playful iconography and palette of colours characteristic of postmodern architecture. The drawing frames a dialogue between visual languages as well as between the city and nature, notably in Riva's insertion of a beach, palm tree, and sunset. In contrast to the exuberance of the drawing, the materials and finishes of the built project are subdued, but the vision that Riva articulates in two dimensions captures an idea of secluded comfort that defines this housing development.   SC

Remo Riva (born 1946, Switzerland)
Axonometric drawing for houses at Sassoon Road (1976–1979)
1976
Graphite, ink, and watercolour on paper
40.6 × 42.1 cm
Gift of Remo Riva, 2013
CA12/1/2

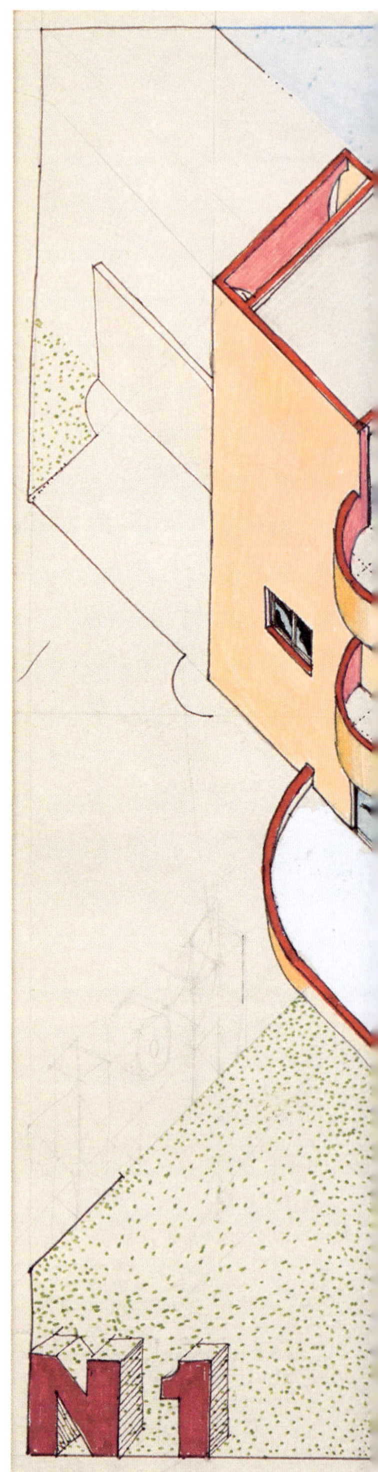

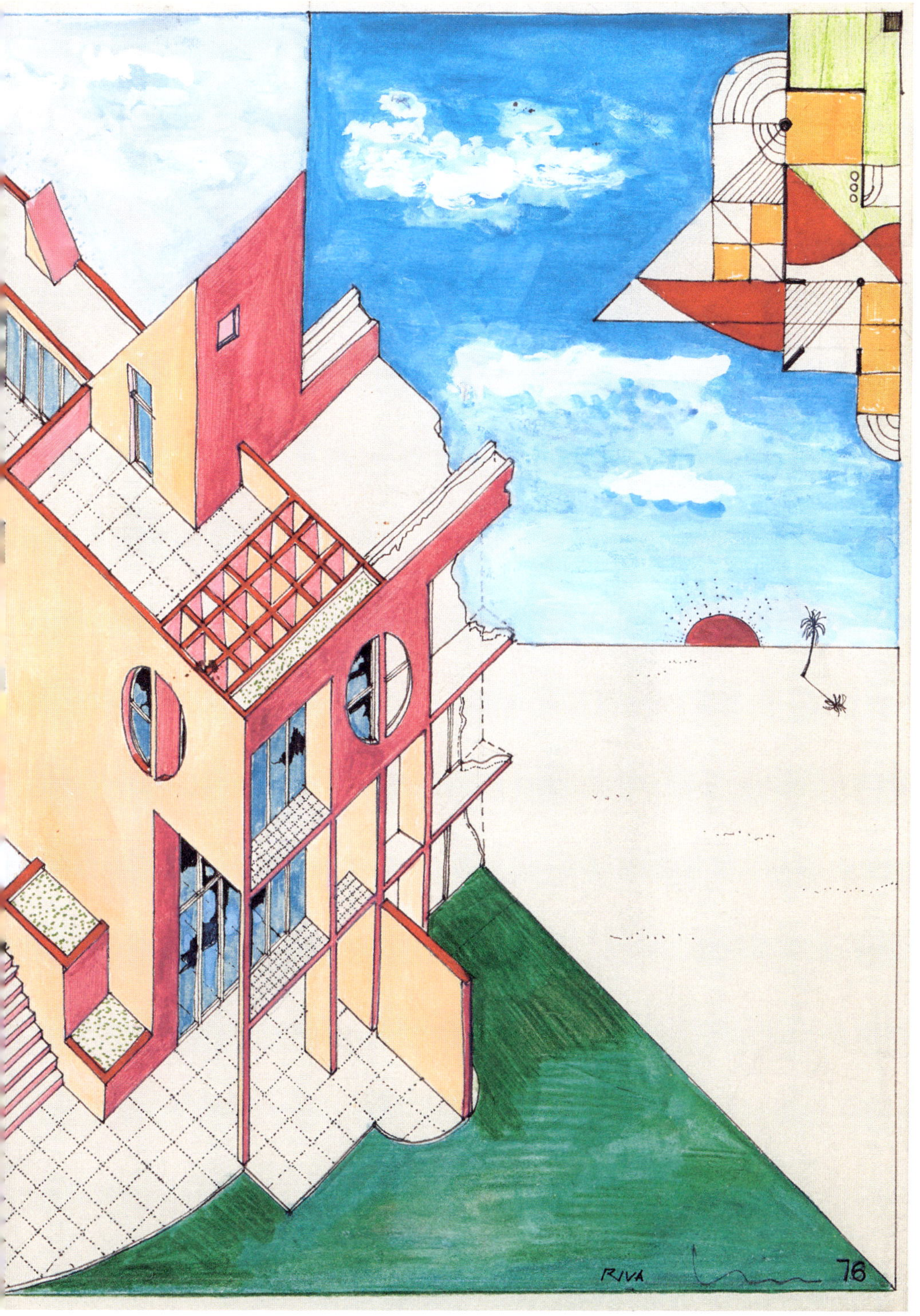

RIVA
76

For more than twenty years, the Legislative Council occupied the Old Supreme Court Building in Central. The need to integrate the work of different government departments more seamlessly prompted the development of a new purpose-built complex on a waterfront site in Tamar, a historical naval base in Admiralty.

The site lies in close proximity to the central business district and other political, juridical, and military offices. The design by Rocco Yim brings together the Central Government Complex, the Legislative Council Complex, and the Chief Executive's Office. Yim aimed to connect Admiralty to Victoria Harbour, emphasising openness and circulation. The two wings of the government complex are connected at the upper levels, creating a structure that symbolises a gateway. The Chief Executive's Office and the Legislative Council Complex sit on either side of Tamar Park, allowing for pedestrian movement between the city and the harbourfront. Yim articulates an idea of transparency for government, one that is meant to inform its relationship with the people. During large-scale demonstrations, the Legislative Council Square has become a space of contention.   TP

Rocco Yim (born 1952, Hong Kong)
Rocco Design Architects (established 1982)
Model for Hong Kong Special Administrative Region Government Headquarters (2007–2011)
2011
Cardboard and acrylic
44.5 × 91.2 × 136 cm
Gift of Rocco Design Architects Associates Ltd., 2013
2014.157

Concept sketch for the 'open door', Hong Kong Special Administrative Region Government Headquarters (2007–2011)
ca. 2007
Print on paper
21 × 29.8 cm
Gift of Rocco Design Architects Associates Ltd., 2013
CA2/11/1

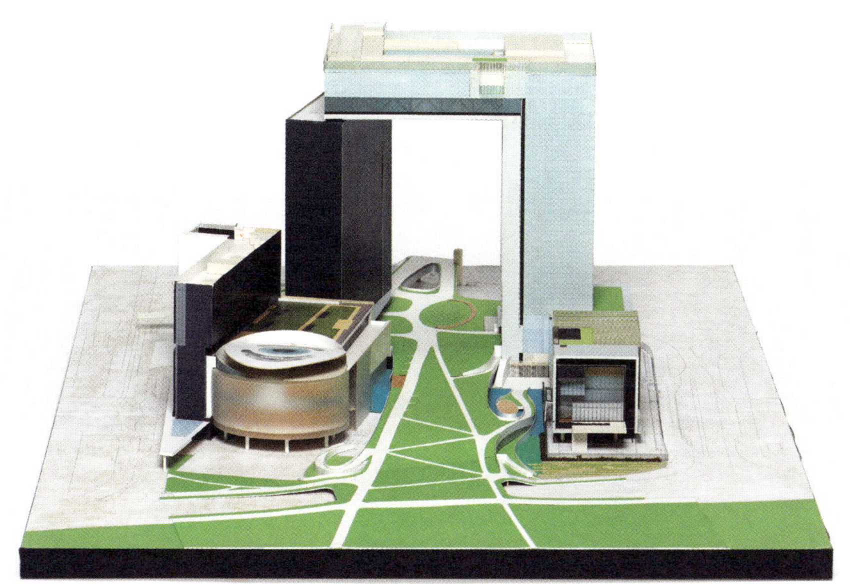

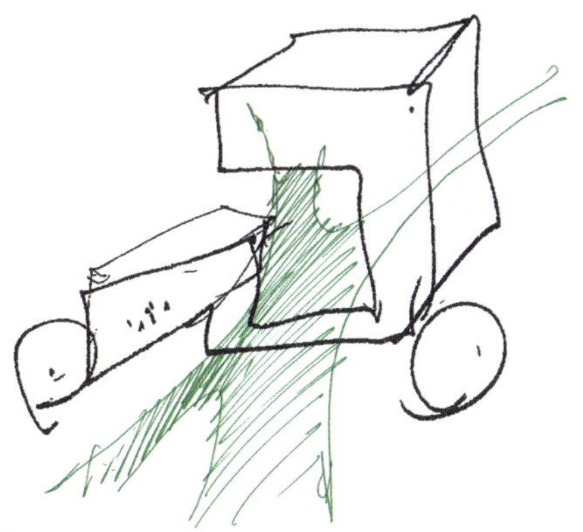

The Hong Kong University of Science and Technology was conceived in response to the increasing demand for specialised skill sets in the city's new service economy. The competition for the design of the campus at Clear Water Bay galvanised the architecture community. It was won by LOTUS Architects, led by Eric Lye and Joan Leung, with a project for a compact, adaptable building system that responds to the topography and natural context. Specifically, LOTUS's design relies on platforms that react to the contours of the land and minimise disturbance of the site. The scheme has two types of platforms: large, regular, and concentrated on the one hand, and small, irregular, and dispersed on the other. The architects exploit these variations to distinguish between the main academic building on the large platforms and the less formal arrangement of housing and recreational facilities on the small platforms. The plan is organised along two parallel axes that are defined by the main academic building and an artificial ridge with elevated vegetation. Buildings descend towards the sea, with their heights delimited by the inclined plane of the hillside, preserving views of the natural surroundings.

Although LOTUS's project was selected as the winner of the competition, it was the proposal by Simon Kwan that was eventually built. Like LOTUS's design, Kwan's project responds to the site's topography, but it provides a less open-ended, more fixed network of clusters of academic spaces, accommodating the university's vision for distinct, interconnected facilities. Kwan's design positions the entrance plaza and the academic block on the site's promontory along a central axis, which intersects with paths leading to university residences arranged on a sequence of descending platforms.   SC

Eric Lye (born 1934, British Malaya (now Malaysia); died 2003, Malaysia)
LOTUS Architects (established 1987)
Drawing for Hong Kong University of Science and Technology
1987
Ink on transparent paper
75 × 52.6 cm
CA3/1/1

Simon Kwan (born 1941, Hong Kong)
Simon Kwan & Associates (established 1973)
Sketch for Hong Kong University of Science and Technology (1987–1993)
1987
Ink on transparent paper
38 × 75.2 cm
Gift of Simon Kwan & Associates Limited, 2014
CA15/3/4

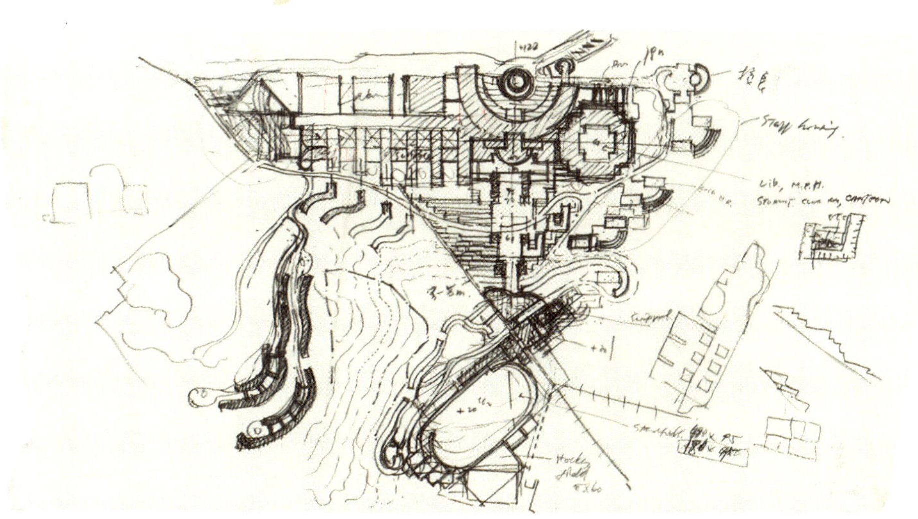

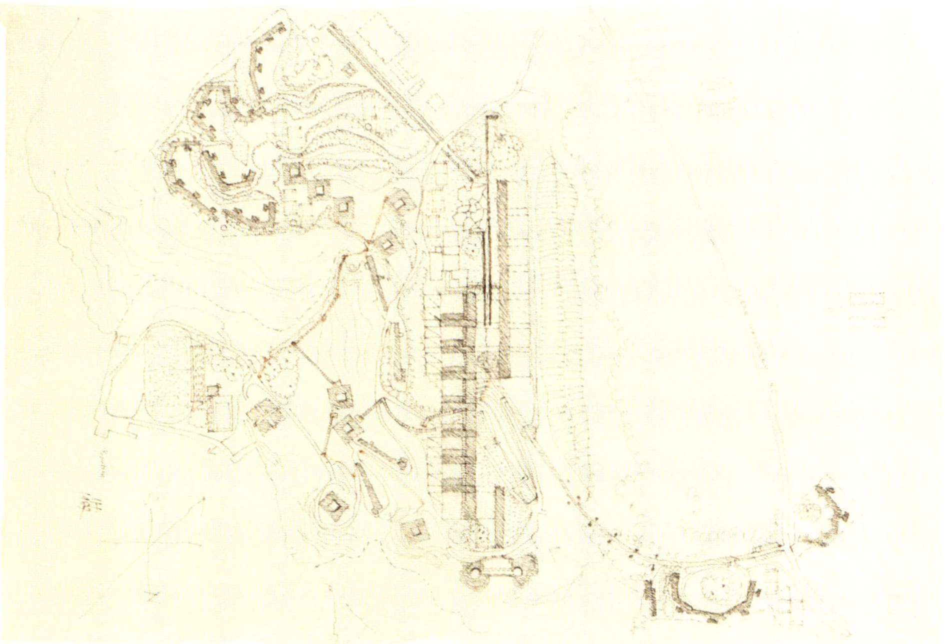

Located in Sai Wan Ho, the home of the architect Gary Chang is perhaps the most famous design for a small residential space in Hong Kong. Known as the Domestic Transformer, it is the result of years of experimentation in the thirty-two-square-metre apartment that has been Chang's home since he was a child. Taking as a point of departure the assumption that we can only perform one activity at a time, Chang matches space with function. This set of models shows ten of the apartment's twenty-four transformations, which include a kitchen, laundry, office, screening room, dining area, spa, and bedroom. The series of custom-built movable walls and components includes multifunctional prefabricated mobile furniture, blurring the boundaries between building envelope, interior, and furnishing. Chang proposes an ingenious solution in response to the constraints of compact living in a hyper-dense urban environment—a context that is increasingly prevalent around the world.   SS

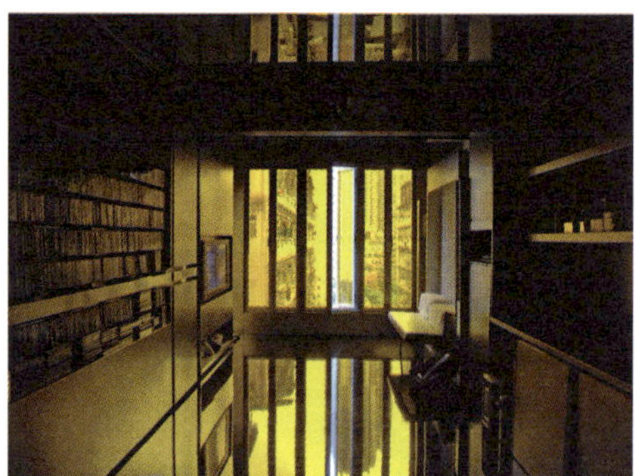

Domestic Transformer, as bedroom and living room

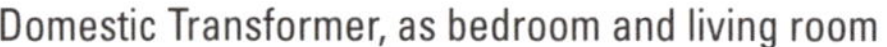

Gary Chang (born 1962, Hong Kong)
EDGE Design Institute (established 1994)
Model for Domestic Transformer (2006–2007)
2015
Acrylic
22.3 × 120 × 5.5 cm
2020.6

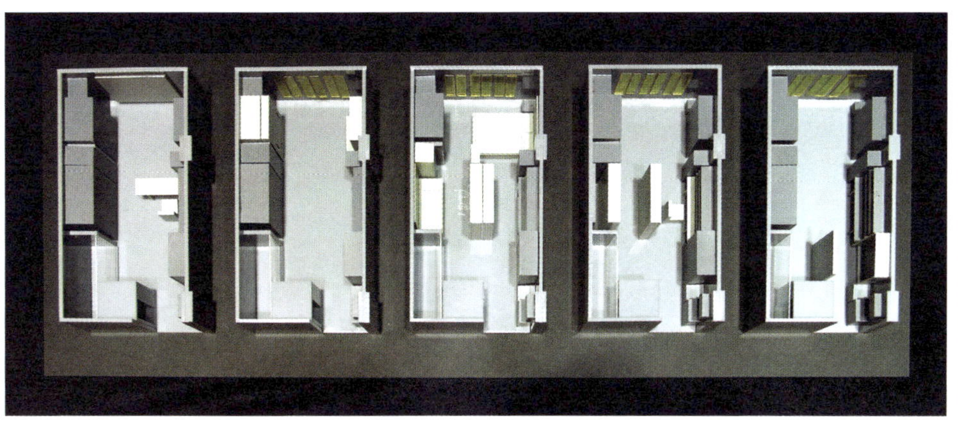

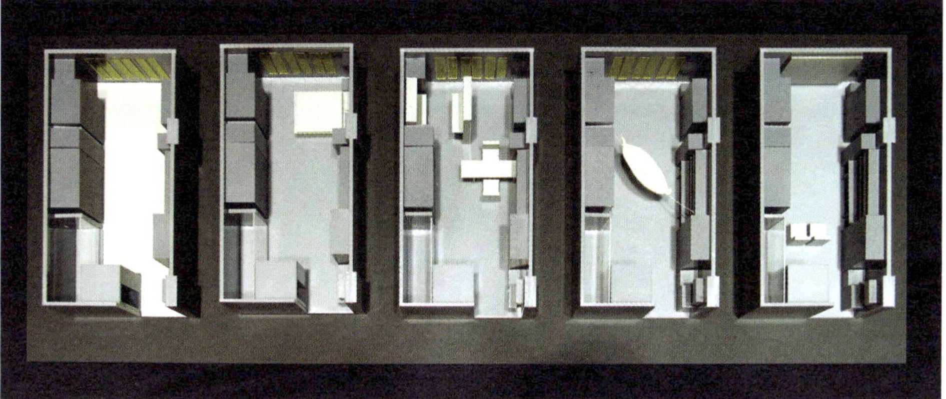

Ten configurations of Domestic Transformer

In 1983, the young Baghdad-born, London-based architect Zaha Hadid won an international competition to design a recreational club and residential complex on Victoria Peak. Hadid's design simultaneously translates the density of the city below and provides relief from this condition. The competition was organised by the entrepreneur and property developer Alfred Siu and the project established Hadid's reputation for formal experimentation. The design involved levelling part of the site and using the extracted stone to clad what Hadid called a 'man-made polished granite mountain'. In a series of paintings, she used the technique of imploding and fracturing geometries—inspired by Russian Suprematism—to depict layers of residential and leisure spaces erupting from the rocky hillside around a central void that houses the club's facilities. The fragmented, levitating planes of walls, floors, and ceilings both blur and accentuate the lines between the structure and the topography. The clubhouse was never built, in part because Hadid's proposal proved impossible to realise before the advent of computer-aided design. The project is a vivid illustration of her pioneering development of an architectural language that digital tools would later make possible. It also reflects the giddy optimism of the property market of 1980s Hong Kong.   SS

Zaha Hadid (born 1950, Iraq; died 2016, United States)
Study for overall isometric night view, the Peak project, Hong Kong (1983 Competition)
1991
Acrylic and inkjet print
124.8 × 187.8 × 6.1 cm
2015.19

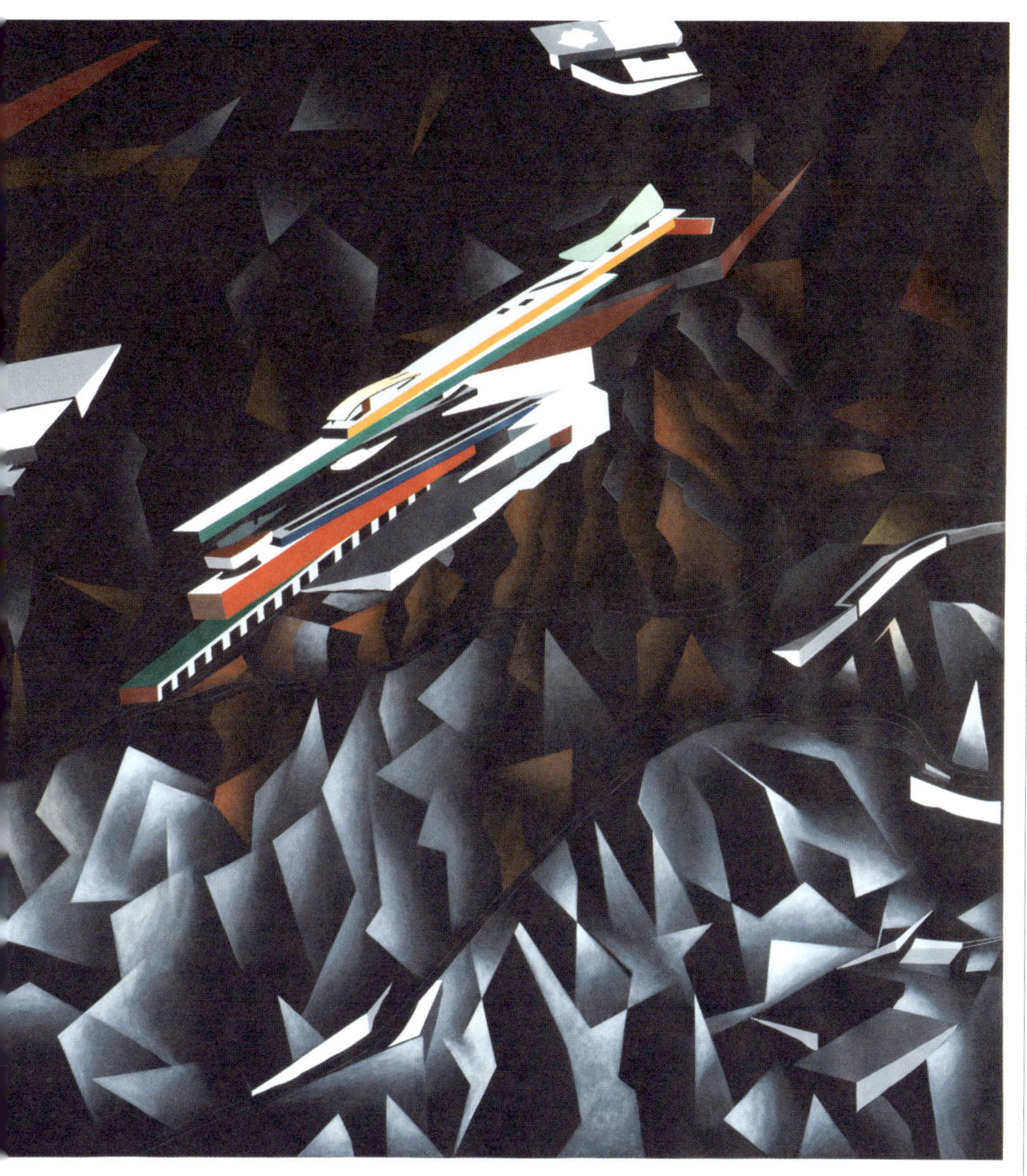

In 1988, the architect Tao Ho designed an innovative proposal for a land reclamation project around the Yau Ma Tei Typhoon Shelter, an area now adjacent to the West Kowloon Cultural District. Developed in collaboration with architecture and urban design students at the University of Hong Kong, Ho's design moves beyond the project's brief. Rather than accepting the reality of designing on reclaimed land, Ho proposed a flexible solution that extends from the land onto the water. The design is organised around a central spine that links Yau Ma Tei with Tsim Sha Tsui, a large concrete deck supported by caissons anchored on the seabed. The deck would accommodate transportation and high-rise commercial developments including offices, hotels, and cultural and recreational amenities, adapting to future growth both horizontally and vertically. The design envisions an urban environment that can be programmed and structured for change. It recalls the modular, transformable, and floating megastructures conceived in the 1960s by architects such as Archigram and the Metabolists. Ho's project also draws from the structural logic of the vernacular waterfront architecture of Hong Kong fishing villages.   SS

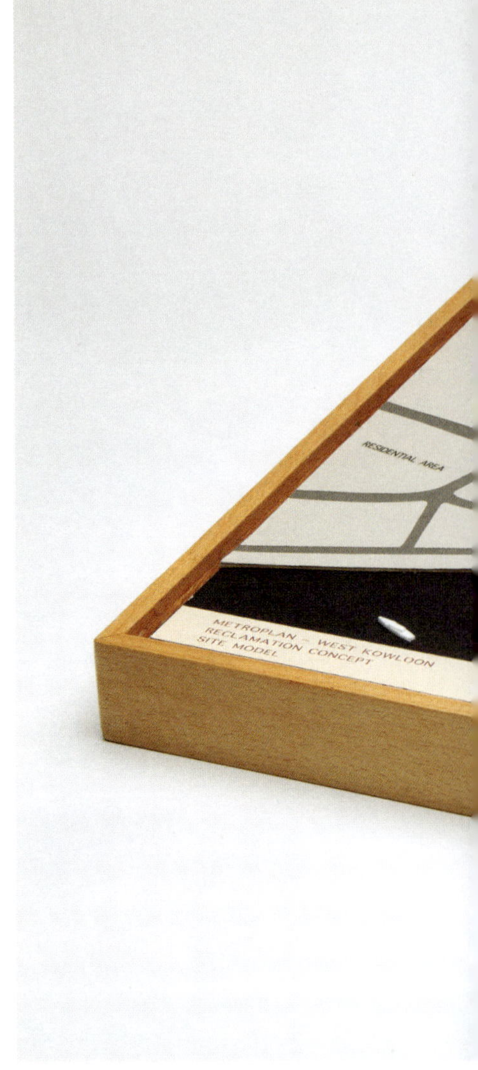

Tao Ho (born 1936, Shanghai; died 2019, Hong Kong)
Taoho Design (established 1968)
Model of Metroplan West Kowloon Reclamation Concept
Designed 1988, made 2013
Acrylic and cardboard
39.7 × 53 × 56.7 cm
2013.160

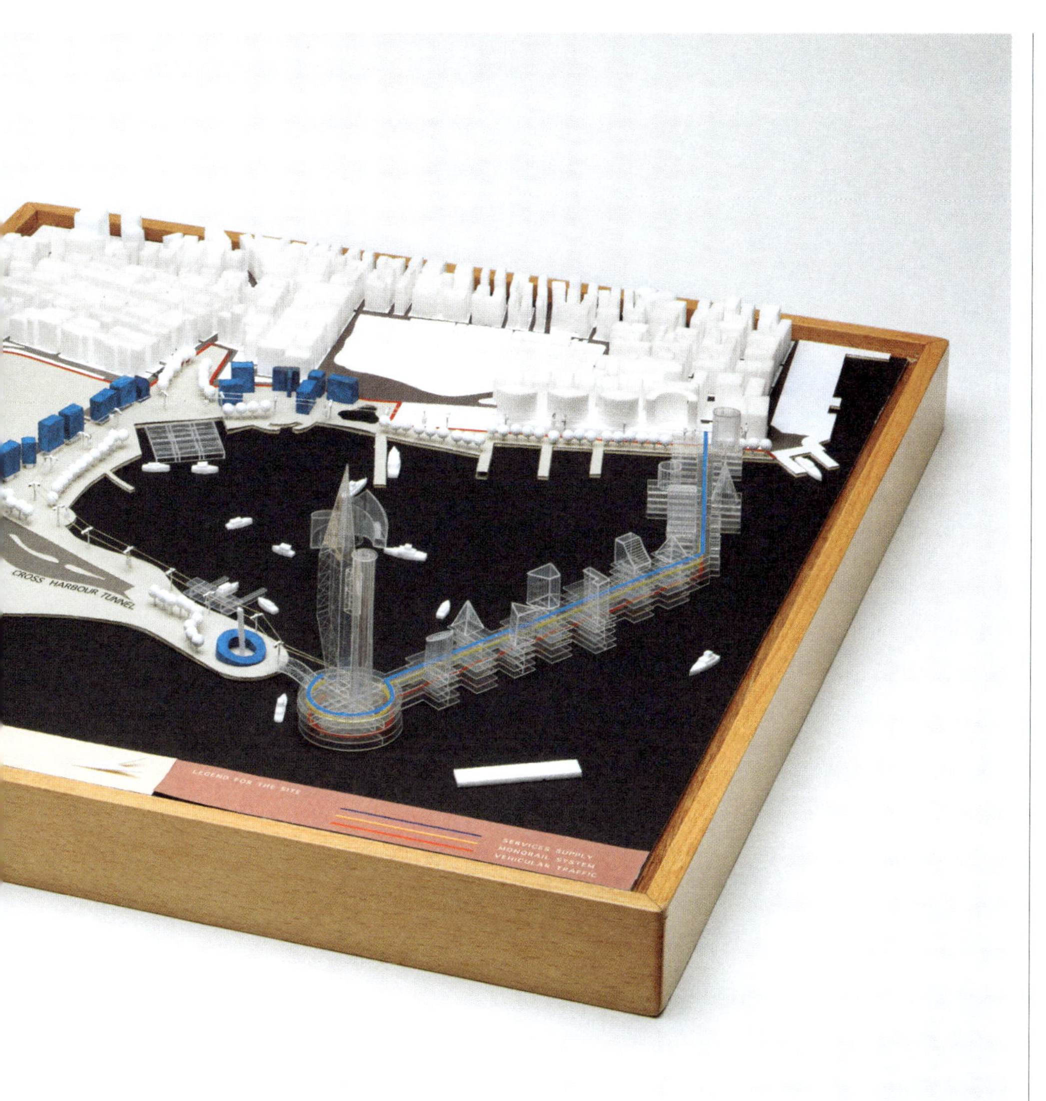
CROSS HARBOUR TUNNEL
LEGEND FOR THE SITE
SERVICES SUPPLY
MONORAIL SYSTEM
VEHICULAR TRAFFIC

The facade of the Bond Centre in Admiralty disrupts the conventional form of the glass curtain wall that characterises neighbouring office towers. The building's cantilevered floor plates produce protruding volumes that result in its distinctive texture. Designed by American architect Paul Rudolph in collaboration with Hong Kong firm Wong & Ouyang, the development quickly became an important node within Hong Kong's extensive network of raised walkways and ground-level pedestrian arteries. The Bond Centre—today known as the Lippo Centre—defines multi-level connections with adjacent buildings through footbridges at each of the four corners of its elevated podium. The design illuminates Rudolph's long-standing interest in buildings as condensers of urban energy and in creating dynamic semi-public spaces, ideas that he also explored in late-career projects for high-rises in Jakarta and Singapore.   SC

Paul Rudolph (1918–1997, United States)
Nora Leung (born 1955, Hong Kong)
Wong & Ouyang (established 1972)
Exterior perspective drawing for Bond Centre (1984–1988)
ca. 1985
Chromogenic print
25.4 × 20.4 cm
Gift of Wong & Ouyang (HK) Ltd., 2017
CA16/7/40

Drawing for Bond Centre (1984–1988)
1985
Print on paper
26.8 × 38.2 cm
CA8

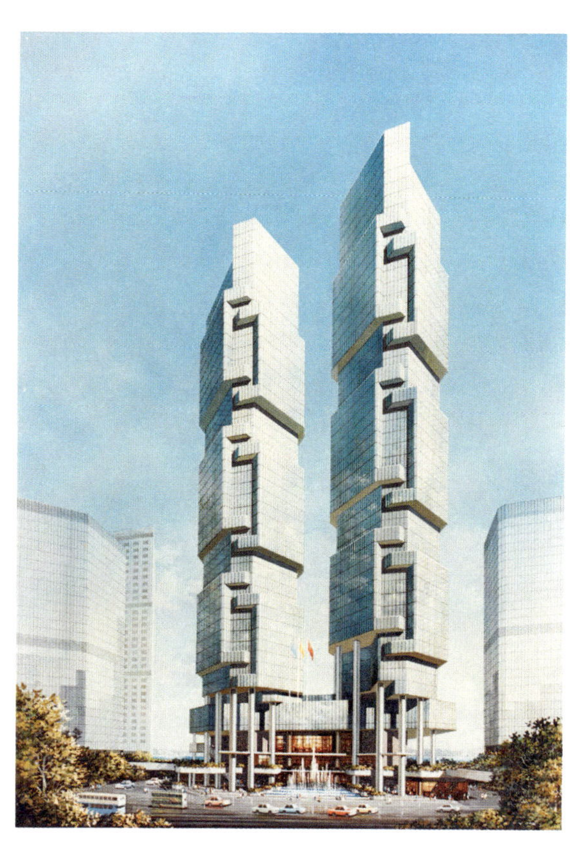

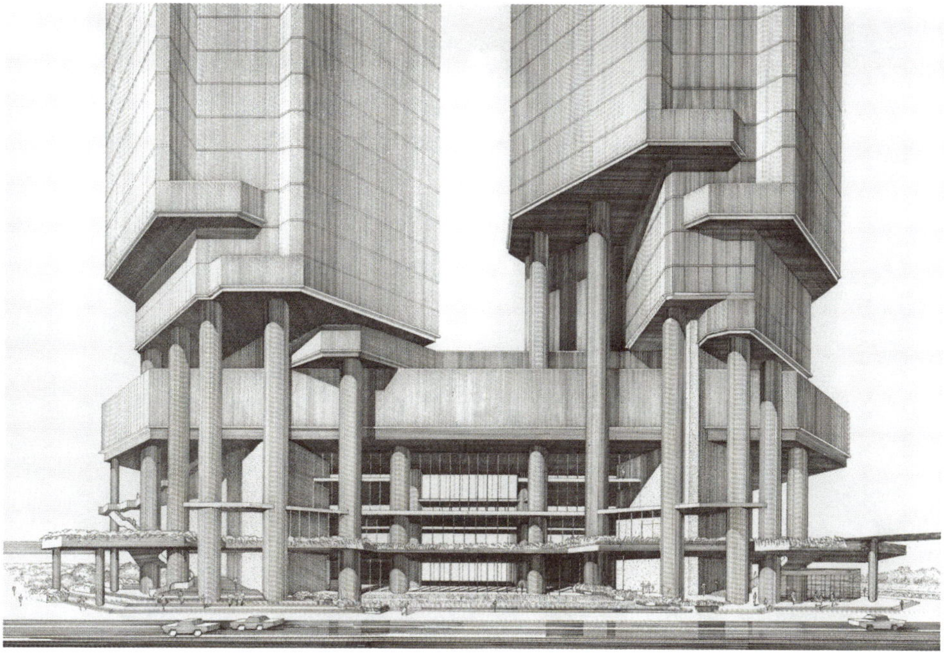

Good Afternoon Hong Kong comprises eight scenes of the city, including the Airport, the Mandarin Oriental Hotel, the clock tower at the old Star Ferry Pier, and Lion Rock. The artist Chihoi painted the scenes in an expressionistic style that lends the work a cinematic or narrative quality. He collaborated with the German manufacturer Plastiskop to produce an artist's book in the form of film stills. The slides are meant to be viewed through a palm-sized picture viewer that mimics the form of a mid-century television set. With 'Hong Kong' printed on it, the picture viewer both harks back to the city's heyday as a centre of plastic toy production and becomes a window onto the past and the present. During the 1980s and 1990s— the years of Chihoi's childhood and adolescence—viewfinders were highly popular as a way of exploring monuments and landmarks from around the world through touristic photographs. This work presents images of Hong Kong as an allusive private viewing experience. *Good Afternoon Hong Kong* exemplifies Chihoi's interest in challenging conventions of publishing and printed mediums.   CC

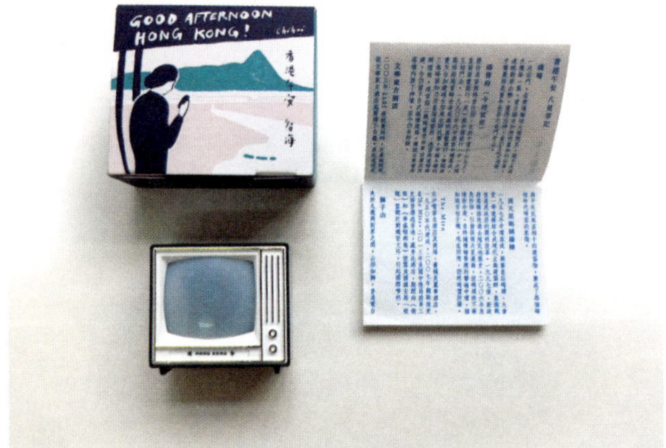

Plastic slide viewer in package with booklet

Chihoi (born 1977, Hong Kong)
Good Afternoon Hong Kong
2017
Acrylic on paper
26 × 29.5 cm (each drawing, set of eight)
2020.483–2020.490
Plastic slide viewer with booklet
6.5 × 8 × 3 cm (package)
2020.491

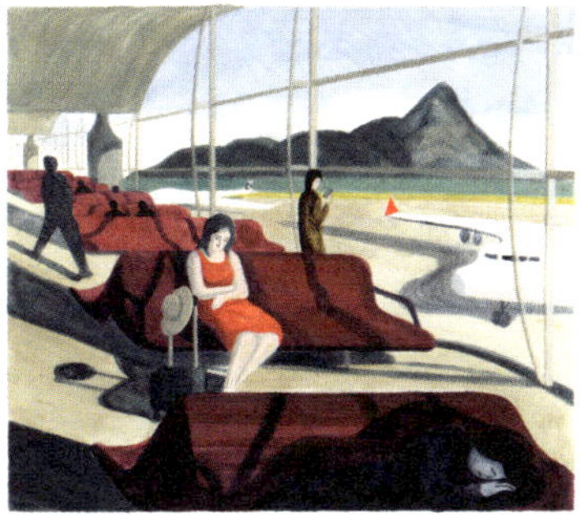

Hong Kong International Airport

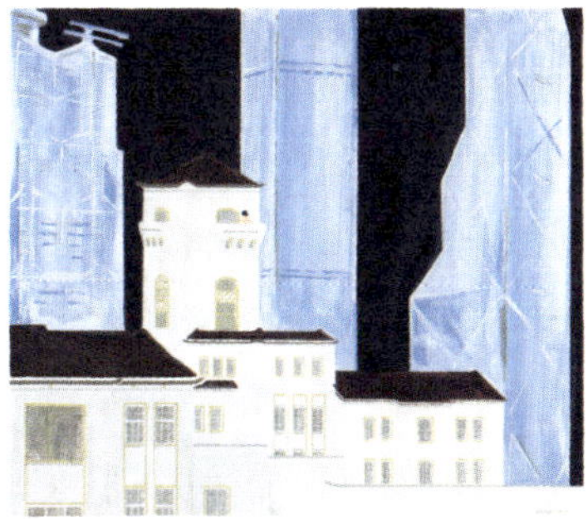

Government House

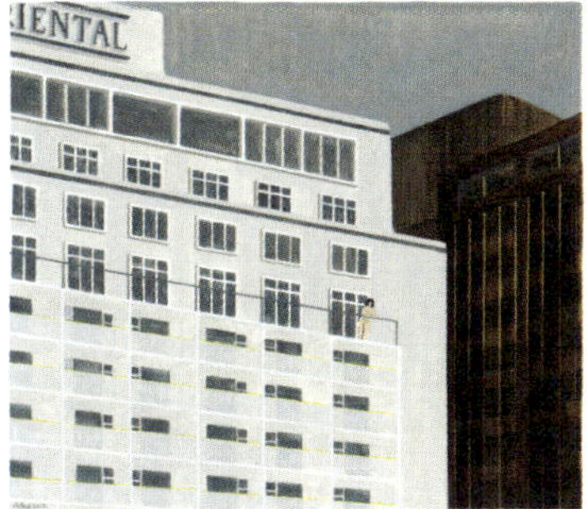

The Mandarin Oriental

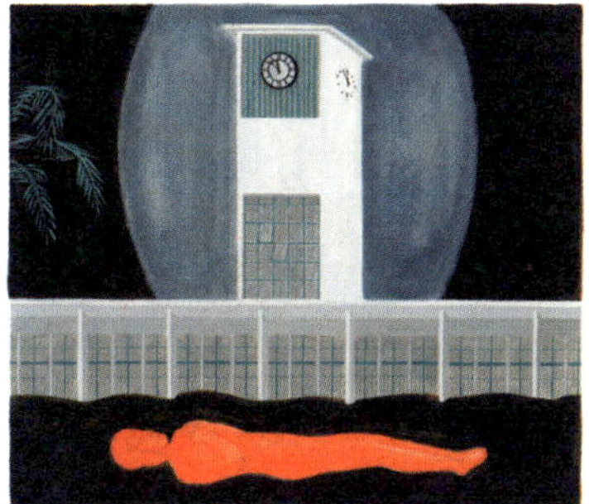

The Star Ferry Clock Tower

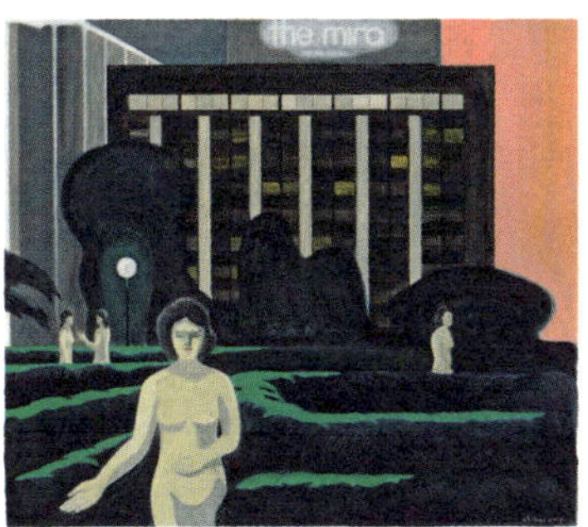

The Mira

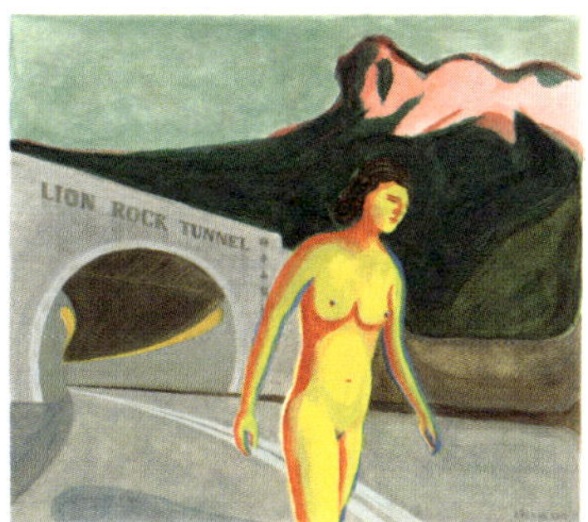

Lion Rock

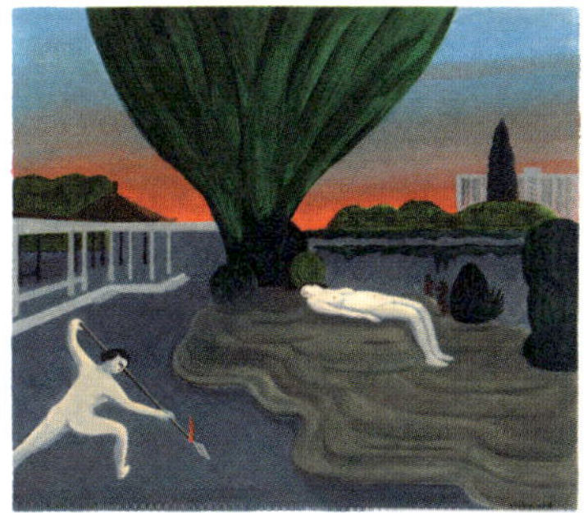

Sha Tin Park

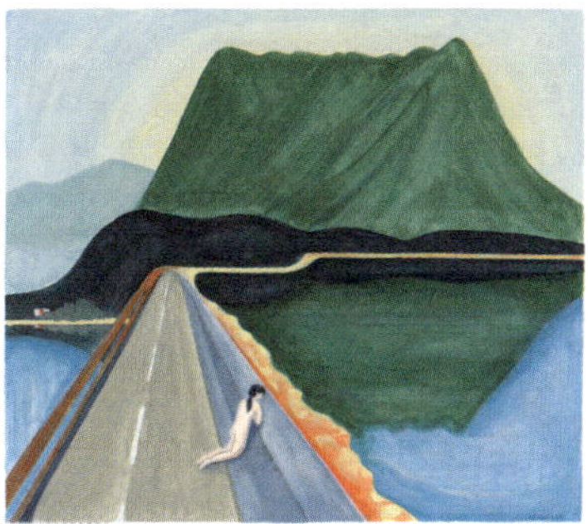

Pak Sin Leng Mountain

GIVE US A CALL, WE HAVE LOTS TO TALK ABOUT

Branding Hong Kong at home and abroad

In the early 1960s, international tourism grew with the advent of affordable jet travel. Commissioned by the Hong Kong Tourist Association, Dong Kingman's watercolour illustration depicts the firing of the Noonday Gun on the Causeway Bay harbourfront. The gun is fired by an employee of Jardine Matheson—one of the earliest *hongs*, or trading houses—which owns the site. The Noonday Gun remains a tourist attraction to this day. The poster also features the Edwardian neoclassical clock tower in Tsim Sha Tsui, Chinese sailboats, rickshaws, and men fishing in small vessels, conveying an enticing combination of experiences that can only be encountered in Hong Kong. The city is presented as an exotic destination, in an image whose colours and jaunty illustrative character reflect the visual language of mid-century travel posters.

Parallel to the development of tourism as a new growth industry was Hong Kong's ambition to position itself as a manufacturing hub. In 1973, the Hong Kong Trade Development Council commissioned the graphic designer Henry Steiner to create the visual identity for a campaign promoting Hong Kong's textile and clothing manufacturing for an international trade fair in Paris. The model in Steiner's provocative design is 'clothed' in bright pink cut-outs, a sexualised, objectified Asian woman that plays on the image of a child's paper doll. The combination of the vibrant colour with the minimal, spare design introduces an internationalist sensibility to Hong Kong's image as a centre of textile production.   TP

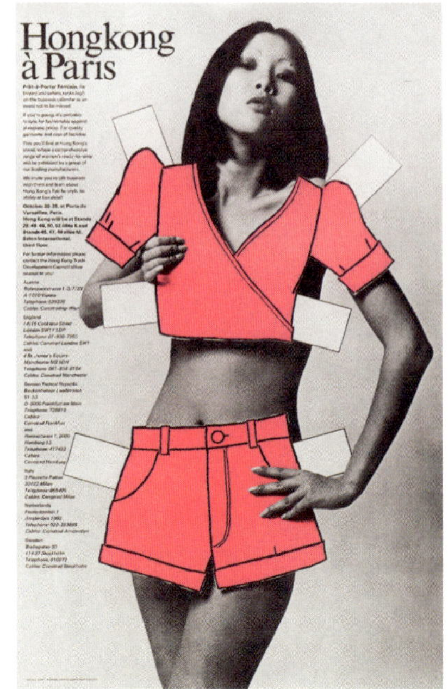

Henry Steiner (born 1934, Austria)
Graphic Communication (established 1964)
Poster for Hong Kong Trade Development Council, 'Hongkong à Paris'
1973
Offset lithograph
65.5 × 51 cm
2020.94

Dong Kingman (2000–2011, United States)
Poster for Hong Kong Tourist Association, 'The Noon Day Gun in Hong Kong'
1961
Offset lithograph mounted on linen
88.8 × 59.3 cm
2018.36

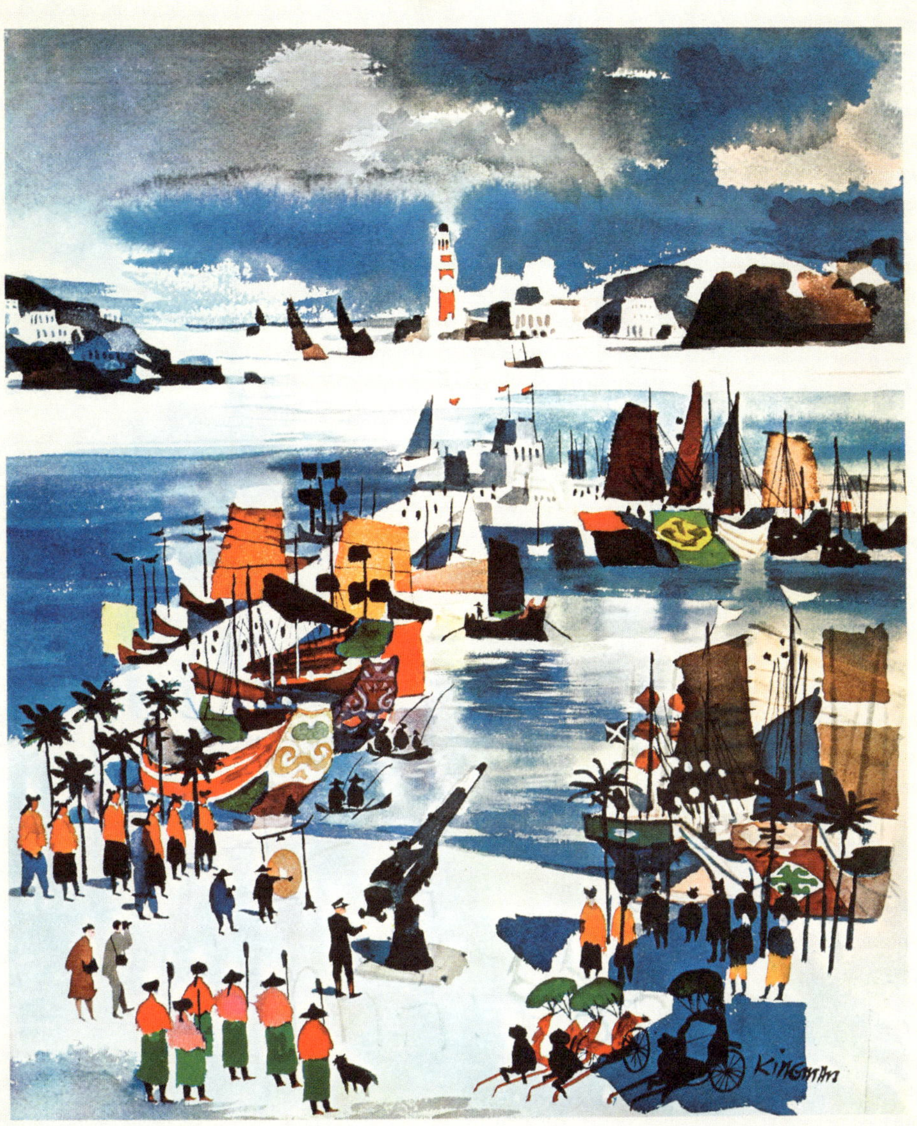

THE NOON DAY GUN IN HONG KONG
PRINTED IN HONG KONG FOR THE HONG KONG TOURIST ASSOCIATION

The Peak Tramways Company commissioned the Peak Tower in 1967, a year of political and social unrest in Hong Kong. Architect Chung Wah Nan designed the building to create the appearance of a floating structure, embedding the base in the site's slope. The form recalls a watchtower on ancient Chinese fortifications, embodying Chung's interest in developing a culturally situated language of architectural modernism. The tower, the terminus of the Peak Tram, contained restaurants, shops, and indoor and outdoor rooftop observation decks, and quickly became one of the city's most popular tourist destinations—even appearing on the 500 Hong Kong dollar banknote. The project was a statement of confidence in Hong Kong's future and a prominent addition to the city's skyline. Despite the Peak Tower's status as an icon, it was demolished in 1993 and replaced with a larger building housing a shopping centre, designed by British architect Terry Farrell.   SC

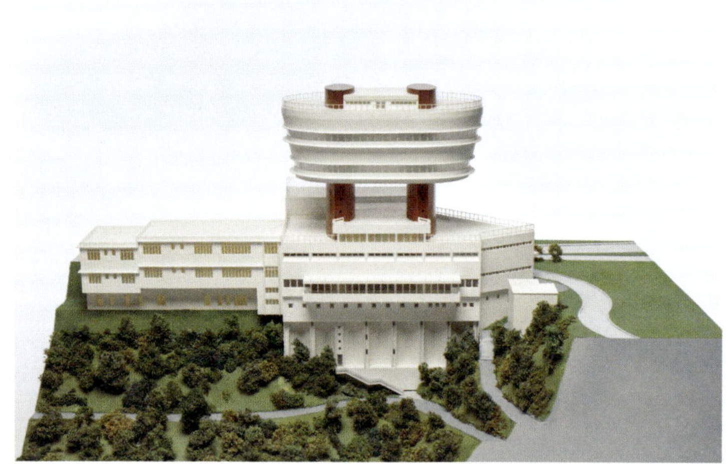

Chung Wah Nan (1931–2018, Hong Kong)
Chung Wah Nan Architects (established 1964)
Model for Peak Tower (1967–1972)
1969, reproduced 2013
Wood, plastic, paper, metal, and paint
98 × 111.3 × 66 cm
2013.215

Aerial view of Peak Tower (1967–1972)
ca. 1971
Chromogenic print
15.1 × 10.1 cm
Gift of Chung Wah Nan Architects Limited, 2014
CA10/1/5/8

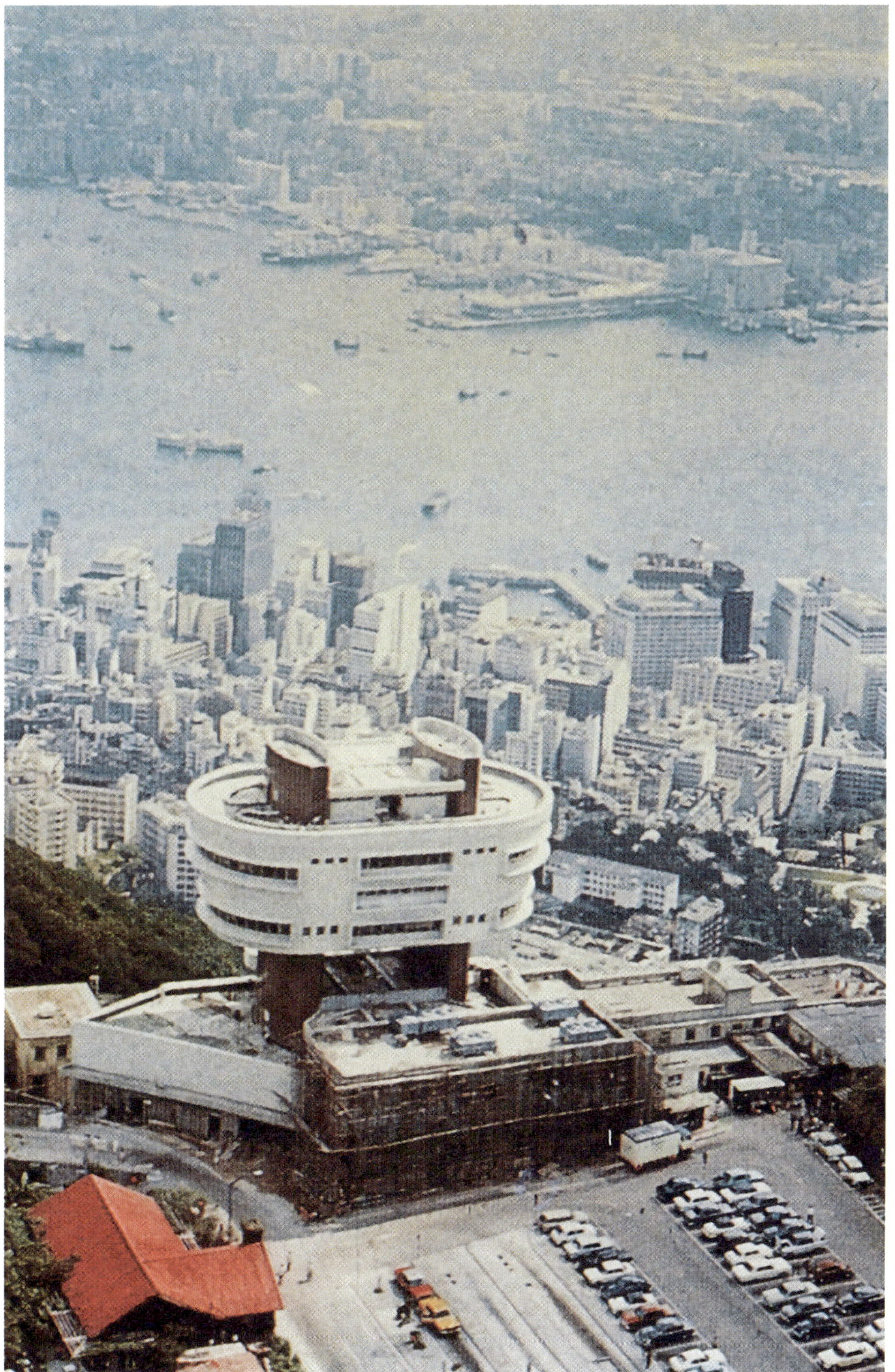

Occupying a prominent position at the junction of Garden Road and Queensway in Central, the five-star Hilton Hotel represented the height of modern luxury, glamour, and culture in Hong Kong. It was an icon of the city's identity as an international business hub and, at twenty-six-storeys, of its high-rise development. Designed by James H. Kinoshita of Palmer & Turner and completed in 1963, the Hilton in Hong Kong pioneered a modern typology for hotels, featuring a two-storey shopping arcade integrated into the lobby, a swimming pool and cabanas on the podium roof, and in-room minibars. Frequented by international travellers and local celebrities, it was the site of a wide range of cultural events.

For his branding strategy for the Hilton, Hong Kong designer Henry Steiner drew inspiration from Chinese latticework to create the double-H logo. His total design approach used a single typeface across many of the hotel's elements to reinforce its identity. In advance of its opening, local artists including Douglas Bland, Cheung Yee, and David Lam were commissioned to produce works for its spaces, signalling the American hotel's intention to engage with cultural production in Hong Kong. The interiors were designed by Dale and Patricia Keller, who shaped the character of many international chain hotels in Asia from the 1960s through the 1980s. The Hilton was demolished in 1995 to make way for the towering Cheung Kong Center designed by César Pelli, but it retains a place in popular memory. Perhaps most famously, it was a site of refuge as well as protest during the 1967 unrest, when leftist demonstrators demanded that the hotel take down its American flag.   SC

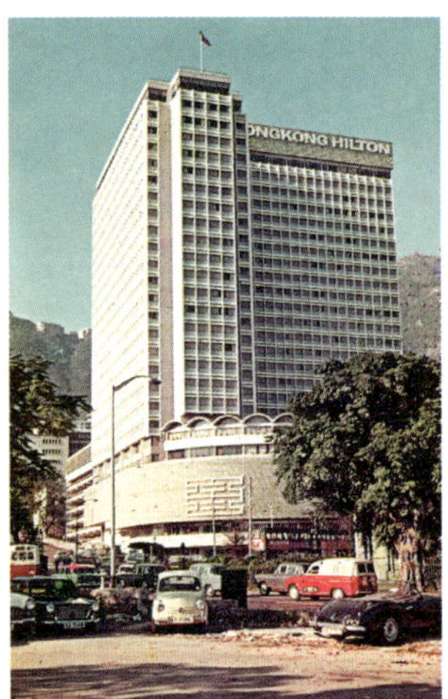

View of the Hong Kong Hilton, ca. 1962

Henry Steiner (born 1934, Austria)
Graphic Communication (established 1964)
***Hong Kong Hilton Magazine*, vol. 1, no. 2**
May 1963
Offset lithograph
23 × 21.2 × 0.3 cm
CA31

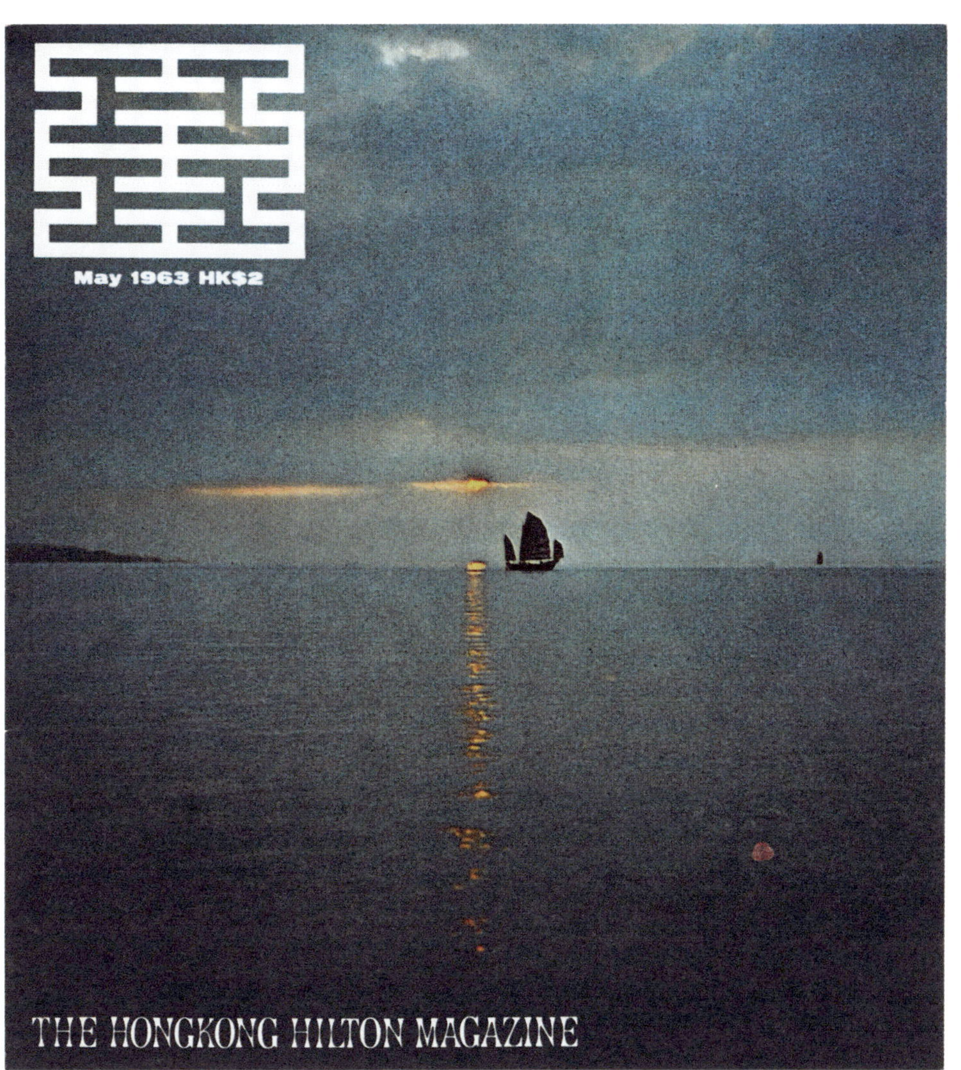
May 1963 HK$2
THE HONGKONG HILTON MAGAZINE

Henry Steiner moved to Hong Kong in the 1960s to set up the new headquarters for *The Asia Magazine* in the city. He quickly established himself through an emphatically cross-cultural approach to graphic design that engaged with Chinese and Euro-American visual traditions, emphasising the languages distinct to each. Steiner developed a strategy in the 1960s that created unity through contrast and that has become deeply influential. His approach reflected Hong Kong's position as Asia's transcultural centre. In addition to his editorial work, Steiner created identities for some of the city's most influential brands and institutions, accentuating elements of cultural and corporate histories. The now-iconic red-and-white hexagon of his HSBC logo derives from the diagonals of the bank's saltire (diagonal cross) flag and alludes to the triangular components of the Chinese tangram puzzle. Steiner's design for the double-H logo for the Hong Kong Hilton is inspired by Chinese latticework, while his rendering of the H in the logo of Hongkong Land resembles the Chinese character *shou*, meaning 'longevity', as well as floor plans—a fitting reference for a property developer. For Dairy Farm, Steiner reflected his client's mass appeal by giving absolute parity to the brand's English and Chinese names.   SS

Henry Steiner (born 1934, Austria)
Graphic Communication (established 1964)
Corporate identity leaflet for Hongkong Bank
1983
Offset lithograph
21.1 × 9.9 cm
CA31

1973 annual report for Hongkong Land Company
1974
Offset lithograph
29.9 × 20.9 × 0.3 cm
CA31

Graphic Design Standards Manual for Dairy Farm
1986
Offset lithograph
24 × 30.7 × 1 cm
CA31

Stirrer for the Hong Kong Hilton Hotel (1963–1995)
Mid-1960s
Plastic
5.1 × 3.3 × 0.6 cm
2020.125

The new Corporate Identity consists of: a distinctive, typographically styled name or **Logo**; an abstract, geometric symbol or **Hexagon**; and a standard colour to be known as **Bank Red**. Together the Logo and Hexagon make up the corporate **Signature**.

1. The **Logo** is a shortened single-word version of the full, legal corporate name and is to be used in an auxiliary manner. It will however serve a prime *identificational* purpose. In North America it would be called a "service mark". The full name of the corporation remains "The Hongkong and Shanghai Banking Corporation" and will continue to be used in formal documents and elsewhere as appropriate. The lettering of the Logo is a completely re-drawn version of the typeface Times New Roman.

2. The **Hexagon** is derived from the traditional HSBC house flag, a white rectangle divided diagonally to produce a red "hourglass" shape. Like many other Hong Kong company flags originating in the last century, the form of the Bank's flag was derived from the Cross of St Andrew. This new symbol adopts and extends the geometry of the flag into a unique and internationally acceptable form. It may be used to convey many meanings such as expansion, interdependence and communication.

3. **Bank Red**, the corporate colour, along with white, has always been the colour of the flag. In most of the regions historically associated with the Bank, the colour red has auspicious connotations of boldness and good fortune. In monochrome or standard black and white printing, as in most newspapers, the Hexagon printed in black remains easily identifiable due to its distinctive form.

4. & 5. The full **Signature** can be used in either a centred or single line version depending on the typographic circumstances. The Signature on most international advertisements will include the full corporate name and, below it, the names of members of the group as appropriate.

6. Affiliation with the group will be indicated by the use of a modified signature, in black, incorporating for example an outline version of the Hexagon, printed at the lower right corner of letterheads where the Hexagon in Bank Red at the top would be incompatible with current stationery designs.

Outlines:

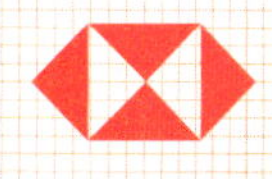

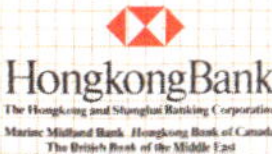

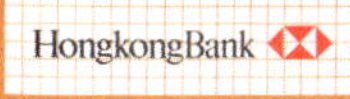

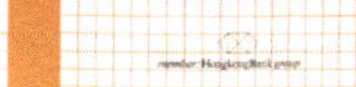

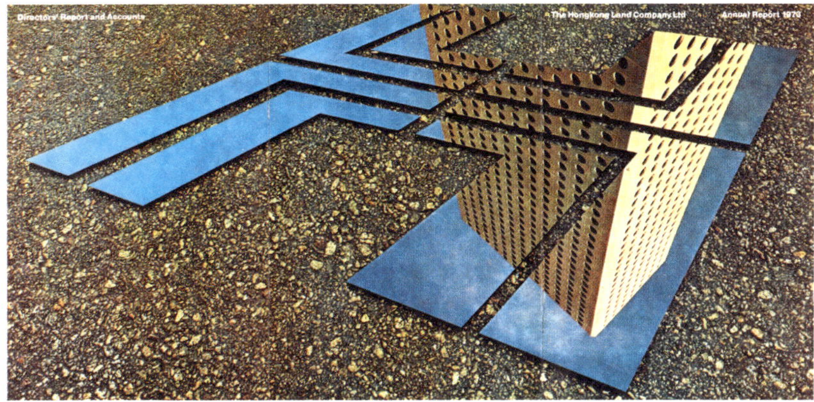

Logotype: Correct Uses

1.4 There are two versions of the Dairy Farm Logotype: **solid** and **outline**. These versions have been developed for different purposes to provide flexibility of application in various media. The two versions are not to be used in the body of any text.

Whenever possible the Logotype should appear in the normal stacked, two colour version. In adverse conditions such as weak visibility of the Logotype, it is recommended to allow a one line version in order to retain maximum visibility.

It is important that this one line version should never appear on general correspondence applications especially in combination with the outline version of the Logotype.

When the use of two colours is not practicable, as on some printed material, the entire Logotype should preferably be printed in Dairy Farm Blue. Other single colours may be used, but under no circumstances should a *combination* of colours other than the two Dairy Farm colours be used.

Solid Version: *English*
For most general applications and on signage

Solid Version: *Chinese*

Outline Version: *English*
For most correspondence applications

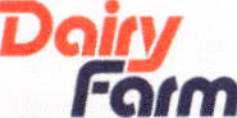

Outline Version: *Chinese*

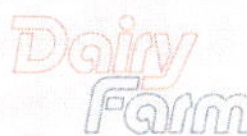

One Line Version: *English*
For use as an alternative to the stacked version
This version may be used when vertical space dictates

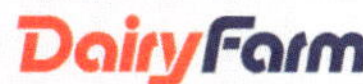

One Line Version: *Chinese*

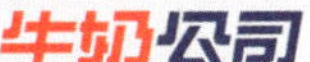

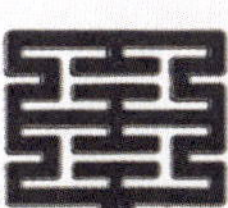

The Festival of Hong Kong, which took place in 1969, 1971, and 1973, was a government-sponsored initiative that included cultural and other entertainment events held across districts. The festival's aim was to generate social cohesion and raise the spirits of city dwellers, in particular its youth, following the turmoil and social division caused by the anti-colonial riots of 1967. The visual identity of the publicity campaign was designed by Arthur Hacker of the Information Services Department and included a distinctive circular logo that references the *Bauhinia x blakeana*, or Hong Kong orchid tree, a symbol of the city. The logo was used across all marketing materials, including posters and street banners, and the simplicity and flexibility of Hacker's design allowed it to be adapted to suit each surface. In this poster, the large central logo is surrounded by eight smaller versions on the bells of trumpets. The colours and dynamic composition call to mind British psychedelia of the late 1960s, a visual language with which Hacker was familiar from his years as an art director in London.   FT

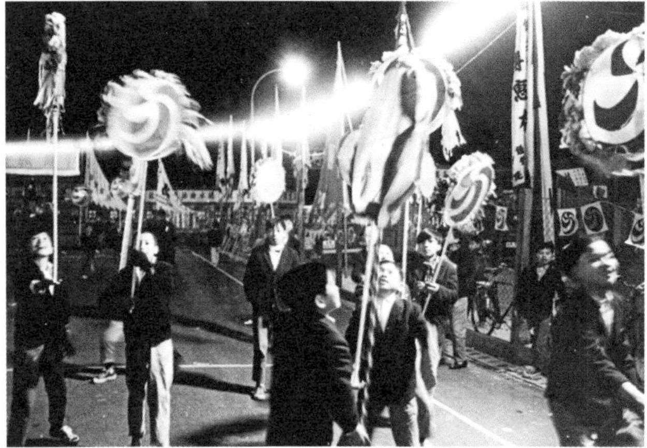

Festival of Hong Kong, 1969

Arthur Hacker (born 1932, United Kingdom; died 2013, Hong Kong)
Information Services Department, Hong Kong (established 1959)
Poster for Festival of Hong Kong Pageant
1971
Offset lithograph
72.9 × 47.4 cm
Gift of the Estate and family of Arthur Hacker in his honour, 2019
2019.90

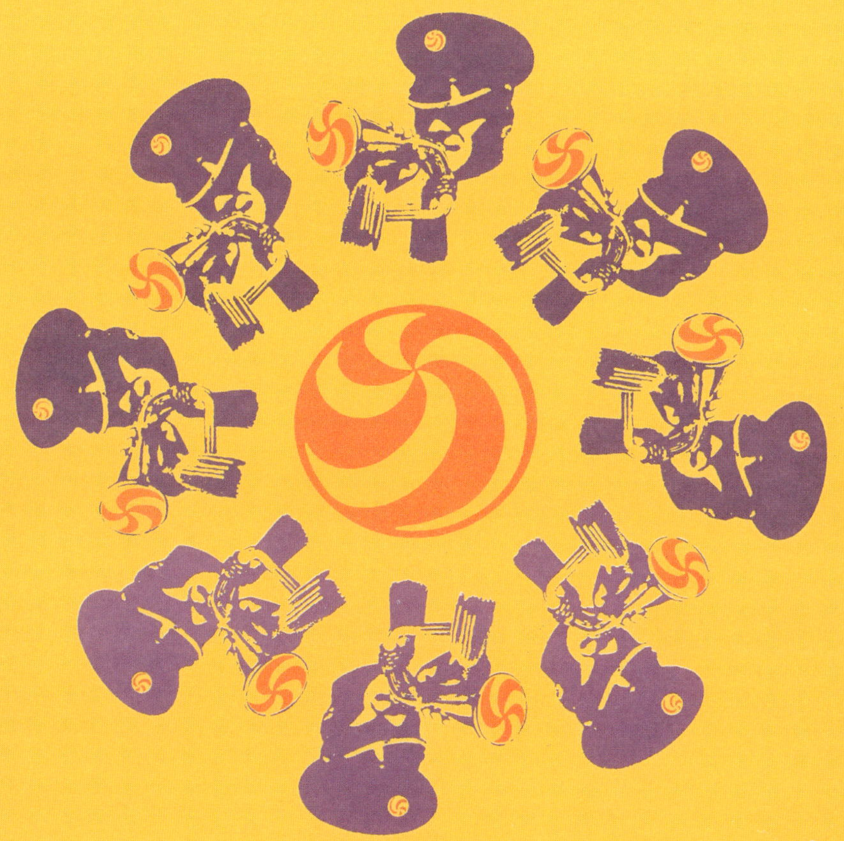
FESTIVAL OF
HONG KONG
PAGEANT
Government Stadium 8:00 p.m. 27th Nov.,–1st Dec.,1971.
Seats: Open Stands: $1; Covered Stand: $5; Reserved: $10
香港節聯歡晚會
地點：政府大球塲舉行　時間：每晚八時開始
日期：一九七一年十一月二十七日（星期六）至十二月一日（星期日）
座位：普通看台:門券一元正 ■ 有蓋看台:門券五元正 ■ 有蓋看台編定座位:門券十元正

Expo '70 in Osaka was the first World Exposition to take place in Asia. Hong Kong's participation was an effort to restore international confidence in the city's progress following the anti-colonial unrest of 1967. Commissioned by Hong Kong's Information Services Department and the Trade Development Council, the pavilion was intended to underscore the city's transformation from a regional entrepôt in a colonial network to a global manufacturing hub. In the built result, the pavilion's design presented an alluring yet conflicted image of Hong Kong.

Located at a prominent site near the United Kingdom Pavilion and designed by Alan Fitch—one of the architects of Hong Kong's modernist City Hall—the 3,300-square-metre Hong Kong Pavilion consisted of timber-and-steel islands on a shallow reflecting pool. It was topped with thirteen batwing sails made of nylon fishing netting without knots and a cluster of masts sunk through its roof. At night, the sails could be backlit in red and orange, and elevated by a hydraulic system of winches and cables to create a spectacle for special events. The pavilion's islands, evoking Hong Kong's geography, were connected by bridges linking various programmes: a floating stage for performances; a Chinese restaurant; and three indoor exhibitions, titled *Social Progress*, *Industrial Progress*, and *Culture and Tourism*.

The pavilion's design exemplifies the colonial government's instrumentalisation of both modern architecture and an idea of Chinese tradition. However, the inclusion of the sails—the pavilion's most prominent feature—makes an explicit reference to junk boats, conjuring a postcard idea of Hong Kong as a picturesque backwater rather than a centre of industrial production and trade. This unintended paradox reflected the state of Hong Kong's shifting cultural and political identities.   SS

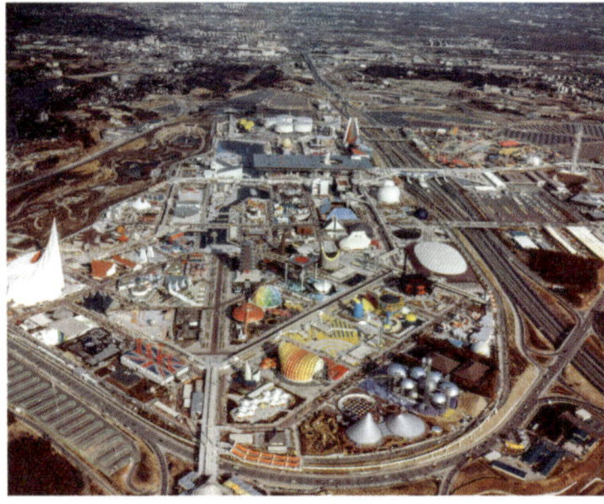

View of the Expo '70 site

Alan Fitch (born 1921, United Kingdom;
died 1986, France)
W. Szeto & Partners (1948–1998)
Photograph of model for Hong Kong Pavilion at Expo '70 (1968–1970), Osaka
1969
Chromogenic print mounted on paperboard
12.3 × 22.3 cm
Gift of Family of Alan Fitch , 2014
CA35/3/3

Exterior view of Hong Kong Pavilion
1970
Chromogenic print
Gift of Family of Alan Fitch, 2014
CA35/3/6

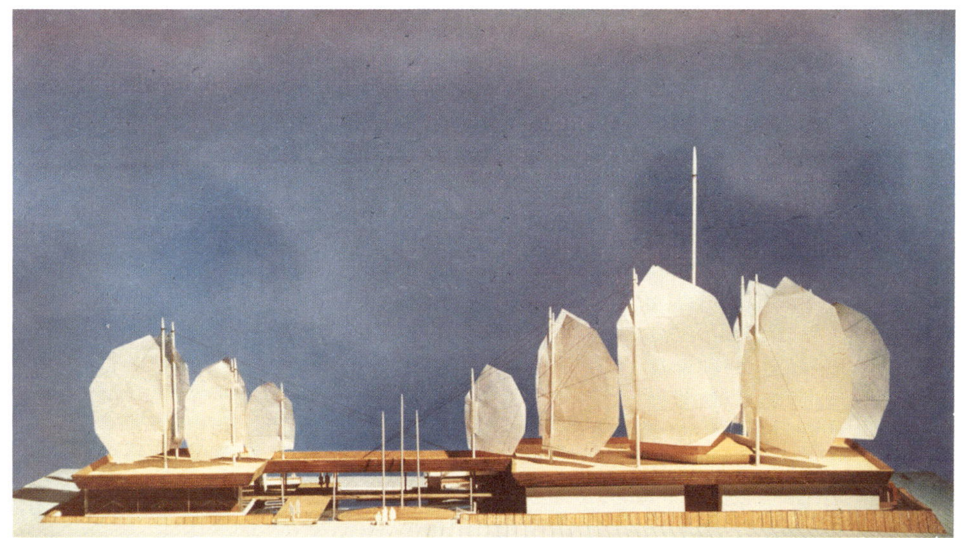

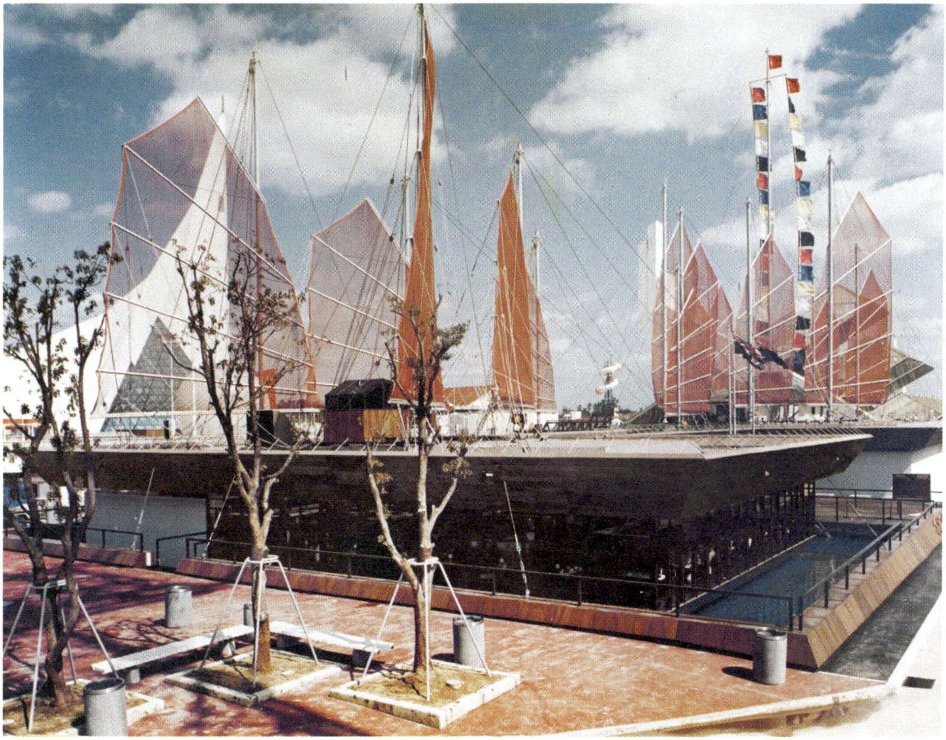

Founded in New York in 1961 by the journalists Norman Soong and Adrian Zecha, *The Asia Magazine* articulated a transnational perspective on Asia as a region of global political and cultural significance. The magazine was a highly circulated colour supplement to English-language newspapers in Asia's capital cities and reported stories that emphasised affinities and heterogeneity in the context of decolonisation and the Non-aligned Movement. Recognised for its editorial clarity and powerful graphic identity, *The Asia Magazine* was printed in Tokyo by leading printing house Toppan and was read by Asia's influential English-speaking elite. Henry Steiner, the magazine's art director, relocated to Hong Kong when the publication moved its headquarters to the city. Steiner's sensitivity to the histories, languages, and cultures of the region is evident in his narrative approach to the magazine's design from 1961 to 1988, which included the masthead, the editorial layout, advertisements for the publication, and even rate cards. Steiner integrated and juxtaposed the complexity of Asian vernacular cultural motifs with the simplicity of modern design and typography. His work for the magazine shaped his approach to design for cross-cultural contexts in Asia.   SS

Henry Steiner (born 1934, Austria)
Cover of *The Asia Magazine*, January 1962
Offset lithograph
34.1 × 26.3 cm
CA31

House advertisement of *The Asia Magazine*
ca. 1962
Offset lithograph
34 × 25.9 cm
CA31

House advertisement of *The Asia Magazine*, March 1964
Offset lithograph
32.2 × 26 cm
CA31

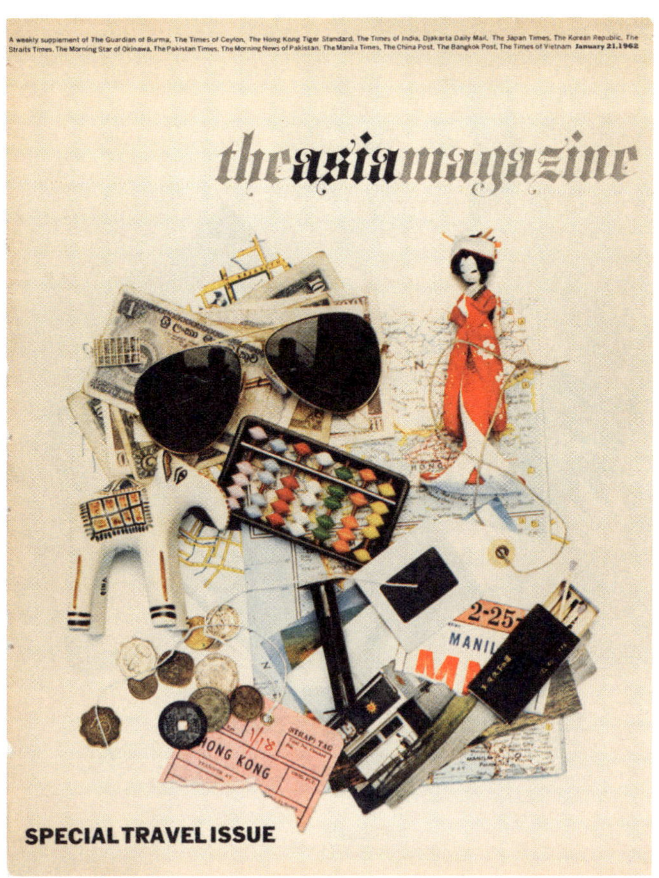
A weekly supplement of The Guardian of Burma, The Times of Ceylon, The Hong Kong Tiger Standard, The Times of India, Djakarta Daily Mail, The Japan Times, The Korean Republic, The Straits Times, The Morning Star of Okinawa, The Pakistan Times, The Morning News of Pakistan, The Manila Times, The China Post, The Bangkok Post, The Times of Vietnam January 21, 1962
the asia magazine
HONG KONG
MANILA
SPECIAL TRAVEL ISSUE

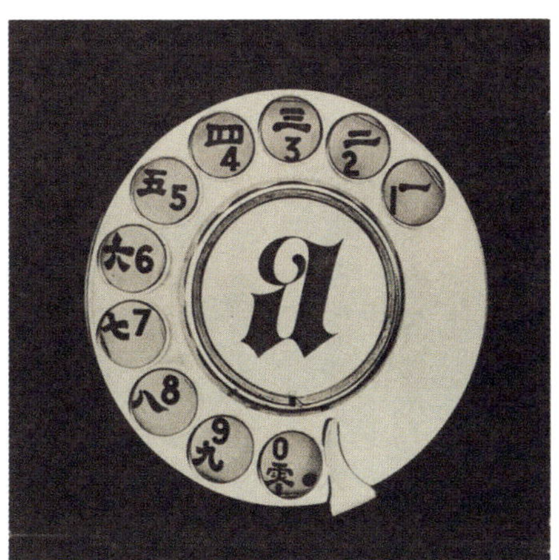
Dial 三六七一零

It's as easy as that to talk to 752,000 Asian families. Call up The Asia Magazine's Hong Kong headquarters (or any of its six advertising offices in Europe, Asia and North America) and place an advertisement in this new, text-and-picture magazine. Each Sunday The Asia Magazine goes directly into the homes of 752,000 English-reading able-to-buy Asians in 14 key markets — from Pakistan in the west to Japan in the east to Indonesia in the south. This is the biggest circulation, the broadest coverage,

the deepest penetration you can buy in Asia. And at a cost-per-thousand readers one-third that of the next largest magazine. Give us a call; we have lots to talk about.

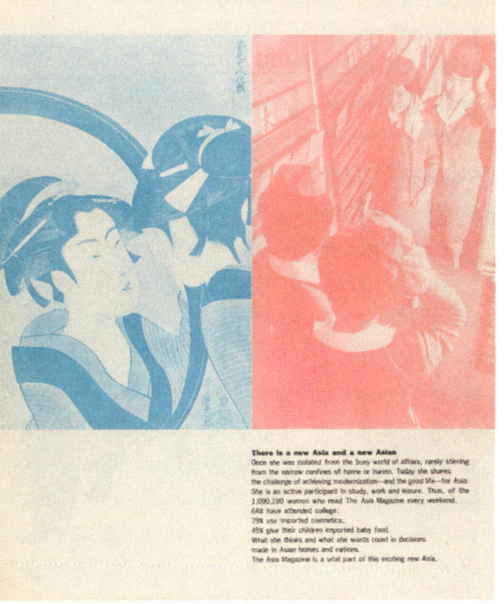
There is a new Asia and a new Asian
Once she was isolated from the busy world of affairs, rarely stirring
from the narrow confines of home or harem. Today she shares
the challenge of achieving modernization—and the good life—for Asia.
She is an active participant in study, work and leisure. Thus, of the
1,090,100 women who read The Asia Magazine every weekend,
64% have attended college.
79% use imported cosmetics.
45% give their children imported baby food.
What she thinks and what she wants count in decisions
made in Asian homes and nations.
The Asia Magazine is a vital part of this exciting new Asia.

During his years as an art director with the Hong Kong government's Information Services Department, Arthur Hacker shaped messaging for the full spectrum of official policies and public health and safety campaigns. Trained at the Royal College of Art in London, he developed a distinctive approach to poster design, involving playful combinations of typography and images. The 'Keep Hong Kong Clean' campaign was Hacker's most successful and enduring, defined by the character Lap Sap Chung, a green monster with red warts who was meant to encourage citizens to keep their city clean. This poster features an image of Lap Sap Chung looming over a photograph of a housing estate, a comically striking visual dissonance.

Hacker's design for a recruitment poster for the Hong Kong Police Force consists of a black-and-white photograph of a policeman seated astride a sharply foregrounded motorcycle, with the headline 'Manhood'. Shot from a low angle, the subject of the image is presented as a guardian of the community, a message that is reinforced in the tagline: 'Maintain public order, benefit society, help the people, become a policeman.'

Hacker's designs reflect a concern with the concise deployment of language. In the bilingual 'Clean Our Buildings' poster, the message is summarised in four Chinese characters and three English words. The Chinese is presented in large type to ensure legibility. The bold Chinese font selected for the 'Manhood' poster, on the other hand, suggests solid reliability while also projecting a striking Pop sensibility to attract the attention of young potential recruits. The posters exemplify the breadth of Hacker's approach, encompassing both playful humour and seductiveness.   FT

Arthur Hacker (born 1932, United Kingdom; died 2013, Hong Kong)
Information Services Department, Hong Kong (established 1959)
Poster for 'Keep Hong Kong Clean' campaign, 'Clean Our Buildings'
1973
Offset lithograph
73.9 × 48.2 cm
Gift of the Estate and family of Arthur Hacker in his honour, 2019
2019.69

Recruitment poster for Hong Kong Police Force, 'Manhood'
1960s–1970s
Offset lithograph
73.7 × 48.4 cm
Gift of the Estate and family of Arthur Hacker in his honour, 2019
2019.78

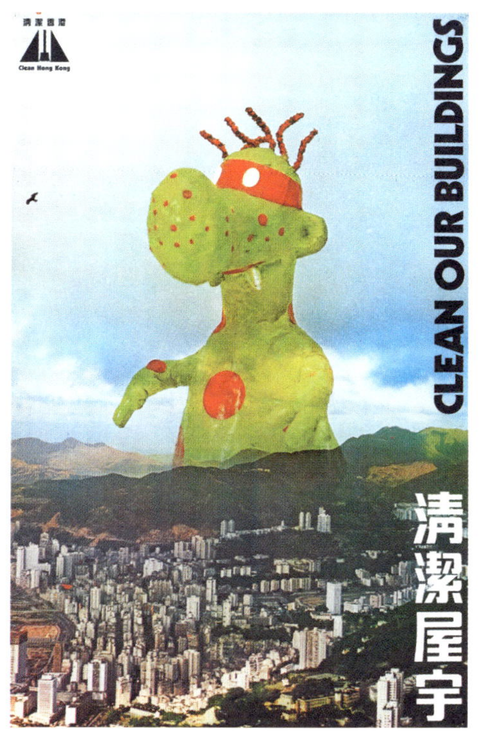
Clean Hong Kong
CLEAN OUR BUILDINGS
清潔屋宇

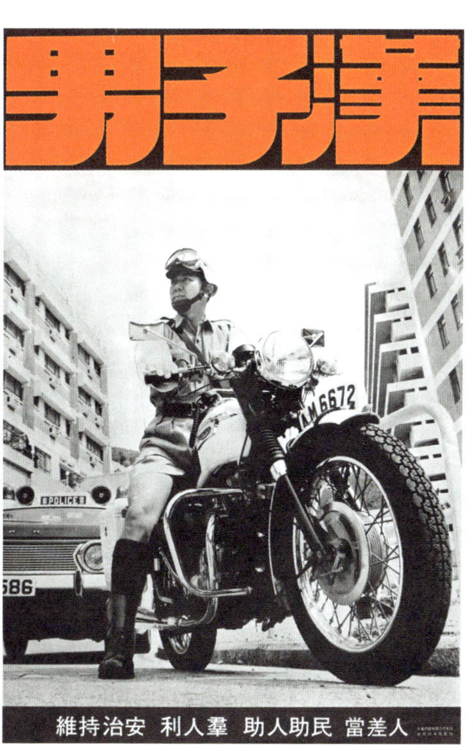
男子漢
維持治安　利人羣　助人助民　當差人

With a face value of ten cents, the yellow-and-red definitive stamp designed by Arthur Hacker for the colonial Post Office of Hong Kong conveys a parity between British and Chinese influence. A portrait of Queen Elizabeth II is flanked by a lion on the left and a dragon on the right to represent the two cultures. 'Hong Kong' is written in Chinese at the top and in English at the bottom, framed in Hacker's signature curlicue motif.

Ian Y. Y. Leung's six first-day-of-issue stamp designs, with the slogan 'Hong Kong Building for the Future', feature images of new construction projects, a theme that finds an echo in the bamboo scaffolding on the cover. This series highlights the city's development, promoting a government that is actively building for future prosperity. The two stamp collections were released in the years immediately before and shortly after the signing of the Sino-British Joint Declaration of 1984, a time when the future of Hong Kong was being shaped by the negotiations between the Chinese and British governments.   FT

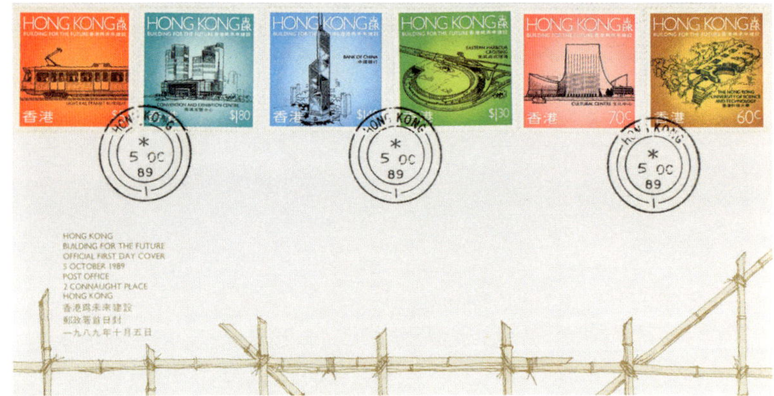

Hong Kong Post Philatelic Bureau
(established 1974)
Official first-day cover, *Hong Kong Building for the Future*
5 October 1989
Offset lithograph
11 × 22 cm
Gift of Simon Kwan & Associates Limited, 2014
CA15/4/4

Arthur Hacker (born 1932, United Kingdom; died 2013, Hong Kong)
Information Services Department, Hong Kong
(established 1959)
Hong Kong definitive stamps, ten cents
ca. 1982
Print on gummed paper
24.2 × 19.9 cm
Gift of the Estate and family of Arthur Hacker in his honour, 2019
2019.54

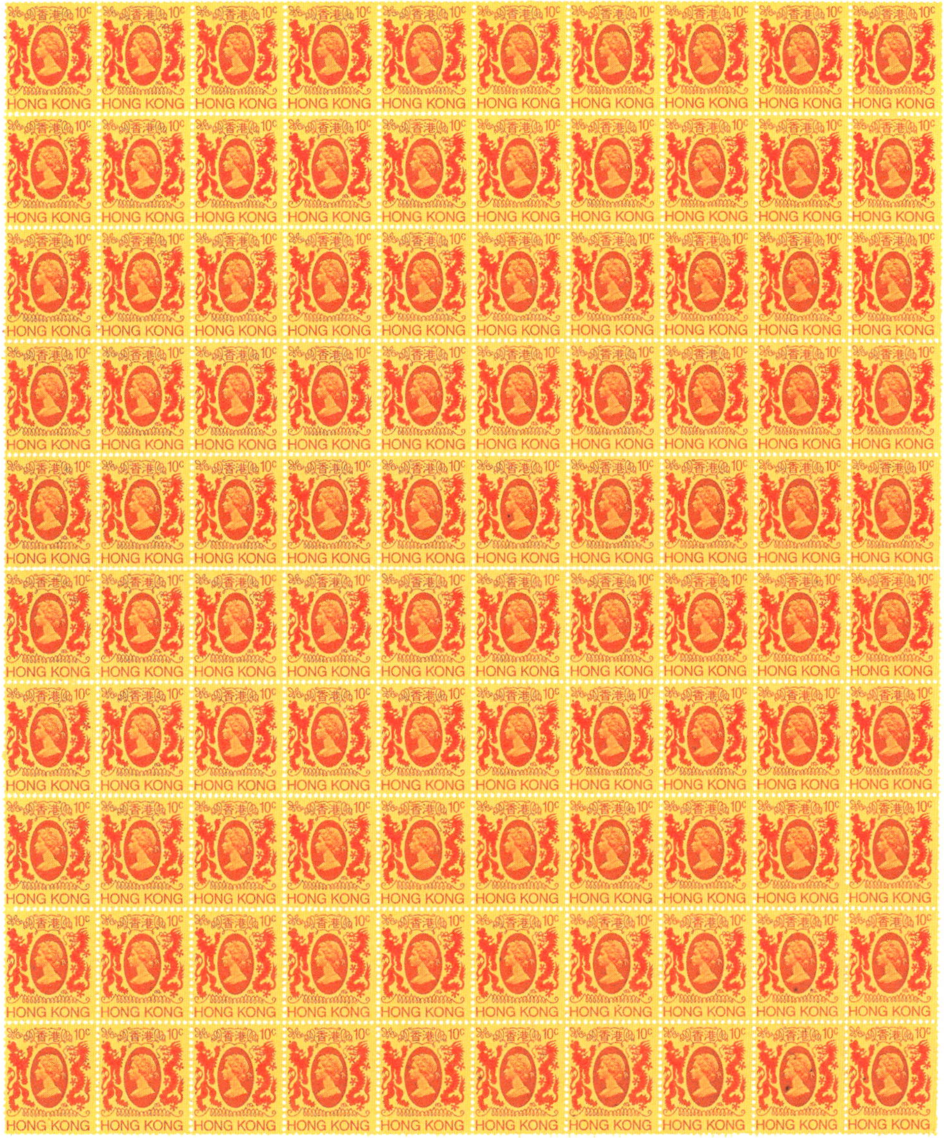

These posters, designed by Freeman Lau, bookend the decade in which he became one of Hong Kong's leading designers and brand consultants as a partner at Kan & Lau Design Consultants. In his early career, he designed for multiple cultural projects. His design for the Chung Ying Theatre Company's play *I Am Hong Kong* captures the anxieties in Hong Kong following the signing of the Sino-British Joint Declaration in 1984. Written by Raymond To Kok-wai and Hardy Tsoi Sik-cheong, the dialogue of the fifteen-act play incorporates Cantonese, Mandarin, and English to explore the transformations of the city's identity from a small fishing village to a modern financial capital. Using a system of cultural dichotomies, Lau highlights the conflicted nature of this inquiry: a figure seated on a chair that is half-Chinese and half-Western in design, against a bilingual, two-tone background. For Lau, the chair embodies Hong Kong's position at the crossroads of multiple languages and cultures.

Chairs became a recurring and flexible motif in Lau's subsequent artistic practice. He created a set of nine posters for *People*, the first exhibition of the short-lived Hong Kong Poster League, in 2000. Lau's posters encapsulate his interest in anthropomorphising chairs to examine group dynamics, social status, and the pursuit of political power, as well as to explore personal relationships. The yin and yang chairs in *Ming Intertwined – 2 in 1*, representing female and male, connect like puzzle pieces and recall Lau's sculptural work, begun in the late 1990s, specifically his *Chairplay* series. Lau's posters signal the position of this form as a highly visible platform for graphic expression and communication.   JW

Freeman Lau (born 1958, Hong Kong)
Poster for Chung Ying Theatre Company, *I Am Hong Kong*
1985
Offset lithograph
57.5 × 40.9 cm
Gift of Lau Siu Hong Freeman, 2019
2019.586

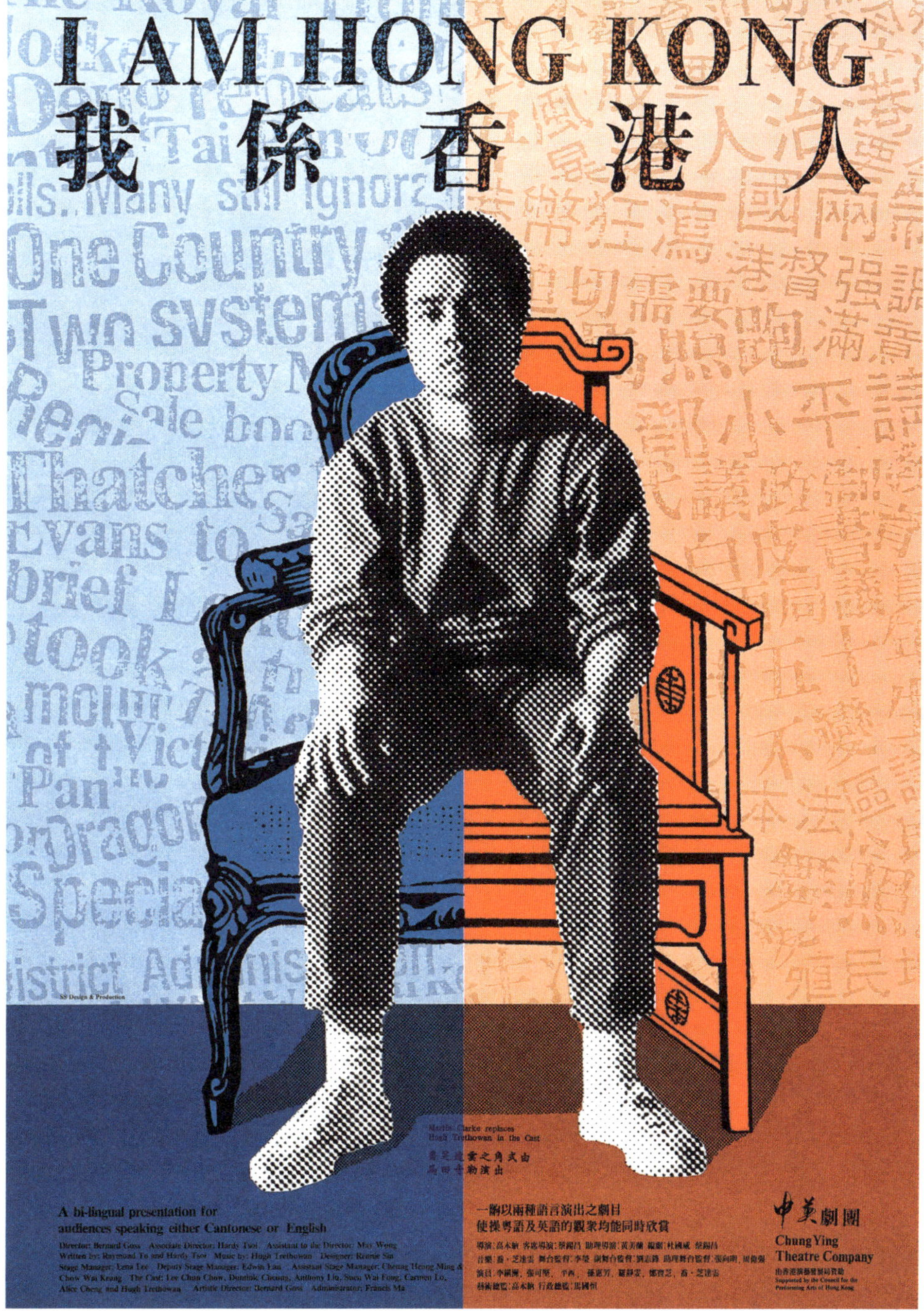

I AM HONG KONG
我 係 香 港 人
A bi-lingual presentation for
audiences speaking either Cantonese or English
Director: Bernard Goss Associate Director: Hardy Tsoi Assistant to the Director: Max Wong
Written by: Raymond To and Hardy Tsoi Music by: Hugh Trethowan Designer: Reenie Siu
Stage Manager: Lena Lee Deputy Stage Managers: Edwin Lau Assistant Stage Manager: Cheung Heung Ming &
Chow Wai Keung The Cast: Liv Chan Chow, Dinthik Cheung, Anthony Liu, Suen Wai Fong, Carmen Lo,
Alice Cheng and Hugh Trethowan   Artistic Director: Bernard Goss Administrator: Francis Ma
Chung Ying
Theatre Company
Supported by the Council for the
Performing Arts of Hong Kong

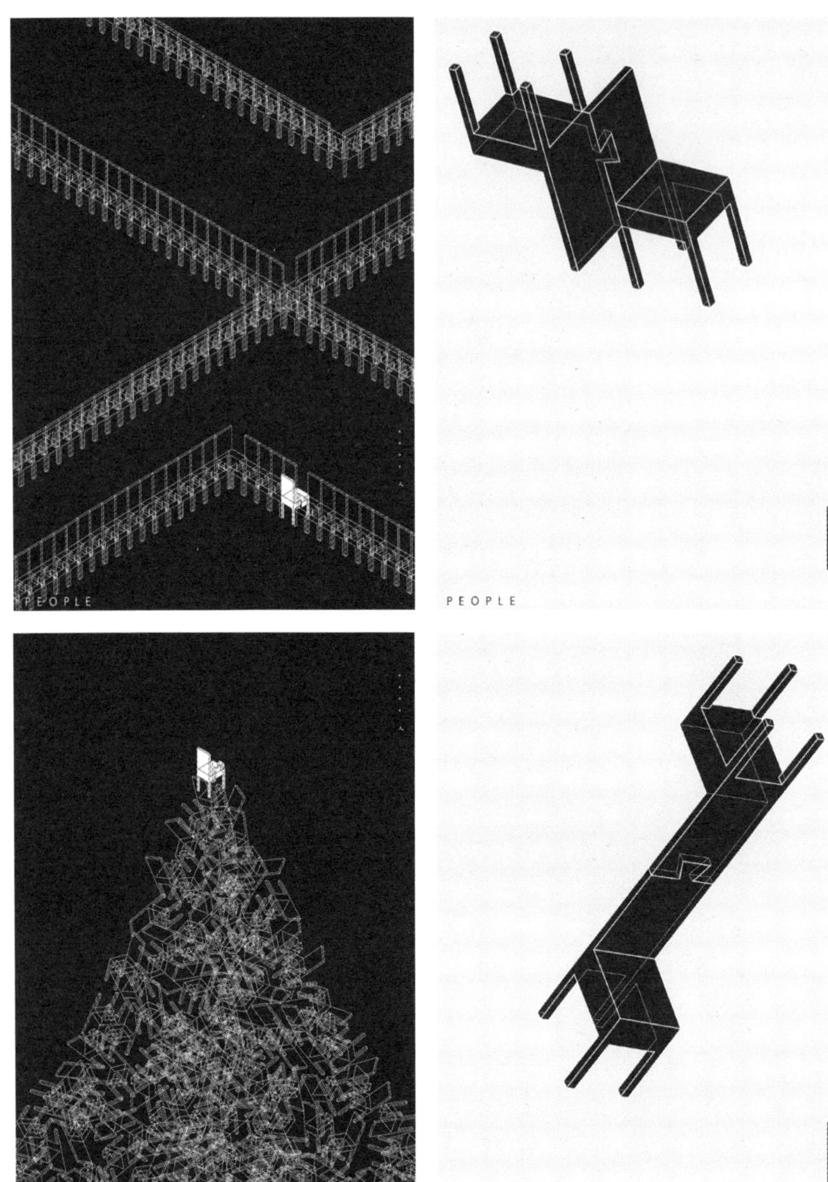

Posters for Hong Kong Poster League Episode I: *People*
2000
Offset lithograph
100 × 70 cm (each, set of nine)
Gift of Lau Siu Hong Freeman, 2019
2019.600, 2019.602–2019.604

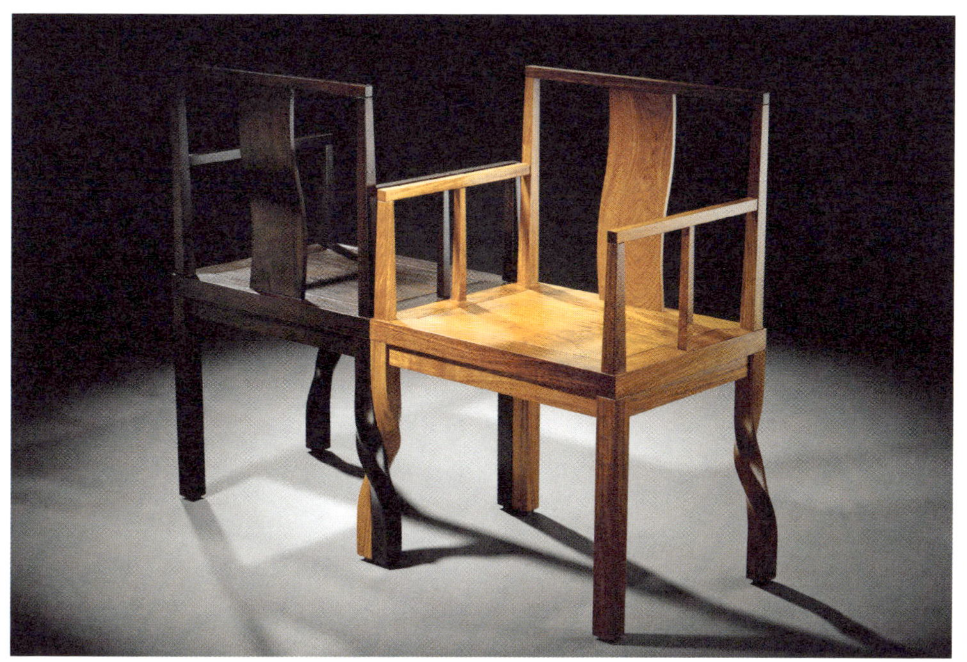

Ming Intertwined – 2 in 1
2011/2015
Padauk and *dispyyosspp* wood
86 × 112 × 43 cm
2019.513

TIDES OF TIME

Artists react to ideas of the past in the present

In the 1960s, Lui Shou-kwan was at the centre of the New Ink Movement, a group of artists whose work came to define a distinct artistic identity for Hong Kong. He considered that ink painting could survive only by engaging with developments in Euro-American contemporary art, and he is best known for his abstract, gestural *Zen* paintings, which experiment with the expressive potential of ink in a spirit of radical enquiry. He was raised in Guangzhou, learning to paint from his father Lui Canming and artists associated with the Chinese Painting Research Society. In 1948, he moved to Hong Kong, where he was directly exposed for the first time to the work of artists and movements from the West. An influential teacher and theorist as well as an artist, he departed from traditional pedagogical methods that emphasise study through imitation of the styles of established masters.

Before he made his breakthrough paintings of the late 1960s and 1970s, Lui returned time and again to Hong Kong as a subject for his compositions. Through his position as an inspector with the Hongkong and Yaumati Ferry Company, he explored the city extensively, experiencing its changing textures and appearance under different weather conditions and at different times of day. Lui captured the city as it was, which created a fertile ground for experimentation. Government House, overlooking the central business district, was the seat of colonial power until the handover of 1997. Lui depicts this subject in a spare composition with an unusual elevated perspective. *Hong Kong at Night* is a depiction of the modern city alive with night-time activity. Dark, inky washes cover the picture surface and contrast with the grid-like lines and light emanating from buildings, an effect that locates the urban environment within the landscape. Lui's portrayal of recognisable landscape subjects in new ways is an articulation of his belief that abstraction derives directly from nature.

Lui's abstract *Zen* paintings span from large, immersive gestural works executed in watery ink and colour, to those in which compositional elements are reduced and controlled. *There Were No Methods in Antiquity* is a representation of a landscape in which a simple red dash evokes a sun. The painting's minimalism is offset with an inscription of a passage from the influential early-Qing painter and Buddhist monk Shitao's *Huayulu*, 'Comments on Painting', which espouses a connection between mind and body in the act of painting. Lui signed his painting 'Zen monk in Hong Kong' as an expression of his reverence for ink tradition, which always underpinned his abstract work. Significantly, *There Were No Methods in Antiquity* is one of two paintings by Lui selected for exhibition at the 1970 World Exposition in Osaka, encapsulating his position at the vanguard of contemporary art in Hong Kong.   TP

Lui Shou-kwan (born 1919, Guangdong; died 1975, Hong Kong)
There Were No Methods in Antiquity
1968
Ink and colour on paper
120 × 59.7 cm
2018.14

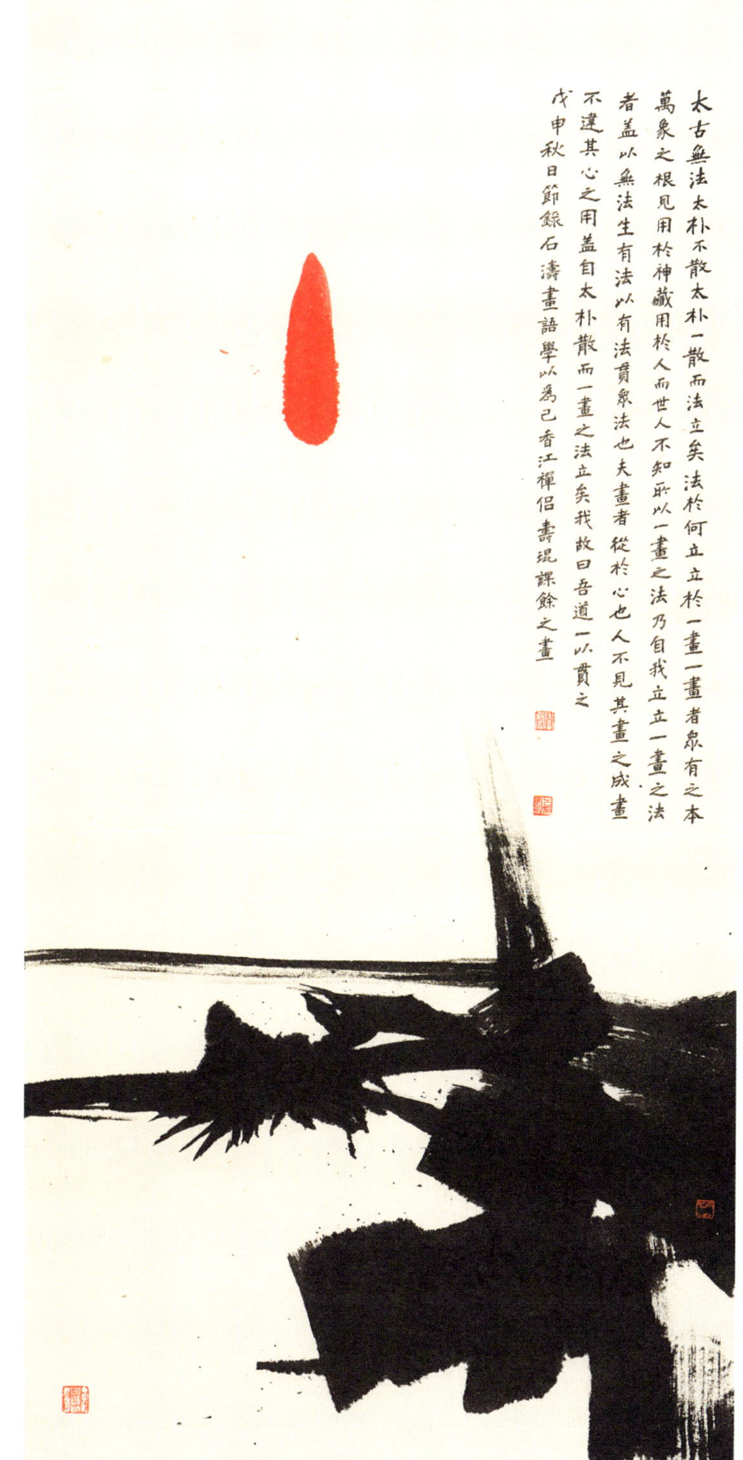

太古無法太朴不散太朴一散而法立矣法於何立立於一畫一畫者眾有之本
萬象之根見用於神藏用於人而世人不知所以一畫之法乃自我立立一畫之法
者盖以無法生有法以有法貫眾法也夫畫者從於心也人不見其畫之成畫
不違其心之用盖自太朴散而一畫之法立矣我故曰吾道一以貫之
戊申秋日節錄石濤畫語學以為己香江禪侶壽琨課餘之畫

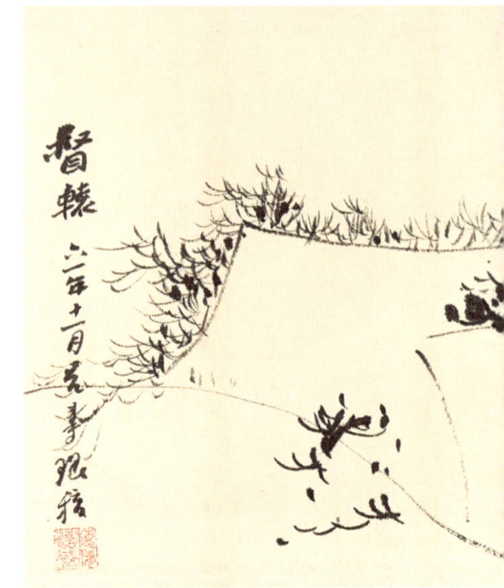

Government House
1961
Ink on paper
29.3 × 84.6 cm
2014.73

Hong Kong at Night
1961
Ink and colour on paper
42.4 × 94.8 cm
2016.685

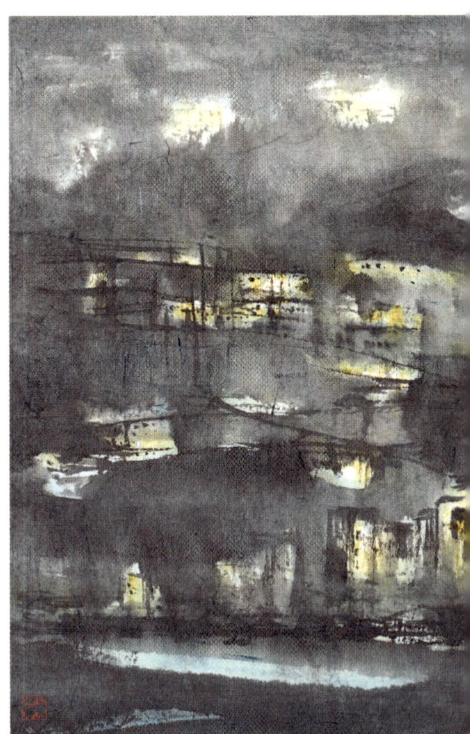

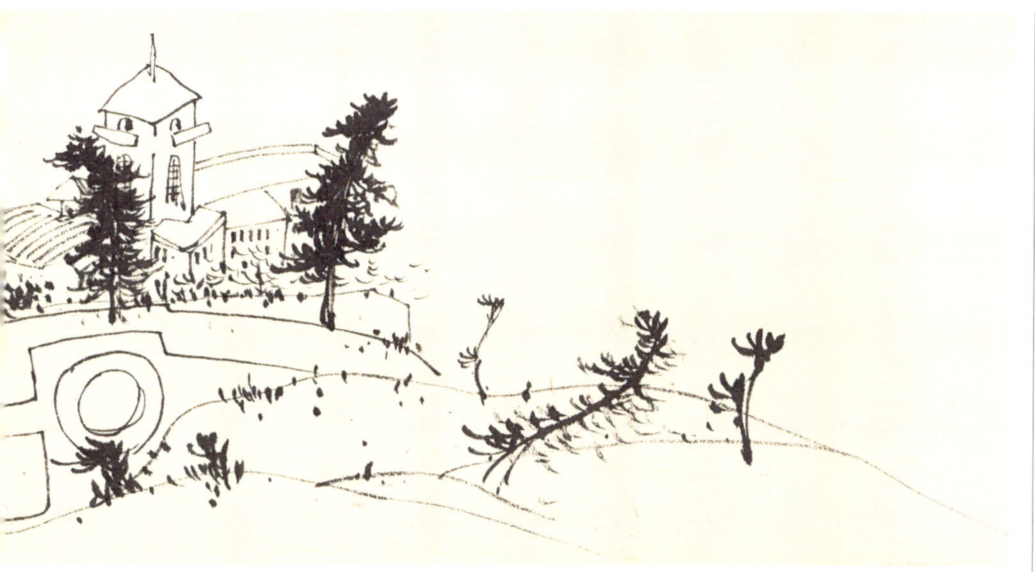

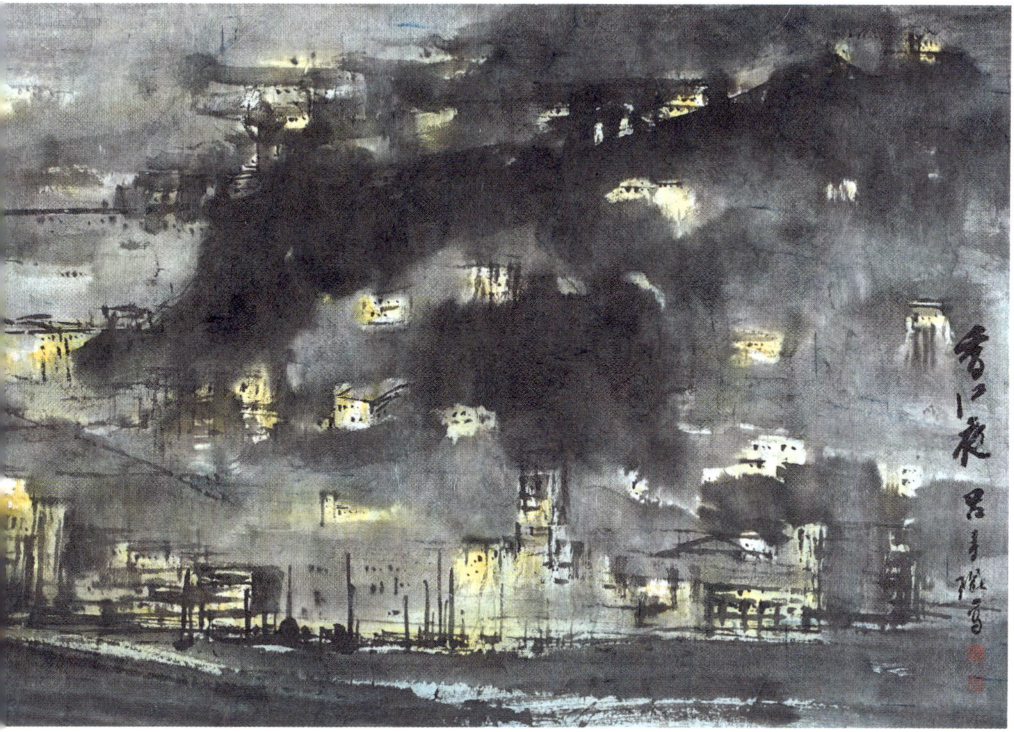

This street scene depicts two women dressed in fitted *cheongsam*, a style that was popular in Hong Kong in the early 1960s. The garments end at the knee, reflecting the influence of Western tailoring on Hong Kong fashion. Yau Leung's photograph directs an objectifying male gaze on the female subjects, but it also alludes to the transformation of women's roles in society. This style of *cheongsam* was a marker of the professional classes, and the women in the image can be seen to embody an educated, confident sophistication as they move through the arcade along Wan Chai's Gloucester Road. Yau took advantage of the increased availability of compact, portable cameras, producing street photographs that capture scenes of urban life with a narrative and even cinematic character. He worked as a set photographer for the entertainment production company Cathay Organisation between 1965 and 1970 and accompanied cast and crew to locations around the city. His photographs contributed to the construction of an idea of Hong Kong—both within the city and for outside observers—as a place that moves seamlessly between East and West and between tradition and modernity. In this light, *Two Women (Gloucester Road)* can be read alongside the image of Nancy Kwan in the 1960 film *The World of Suzie Wong*, which placed the fitted *cheongsam* within the wider popular imagination.   BW

Yau Leung (1941–1997, Hong Kong)
Two Women (Gloucester Road)
1961
Gelatin silver print
46 × 34.3 cm
2012.1806

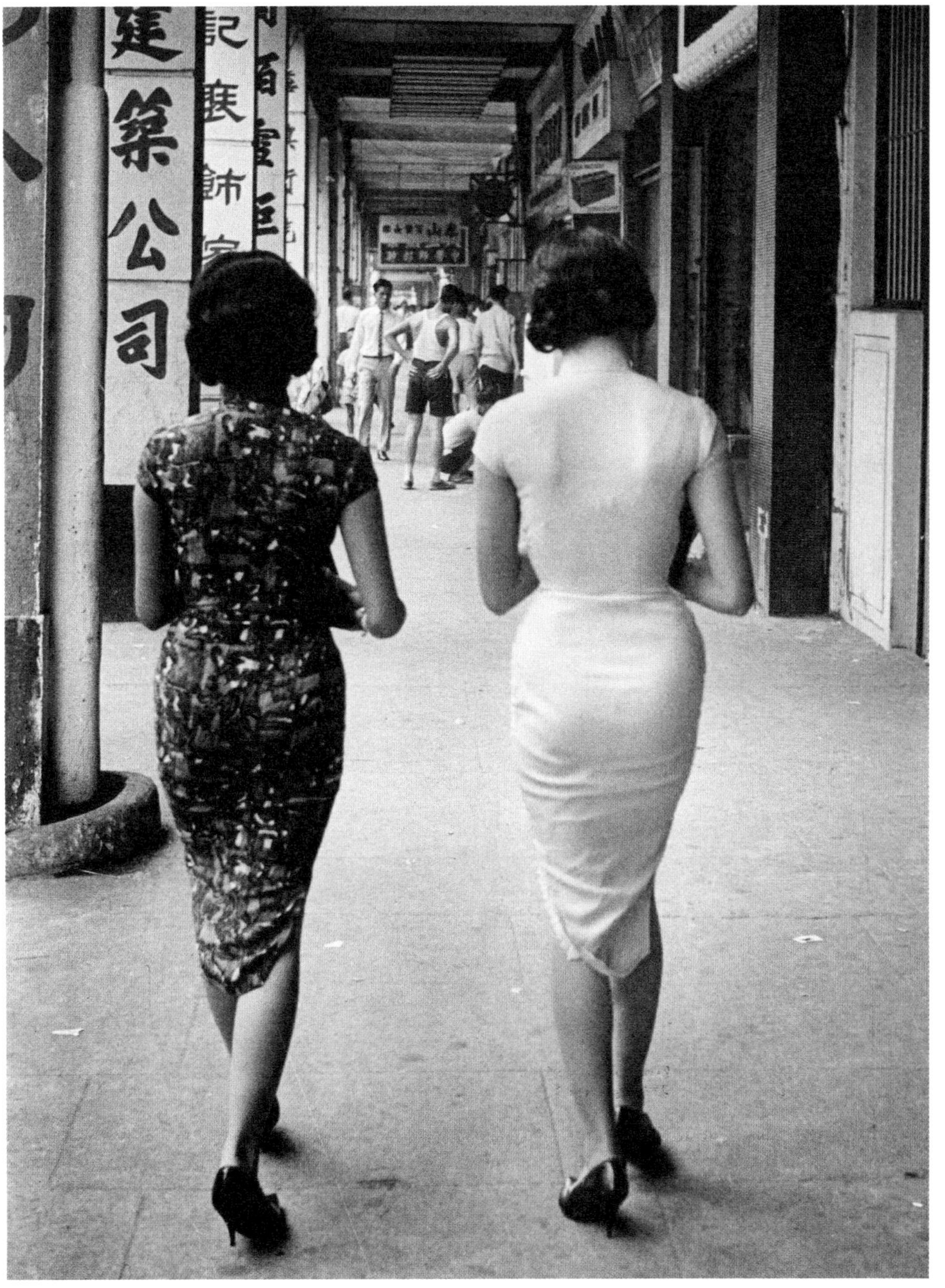

In the 1950s, Fan Ho established a style of photography that crossed the appearance of snapshots of urban life with staged and manipulated images. Ho moved to Hong Kong from Shanghai with his family in 1949 and was given a twin-lens Rolleiflex camera by his father. Over the course of the following decade, he produced a body of work that constitutes an extended exploration of his new home, approaching the city as a theatre of endless possibilities. His images elevate the commonplace into something theatrical. He is indebted to Henri Cartier-Bresson's idea of the 'decisive moment', a photograph that captures the essence of a situation, but unlike Cartier-Bresson's, his images result from precisely staged and constructed compositions. For *Approaching Shadow*, Ho asked his cousin to perform a meditative pose against a wall at Queen's College in Causeway Bay. In order to increase the drama of the photograph, Ho created a diagonal shadow across the left side of the negative image in the darkroom. The originality of the graphic composition and Ho's skill in darkroom manipulation exemplify his experimental approach that nevertheless remains faithful to the silver gelatin process. The image exemplifies Ho's dramatic and often romantic reading of Hong Kong as a city in transformation.   BW

Fan Ho (born 1931, Shanghai; died 2016, United States)
Approaching Shadow
1954, reprinted 2013
Inkjet print
30.6 × 21.9 cm
Gift of Fan Ho, 2012
2015.446

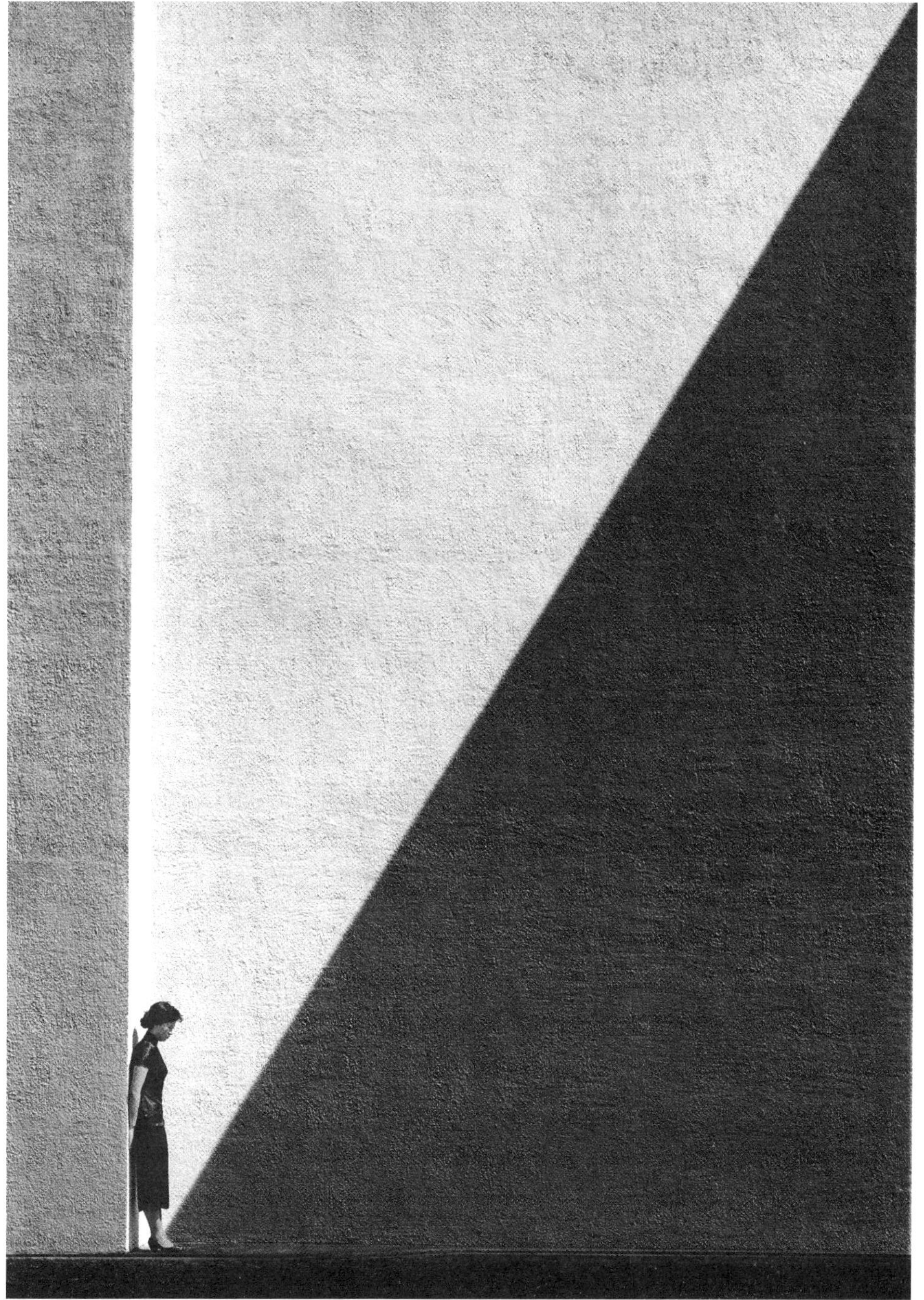

The Kowloon Walled City was an urban anomaly, a self-governing, unplanned enclave that was outside the jurisdiction of both China and British Hong Kong. Originally built as a military fort, the walled city was an enclosed area left outside of the Qing government's 1898 lease to Britain of northern Kowloon, which became known as the New Territories. By the 1980s, the unplanned settlement on 2.7 hectares had become the most densely populated plot of land in the world. The walled city's informal residential and commercial architecture was woven together by narrow alleyways and elevated passages providing points of connection on upper levels. The city defined a unique urban condition that attracted artists and architects as a subject of study, particularly in the years before its demolition began in 1994.

Between 1991 and 1992, architect and urban designer Suenn Ho carried out a ten-month research project in the Kowloon Walled City. Her team created detailed documentation of the city's architecture and interviewed residents, ultimately producing a large body of research materials that includes extensive video footage. During her research, she used a map drawn by Chan Cheung Chuen, a volunteer at the Kowloon Walled City Kai Fong Welfare Association. Although Chan was not a professional illustrator, he devised a system of symbols to represent the complex, multi-level walkways that aided navigation through the city. For example, dotted lines are used to represent overpasses, arched black lines denote unconnected roads, and triangles stand for building entrances. The drawing remains the only map of the walled city with any degree of detail. Chan created it to help residents negotiate with the government for compensation for being evicted in advance of the walled city's demolition. Made entirely out of a practical need, it inadvertently became a crucial reference for research into this unique urban phenomenon.

British architect Ian Lambot and Canadian photographer Greg Girard spent five years documenting the city's changing landscape in photographs, research that they published in 1993 as *City of Darkness: Life in Kowloon Walled City*. Lambot's aerial view from the south-west captures the compression of the enclave in relation to its surroundings. Girard, on the other hand, focuses on the lives of the city's residents. This image captures the dynamic relationship between the built environment and its inhabitants, portraying the walled city as both an architectural curiosity and a home.   CC

Ian Lambot (born 1953, United Kingdom)
Kowloon Walled City, aerial view from the south-west
1989, printed 2013
Inkjet print face mounted to acrylic and aluminium
91.7 × 120 × 2.6 cm
2013.143

Kowloon Walled City, south elevation
1990, printed 2015
Inkjet print
39.9 × 80.3 cm
2017.412

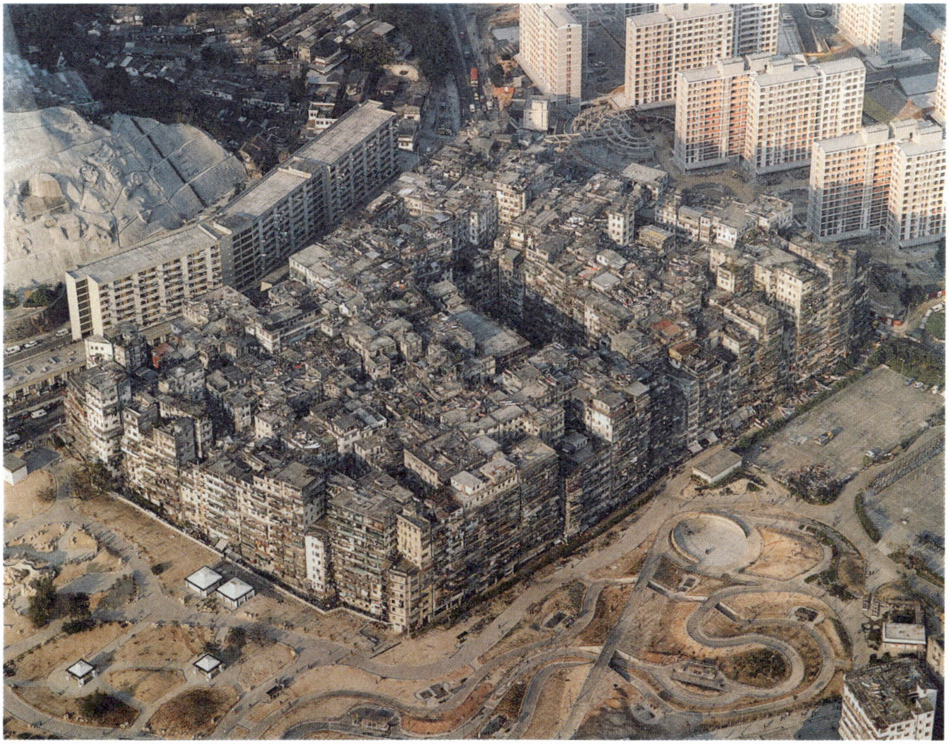

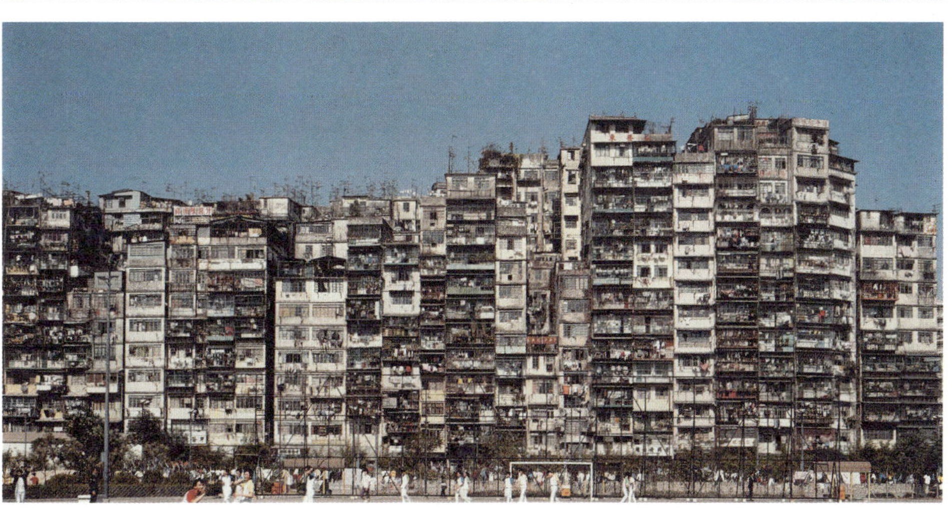

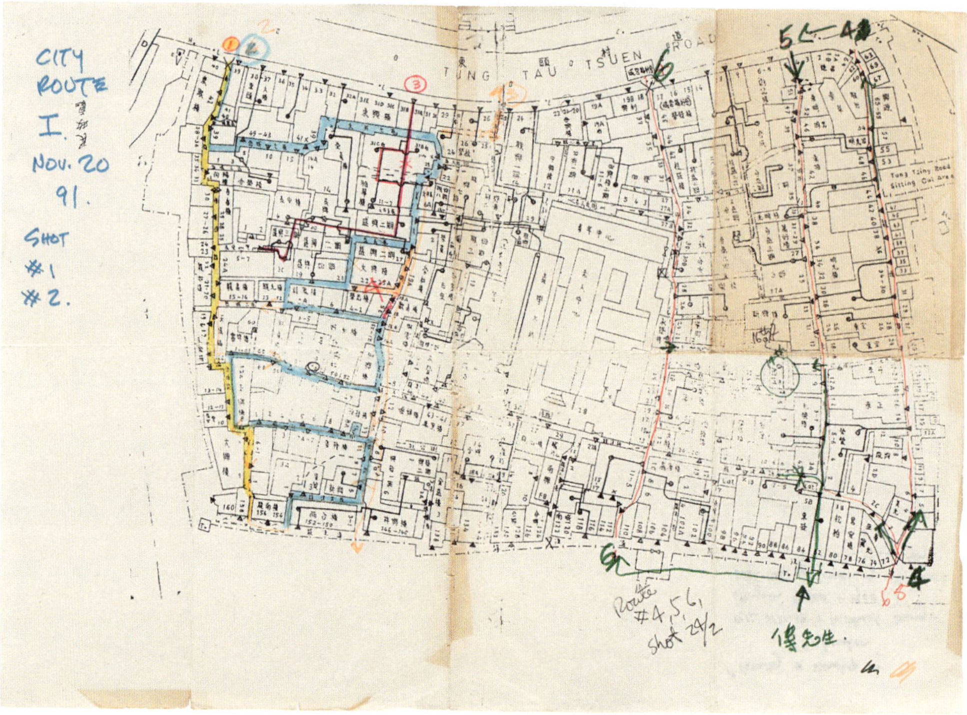

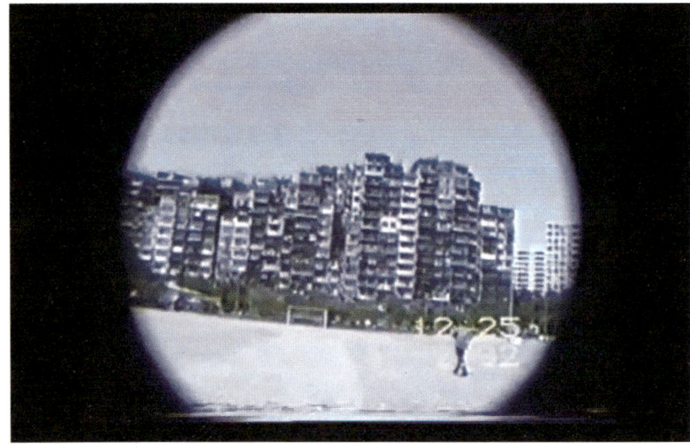

Suenn Ho (born 1961, United States)
**Route map of Kowloon Walled City research
project**
1991–1992
Photocopy, ink, and marker ink on paper
29.7 × 41.6 cm
Gift of Suenn Ho, 2015
CA17/2/1

**Kowloon Walled City research
project video documentation (still)**
1989–1991
Single-channel VHS tape transferred to digital
video (colour, sound)
90 min. 22 sec.
Gift of Suenn Ho, 2015
CA17/1/1

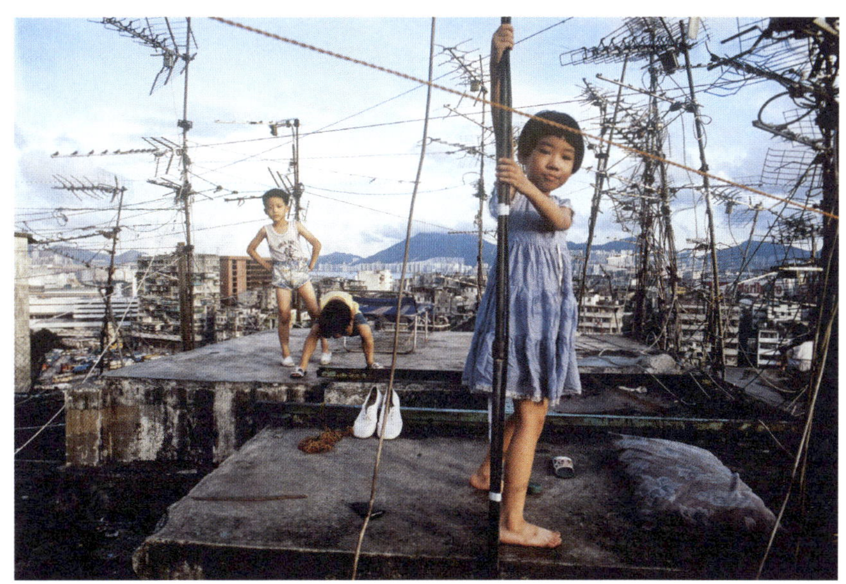

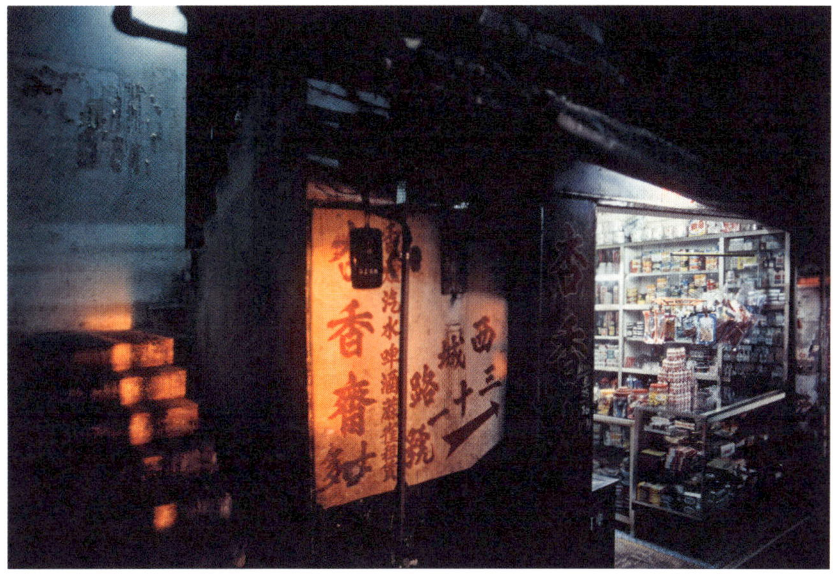

Greg Girard (born 1955, Canada)
Kowloon Walled City – Children on Rooftop
1989, printed 2015
Inkjet print
40 × 59.9 cm
2018.2

Kowloon Walled City – Alley View #3
1990, printed 2015
Archival digital print
40.1 × 59.9 cm
2018.3

This work is part of Tiffany Chung's ongoing series entitled *the unwanted population: The Vietnam Exodus – Hong Kong chapter* (1975–2000), which documents the history of the Vietnamese boat people and their treatment in Hong Kong. Painted in rich, jewel-like tones, the work records the movement of these refugees into and out of the city over a twenty-year period using the aestheticising conventions of data visualisation. Chung's use of data highlights the ways in which cold statistical analysis can trivialise the human consequences of forced migration. Compelled to flee Vietnam in the aftermath of the two decades of war that devastated the country's population, infrastructure, and economy, some eight hundred thousand migrants escaped by sea. Chung experienced the post-1975 exodus of refugees from her homeland at first-hand. However, her research began as an investigation into the historical precedents for international policies towards contemporary refugees, specifically those displaced from Syria.

Vietnam's immediate neighbours in Southeast Asia responded to the refugee crisis by closing their borders. In contrast, Hong Kong declared itself a 'port of first refuge'. Conditions in Hong Kong were initially favourable, with those applying for asylum in third countries housed in open camps and allowed to work while awaiting resettlement. By the early 1980s, Hong Kong's status as a haven attracted around three hundred refugees per day. The rise in the number of refugees arriving in Hong Kong corresponded with a decline in the number of countries willing to offer resettlement and, as the refugee population grew, tensions with local communities increased. The government introduced a system of closed camps across Hong Kong, which were often described as resembling detention centres. In Chung's work, the numbers of refugees arriving and departing over the period in question are overlaid against a map of Hong Kong in which the locations of refugee camps are marked using white triangles, and detention centres are indicated by white circles. Beginning in the late 1980s, Hong Kong introduced a highly criticised programme of repatriation. Locally, the plight of the Vietnamese was dramatised by New Wave director Ann Hui in her Vietnam trilogy, the first part of which was filmed for Radio Television Hong Kong's long-running *Below the Lion Rock* docudrama series in 1978. In her work, Chung documents this period of history that, despite its proximity to the present moment, is almost forgotten today. Her work offers a cautionary commentary on how fragile and fragmentary knowledge of shared histories can become.   TP

Tiffany Chung (born 1969, Vietnam)
HKSAR Statistics on Yearly Arrivals and Departures of V-refugees from 1975–1997
2016
Acrylic, ink, and oil on vellum and paper
79 × 99.7 cm
Brown Family Annual Acquisition Fund, 2016
2017.9

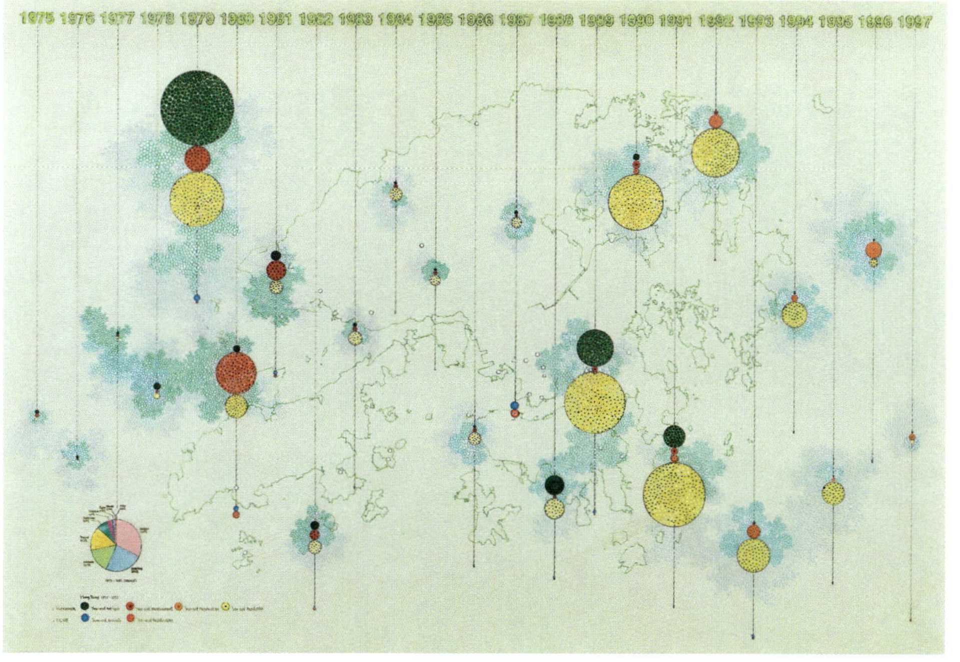

The Tides of Time, an installation including a video and a ceramic object, refers to the title of the book by Hong Kong historian Cheng Po-hung that is at its centre—both conceptually and physically. The video records the process of creating the final object, in which Annie Wan uses clay slip to paint over the pages one by one. Wan transforms this book on Hong Kong's history into a poetic exploration of the past and the instability of historical narrative. Once every page of the book was covered, it was fired at more than 1,000 degrees Celsius. During the firing the pages burned away while the clay hardened into the sculptural form of a ceramic book. Wan considers the casting process—through which the original object is replaced by a fragile shell—in terms of French semiotician Roland Barthes's reading of a photograph as a witness to a moment in time. In this sense the video acts as a witness to the material's transformation and calls into question the endurance of an image and a memory.   CC

Annie Wan (born 1961, Hong Kong)
The Tides of Time
2016
Single-channel digital video (colour, sound) and ceramic
81 min. 24 sec.
23 × 24 cm
Gift of William and Lavina Lim, 2019
2020.366

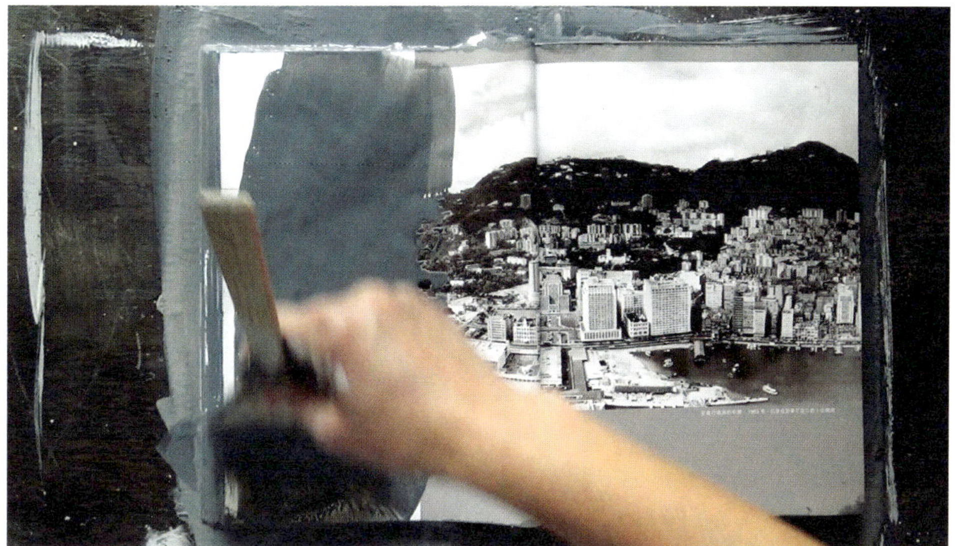

Still from the video

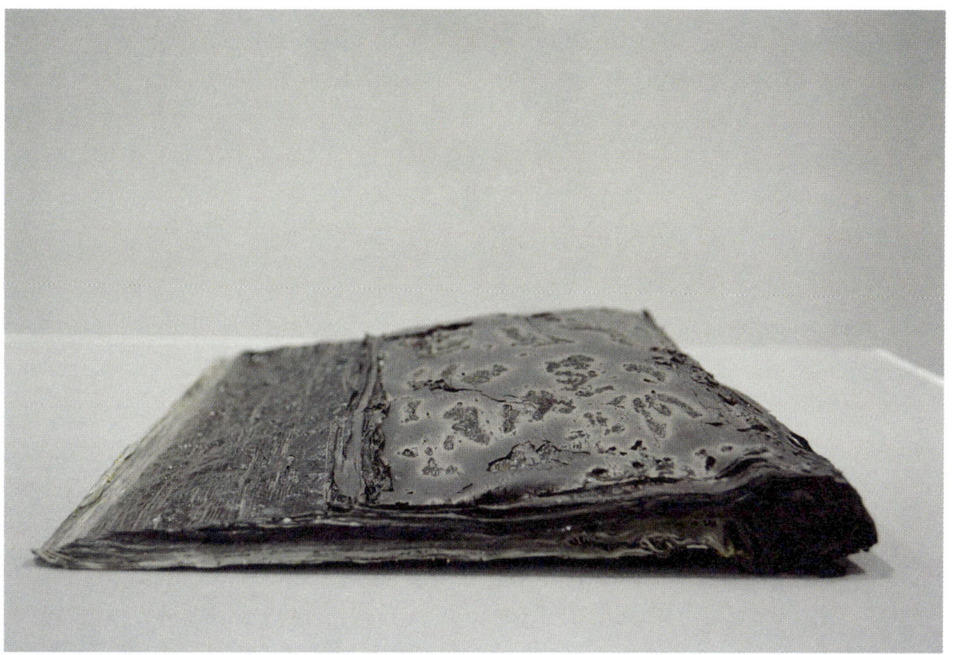

Ceramic book

Chu Hing Wah's depiction of a fruit market in Yau Ma Tei shows shoppers going about their daily activities. In Chu's signature naive style of painting, market stands, fruit boxes, and high-rise buildings are represented in weathered colours and a flat perspective. Chu's skill is in creating complex scenes and characters with economy, in order to portray his subjects with tenderness and familiarity. In the foreground, the curve of a man's back speaks to a lifetime of labour, while two women are deep in conversation as they walk towards a fruit stand whose trader looks on. The simplicity of the image seems to suggest a simpler time. But the air of comforting nostalgia is disturbed by the muted tones of the painting, as if night were falling over the city.

Trained as a psychiatric nurse in London in the 1960s, Chu taught himself to draw and paint between work and classes. Throughout his career Chu has worked in a style of human-centred painting unusual among his contemporaries, one that privileges everyday experiences and interactions and the environments in which he lives.   TP

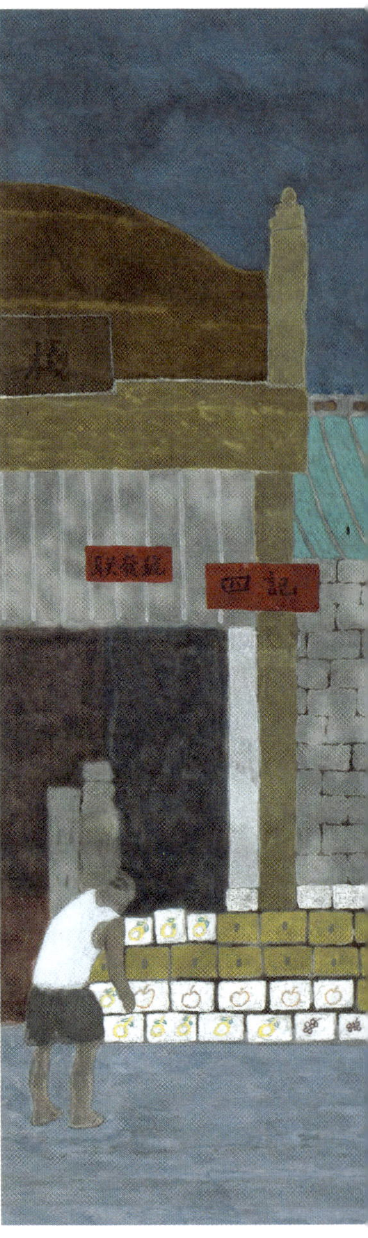

Chu Hing Wah (born 1935, Guangdong)
Yau Ma Tei Fruit Market
2004
Ink and colour on paper
53.1 × 66.8 cm
Gift of the Yiqingzhai Collection, 2019
2019.176

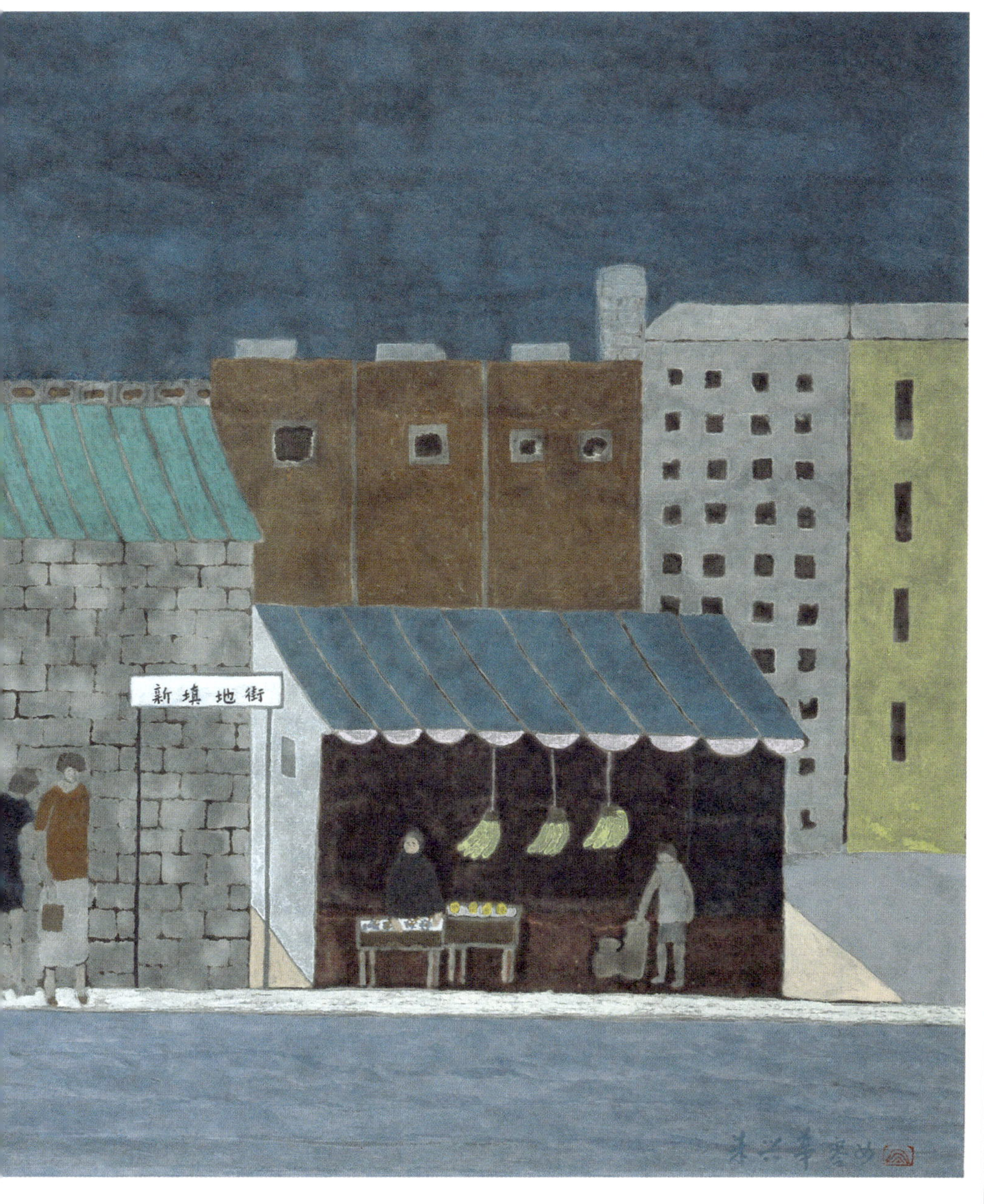

新填地街

Time Traveller is an installation comprising objects that Sara Tse has collected to create a fictional domestic space. She weaves together the histories of the individual objects with her own background to propose a way of viewing personal experiences in a larger shared context. Some of the furniture in *Time Traveller* was salvaged from the home of a widower who had preserved the interiors as they were when his wife died in the 1950s. This decade is referenced in a more personal way with a sewing machine and diary that belonged to the artist's late mother. Like many women of her generation, she was employed in the garment industry and worked from home in order to care for her young children. Tse memorialises some of the objects in the installation—including her mother's diary—by transforming them into delicate white porcelain. The process of coating the objects in slip and then firing them destroys the object, leaving behind a fragile porcelain shell that is a melancholy trace of the original, and a fitting metaphor for the ravages of time and the fragility of memory. *Time Traveller* is Tse's tribute to her mother, but also to a generation of women living in Hong Kong in the 1950s.   FT

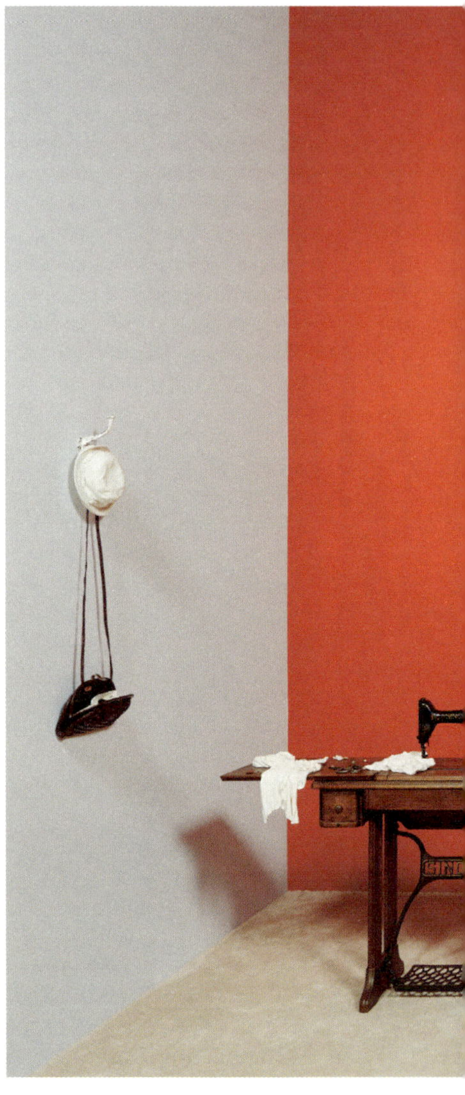

Sara Tse (born 1974, Hong Kong)
Time Traveller
2014
Wooden furniture, found objects, and porcelain
Dimensions variable
2015.590

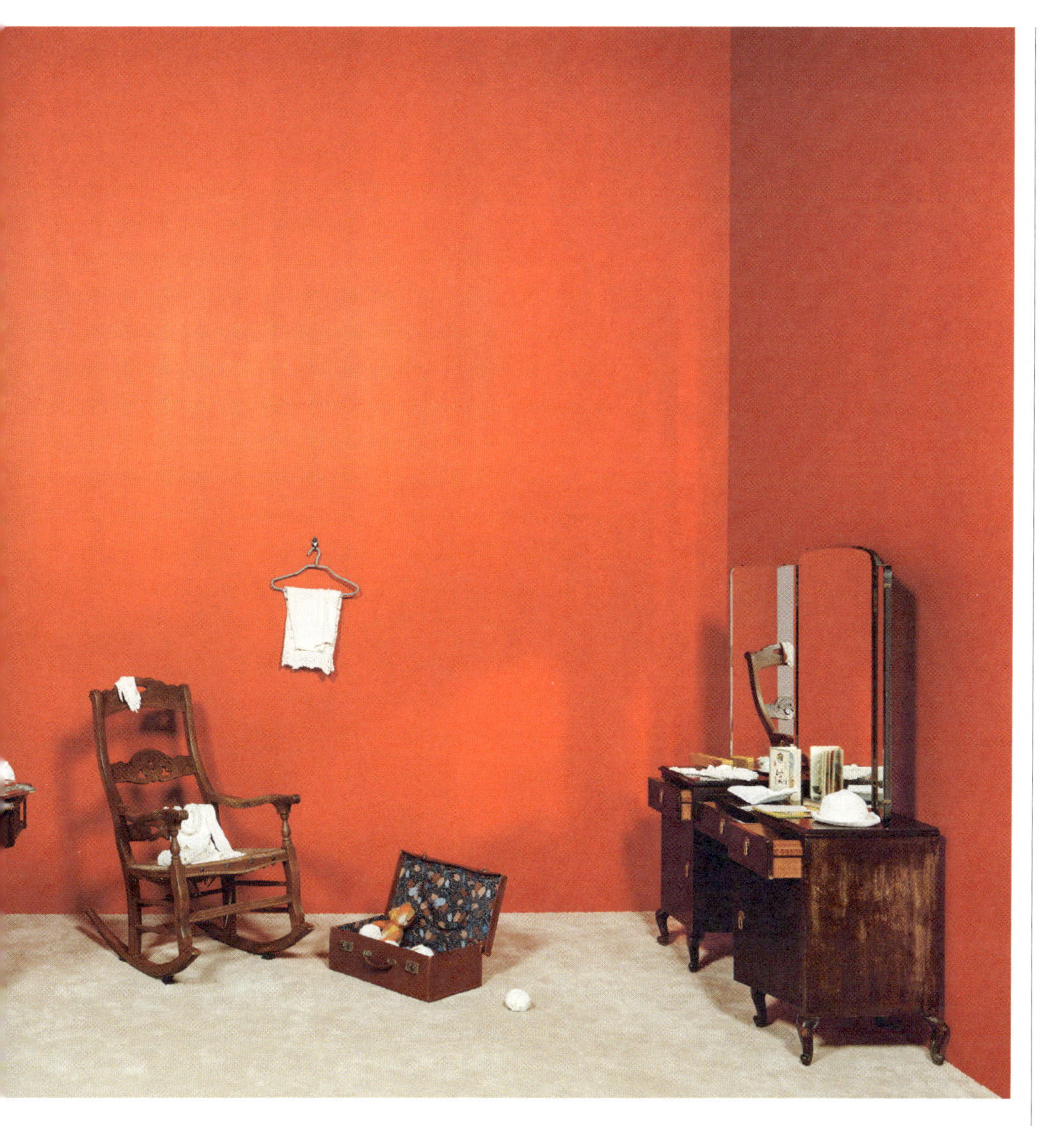

Wong Wo Bik created the experimental, autobiographical *Wyncote studio series* during her years as a student in Philadelphia in the late 1970s. This tender, contemplative, and meticulously constructed self-portrait contrasts with the large-format photographs of fading architectural spaces in Hong Kong for which she is better known. It nevertheless demonstrates the attention to detail and interest in fragments that characterise her later work. The image addresses Wong's identity as a Chinese woman in a foreign land, with a scene lit using both natural and artificial light to create a surreal intimacy.

The objects in the composition have personal significance, including the Chinese-style cotton-padded silk jacket given to Wong by her mother before she left for her studies and the necklace she received as a birthday gift. She inserts an image of her face into the neckline of the jacket, enhancing the theatricality of the portrait. Wong arranged her belongings to communicate aspects of her emotional life, playing the roles of author, director, actor, and set designer. Using the language of staged photography, she questions the authenticity of her medium and explores its cinematic potential.   BW

Wong Wo Bik (born 1949, Hong Kong)
Wyncote studio series – self portrait
1978–1979
Chromogenic print
39 × 26.5 cm
2018.305

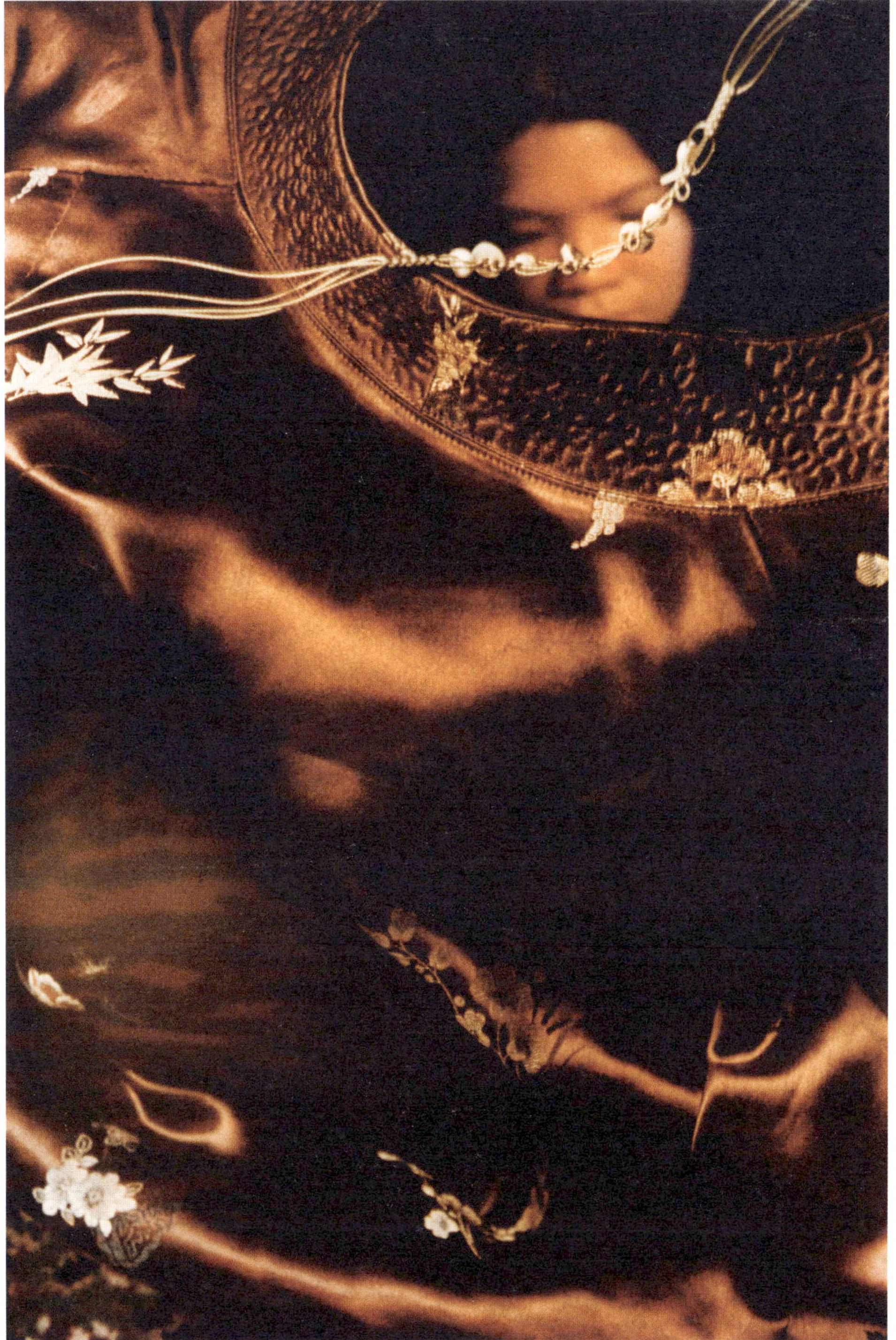

Begun in 2010, Trevor Yeung's *Sleepy Bed* series of photographs depicts people with whom he shared a room in hostels around the world, including New York, Singapore, São Paulo, and Frankfurt. The images are a record of his journeys—geographic, emotional, and sensual—that express a sense of anxiety as well as a deep longing for intimacy. He surreptitiously captures strangers at their most vulnerable, in the intensely private state of sleeping. His low-lit, close-up views of spaces and bodies convey an ache at the dissonance between proximity and intimacy. He engraves the glazing of the images' frames with geometric patterns, both emphasising the body as an element within the composition and objectifying it. These voyeuristic works illustrate the complexity of his position as an observer, documenting stolen moments as records of unrequited desire.   CC

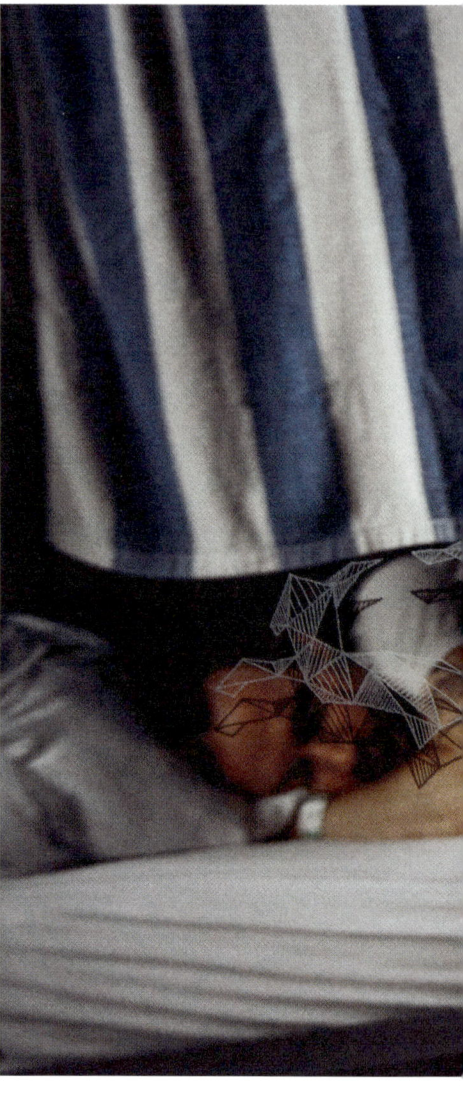

Trevor Yeung (born 1988, Guangdong)
Sleepy Bed (Frankfurt Hostel 1)
2014
Inkjet print with engraved glass
29.3 × 45.3 cm
2016.271

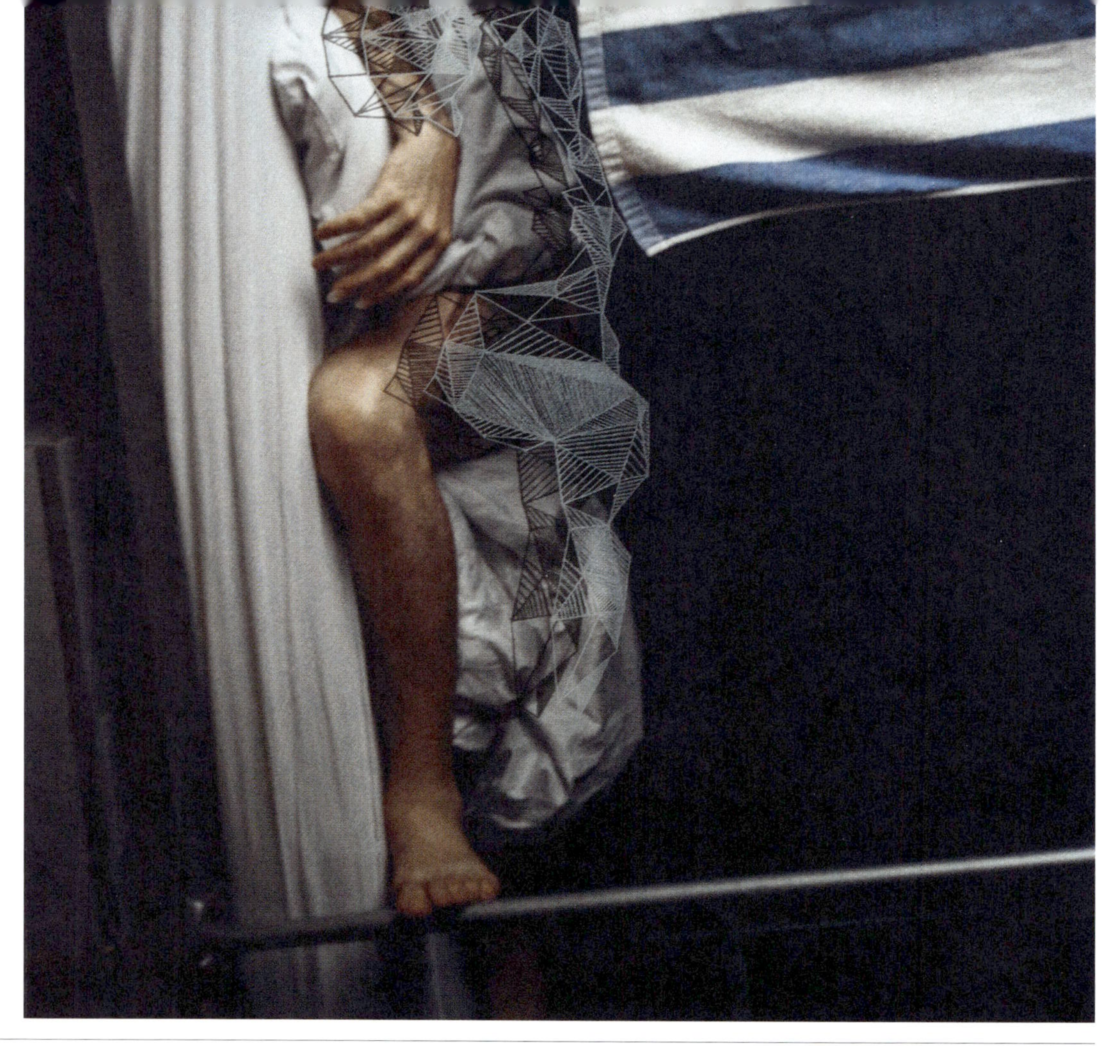

She Said Why Me features a blindfolded woman feeling her way through the crowded streets and colonial architecture of central Hong Kong and through a deserted rural village. The protagonist's journey across these two places reflects Hong Kong's ambiguous position between two cultural and political identities. Filmed at a time of political uncertainty, after the signing of the Sino-British Joint Declaration in 1984 and before Hong Kong's handover in 1997, the work reflects the anxieties of a generation. As the protagonist turns to gaze into the camera, the video cuts to a montage of archival footage of women participating in political demonstrations, offering a feminist perspective on the city's layered histories.

An artist, educator, and curator, May Fung co-founded the artist collective Videotage with Ellen Pau, Wong Chi Fai, and Comyn Mo in the 1980s. She also frequently collaborated with the experimental theatre group Zuni Icosahedron, whose multidisciplinary performance practice had a profound influence on her video works.   CC

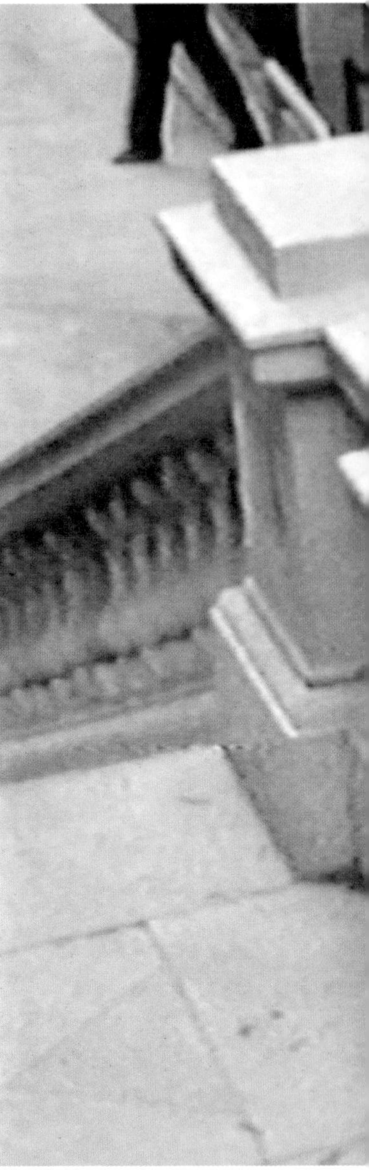

May Fung (born 1952, Hong Kong)
She Said Why Me (still)
1989
Single-channel VHS tape transferred to digital video (colour, sound)
8 min.
2018.349

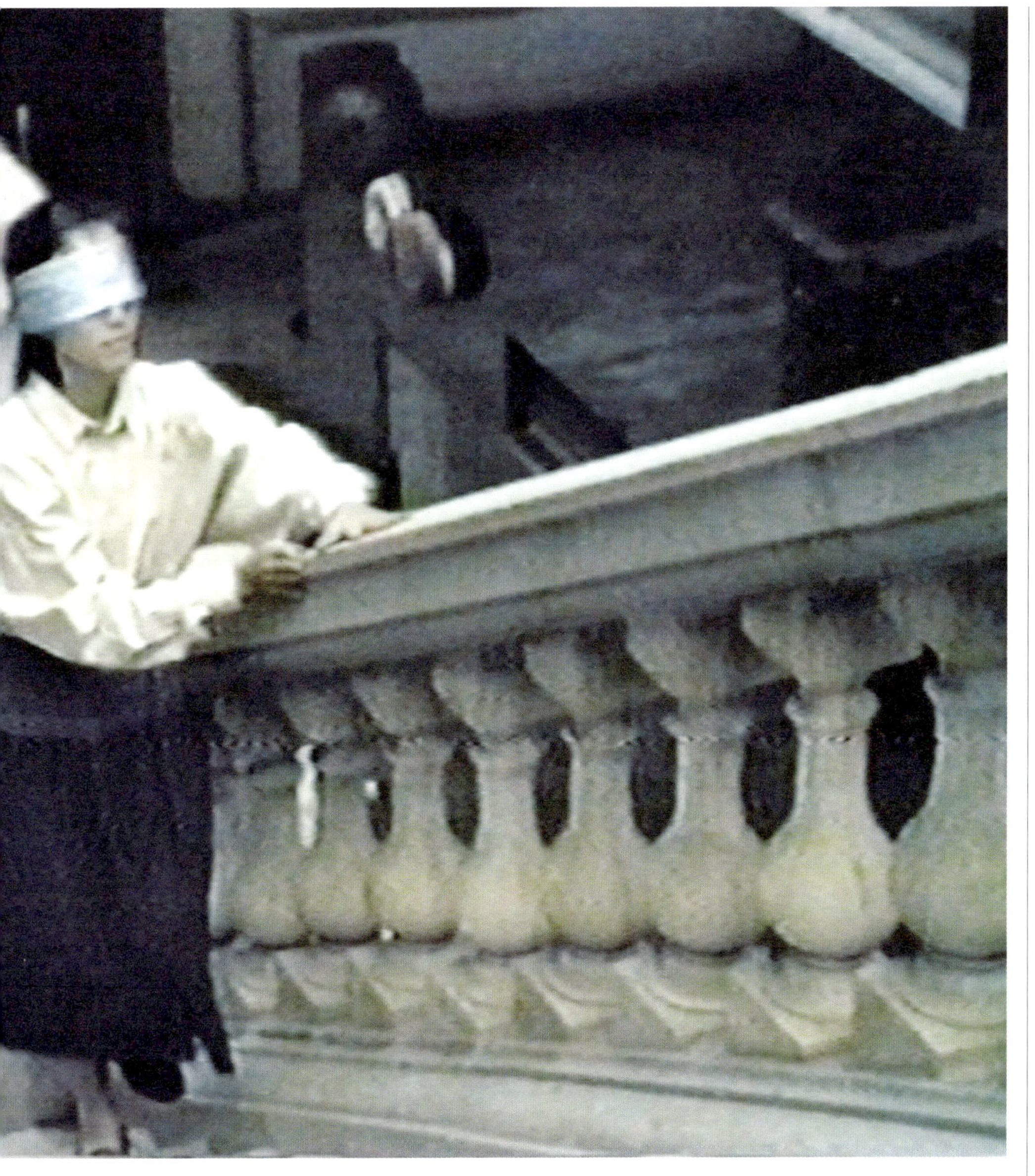

Benny Lam created this portrait of domestic life using an aerial technique that emphasises the compact conditions of subdivided housing units. Commissioned by the Hong Kong Society for Community Organisation (SoCO) to document the housing crisis that is endemic to the city, Lam photographed the homes of families living in subdivided units in Sham Shui Po, Mong Kok, and Yau Ma Tei between 2012 and 2015. According to the Hong Kong Census and Statistics Department, in 2016 there were approximately 92,700 subdivided units housing some 210,000 people, with a median per capita floor area of 5.3 square metres. In 2016, SoCO exhibited Lam's photographs and published them in the monograph *Trapped*. These images have become a powerfully direct way through which to sharpen public consciousness about urban poverty.   BW

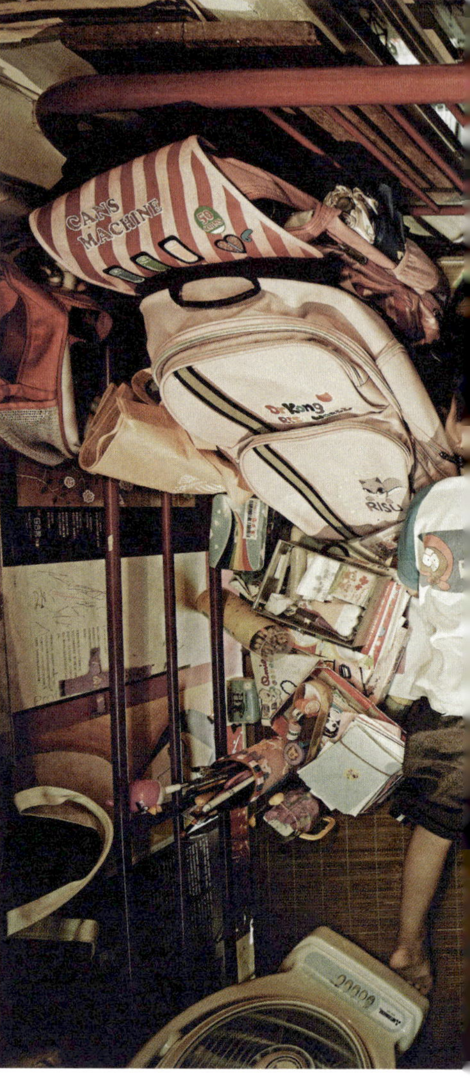

Benny Lam (born 1967, Hong Kong)
Trapped – sub-divided units 01
2012
Inkjet print
151 × 229 cm
Gift of Benny Lam, 2018. Commissioned by Society for Community Organization
2019.556

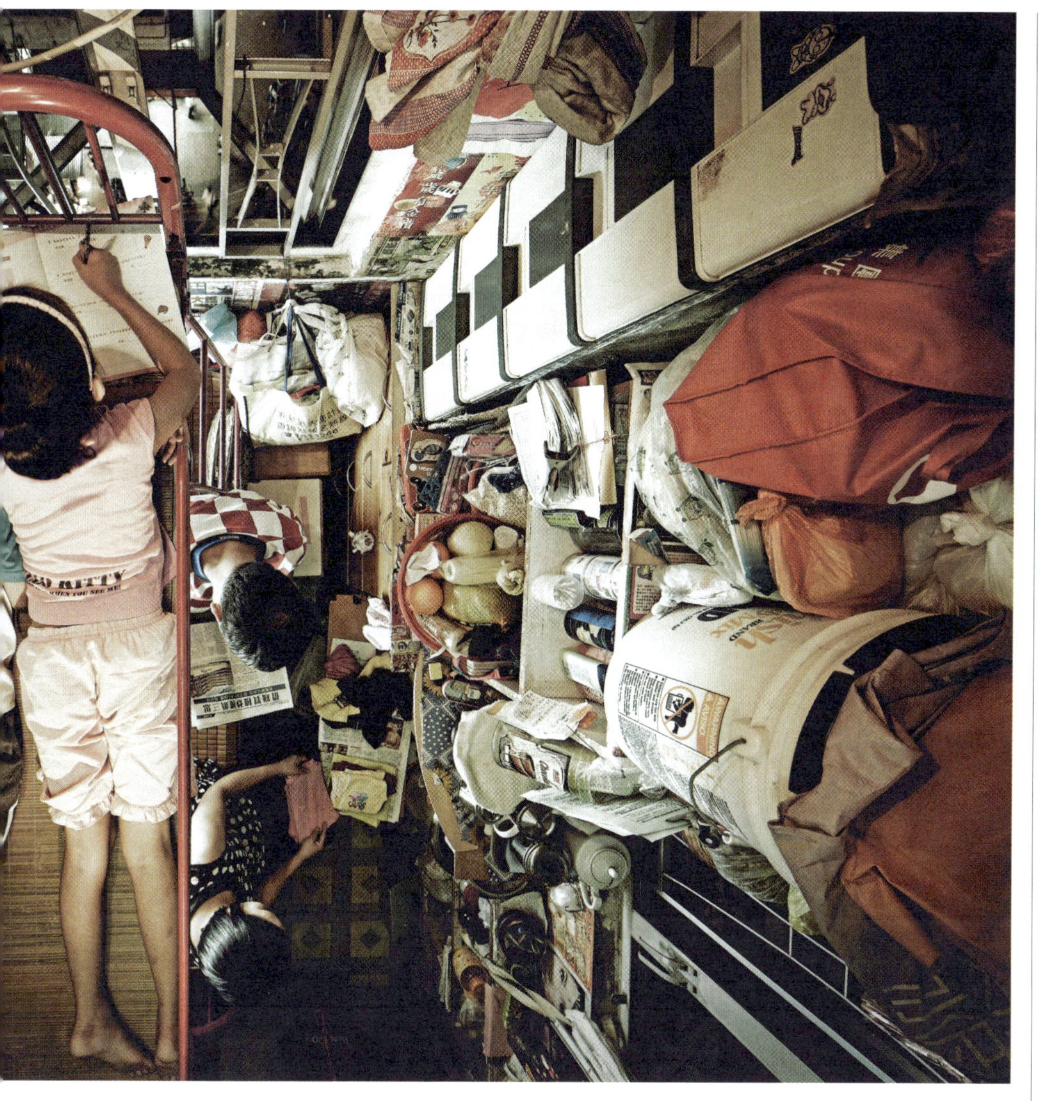

Made when Yau Ching was studying in New York, *Flow* is an experimental documentary that questions the form of biographical narrative. The work is constructed around conversations between Yau and Hou Wenyi, an artist based in New York who had been part of the '85 New Wave art movement in China. Presenting the work as a documentary about Hou's life, Yau asks the artist about her thoughts on country and identity. Hou's response—'My identity is having no identity'—prompts Yau to reflect on the identity of Hong Kong citizens following the handover in 1997. The film also centres on notions of alienation and marginalisation, in both the United States and China. Interspersing the dialogue with documentary and news footage of the Chinese Civil War and police shootings of Black Americans, Yau's postmodern structure introduces a complex cultural plurality to the film's historical narrative.   CC

Yau Ching (born 1966, Hong Kong)
Flow (stills)
1993
Single-channel digital video (colour, sound)
38 min. 24 sec.
2019.150

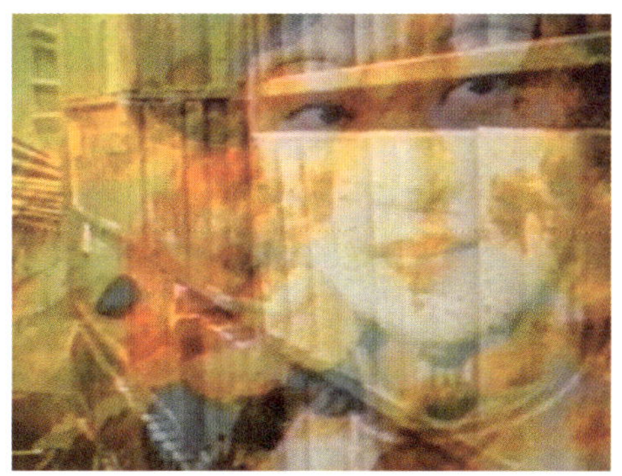

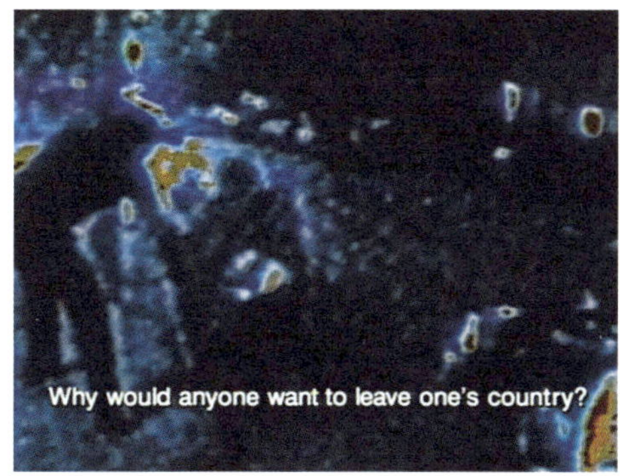
Why would anyone want to leave one's country?

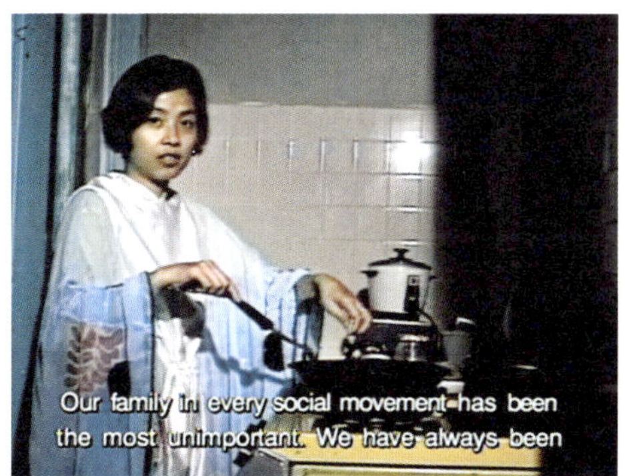
Our family in every social movement has been
the most unimportant. We have always been

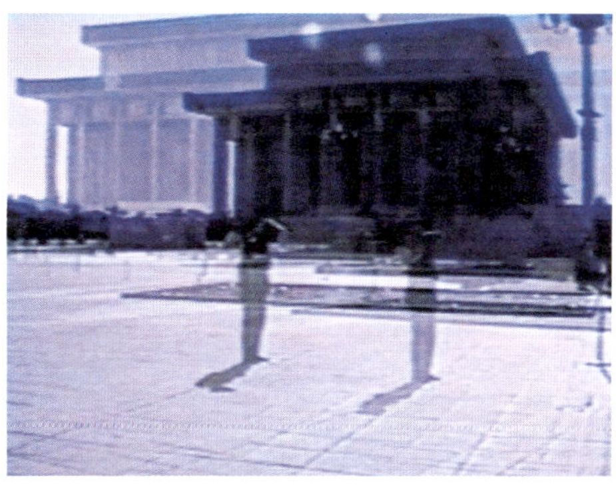

Since the beginning of her career in the 1980s, Ellen Pau has consistently adopted an unconventional approach to the production techniques and viewing experience of video art. For *Recycling Cinema*, she uses the aesthetic of surveillance video, taking inspiration from Dziga Vertov's 1929 *Man with a Movie Camera*, an experimental film that documents life in cities in the Soviet Union. Pau mounted a camera on a mechanised tripod in order to document the Island Eastern Corridor expressway over a twenty-four-hour period. Traffic and camera move independently of each other in disorienting imagery that prompts the viewer to play an active role. The pace of the footage is broken by the camera's zooming in on cars as well as a night view of Victoria Harbour. The ending expands on the poetic quality of the visuals, with the lyrics 'love is real, real is love' from John Lennon's 1970 song 'Love' becoming both an expression of affection and an articulation of loss.

While she was in Europe for the Venice Biennale, Pau visited Berlin, where she took many photographs. The images formed the point of departure for her 2003 work *For Some Reasons*. This video exemplifies Pau's approach to moving image as a narrative medium and her integration of text and image in essayistic videos. It forms an expression in response to the legislation of Article 23 of the Hong Kong Basic Law, which prohibits acts of treason and sedition against the Chinese government, and other controversial social issues. Pau paired photographs of streetscapes, urban life, and popular culture in Berlin and Hong Kong with twenty-three phrases including 'cannot', such as 'cannot play' and 'cannot think'. Changing the first Chinese word of each phrase leads to a shift of meaning. By juxtaposing images of the former East Berlin, once within the Soviet-led Eastern Bloc, with views of contemporary Hong Kong, the work proposes dialogue and comparison between two distinct situations.   CC

Ellen Pau (born 1961, Hong Kong)
Recycling Cinema (stills)
1998
Single-channel video installation (colour, sound)
11 min. 36 sec.
2016.888

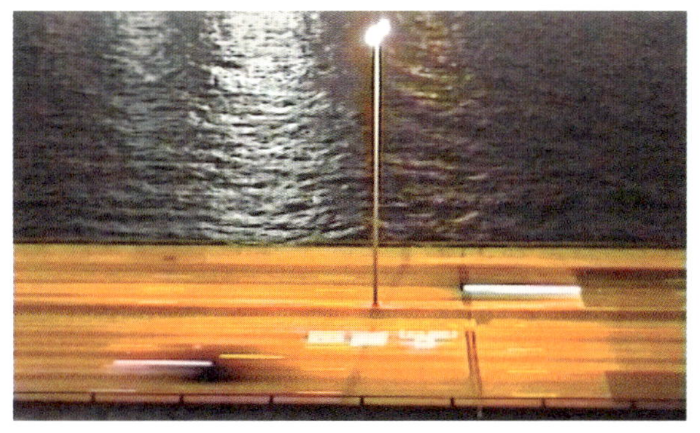

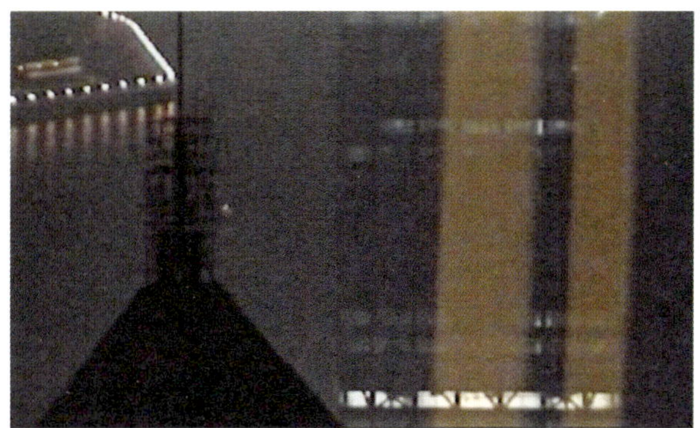

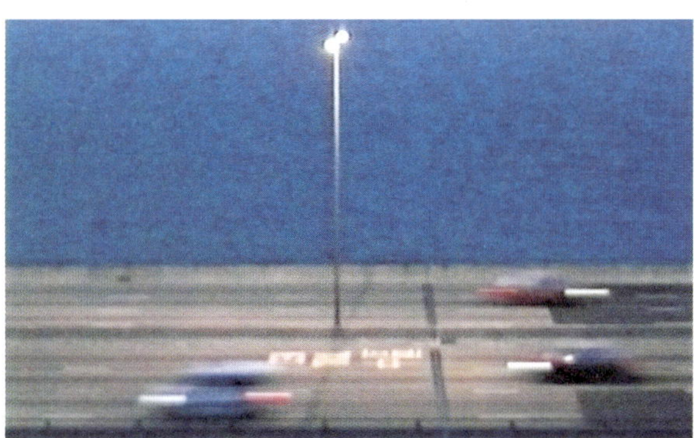

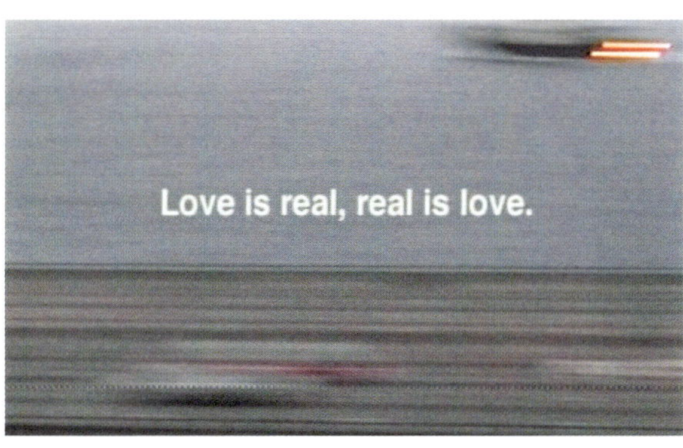
Love is real, real is love.

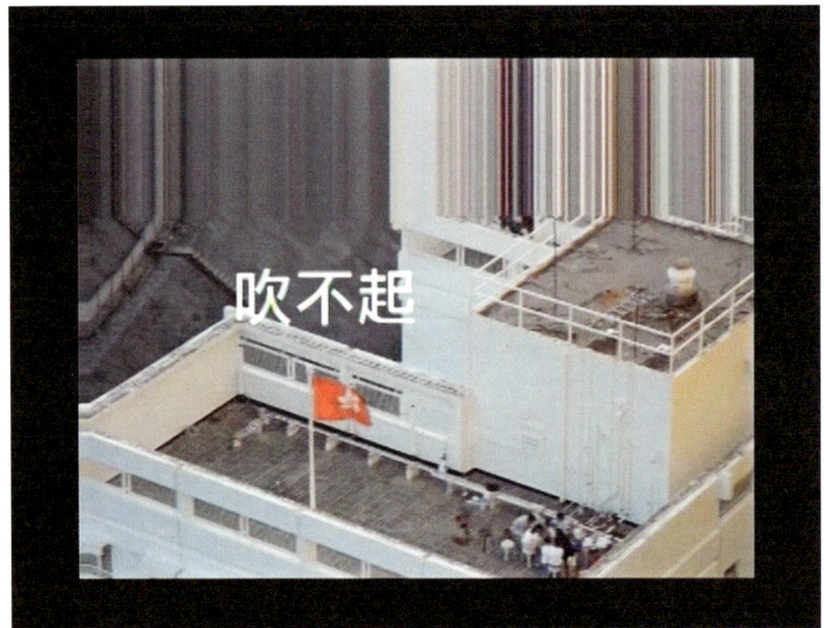

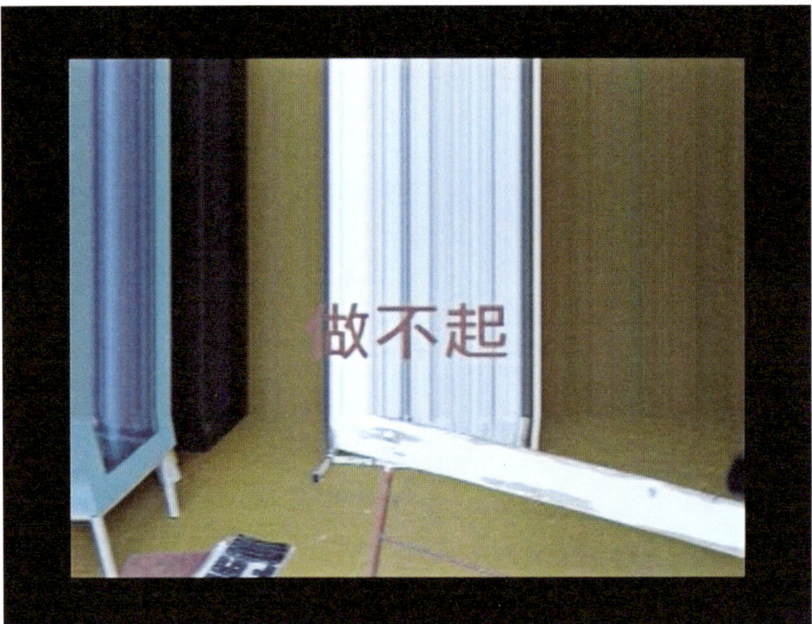

For Some Reasons (stills)
2003
Single-channel digital video (colour, sound)
6 min. 40 sec.
2016.889

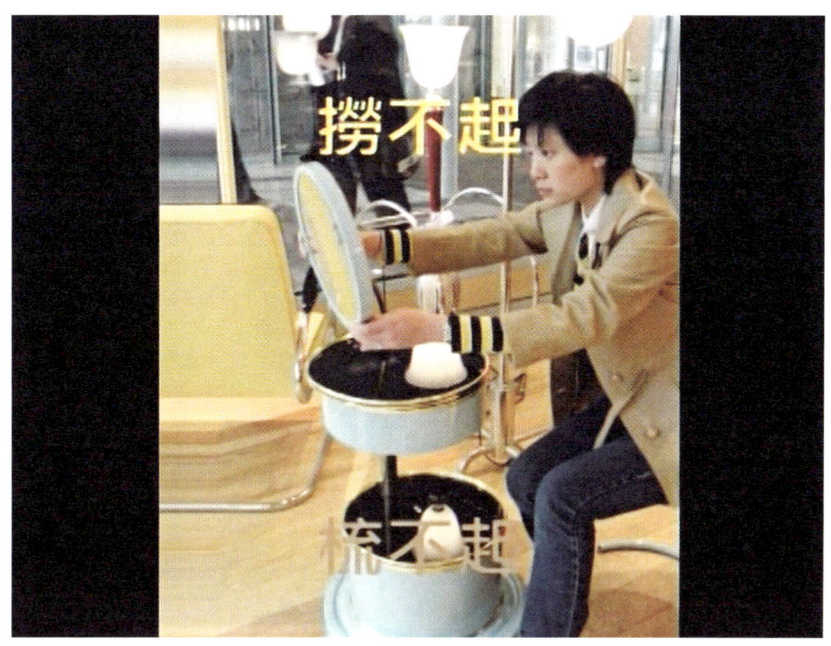
捞不起
梳不起

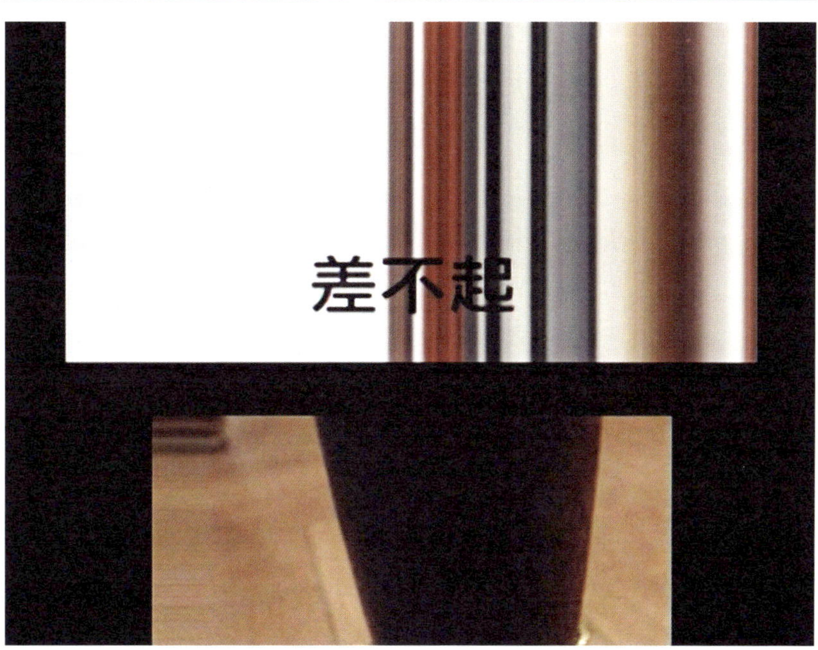
差不起

In 1999, when Luke Ching was teaching at a primary school, he rented a room in nearby Pok Fu Lam Village. Located on the site of a dairy farm established in the 1880s, the community is one of the oldest remaining villages in Hong Kong. Ching transformed this room into a pinhole camera, covering the windows, leaving only a small hole for light to enter, and lining the wall facing the windows with light-sensitive film to capture the view outside. He produced a set of images through the pinhole technique, a method that predates photographic technology and has its roots in antiquity. Ching returned years later only to find that the house was no longer standing. His images document a way of village life in Hong Kong that is now fast disappearing.

Ching's Pok Fu Lam Village project is part of a series of works made between 1998 and 2006 in which the artist transformed rooms across the city into pinhole cameras. This work is unique in the series, in that it not only documents the site—the village and aspects of its informal architecture—but also includes an autobiographical resonance, tracing Ching's experience as a teacher. The project uses a documentary form to comment on the changes brought about by urban development.   CC

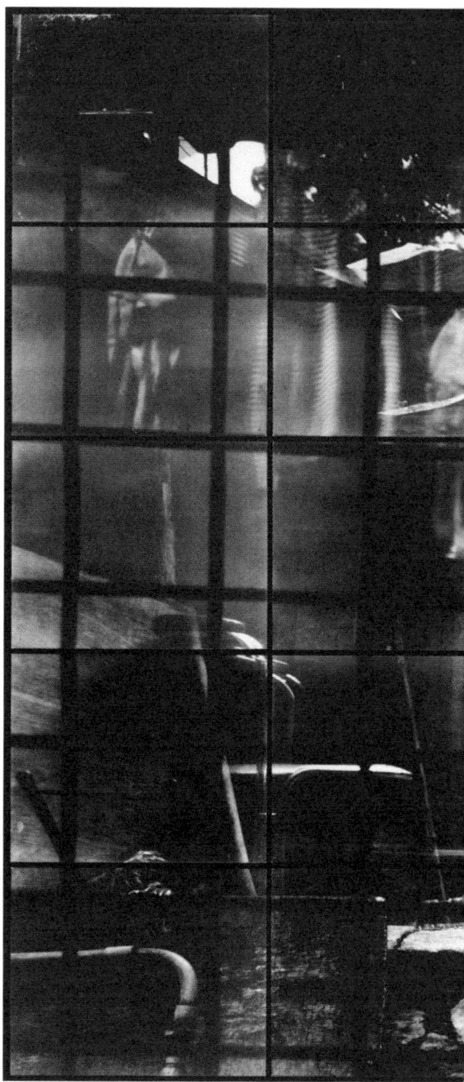

Luke Ching (born 1972, Hong Kong)
Pokfulam Village: View (Positive)
1999
Inkjet print
202.5 × 304.8 cm
2018.247

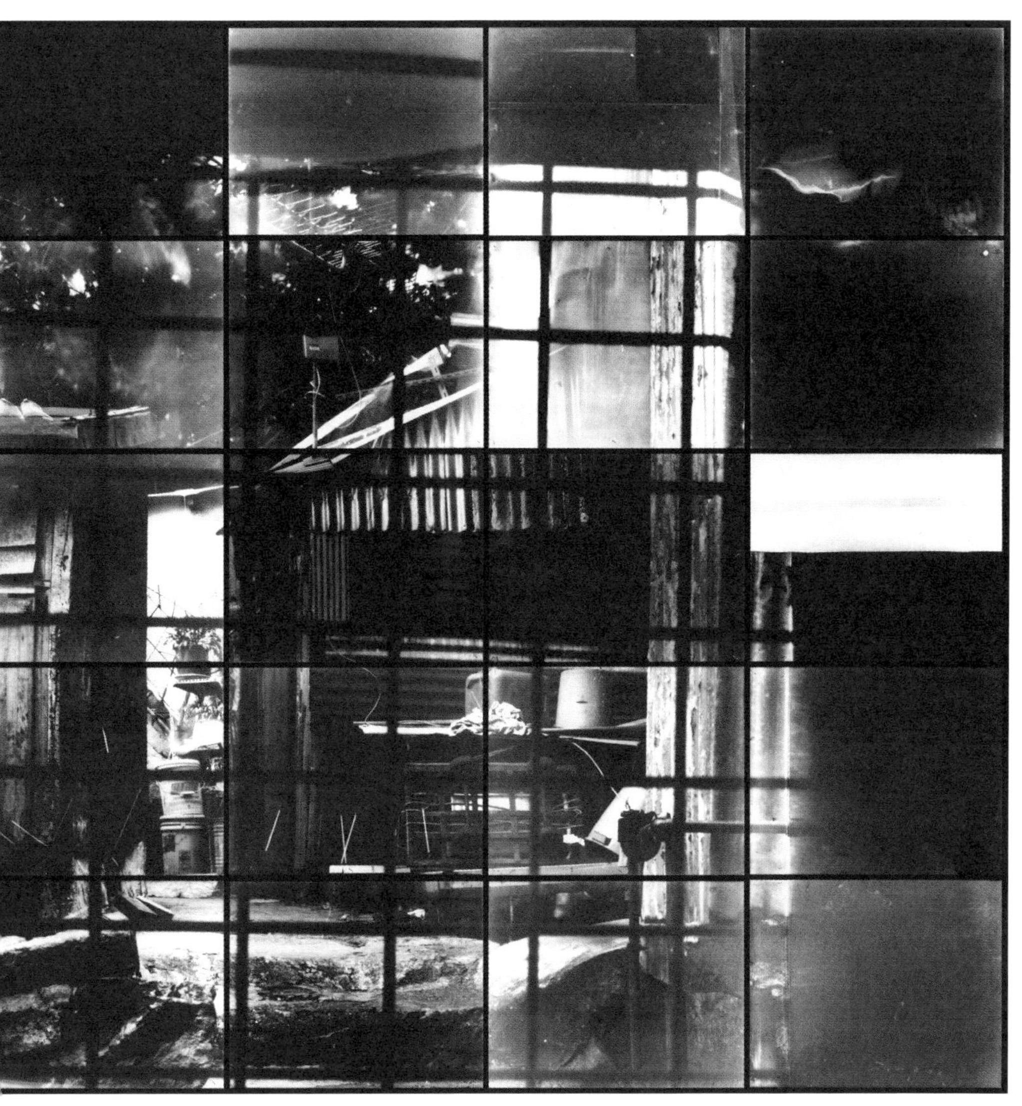

For *On the Edge of a Floating City, We Sing*, Anson Mak invited the Hong Kong indie bands My Little Airport, the Pancakes, and mininoise to play at a location of their choice. Using the selection of songs and locations as a starting point, Mak—herself a former member of the band AMK—interviews the artists about various social issues. These include urban planning, the power of property developers, and a government policy to repurpose under-used industrial spaces. Mak's documentary-style footage is interspersed with poetic episodes filmed on a handheld Super 8 camera, including reflections of the city in Victoria Harbour and pieces of driftwood floating off the Kwun Tong pier. Read alongside the interviews, these visual evocations of the 'floating city' of the title capture the artist's concerns and anxieties about the future for herself and other artists.   CC

Anson Mak (born 1969, Hong Kong)
On the Edge of a Floating City, We Sing (stills)
2012
Single-channel digital video (colour, sound)
120 min.
2017.406

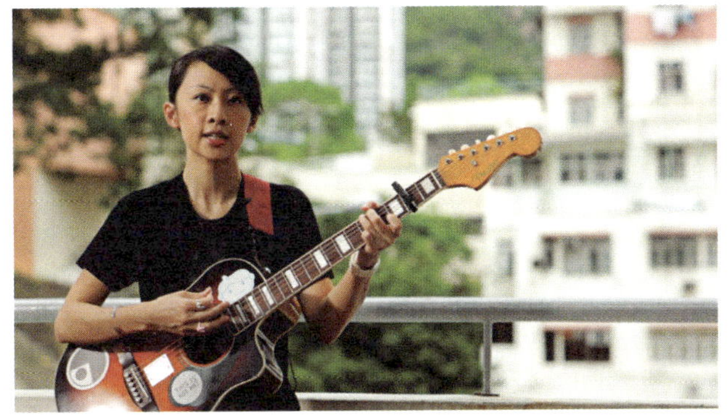

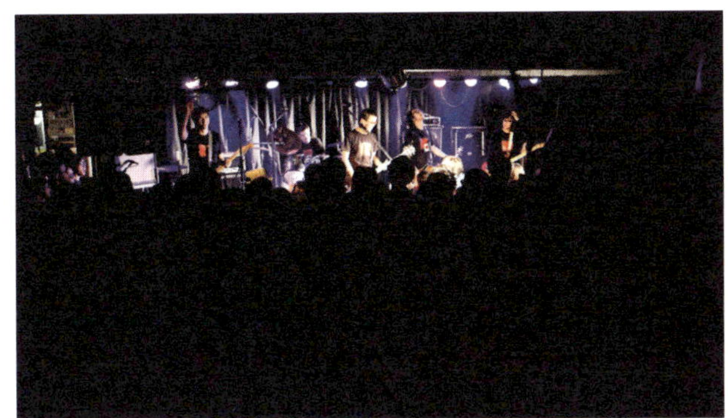

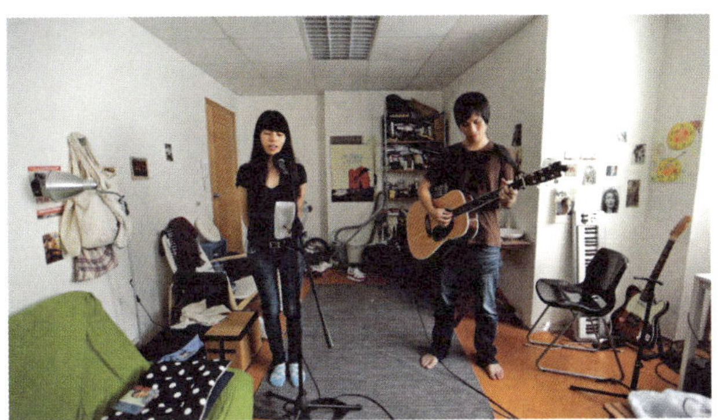

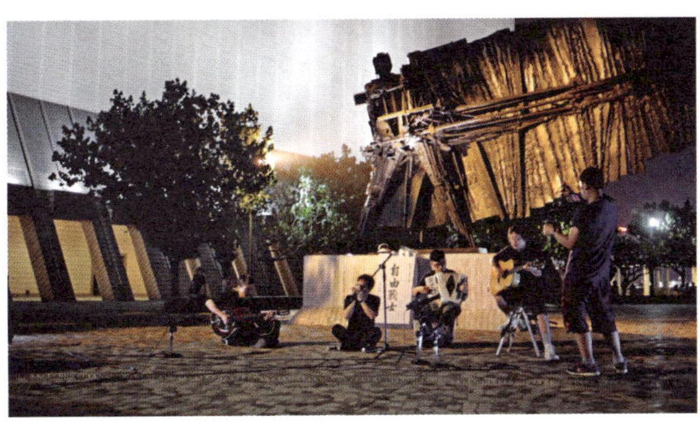

Trained in music composition, Samson Young uses sound to explore and deconstruct issues surrounding politics, culture, identity, and ideology. *Lullaby (World Music)* depicts the artist on a boat on the Pearl River, where Hong Kong meets mainland China, with his back to the camera. The minimal visual information leads the viewer to focus on the video's sound, which consists of Young singing a Cantonese charity single from 1991. The song, adapted from Simon & Garfunkel's 'Bridge over Troubled Water', was originally performed by Hong Kong artists to raise funds for the floods that ravaged eastern China that year. Recalling George Lam's 1986 Cantopop hit 'A Life of Numbers', Young sings a meaningless sequence of numbers rather than the lyrics to the melody. Charity singles were popular in the 1980s, as a way to support humanitarian efforts. Young uncovers the fundamental irony of these songs, as projects that only draw attention to economic disparities— in this case Hong Kong's wealth relative to mainland China in the 1990s. Through a spare, reduced composition of images and sound, he both engages with the past and reflects upon the contemporary relationship between Hong Kong and the mainland.   KW

Samson Young (born 1979, Hong Kong)
Lullaby (World Music) (still)
2017
Single-channel digital video (colour, sound)
6 min. 25 sec.
2019.583

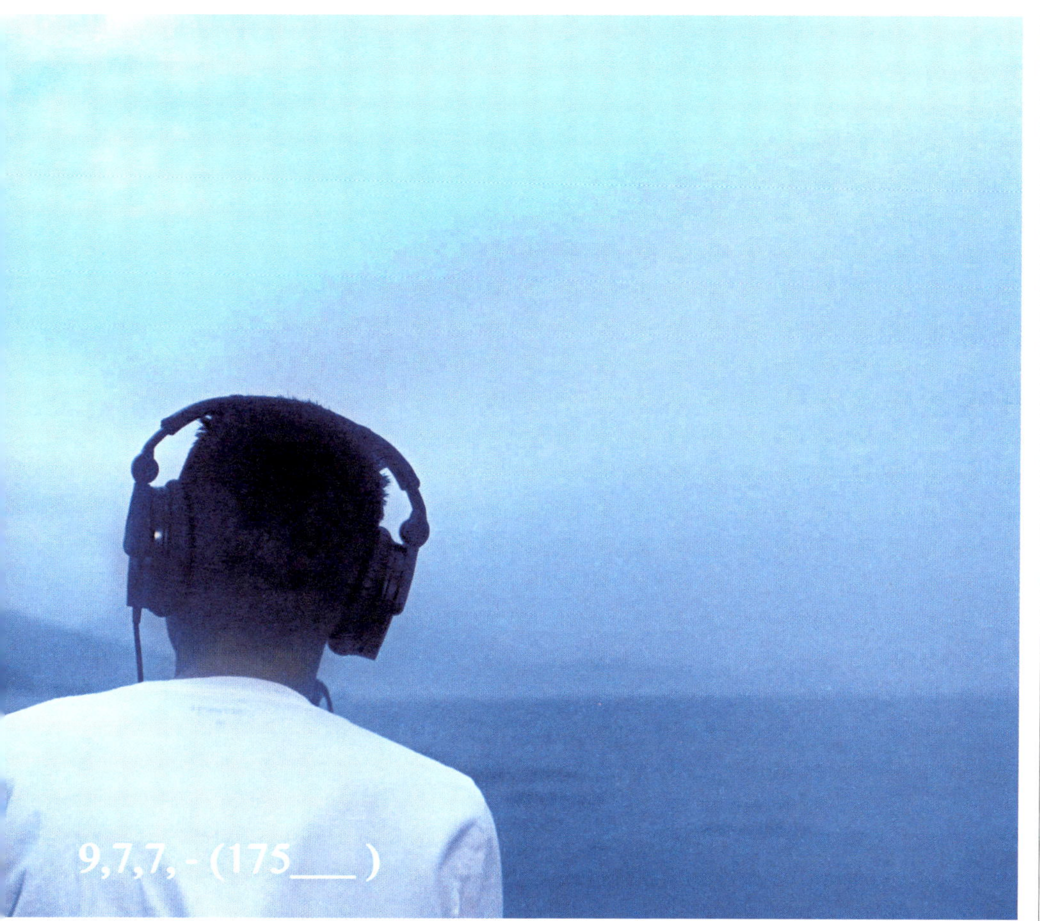
9,7,7, - (175____)

The Hong Kong–based German photographer Michael Wolf took Hong Kong's urban environment as one of his principal subjects, creating a body of work that comprises images of exteriors—notably in his *Architecture of Density* series—as well as interiors. Over four days in 2006, Wolf partnered with a social worker to visit more than one hundred homes, each measuring one hundred square feet (9.2 square metres), at Shek Kip Mei Estate shortly before its demolition. Moving quickly through the corridors, Wolf asked residents for permission to document their home and then took a photograph. He placed his camera on the threshold of the apartment in order to capture the entirety of the interior. Built in 1954 to house the inhabitants of squatter homes in a nearby hillside who lost their homes in a fire in 1953, the small units at Shek Kip Mei represented, for many, vastly improved living conditions. In *100x100*, Wolf shows how the mostly elderly residents had personalised their compact private spaces and incorporated staples such as steel bunk beds and flexible furniture. Television cabinets and ancestral tables frequently take pride of place. Wolf's images reveal the hidden order within the sometimes chaotic interiors of each unit, reflecting his interest in simple, everyday solutions to navigating and inhabiting the city. As an examination of individual ways of living, *100x100* offers insight into diverse definitions of the concept of 'home' and a depiction of a society in microcosm.   BW

Michael Wolf (born 1954, West Germany (now Germany); died 2019, Hong Kong)
100x100
2006
Chromogenic print
22.8 × 34.2 cm (each, set of 100)
2015.542

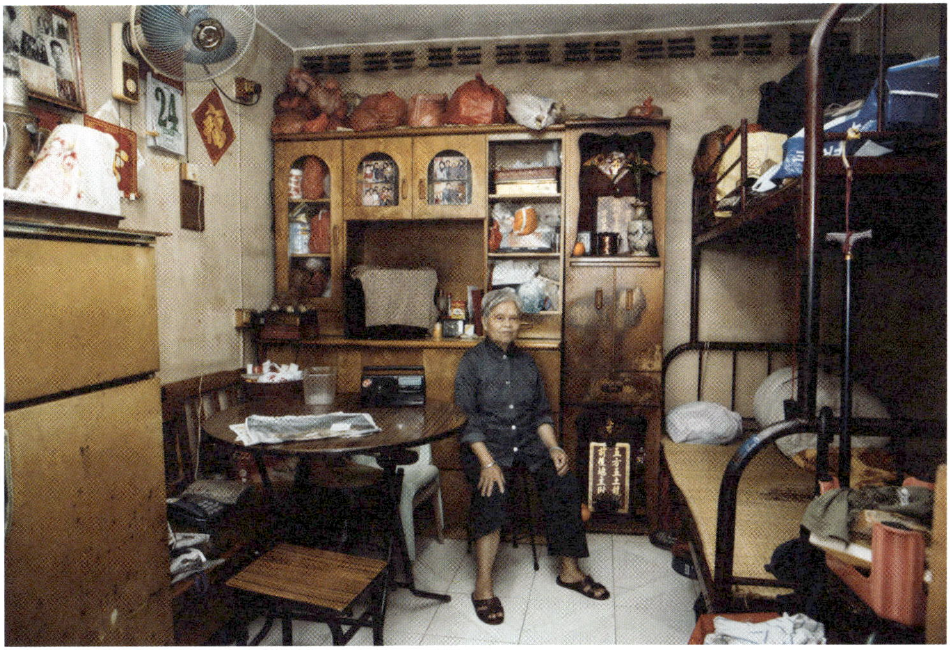

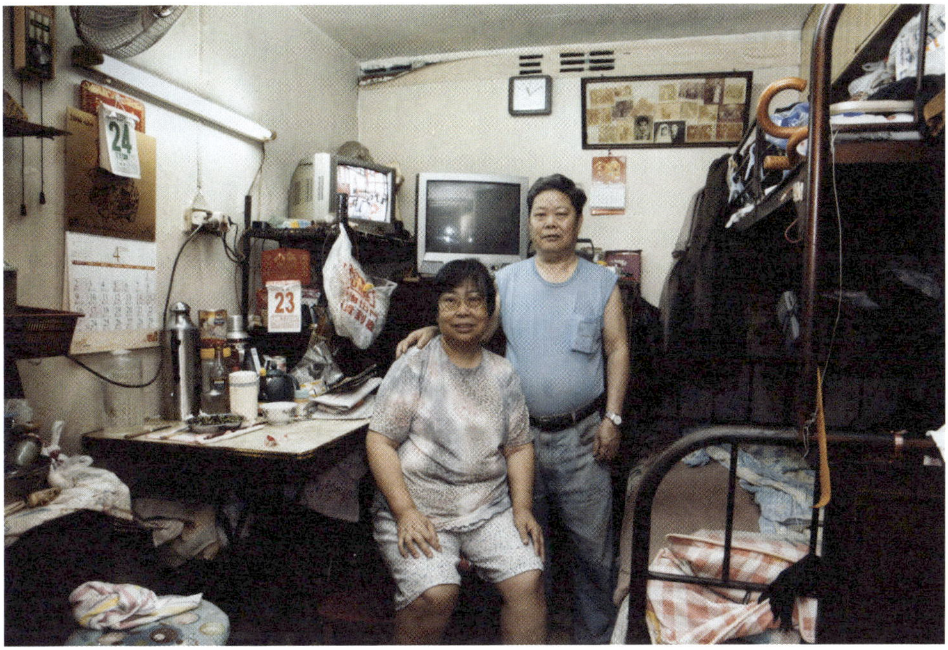

Martin Parr is known for his documentary photographs of people in settings of work and leisure, particularly in the United Kingdom. Beginning in the 1980s, he has captured subjects in candid images that address the relationship between taste and social class, producing a body of work characterised by a pervasive, mischievous irony.

In 2013, Parr was commissioned to produce a series of photographs on Hong Kong. The project resulted in the publication *Hong Kong Parr*, sixty-seven images that form a portrait of contemporary life. Approaching the city from an outsider's perspective, Parr extends his interest in the everyday as well as in how personal taste shapes our choices. In this image, Parr's signature use of saturated colour and direct flash captures a bettor at Hong Kong's historic Happy Valley Racecourse, whose face is almost completely obscured behind a racing form and a pair of binoculars. Parr observes his subject with an anthropological gaze, drawing our attention to the man's exuberant shirt and gold watch to form a wry comment on Hong Kong's gambling culture. As with Parr's larger oeuvre, *Hong Kong Parr* constitutes a theatre of the ordinary. It uncovers vernacular details and registers the often comic friction between appearances and social realities.   BW

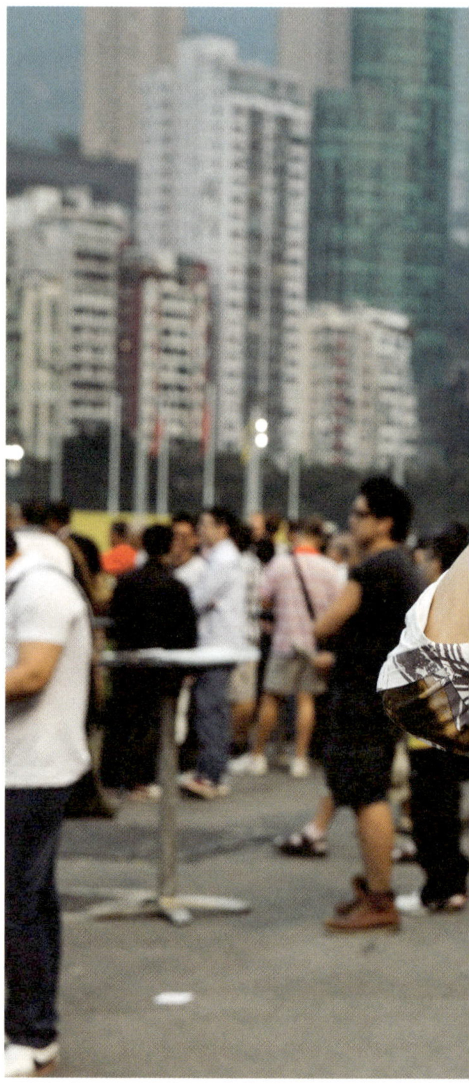

Martin Parr (born 1952, United Kingdom)
Hong Kong (LON156562)
2013
Inkjet print
50.8 × 76.2 cm
2016.16

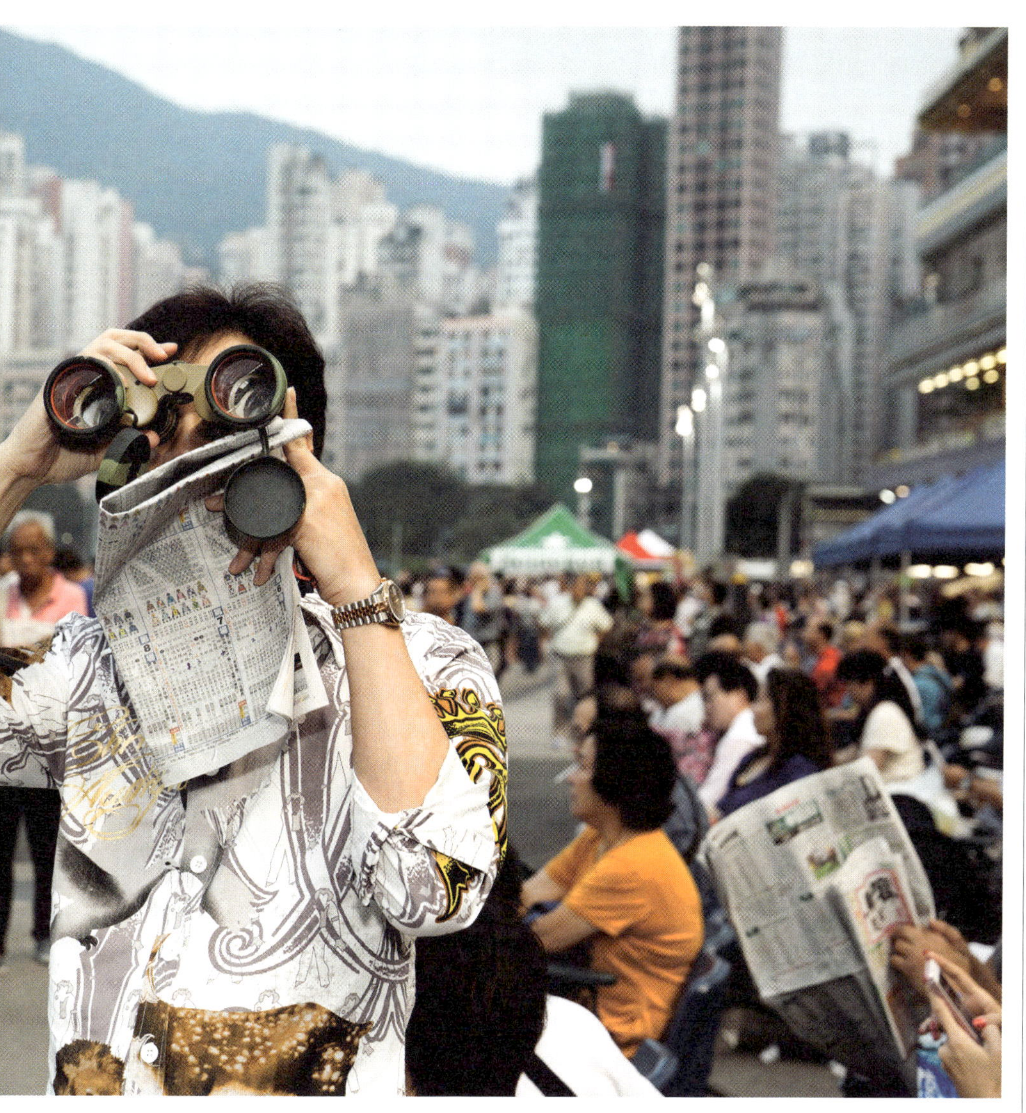

South Ho began his *Every Daily* series in 2013 after moving to Tin Shui Wai, one of Hong Kong's largest satellite towns, in the New Territories. The remote urban setting inspired him to take a subjective and introspective approach to his photographic practice, in contrast to his earlier documentary work. This shift was also informed by the grief he felt following the death of his father several years earlier.

Every Daily 26 juxtaposes a black-and-white photograph of a landscape scene with hand-painted grids of coloured squares raining down from the sky. In the distance, the towering residential blocks that are hallmarks of Tin Shui Wai are visible, while the foreground is dominated by a pond with an incongruous sculpture of a water buffalo at its centre. Ho's painterly intervention is a homage to his father, a graphic artist who painted large posters and advertisements. The image can be read as a poetic statement of Ho's desire for a family reunion with his departed father at his new home.   BW

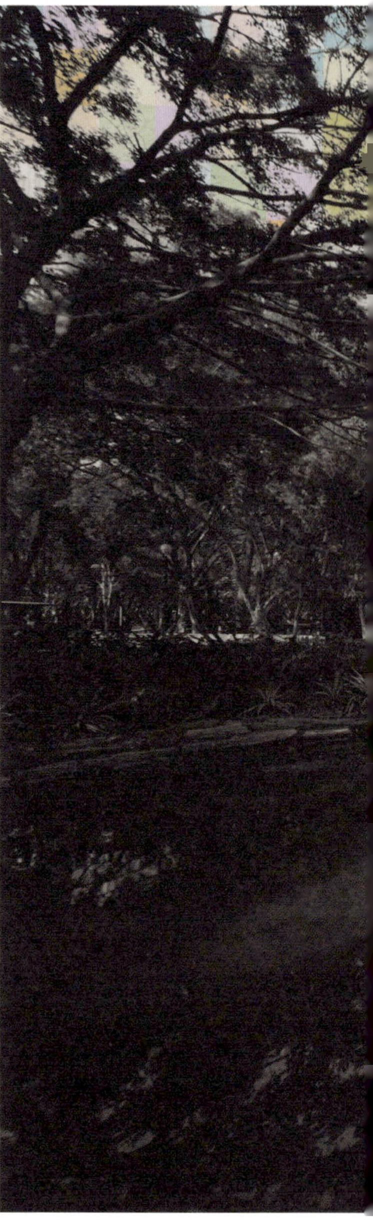

South Ho (born 1984, Hong Kong)
Every Daily 26
2013
Watercolour on inkjet print
64 × 80 cm
M+ Council for New Art Fund, 2019
2019.110

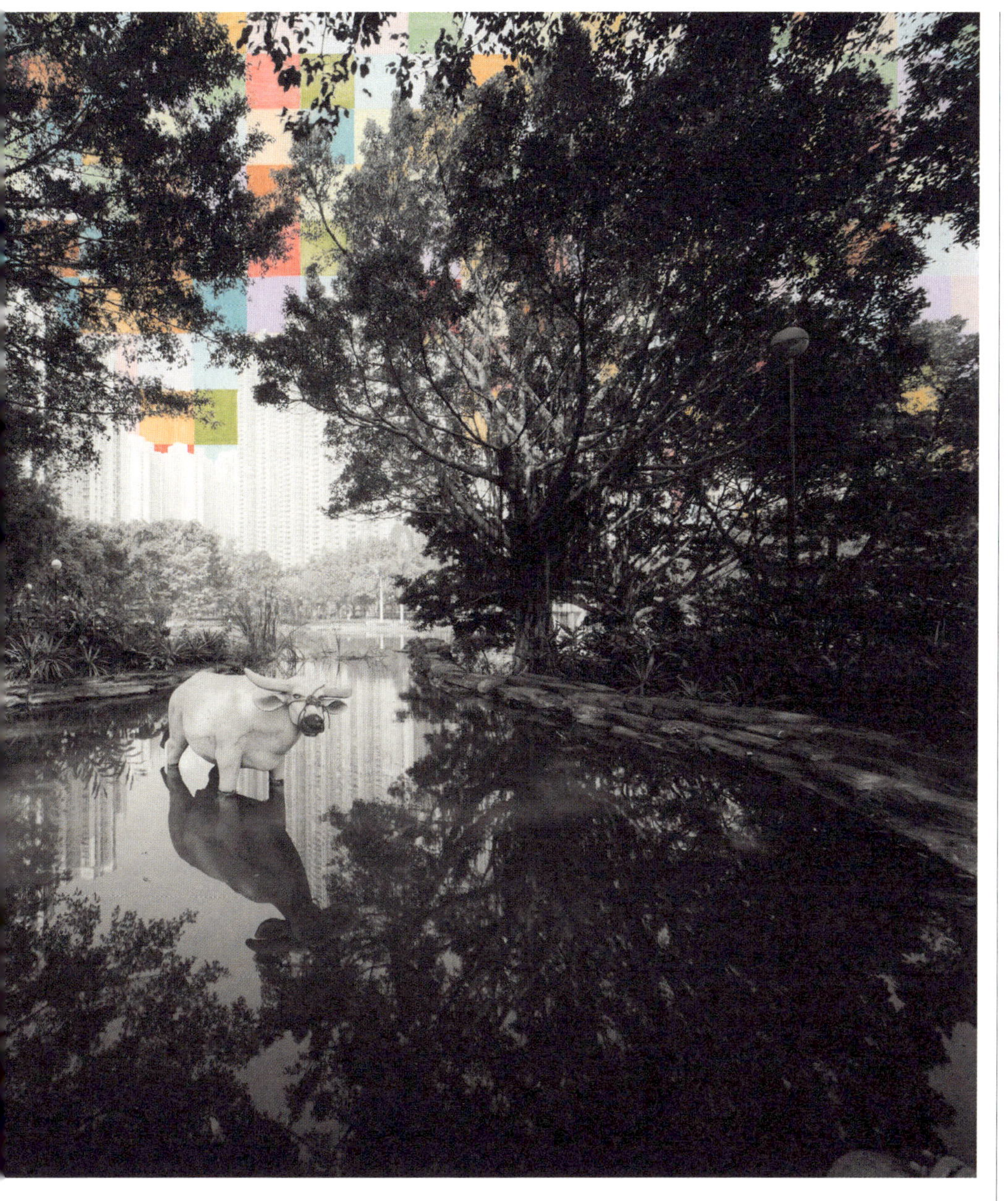

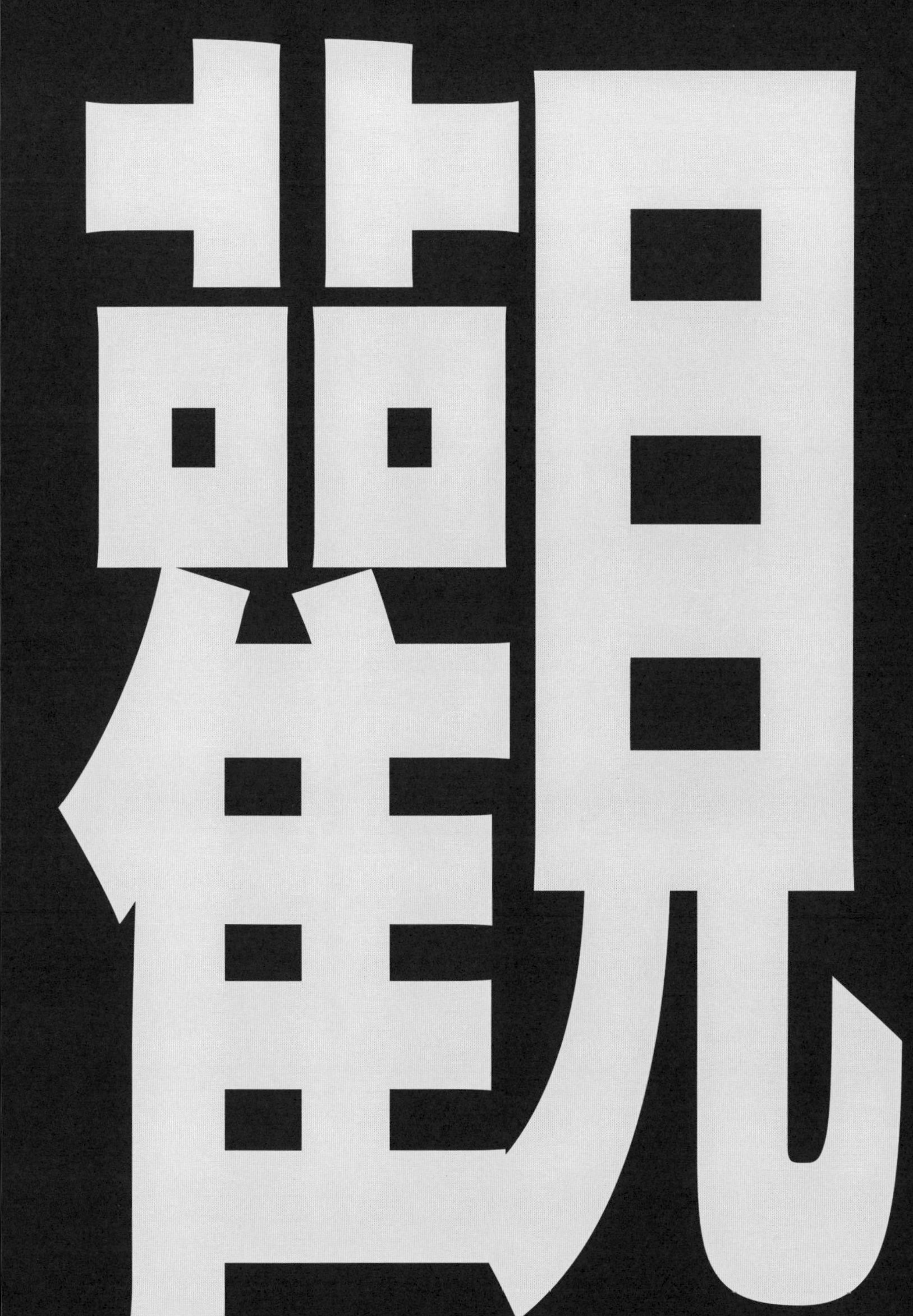

PERSP

CTIVES

The early post-war years in Hong Kong were shaped by tremendous changes, with the arrival of refugees from mainland China and profound economic transformation. Between the 1940s and the 1970s, the city experienced great economic opportunity but had little in the way of an art ecosystem. Nevertheless, artists across generations developed new experiments and forms of expression. Curators, collectors, and gallerists, along with schools and exhibition spaces, formed a network that provided an environment in which artists could thrive. This chapter considers distinct artistic practices and perspectives that are informed by cultural conventions, political and social contexts, and the flow of ideas from around the world.

'Beyond Form', the first section, considers artists who work in different mediums but are united in an endeavour to forge new paths in dialogue with existing conventions. The second section, titled 'Door Games Window Frames', brings together works that mark dramatic shifts in artistic expressions. The third section, 'Quizás, Quizás, Quizás' ('perhaps, perhaps, perhaps'), includes works that confront the uncertainties that were pervasive during the pre- and post-handover period.

The first section is inspired by Leung Kui-ting's abstract gestural painting *Beyond Form*, which breaks with the traditions of ink painting. Irene Chou, in her own departure from ink tradition, introduces an individualistic dimension to the potential of the medium. The fantastical worlds of Luis Chan's artistic imagination are constructed with the materials of ink painting but are filled with a wholly original perspective on contemporary life. Andreas Gursky's portrait of the HSBC building subverts the conventional form of architectural photography that glorifies the building as place-making object, presenting it instead as an icon of global financial labour. Seen together, the artists in this section pioneered unexpected perspectives using familiar mediums.

The second section takes its cue from Linda Chiu-han Lai's video installation *Door Games Window Frames,* a montage that shows the way doors and windows mark moments of transition in Hong Kong films. Szeto Keung's trajectory, spanning Hong Kong, Taiwan, and New York, speaks to the expanded art world of the 1970s and 1980s. Szeto and other artists reckoned with cultural dualities and new modes of expression in response to deep uncertainties about the future.

Wong Yankwai's visceral abstraction evokes the raw emotions of a pivotal point in Hong Kong's transition towards Chinese sovereignty, while Holly Lee combines contemporary cultural encounters with the appropriations of the Qing court. Crossing editorial with artistic practice, Lee Ka-sing's poetic manipulation of images obscures their original meanings and conveys a lack of fixity.

The third section borrows its title, 'Quizás, Quizás, Quizás', from *Angkor Quartet*, Wilson Shieh's affectionate tribute to Hong Kong's popular culture and historical links to Southeast Asia. It includes artists who came of age during the period before and after the handover. Working in conceptual and dematerialised practices such as installation and performance, artists such as Lee Kit, Kwan Sheung Chi, and Wong Wai Yin enact a kind of postcolonial ennui in response to their circumstances. In the medium of painting, Firenze Lai and Lam Tung Pang express similar sentiments and a subtly powerful subjectivity. This chapter, and this book, ends with Kacey Wong's insistence on the inseparability of art and life. He embodies a city that can move, offering a summary statement on a way to read Hong Kong visual culture and to see Hong Kong in the world.

BEYOND FORM

How artists reread tradition and history, and propose new visual languages

Designed by British architect Norman Foster and completed in 1986, the HSBC building was at the time the most expensive architectural project in the world, and HSBC's fourth headquarters in Hong Kong. Built using prefabricated components, it is an articulation of high-tech modernism that presents an image of exposed mechanical systems and structural elements. Massive suspension trusses provide support and allow for a column-free interior on the office floors. The building quickly became both an architectural landmark and a symbol of Hong Kong's position as an international centre of finance.

Beginning with his 1990 photograph of the Tokyo Stock Exchange, artist Andreas Gursky embarked on an extended engagement with spaces of financial work around the world. Here, he strips away the structural and formal innovations of Foster's design, presenting an entirely new reading. The image emphasises the horizontality of the floors against the nocturnal backdrop and draws attention to the activity taking place inside. The monumental scale of the photograph and the decapitated architectural form create a disorienting effect, but one that nonetheless alludes to Hong Kong's place within an international financial network.   FT

Andreas Gursky (born 1955, East Germany (now Germany))
Hong Kong and Shanghai Bank
1994
Chromogenic print
185.5 × 135.5 cm
2013.27

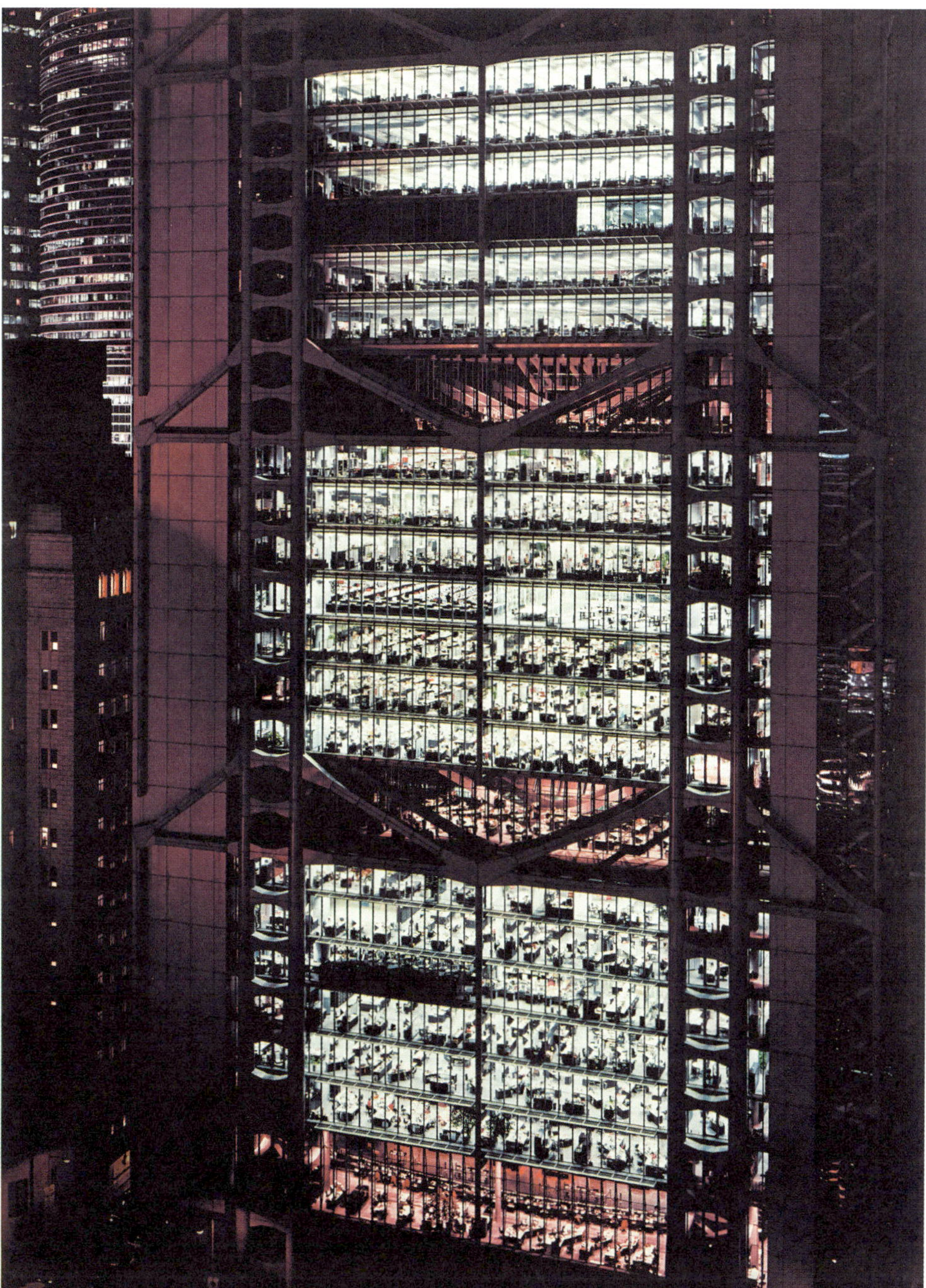

Distant Thoughts No. 19 depicts the Englewood Cliffs along the Hudson River in New Jersey, where Wucius Wong lived in the 1980s and 1990s. The monumental scale, dense dotted marks, and thick brushwork recall the landscape paintings of the Northern Song period. Wong's aerial perspective and use of high contrast across this landscape increase the romantic drama of the scene but also impose an analytical distance. The composition is shaped by the river that runs diagonally through the landscape and by the verticality of the fourfold division of the painted surface. In line with the spirit of experimentation espoused by the New Ink Movement, the work reflects Wong's background in graphic design and his application of principles of design theory to create dynamic tension.   CC

Wucius Wong (born 1936, Guangdong)
Distant Thoughts No.19
1990
Ink and colour on paper
135 × 91.8 cm
2013.275

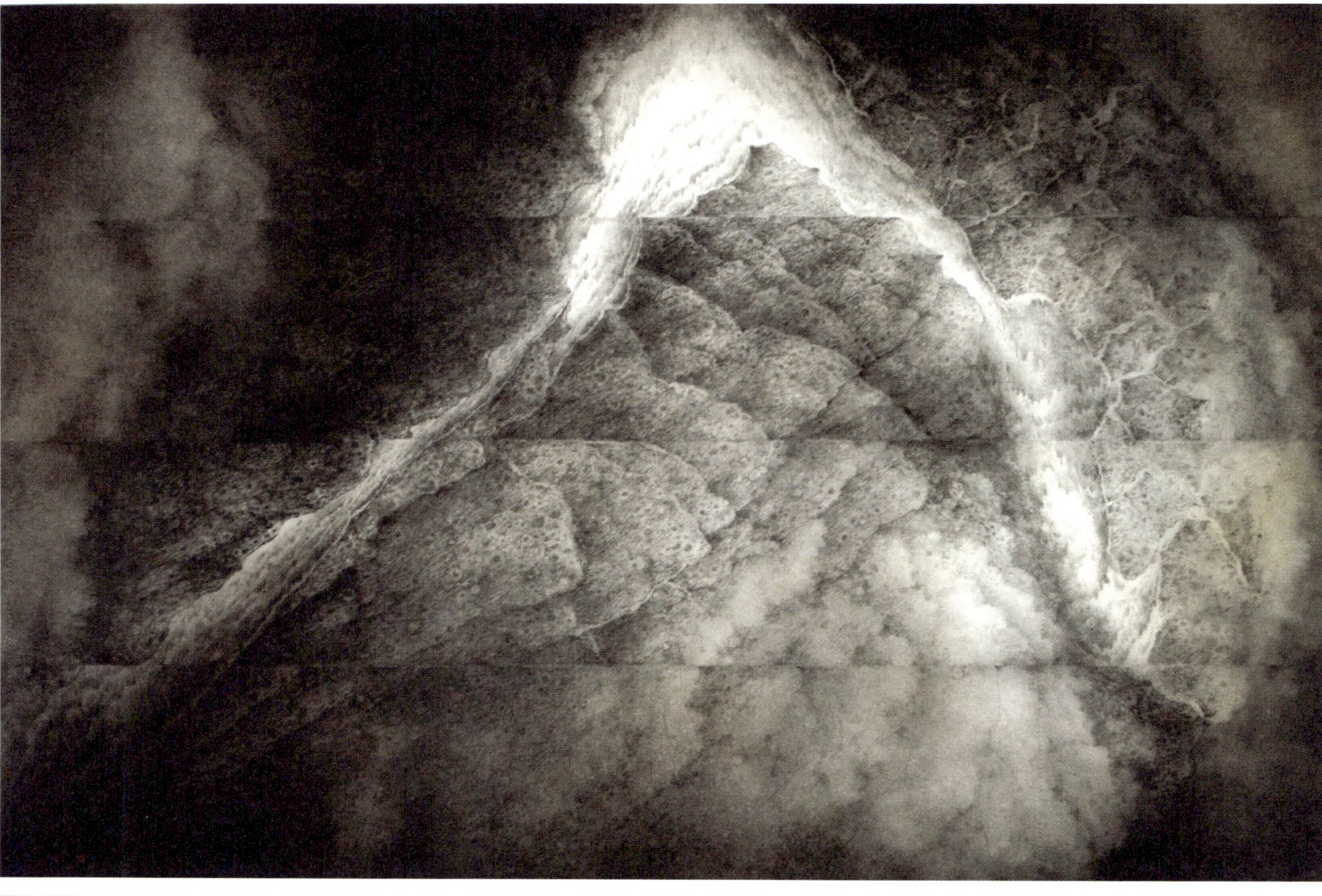

Koon Wai Bong is best known for his meticulous *gongbi* (fine brush) style. Here he applies this technique to depict a canopy of trees in a nocturnal landscape, rendering the rest of the scene in a dense ink wash—an unusual choice in the context of his oeuvre. This work's title refers to a line from the popular Northern Song *ci* lyrical poem *Shuidiao Getou* by Su Shi. The concentration of blue and black ink at the centre of the composition could refer to the silhouette of a dancer, an allusion to the poem. The suggestion of the figure's presence heightens the tension between light and shadow, and action and stillness. Koon's combination of two ink-painting techniques—fine brushstrokes and heavy ink wash—exemplifies his experimentation with tradition, and his appropriation and reconfiguration of an aesthetic to articulate a contemporary creative position.   KW

Koon Wai Bong (born 1974, Hong Kong)
Dancing in Shadows
2014
Ink and colour on paper
242.4 × 120.5 cm
2014.108

Between 2013 and 2015, Hung Fai experimented with water as the primary compositional element in his ink paintings, producing his *Splash* series. What appear to be images made through a process determined by chance are in fact carefully controlled through the artist's manipulation of his materials. To create this composition, he folded a wet piece of *xuan* paper with ink markings on it, resulting in a symmetrical triptych when the paper was unfolded. Although the image calls to mind the inkblot tests developed by Swiss psychiatrist Hermann Rorschach in the 1920s, for Hung it is something more immediate. He sees the encounter between ink and water as a reflection of the interactions between individuals in society, bound by rules and operations but ultimately unpredictable.   CC

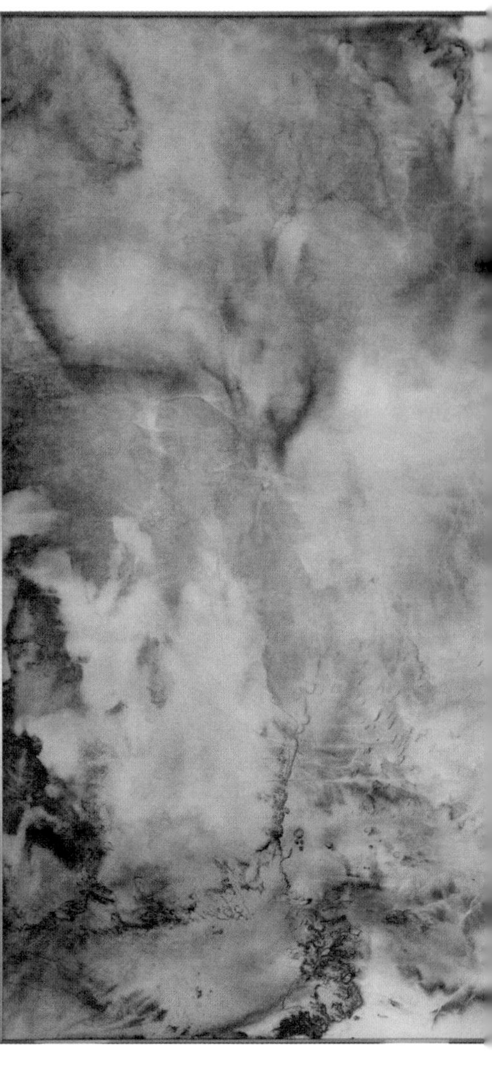

Hung Fai (born 1988, Hong Kong)
Splash VIII
2013
Ink on paper, triptych
179 × 288 cm (total)
2016.477

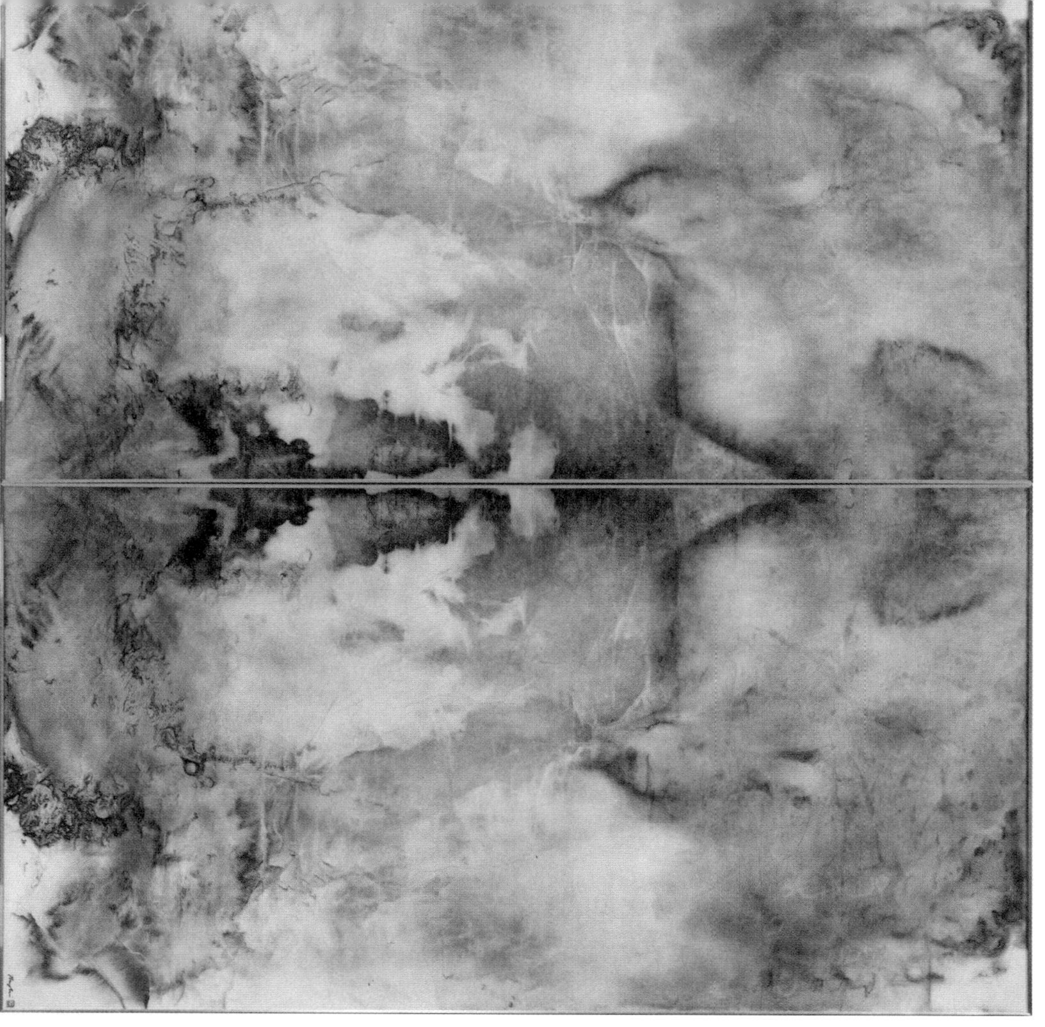

Beyond Form is an experimental work by Leung Kui-ting that combines ink wash and splash techniques, creating a dense composition of contrasting wet and dry layers that offers a record of the unusual overlaid movements of the brush. The work demonstrates his knowledge of and fluency in gestural abstraction. The tight cropping along the edges of the paper reflects the agenda of the New Ink Movement to break with conventional approaches to subject and technique. Leung developed an innovative practice that encompasses printmaking, oils, and sculpture, as well as ink. His primary focus on ink expresses his reading of this medium as both uniquely positioned in tradition and a rich field for experimentation. Unusual in its spontaneity and openness, this work offers insight into the artist's formative development.   KW

Leung Kui-ting (born 1945, Guangdong)
Beyond Form
1969
Ink on paper
135.9 × 80.7 cm
2015.317

Kan Tai-keung began his studies in design with Wucius Wong in 1967 and later enrolled in ink-painting classes with the influential artist and theorist Lui Shou-kwan. Kan's distinctive mode of expression in the medium of ink bears traces of the influence of both figures: Wong's analytical practice informed by a graphic sensibility, and Lui's fundamentally experimental approach.

The form, colour, and composition of this early abstract work follows principles of Chinese landscape painting while connecting with contemporary avant-garde developments. Kan's positioning of red and yellow spheres against a dark-blue and purple background creates an atmosphere of deep cosmic mystery. The floating steps that define the vertical axis suggest his familiarity with the sculptural work of American Minimalist artist Donald Judd. This painting exemplifies a period of experimentation in Kan's art practice, which has since developed into a more direct engagement with traditional landscape aesthetics.   KW

Kan Tai-keung (born 1942, Guangdong)
Stairs
1969
Ink and colour on paper
185.1 × 95.8 cm
2013.255

Hon Chi-fun's airbrushed paintings of circle motifs convey the metaphysical ideas that underpin the artist's practice. These include references to the cycle of life and the relationship between humankind and nature derived from Buddhist and Taoist philosophies. In both form and title, the monumental, immersive *Chasm Forever* evokes the mystery of human existence, as well as an erotic magnetism.

Hon was a founding member of the avant-garde Circle Art Group of the 1960s. Many of his early works, including paintings, mixed-media compositions, collages, and silk-screen prints, incorporate sutras and calligraphic elements. In 1969, he received a fellowship from the John D. Rockefeller 3rd Award, which allowed him to study printmaking at the Pratt Graphic Center in New York and exposed him to developments in Abstract Expressionism. The breakthrough in his practice came with his paintings of circles, as symbols of unity and perfection that resonate across contexts.   TP

Hon Chi-fun (1922–2019, Hong Kong)
Chasm Forever
1971
Acrylic on canvas
188 × 188 × 4.7 cm
2017.324

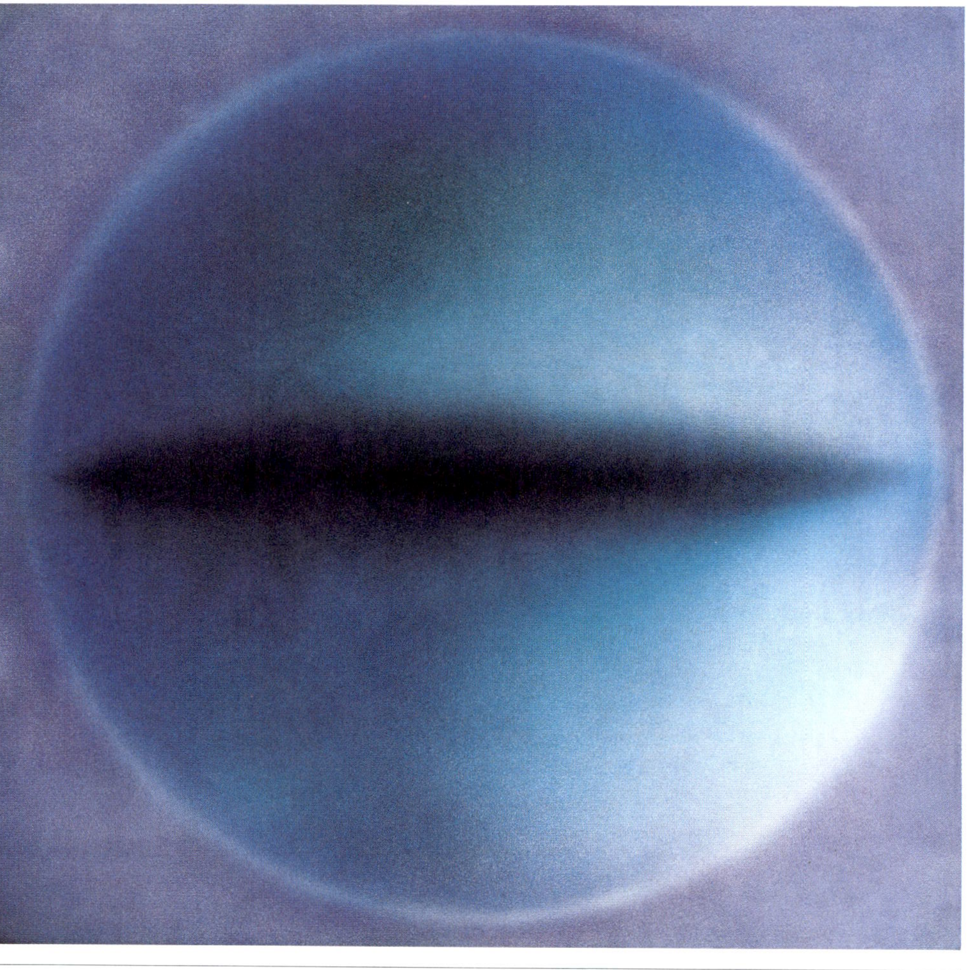

Proximity consists of four individually sculpted forms placed close to one another. The work appears as if it has been sculpted from a single piece of camphor wood and then pulled back apart. Its power lies in the relationship it constructs between form and emptiness, a challenge to conventional ideas of how sculpture occupies space. By drawing attention to the voids, *Proximity* can also be read as a meditation on the nature of human relationships.

Tong King-sum was one of Hong Kong's most prominent sculptors. He achieved wide recognition for his works in wood inspired by natural and abstract forms. He worked throughout his life with live models, documenting how the human body moves. Many of his representations of the body exploit the natural qualities of his materials, communicating the power of their presence and the beauty in their flaws. As a child Tong was diagnosed with tuberculous arthritis, which affected his physical development, but he nevertheless chose to work in one of the most physically demanding mediums. The effort of creation is often evident in the marks on the surface of his sculptures, conveying an intimacy in the processes of both looking and making.   TP

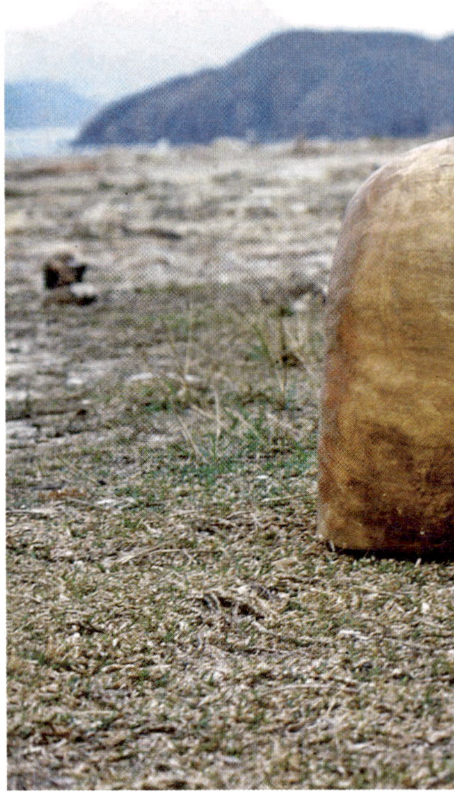

Tong King-sum (1940–2008, Hong Kong)
Proximity
1978
Camphor wood
48.5 × 120 × 47 cm
Gift of Chiu Wai-Yee, 2016
2016.480

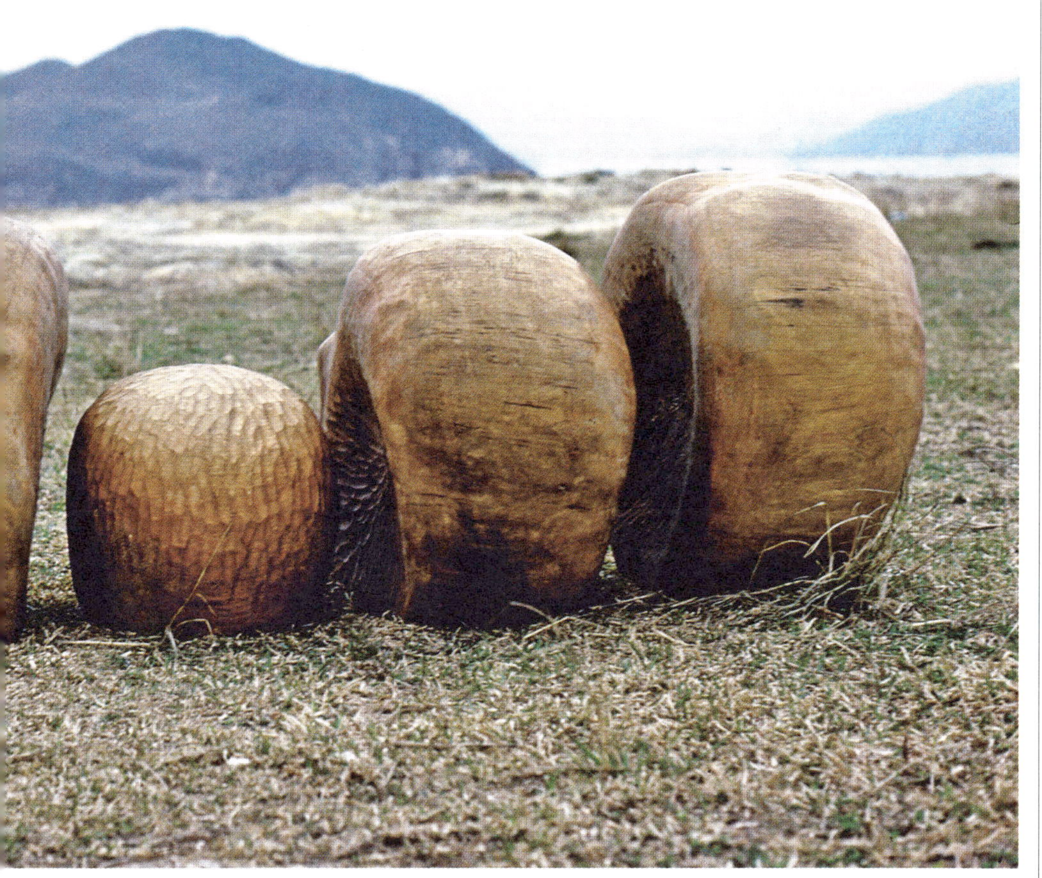

PERSPECTIVES 247

Memory is at the core of Leung Mee Ping's practice. Her body of work involves collecting objects to read a relationship between the individual, their place, and their history, establishing a dialogue with the passing of time. Through gathering what others have left behind—including tea bags, hair, and mailboxes—Leung anchors her practice in ordinary objects.

Monumental in its ambition, *Memorise the Future* consists of ten thousand individual shoes, each between ten and twelve centimetres in length, made of hair collected over a period of seventeen years and from more than one hundred countries. Leung's sources include family members, friends, flight attendants, senior homes, and hair salons. Forming shoes in a size suitable for a child with hair from diverse sources, Leung brings together races, ages, genders, and geographies in a shared purpose. A fallen hair usually evokes regeneration, and by using hair to craft child-sized shoes, the artist highlights the process of loss and growth in individual existence.   CC

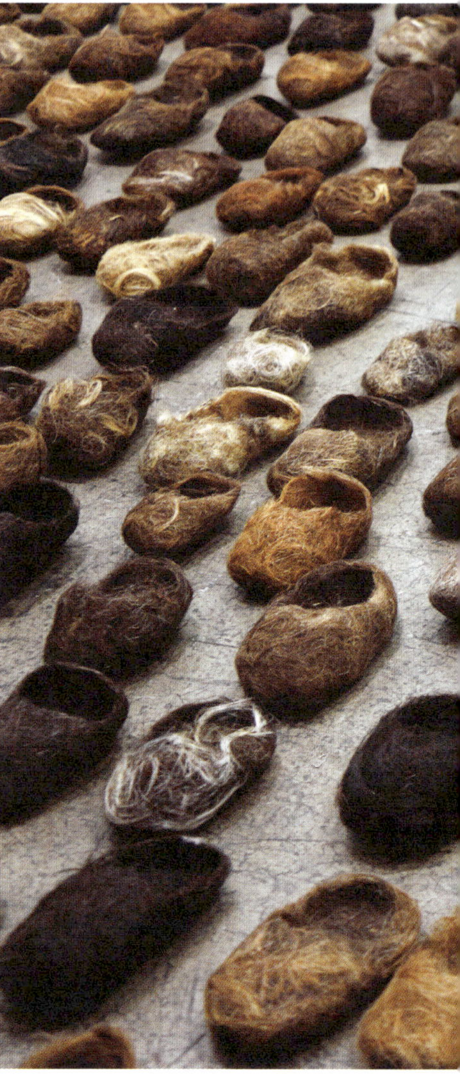

Leung Mee Ping (born 1961, Hong Kong)
Memorise the Future
1998–2015
Human hair
Dimensions variable
2015.721

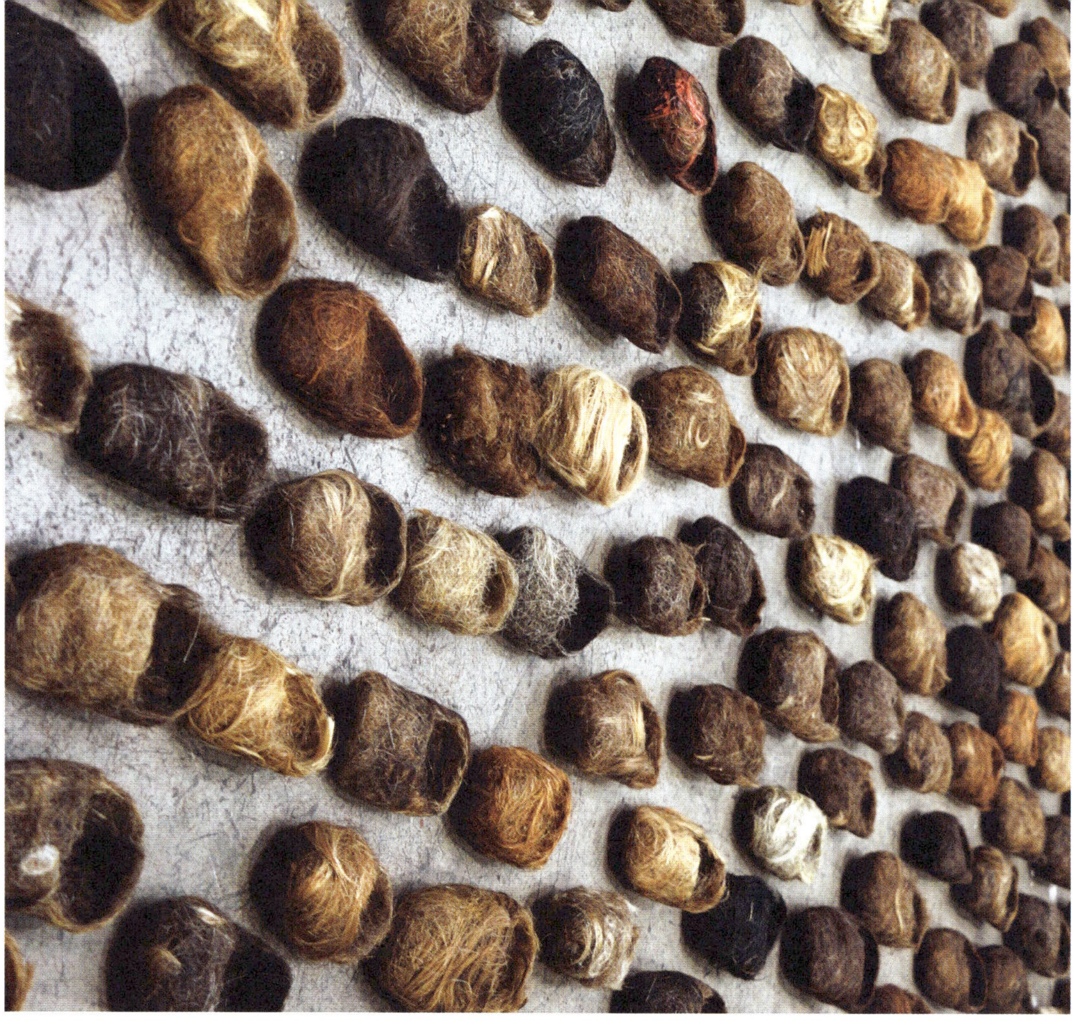

Irene Chou's powerfully idiosyncratic style of ink painting includes linear, splash, and wash techniques. Her works often incorporate spherical and biomorphic elements in abstract compositions that evoke a cosmic universe. Her paintings possess an enigmatic quality that makes them markedly distinct from the work of her contemporaries, and she often referred to her images as representations of her mind.

Chou spent her formative years in Shanghai, where she grew up in a progressive, intellectual household. Her parents introduced her to European and American art and literature, and she went on to study economics at Shanghai's prestigious St John's University. In 1949, in the aftermath of the Chinese Civil War, Chou and her husband, the worldly and sophisticated Yang Yanqi, settled in Hong Kong. While Yang became a successful screenwriter, lyricist, and film director, Chou began to establish herself as an artist. She first studied painting with Zhao Shao'ang, quickly mastering the naturalistic Lingnan style. In the 1960s, she began to study contemporary Euro-American art history with the Chicago-trained artist Kam Ka-lun at the Chinese University of Hong Kong's Extramural Studies Department. She also studied lithography with American artist Joan Ferrer, who had been an assistant to Salvador Dalí.

It was after meeting Lui Shou-kwan, however, that Chou found her artistic voice. By the 1970s, her painting had reached its maturity in works that translate the natural world into dark, sometimes foreboding, abstract compositions. Chou was a committed practitioner of *qigong* and had an enduring interest in spirituality. Early paintings such as the meticulously executed *Christmas Tree* convey spaces filled with mysterious linear and biomorphic elements that draw from the natural world but are clearly not of it.

While the 1970s was a decade of significant artistic achievement for Chou, it was overshadowed by the deaths of Lui and her husband. After a period of deep grief, she emerged with a renewed vigour and optimism, evident in a more spontaneous and expressive method of working centred on what she called the impact motif. This is a physically demanding gestural stroke that produces a directional splash effect. *Impact II* was made at an especially productive and experimental moment. At the composition's centre is a red sphere set off by a dynamic radius of splashed ink and circular brushstrokes. Using both wet and dry techniques, Chou creates a powerful core that seems to exert a gravitational pull on the other elements.

This impact motif forms the dark surface that dominates Chou's *Movement II*, where graduated splashes frame a watery red vortex-like opening that descends towards a red focal point. Erotic and elemental, this work demonstrates how Chou never shied away from depicting aspects of her sexuality. The intimacy of *Movement II* epitomises Chou's unique style of abstract painting as a representation of a profound view of individual consciousness and its place in the universe.   TP

Irene Chou (born 1924, Shanghai; died 2011, Australia)
Movement II
ca. 1985
Ink and colour on paper, hanging scroll
138.7 × 69.6 cm
2012.1637

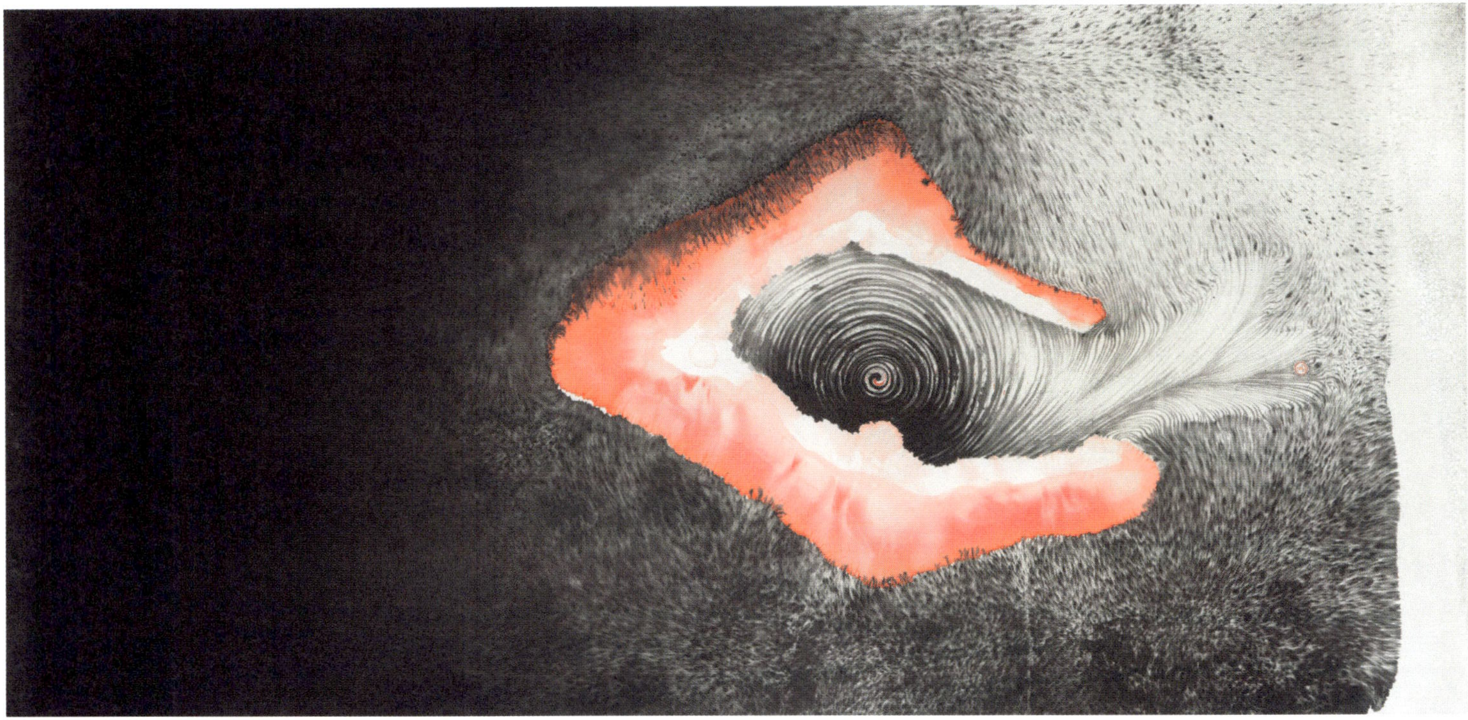

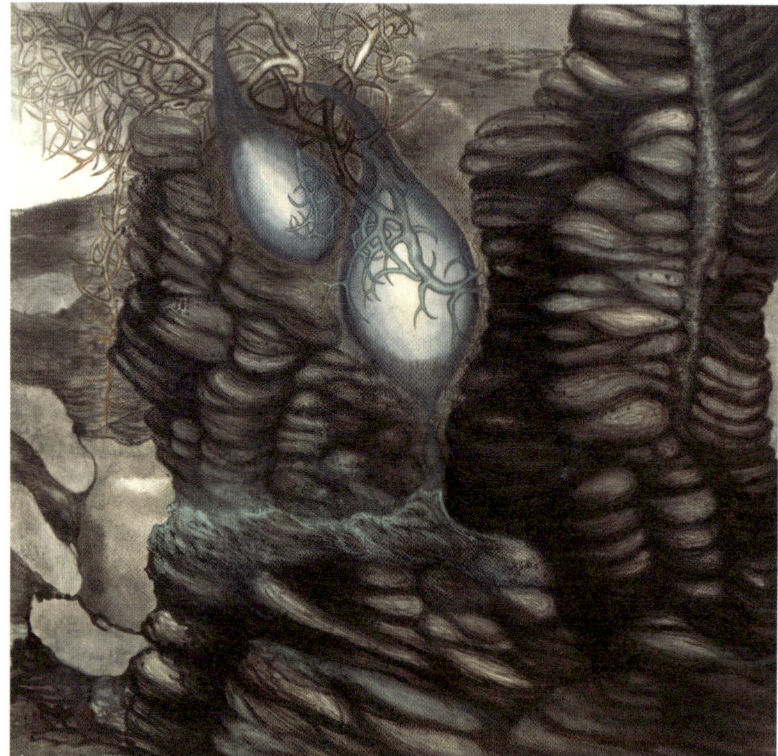

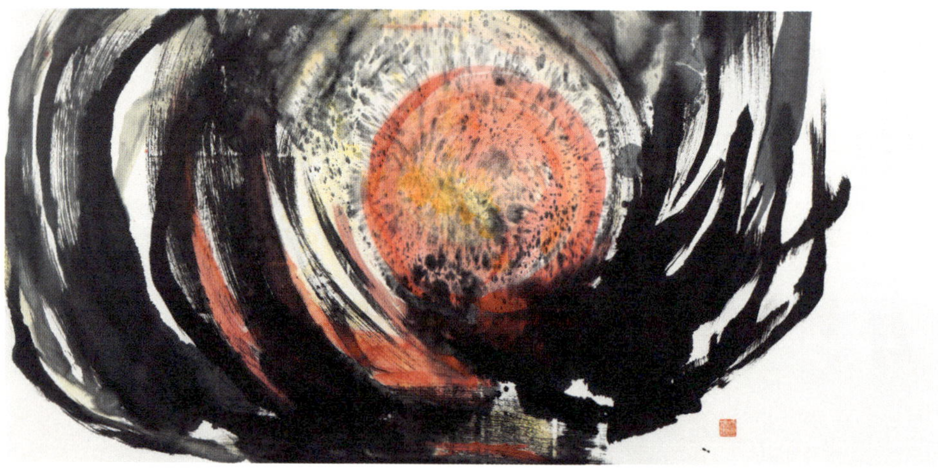

Christmas Tree
1970s
Ink and colour on paper
91.7 × 95.3 cm
2012.1636

Impact II
1977
Ink and colour on paper
66 × 139 cm
Gift of MK Lau Foundation Ltd, 2018
2018.245

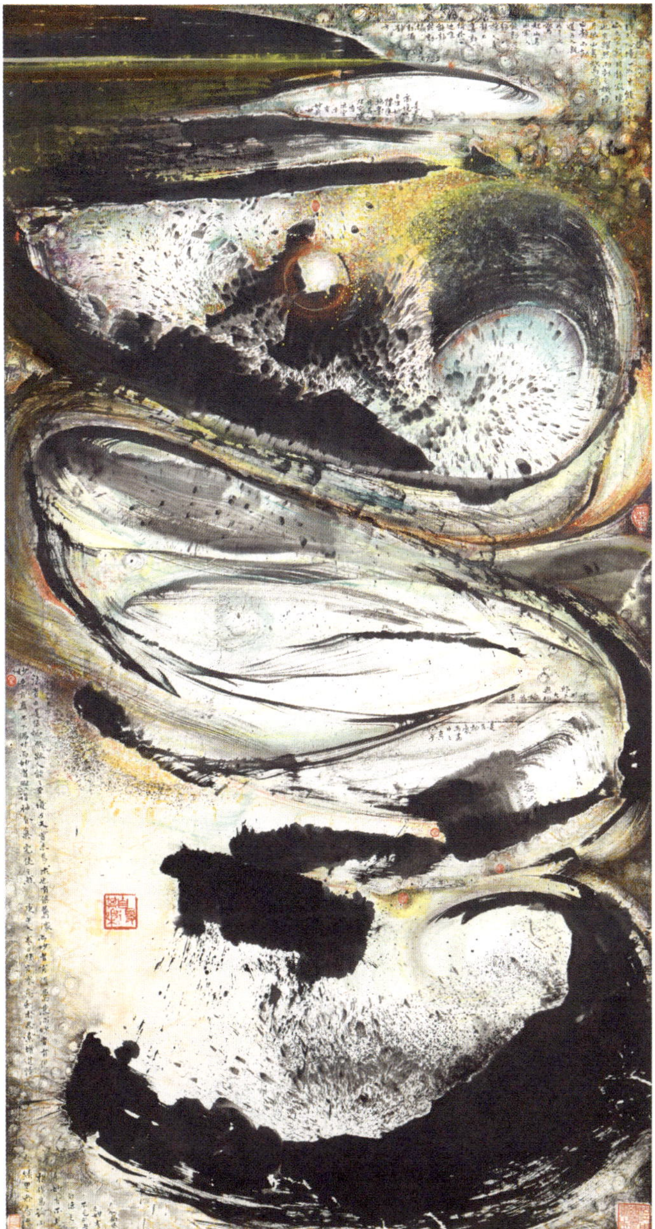

Untitled
1990
Ink and colour on paper
179.7 × 96.6 cm
2017.249

Painted when Luis Chan was eighty years old, this exuberant composition of people gathered for a special occasion is rich in detail yet fantastical and even surreal. Chan was a famously gregarious and active figure on the Hong Kong art scene, and figures in landscapes, both real and imagined, were a favourite subject. The vividly coloured outfits of this crowd lend the painting a festive atmosphere, while the implausibly large fish swimming through the scene could be read as a comparison between a fashionable social life and the exposure of a fishbowl. The title of the painting is playfully inscribed on the green leaf at the top of the composition, a subtle reference to Chan's early interest in typography.

A self-taught artist, Chan was also an influential writer, critic, curator, and teacher whose practice included collages that offer a commentary on exhibition-making and museum displays. He was one of the pioneers of modern art in Hong Kong, with an original and idiosyncratic visual language that constitutes a unique distillation of encounters with a range of styles including the New Ink Movement, Surrealism, Abstract Expressionism, and Pop Art. Often using the materials of traditional Chinese painting, Chan had a spontaneous approach to art-making that suggests free associations of the subconscious mind.   TP

Luis Chan (born 1905, Panama; died 1995, Hong Kong)
Greenleaf
1985
Ink and colour on paper
135.7 × 68.5 cm
2019.478

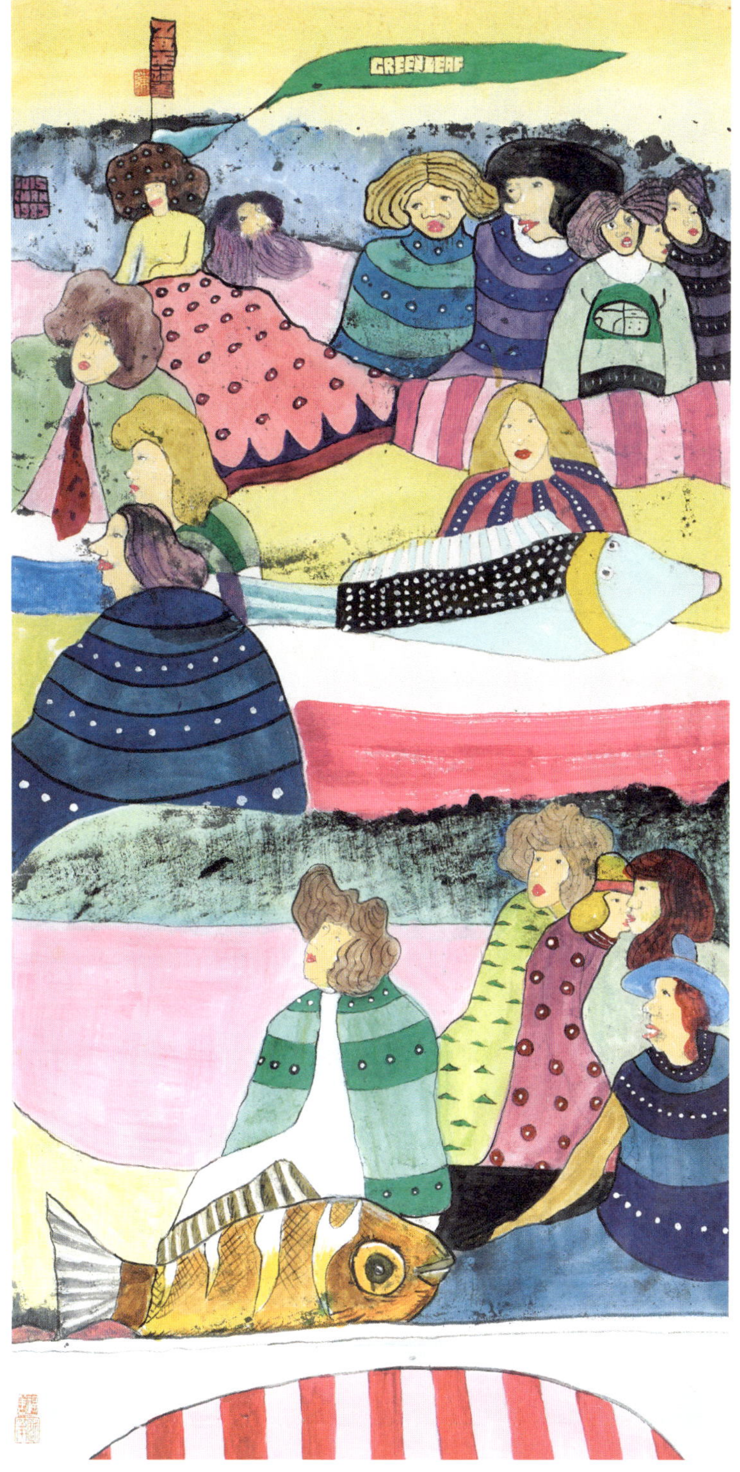

GREENLEAF

In this work, a one-eyed creature is depicted in profile against a dense yellow background, baring the seven teeth of the title. With its geometric markings, three legs, skunk-like tail, oversized jaw, and red gills, Gaylord Chan's fantastic zoomorphic subject recalls the deepest historical origins of visual representation. Looking directly at the viewer, the creature's single eye calls to mind the evil-eye talismans traditionally used across Western Asia to ward off misfortune. Chan's practice of layering colours gives his paintings a complexity of tone and texture that contrasts with the simplicity of his compositions. His representation of an invertebrate at the bottom of the painting has a translucent appearance that suggests the fossilised remains of a prehistoric animal, or the totemic creatures of traditional bark paintings by Indigenous Australian artists.

Taught by the painter Hon Chi-fun and the artist and architect Tao Ho, Chan only began painting seriously at the age of forty-two, when he was employed at Cable & Wireless. He became a singular force in abstract painting, known for his vocabulary of semi-figurative and erotic motifs in bold colours. A tireless innovator, in later years he used digital technologies to expand his practice, to encompass prints, banners, and laser-cut wood paintings.   TP

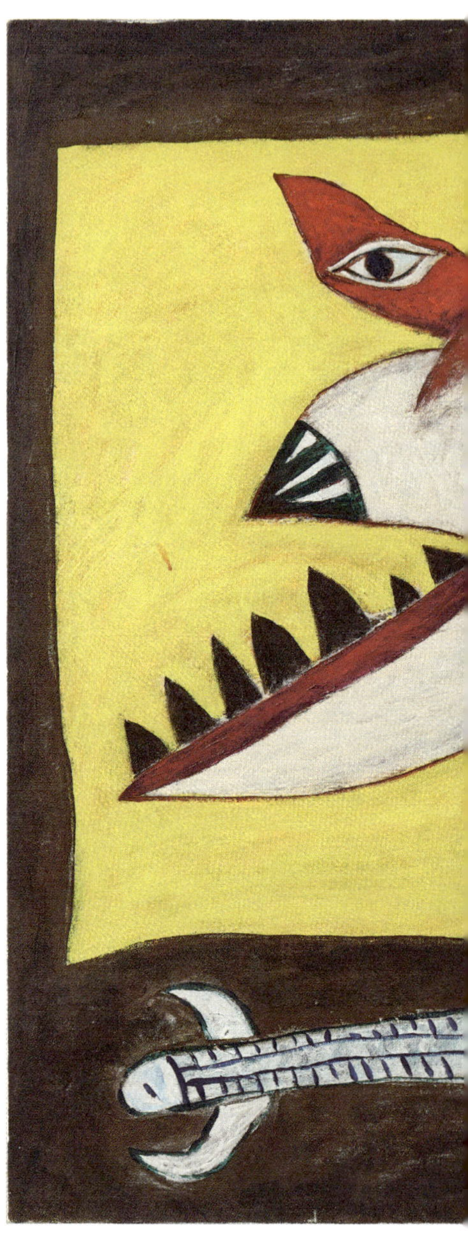

Gaylord Chan (1925–2020, Hong Kong)
Seven Teeth
1999
Acrylic on canvas
91.5 × 122.1 cm
2018.392

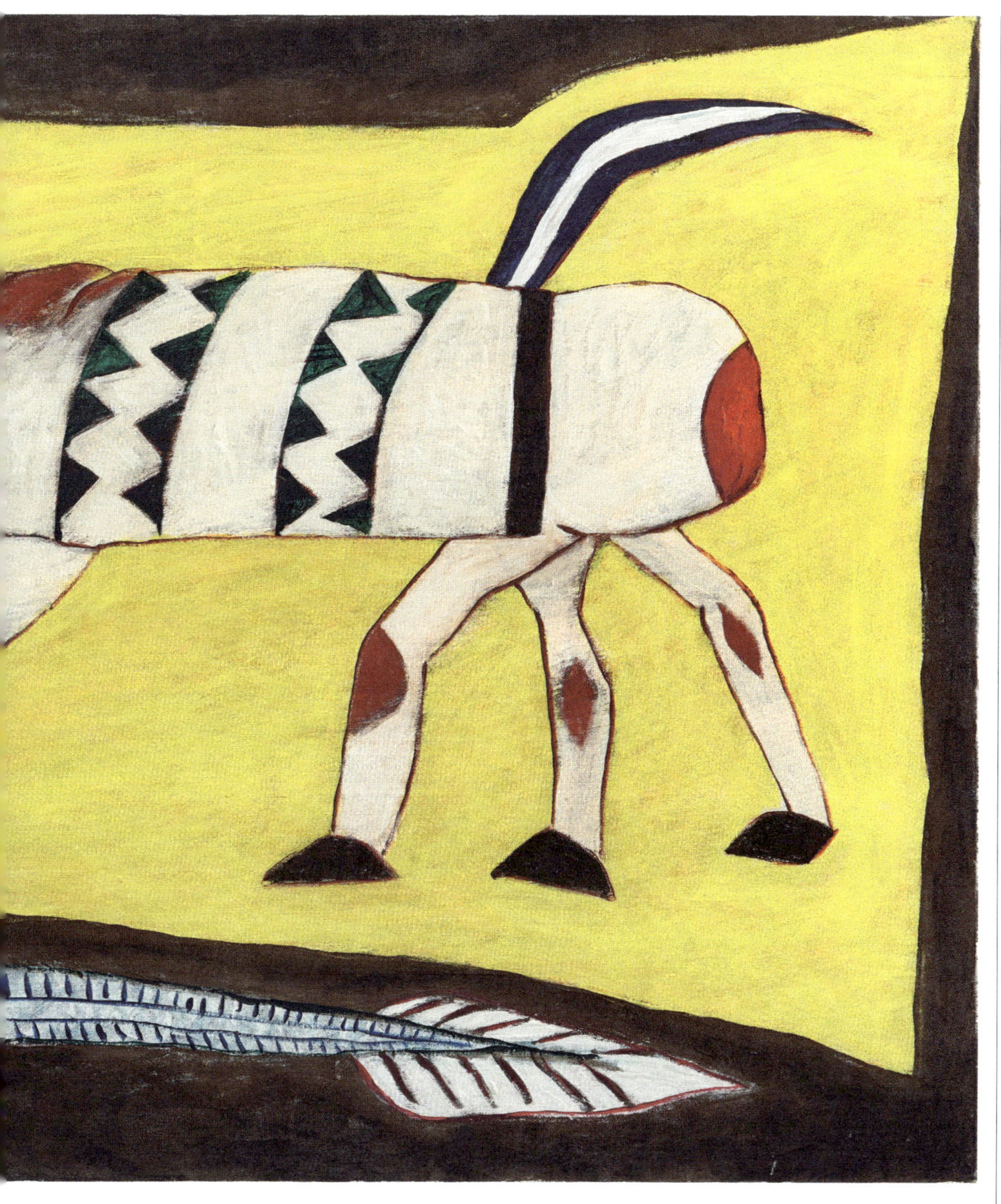

DOOR GAMES WINDOW FRAMES

A city in transition, on canvas and on screen

Using techniques of photorealism and *trompe l'oeil*, Szeto Keung's painting is a homage to Marcel Duchamp's *Tu m'* (1918), one of the most important works in the history of Conceptual Art. It is a layered composition that references the original work—Duchamp's final painting—and Jasper Johns's later interpretation of it, *According to What* (1964). Where Duchamp incorporated a readymade bottle brush into his work, Szeto's objects are meticulously painted to look like readymades. He depicts an accordion-fold colour swatch bursting out of two paper gift bags, clear references to Duchamp's lozenge-shaped colour swatches and an echo of their transformation in *According to What*.

Tu m' after Duchamp is an art history lesson, in which Szeto simultaneously looks back and gestures humorously to the present. The two paper bags each introduce a canonical artist of the twentieth century: Pablo Picasso and Henri Matisse. Matisse's design for the American department store Bloomingdale's is shown inside a larger gift bag from the Museum of Modern Art in New York bearing the partial signature of Picasso. Along the top of this bag, Szeto includes the details of his own painting, inserting himself into a wider art history.

After moving to New York, Szeto was associated with a group of Chinese émigré artists who experimented with photorealistic practices in the 1970s and 1980s. His work stands out for its juxtaposition of images of familiar objects with ideas of identity and memory.   TP

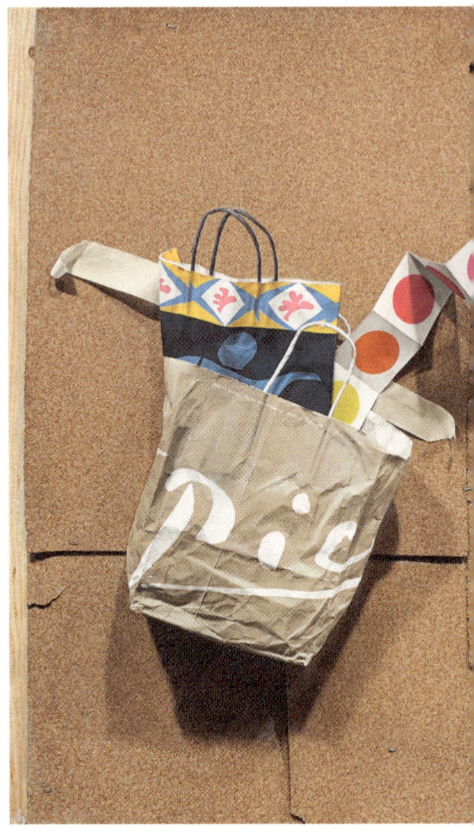

Szeto Keung (1948, Guangdong; died 2011, United States)
Tu m' after Duchamp
1983
Acrylic and mixed media on linen
113.2 × 223.9 × 5.3 cm
2019.380

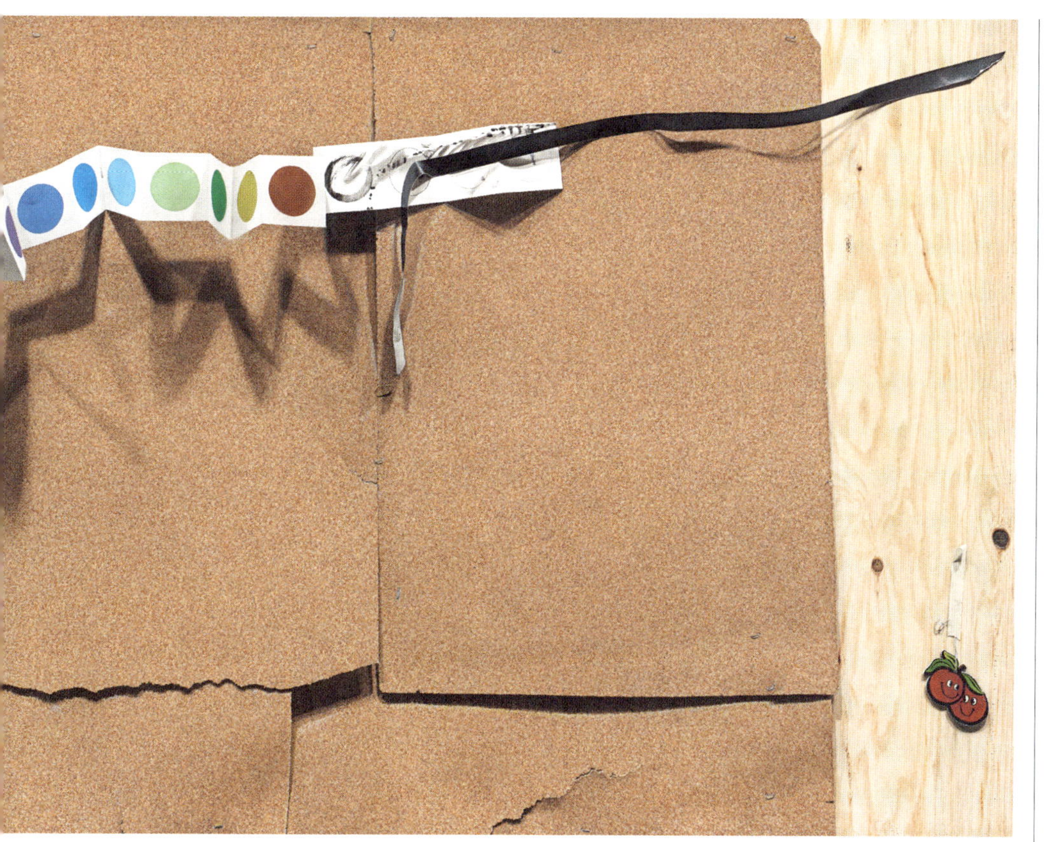

Fire Painting, Butterfly, by Kwok Mang-ho, also known as Frog King Kwok, expresses the artist's career-spanning concern with processes of transformation, in both material and visual terms. A collage of burned Chinese lantern paper fixed in place with lacquer, the composition is part of a small series from the late 1970s that reflects Kwok's interest in alchemical processes and the elements of traditional Chinese divination. His experimental, often performative works include what became known as his fire paintings and sculptures, which are constructed from burned found materials. This body of work articulates a connection with ancient rituals, specifically the reading of oracle bones. In this practice, heat is applied to animal bones to elicit signs from the heavens, which are then interpreted by shamans or diviners. Kwok's fire paintings also refer to the burning of offerings in ancestor worship, an activity believed to influence the fate of the living.

The title of this work evokes the Chinese philosopher Zhuangzi's dream of being a butterfly, and his reflection on the nature of reality. Accentuating the association with shifts between different states of consciousness, the image recalls Rorschach inkblot tests, tools in psychoanalysis meant to access the subconscious mind. Butterflies are the result of one of nature's most spectacular metamorphoses, and Kwok similarly takes his work from one state to another—from ordinary materials to art.   TP

Kwok Mang-ho (a.k.a. Frog King Kwok) (born 1947, Guangdong)
Fire Painting, Butterfly
1978
Lacquer and burnt-paper collage
63.5 × 50.5 cm
2016.260

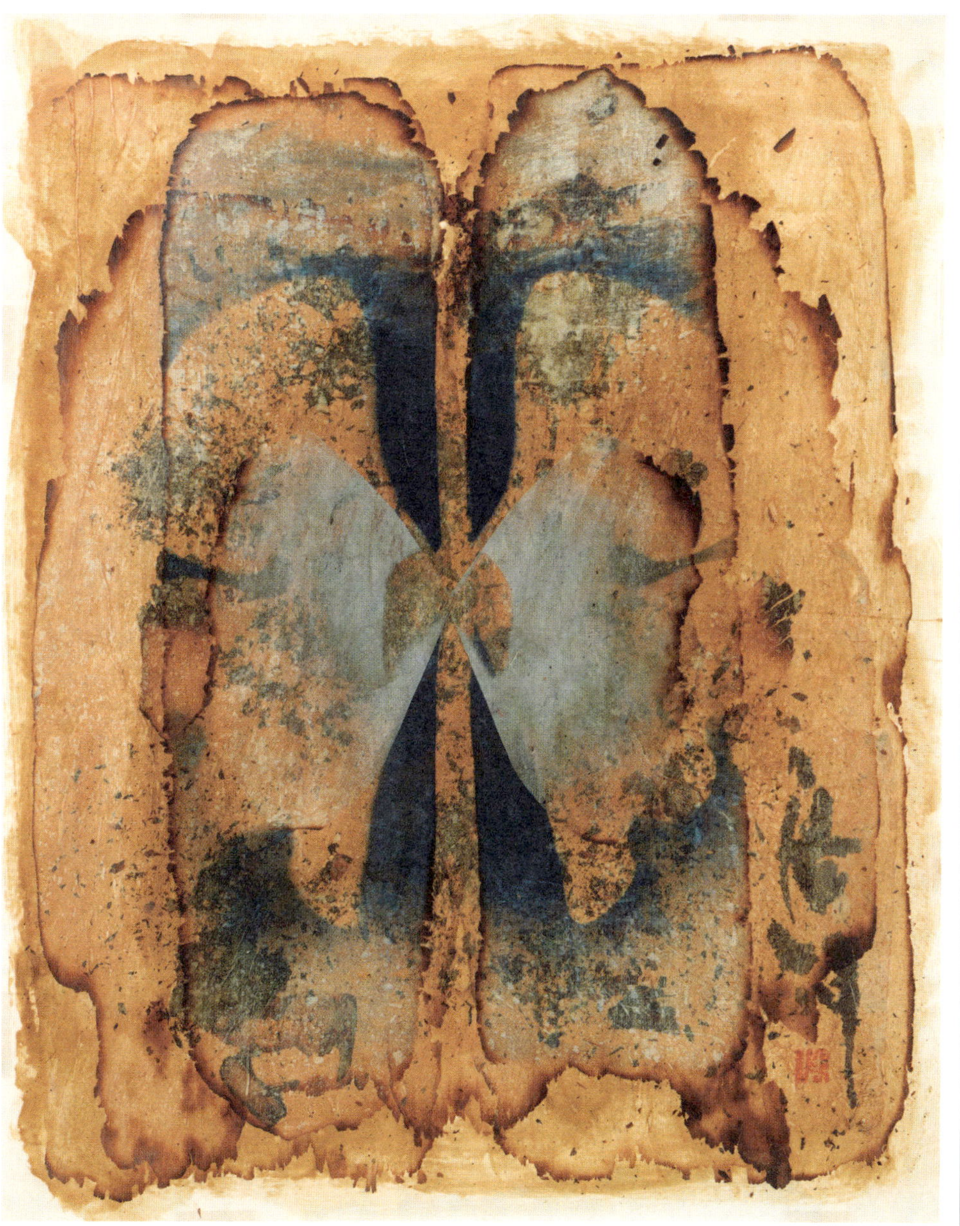

Antonio Mak often addressed dichotomies and oppositions in his work. *Horse and shadow I* is a playful visual pun that has a deeper resonance with the logic of Western perspectival constructions as well as the Taoist concept of yin and yang. The contrast between the white horse and its shadow in the foreground and the black horse on the opposite side of the rectangular divider abruptly transforms perception. The drawing, grounded in reality, precise in its depiction of anatomical detail, but ultimately absurd, encapsulates Mak's enduring interest in the relationship between illusion and the observed world.

Trained at London's Slade School of Fine Art, Mak was a highly skilled draughtsman and depicted his subjects in precise black-and-white drawings in ink and pencil as well as in fluid, confident watercolours. Many of his works contain references to images from traditional Chinese visual culture and European art history, using drawing as a strategy to explore the natural world and to challenge conventional depictions of it. Known primarily as a sculptor, Mak worked with the lost-wax technique and produced relatively few finished sculptures. He did, however, leave a large body of drawings and collages that form an eloquent record of his visual explorations and his artistic thinking.   BW

Antonio Mak (born 1951, Philippines; died 1994, Hong Kong)
Horse and shadow I
1986
Ink and watercolour on paper
27.9 × 38 cm
2017.83

Chang Chao-Tang (born 1943, Taiwan)
Photograph of sculptor Antonio Mak, Taipei, Taiwan, 1985
1985
Silver-print proof
25.3 × 38.1 cm
Gift of Chang Chao-Tang, 2017
2017.211

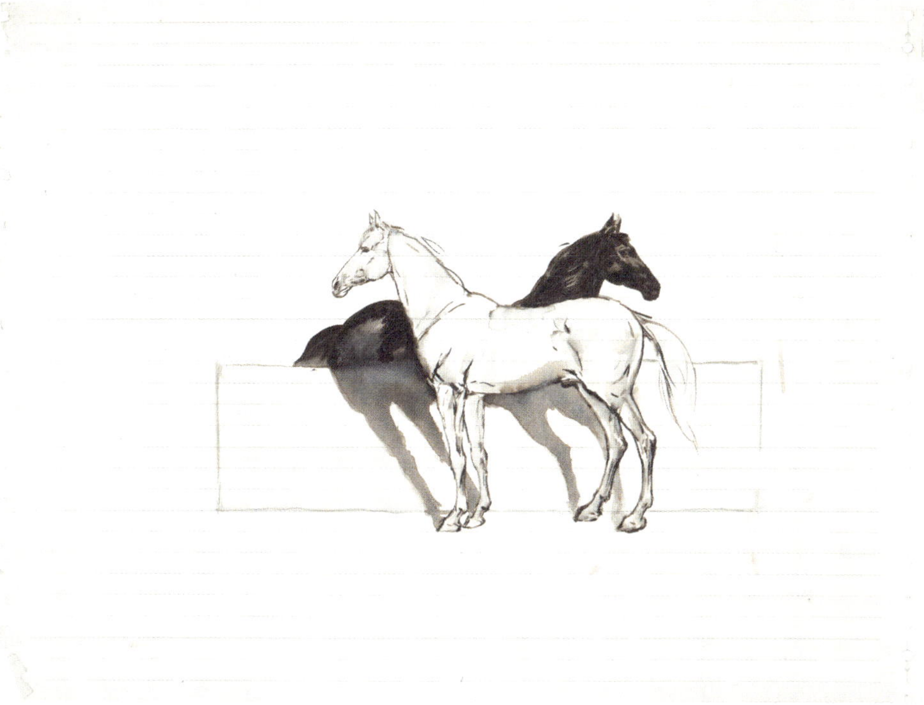

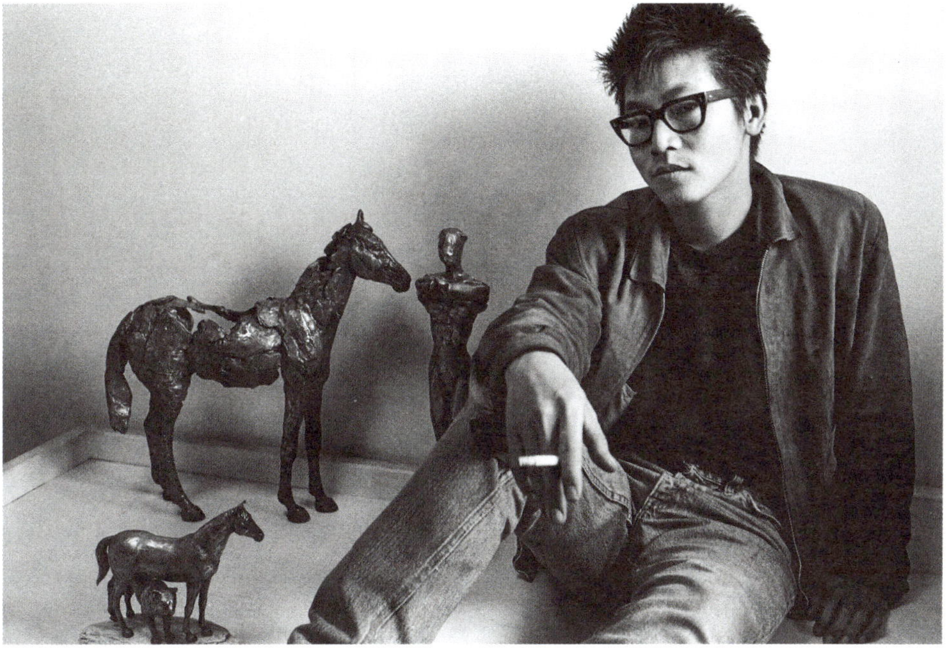

Gravity Hoop is both a sculptural work and an experiential instrument that records Ho Siu Kee's career-long interest in perception, space, and the body. The artist becomes part of the object in what he refers to as body sculpture. Suspending himself upside down from the top of the circular steel structure and positioning his body as the centre of gravity, he challenges the conventional way of understanding the natural order of the world. He explicitly draws on the work of philosopher Maurice Merleau-Ponty, who defines the body as a fundamental instrument of perception. In more recent works, Ho has transitioned from an exploration of the body and perception to a more meditative, spiritual investigation.   FT

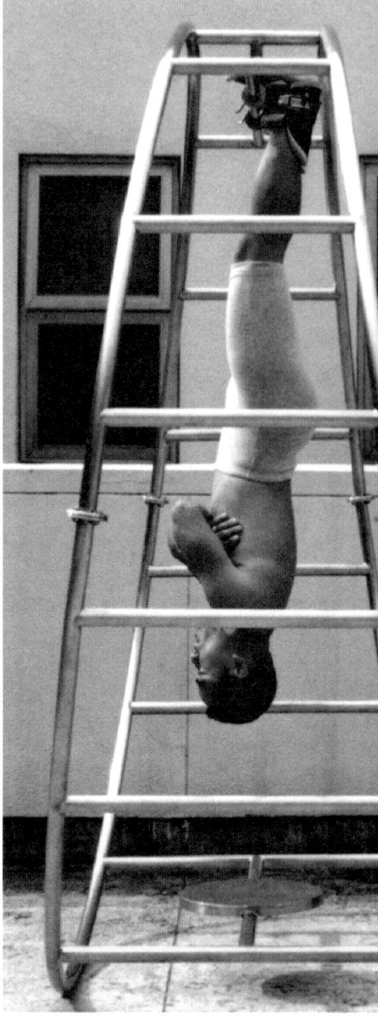

Ho Siu Kee (born 1964, Hong Kong)
Gravity Hoop
1996
Steel and inkjet print
Steel structure: 241.5 × 253 × 98 cm
Photo: 79.3 × 119.2 cm
2015.388

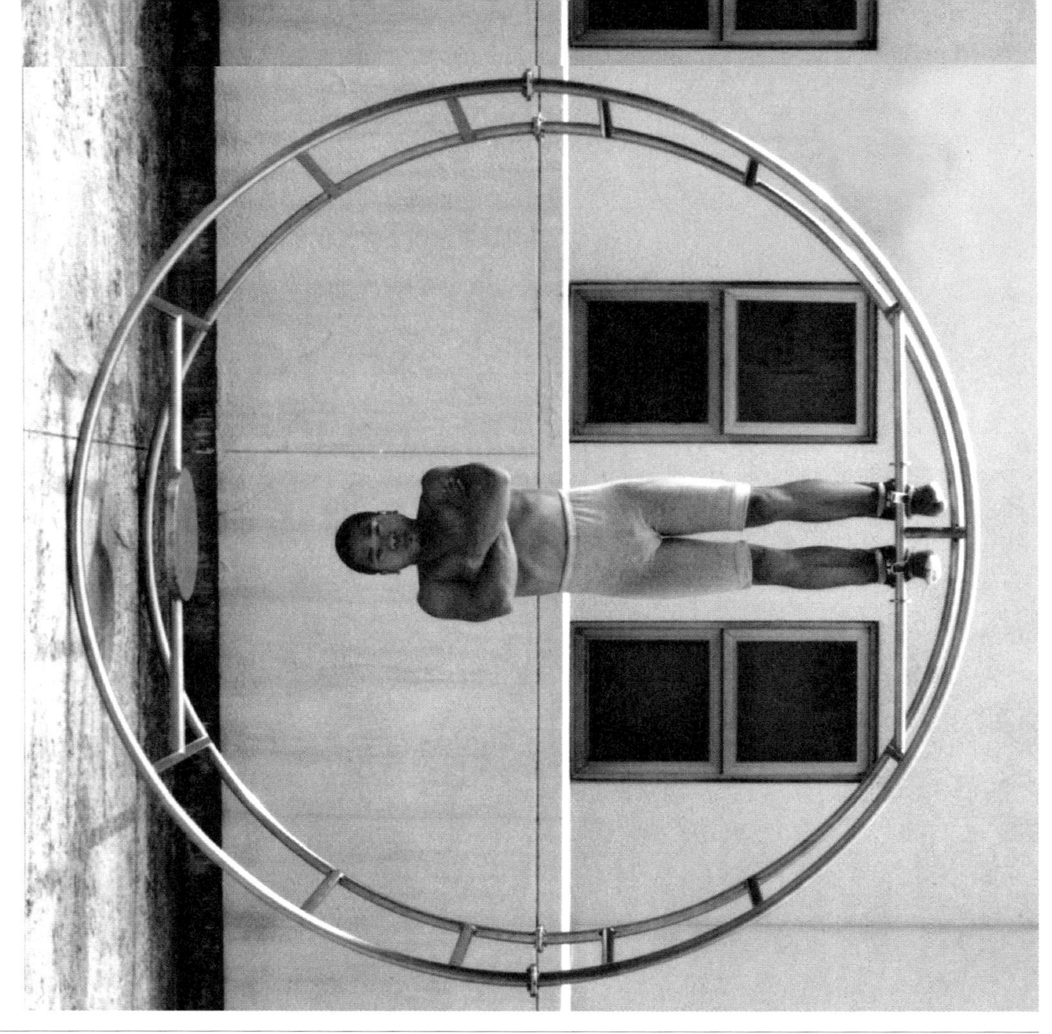

This painting is Wong Yankwai's response to the events of 4 June 1989 in Beijing's Tiananmen Square. Painted in a sombre palette of opaque peacock blue and burnt umber, the abstract forms are enlivened by spontaneous brushwork, linear marks, and symbols. Wong's distinctive technique of layering colour in a non-hierarchical way creates a relationship of tension between foreground and background, a dynamic that is accentuated by the incorporation of paper and bandages into the composition.

Known for his vividly colourful abstract paintings, Wong is also an accomplished writer, poet, photographer, and blues musician, and an award-winning screenwriter and art director for film. He is among the earliest foreign-trained artists in Hong Kong, having studied in France in the 1970s. After his return to Hong Kong in 1979, he was hired by Chan Koonchung to work as an art director for *City Magazine*, a publication that gained recognition for its experimental graphic character. The events of 1989 were an important moment for political consciousness in Hong Kong, inspiring many forms of interdisciplinary artistic expression. Seen in this light, Wong's work conveys a sentiment of solidarity with social movements in Beijing and their implications for Hong Kong.   TP

Wong Yankwai (born 1955, Hong Kong)
Failing to Light Up the Night Sky with Tracer Fire
1989
Acrylic, bandage strips, and paper on canvas
152 × 152 cm
2020.149

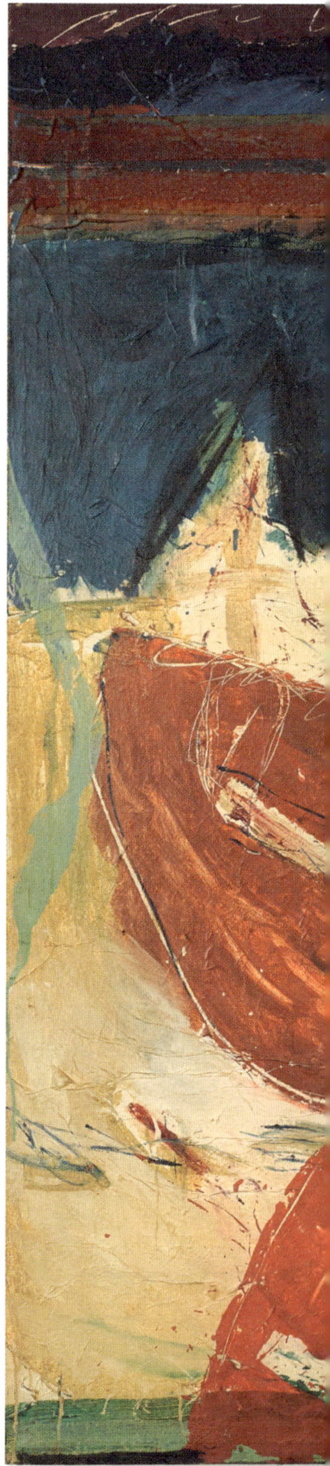

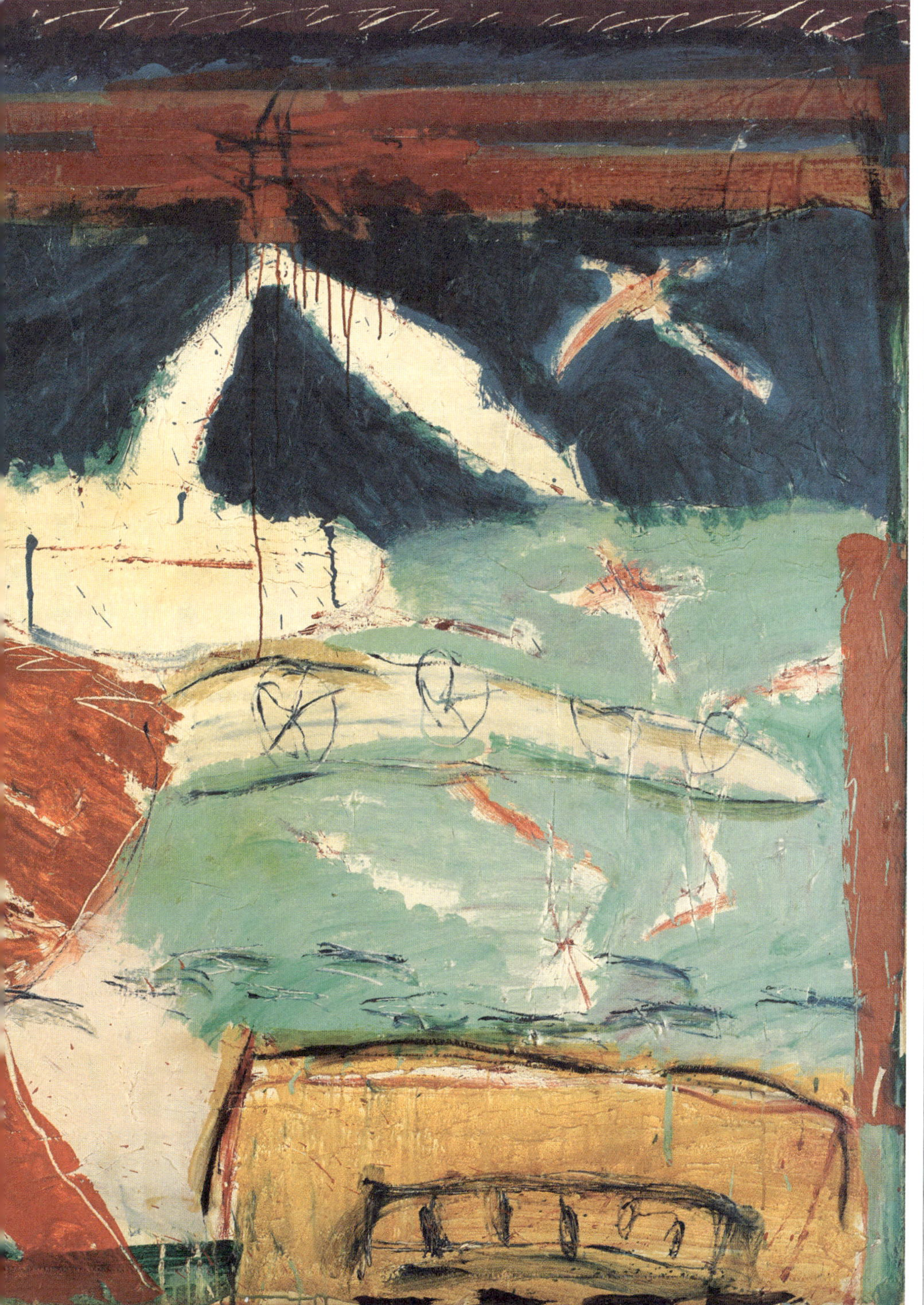

The Floor is an intimate portrait of Yeung Tong Lung's studio in Kennedy Town. At once hyperrealistic and exaggerated, the image expresses the artist's deep familiarity with the space and its intimate connection with his creative work. The studio is depicted as a bright room with well-loved tools and a window looking onto the verdant city. The floor dominates the composition, showing layers of paint marks as traces of a years-long practice. The unusual elongated perspective pushes at the physical limits of the studio. Yeung's practice revolves around observing people, events, and objects in his daily life. Across his body of work, he constructs subjective realities as authentic spaces that exist only in his paintings. Together with Wong Yankwai, Yeung Tong Lung founded an ambitious, though short-lived, avant-garde art group known as the Quart Society in the early 1990s as a critical, discursive, and exhibition platform. Since then his commitment to the medium of painting has made him an influential figure within artistic circles.   KW

Yeung Tong Lung (born 1956, Fujian)
The Floor
2014
Oil on canvas
243.5 × 91.3 cm
2016.35

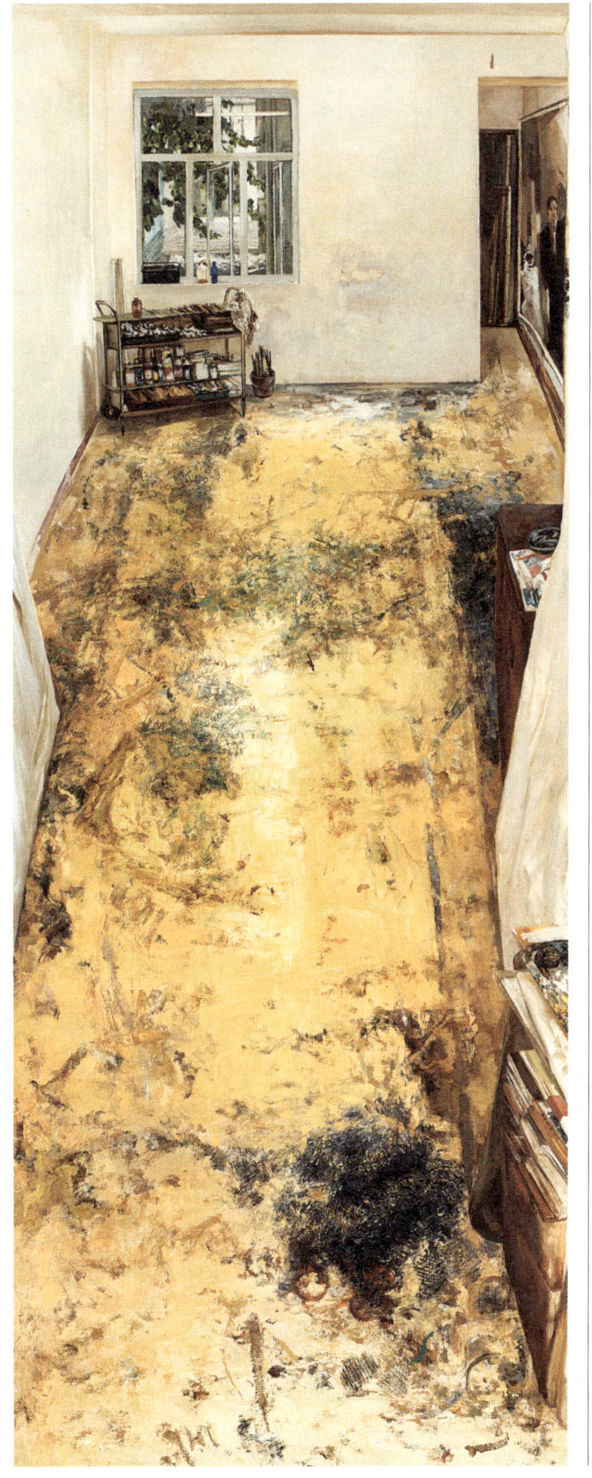

Lui Chun Kwong is known for his spare, analytical compositions of meticulously painted arrangements in muted tones. *The Earth* combines horizontal and vertical trajectories in painterly brushstrokes and drips, clearly expressing the hand of the artist. Divided into three parts, the work's yellow, black, grey, and brown lines seem to mimic the texture of bark or the earth of the work's title. It can be seen as marking a transition between Lui's early figurative paintings and the more precise abstract canvases he would create in later years, which consist of vertical striations. An influential educator, Lui taught for many years in the Department of Fine Arts of the Chinese University of Hong Kong and inspired a generation of artists who approach painting beyond its definition as a representational medium.   FT

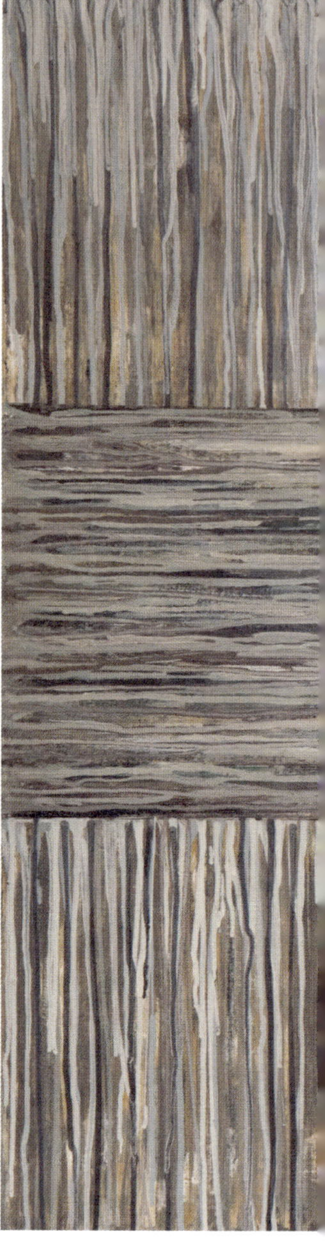

Lui Chun Kwong (born 1956, Guangdong)
The Earth
1994
Acrylic and mixed media on canvas
91.4 × 107.7 × 4.3 cm
2016.838

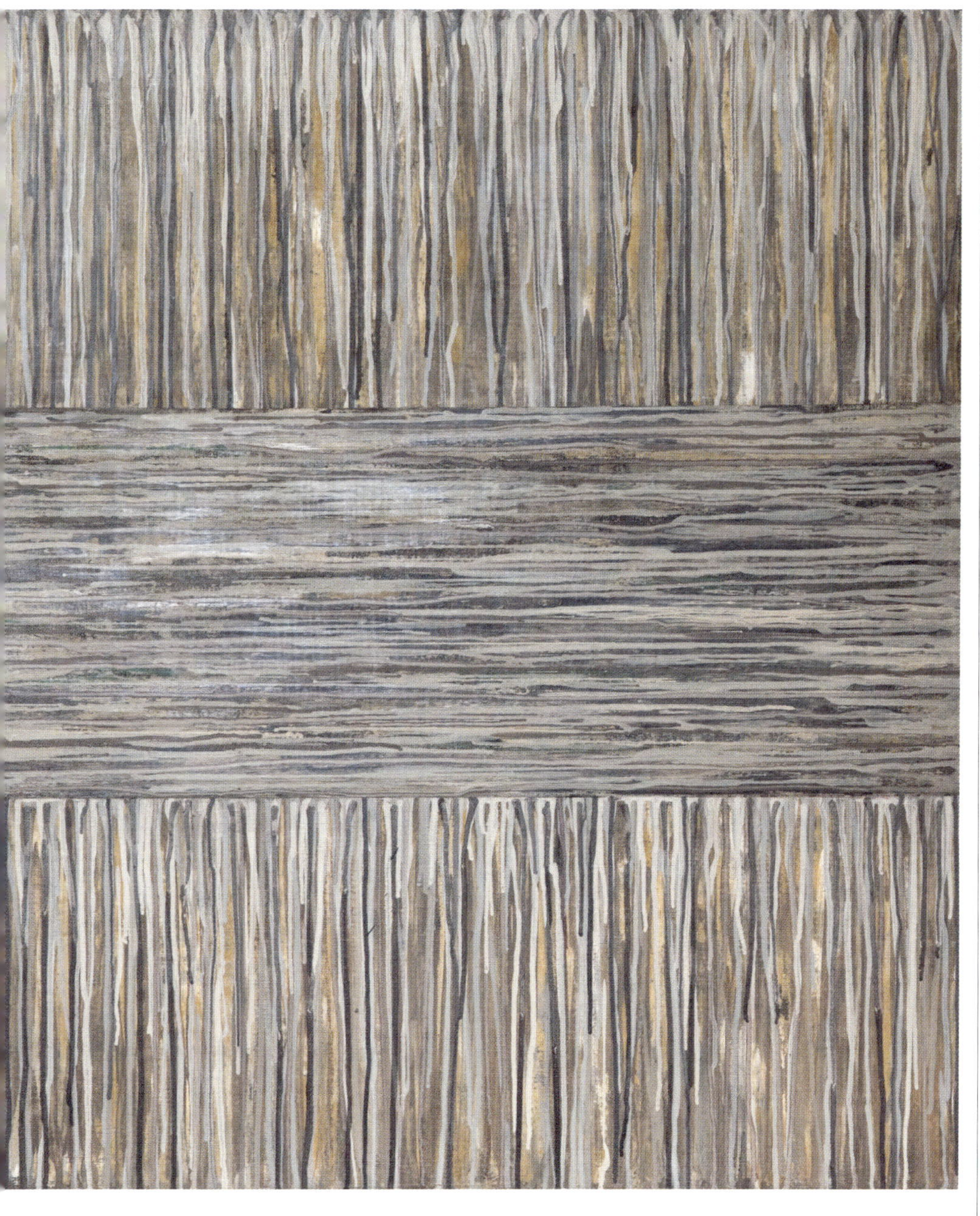

In this three-channel video installation, around five hundred film clips that depict the act of opening and closing windows and doors play in a sequence determined by a computer algorithm. This action is a device commonly used to mark narrative transitions in 1960s Hong Kong cinema, and is especially characteristic of thrillers and melodramas from this period. These seemingly trivial moments offer a point of entry into a deeper reading of the Cantonese cinema of Linda Chiu-han Lai's childhood. The work exemplifies Lai's larger exploration of art mediated by technology, which she articulates as an art historian and curator as well as an artist. Here, she dissects conventional visual elements of dramatic tension: the doors and windows opening and closing, but also close-ups of the facial expressions of the main characters. The random sequences continuously create new visual narratives, inviting the audience to reflect upon their relationship to film.   FT

Linda Chiu-han Lai (born 1957, Hong Kong)
Door Games Window Frames: Near Drama (still)
2012
Three-channel generative digital video projection (black and white, sound)
Continuous
2019.351

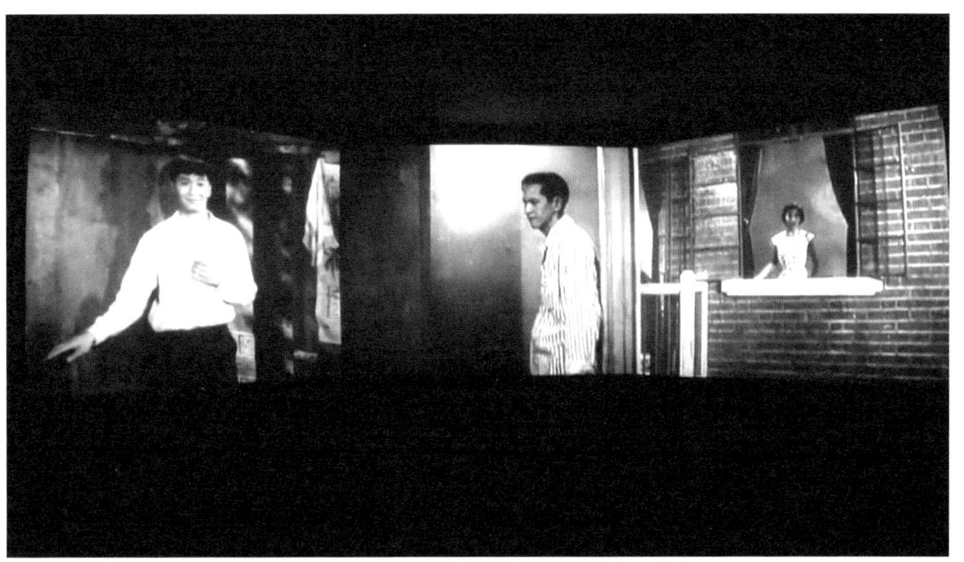

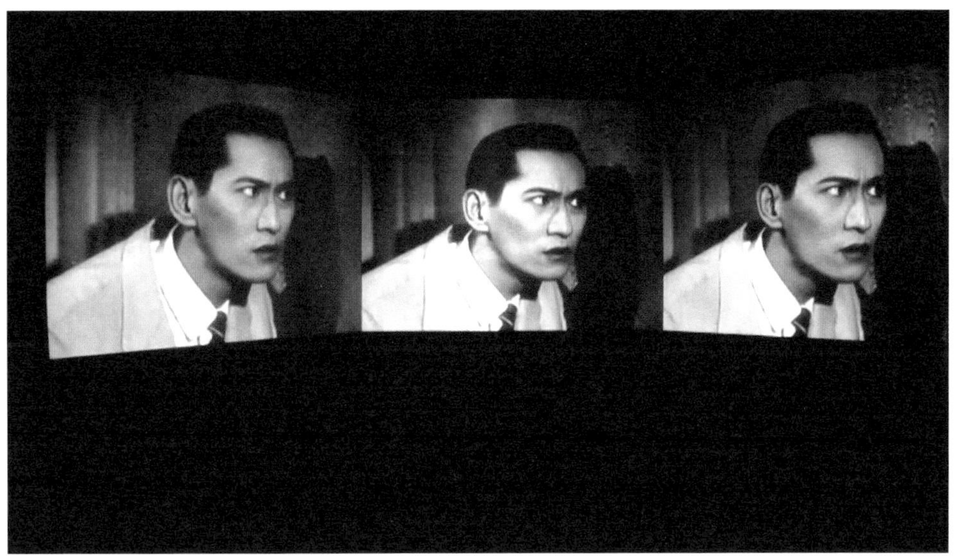

Angela Su's wide-ranging practice expresses her interest in the body as an object of scientific enquiry and curiosity. She frequently examines the transformation of the body and challenges perceptions of physical pain. Su's video *The Assembly Line* explores the connection between the human body and the industrial assembly line. A slideshow of historical photographs juxtaposes images of meat-packing factories, bloody animal carcasses, and workers with prosthetic body parts.

Captions narrate the history of the assembly line: its invention, its proliferation, and its eventual transformation of standard production processes around the world. Su constructs a disturbing story of human and machine, questioning the meaning of existence in the context of capitalist society and technological advances. She seems to ask whether we are autonomous individuals or cogs in the mechanical system of production and consumption.   KW

Angela Su (born 1958, Hong Kong)
***The Assembly Line* (stills)**
2013
Single-channel digital video (black and white, sound)
4 min. 53 sec.
2015.574

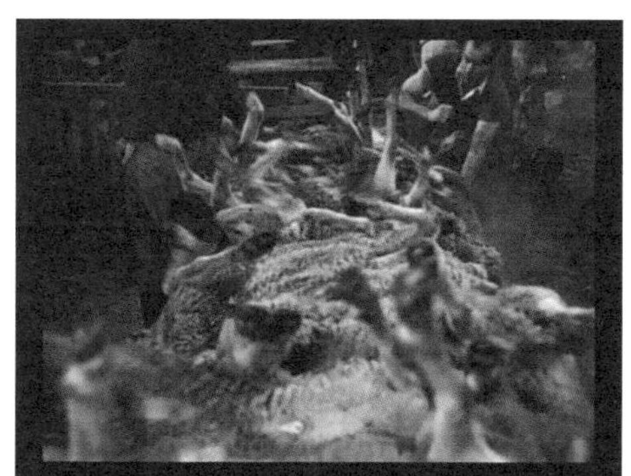

The machine extends the body. The machine amputates the body.

My body that consumes and as a consumable artifact is the extension of the machine.

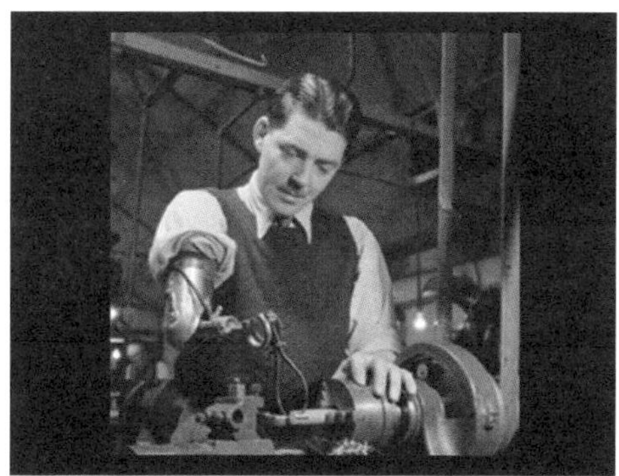

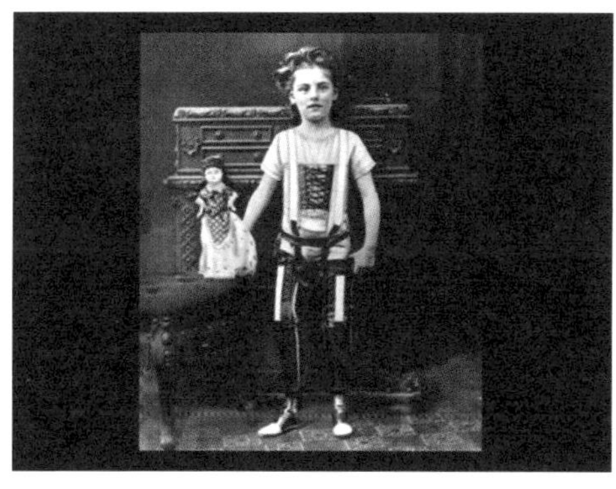

In his conceptual, collaborative practice, Lee Ka-sing uncovers new narrative potential for the medium of photography. Through a number of pioneering projects with poets, musicians, and artists, and editorial activities, including the publication of *Dislocation* magazine, Lee has had a significant influence on artists across many fields. He established OP fotogallery as a curatorial platform that advanced appreciation of photography as an art form in Hong Kong in the 1990s. Many of Lee's works upend the conventional communicative function of graphic design. For example, *In City, 3* is an assemblage of graphic elements and material objects, including a medium-format camera and an orange, forming an anthropomorphic figure that recalls Oskar Schlemmer's costumes for his *Triadic Ballet* at the Bauhaus in the 1920s.

As a connoisseur of early scientific illustrations and traditional Chinese outline drawings, Lee often combines contemporary photographs with historical images to make productive collisions between past and present. He created *City at the End of Time*, one of his most recognised images, for the cover of a bilingual collection of poems by Leung Ping-kwan, a writer with whom he collaborated throughout his career. Leung's poems convey a profound ambivalence towards the 1997 handover, in terms of the apparent instability in cultural identity and the changing sociopolitical landscape. Lee translates Leung's sentiment in visual terms, presenting a complex layering of references to cultural conventions and the urban landscape. Ghostly images of Guanyin (bodhisattva of compassion) in the style of old advertising posters and a Chinese painting are superimposed over aerial views of the modern city, notably Kai Tak Airport.

Think Poetry, one of twenty-five works from Lee's *Forty Poems* series, exemplifies his approach to creating a new reading through unlikely combinations of found objects. Over two wooden blocks, he superimposes a graphic treatment of mathematical diagrams to suggest a cartographic interpretation. The series marked the beginning of Lee's appropriation of his own commercial photographs for new artistic projects. He moved between analogue film photography and the digital image editing and scanning techniques that had emerged in the early 1990s. This extended his career-long interest in constructing narratives through collage and the juxtaposition of multiple views. Across his practice, Lee has expanded lens culture beyond the two-dimensional photographic print and prefigured the visual promiscuity of the post-internet age.   BW

Lee Ka-sing (born 1954, Hong Kong)
City at the End of Time
1992
Chromogenic print
143 × 101.5 cm
2018.228

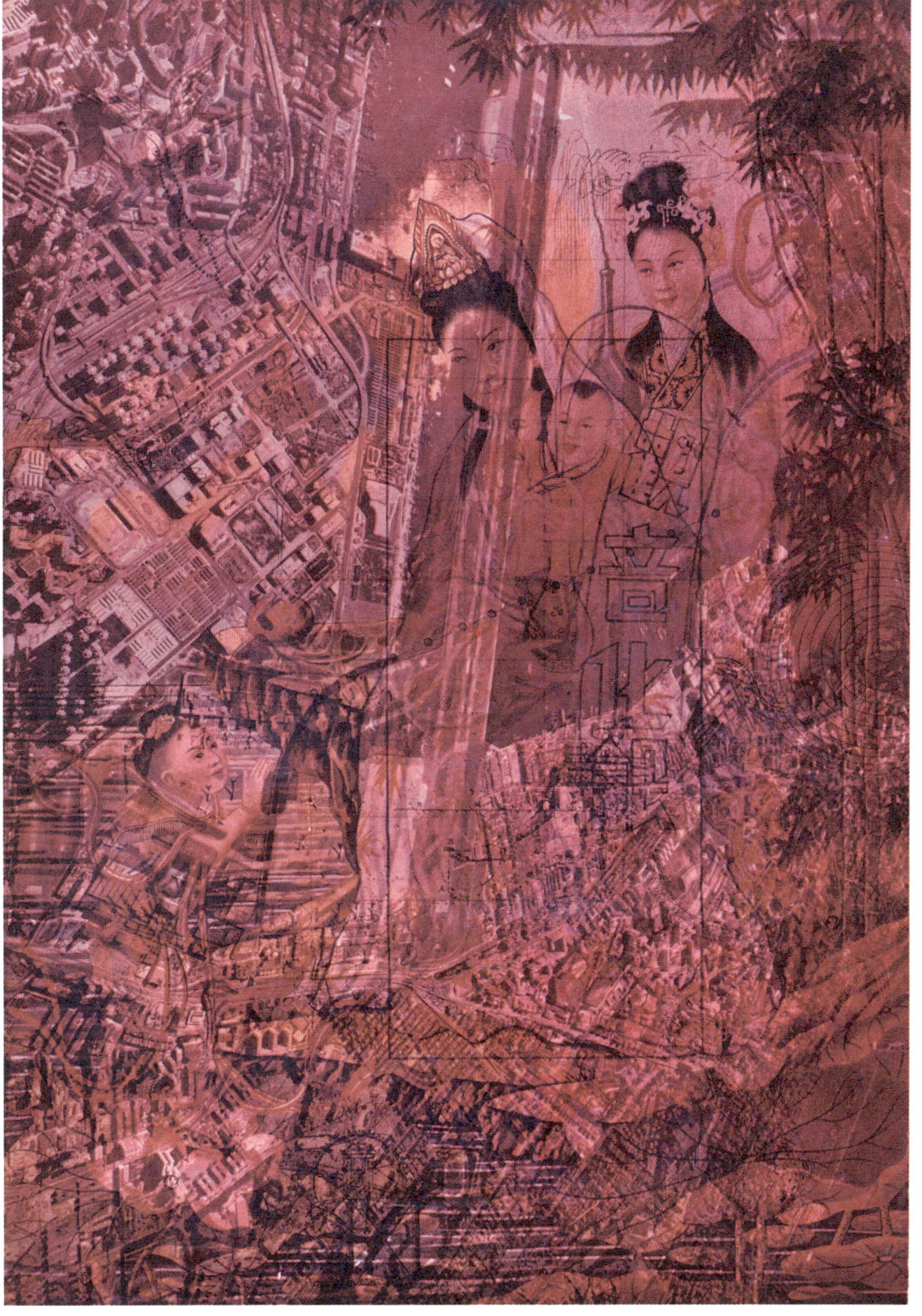

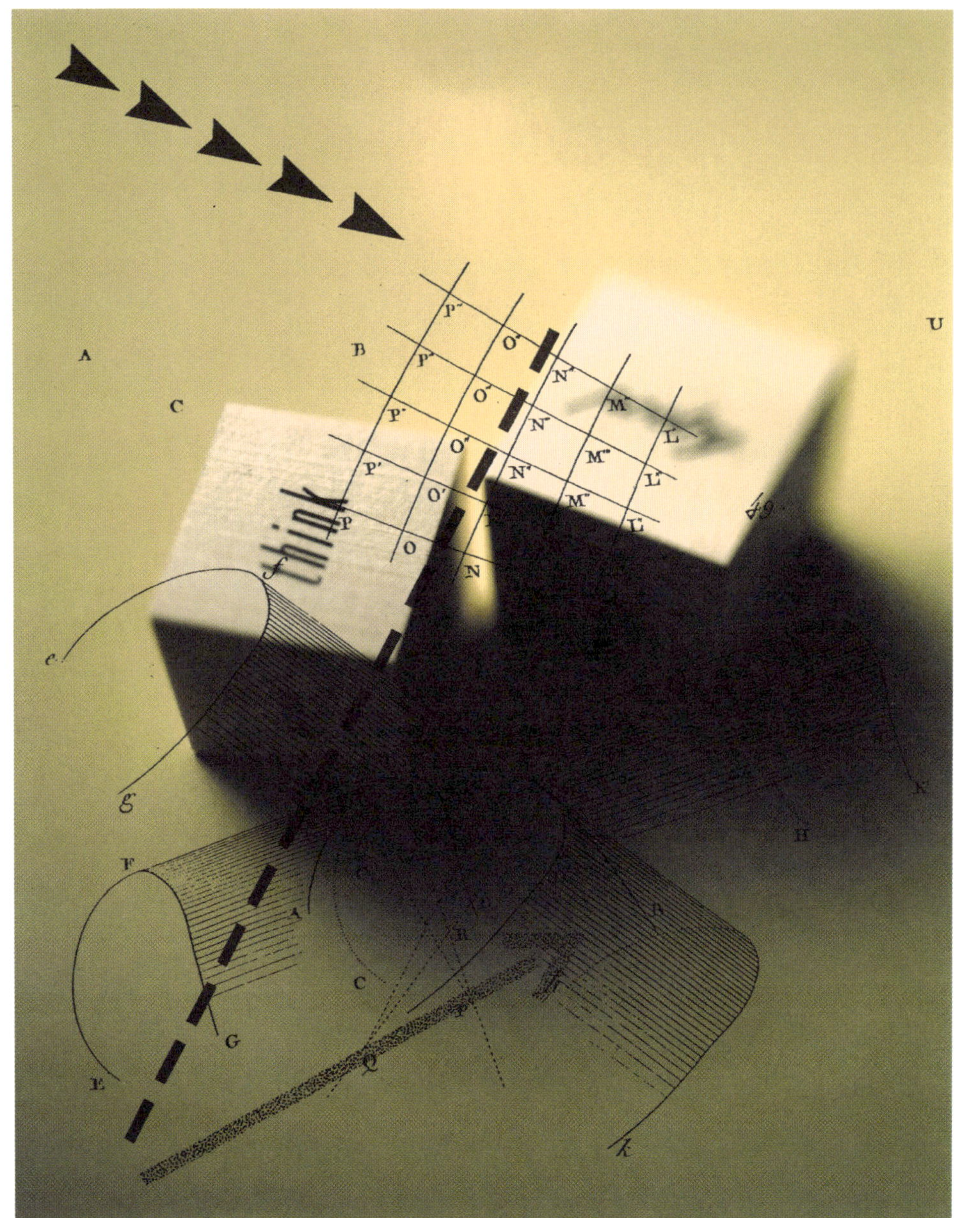

Think Poetry
1995
Instant print
24.2 × 19 cm
Gift of Lee Ka-sing, 2019
2019.162

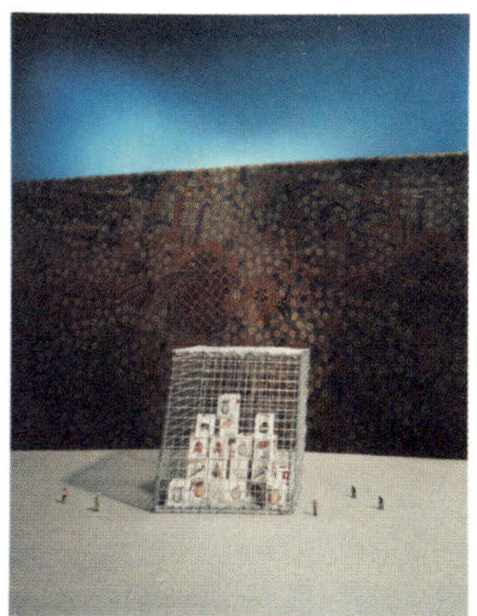

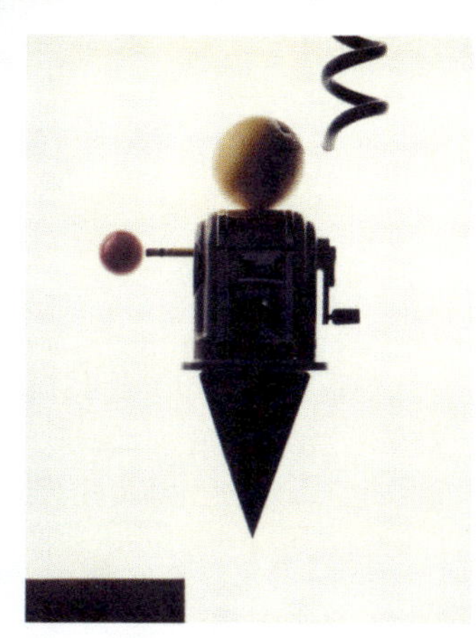

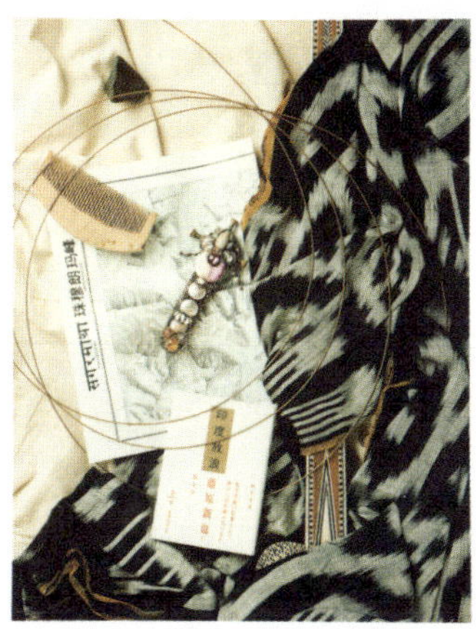

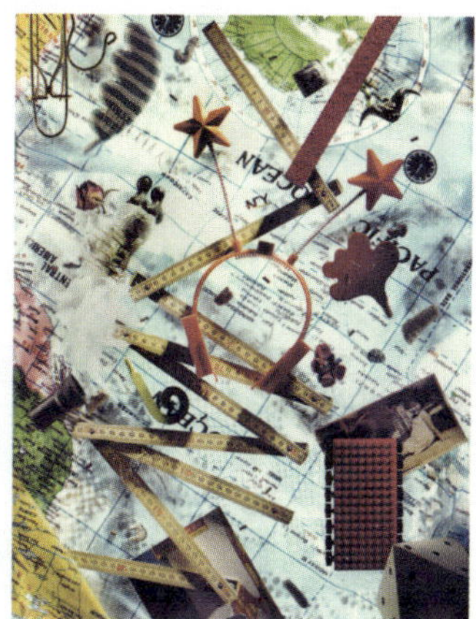

Objects in front of a piece of Indonesian Batik
1986
Instant print
10.4 × 8.7 cm
2017.294

A Portrait of Four Designers
1988
Instant print
10.4 × 8.7 cm
2017.295

In City, 3
1989
Instant print
10.4 × 8.7 cm
2017.293

In City, 6
1989
Instant print
10.4 × 8.7 cm
2017.292

The atmosphere of uncertainty in 1990s Hong Kong, haunted by the end of British colonial rule and the transfer of sovereignty to China, saw an outpouring of creativity. Blues Wong's *Raise the Red Lantern* is a set of five photographic episodes, each consisting of nine Polaroid photographs placed together to form a single image. Inspired by Chinese filmmaker Zhang Yimou's globally acclaimed 1991 film of the same name, *Raise the Red Lantern* is a photographic deconstruction of its cinematic twin. Through the juxtaposition of expressive, abstract, and fragmented images, Wong's work captures the state of suspension experienced before the handover, directly connecting artistic expression with social context. The series of images creates multiple viewpoints and challenges conventional linear narratives to capture a changing reality. Wong's multifaceted work mirrors the fraught heterogeneity of the pre-1997 generation. TP

Blues Wong (born 1966, Hong Kong)
Raise the Red Lantern
1995
Polaroid collage
27.5 × 25.1 cm (each, set of five)
2017.298–2017.302

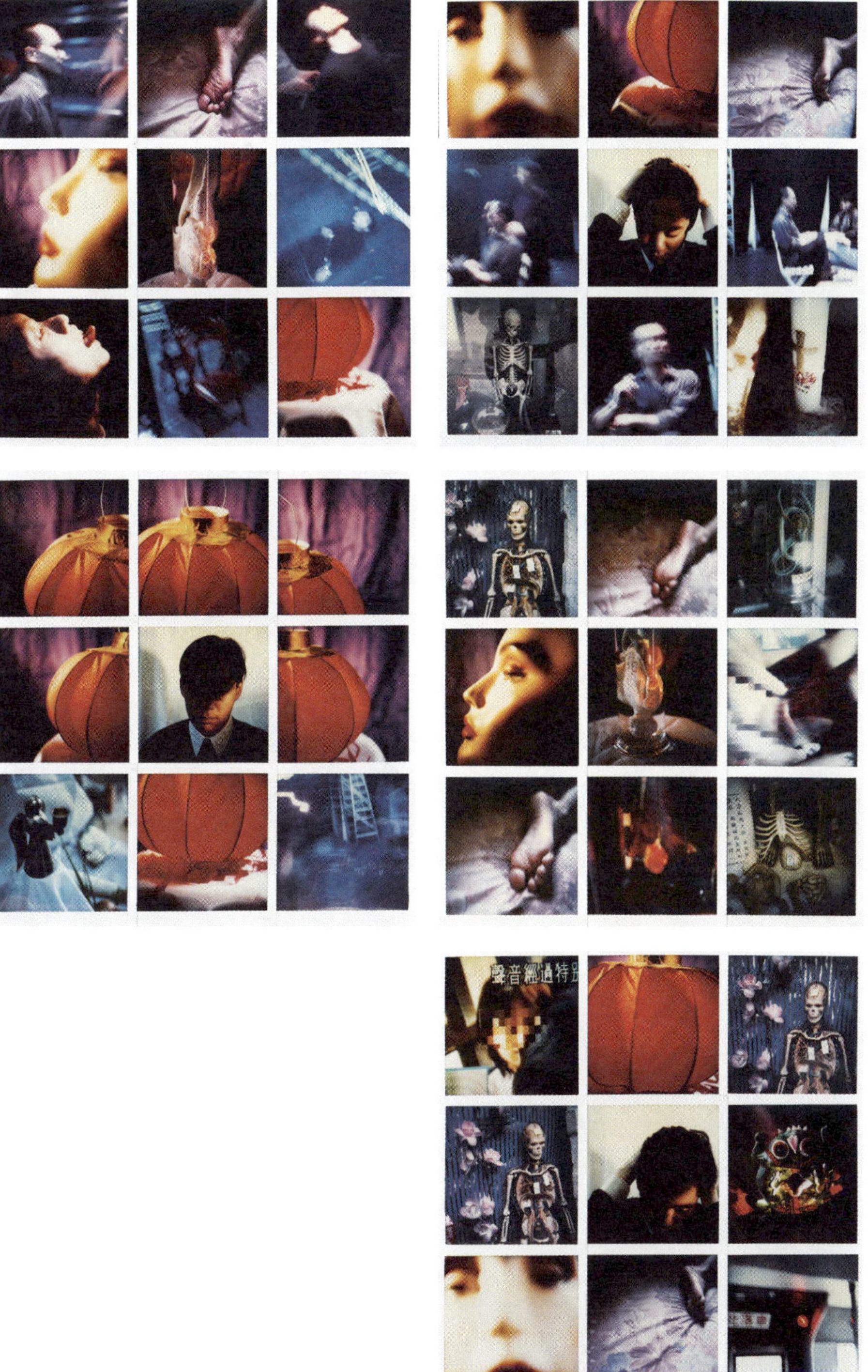

The Great Pageant Show combines art historical references, digital technology, and cultural commentary in a conceptual portrait. Specifically, Holly Lee draws from the Pictorialism movement of the late nineteenth century, which approached photography as a medium with all the expressive and aesthetic potential of painting. A pioneer of experimental digital imaging techniques since the 1990s, Lee used Photoshop to combine the image of a model posing as a winner of the Miss Hong Kong beauty pageant dressed as Queen Elizabeth II with a painting by Giuseppe Castiglione (1688–1766). Castiglione was an Italian Jesuit attached to the Qing court whose work became highly influential for its application of European perspective to Chinese subjects. During the colonial era in Hong Kong, portraits of Queen Elizabeth were a common sight in government offices. Miss Hong Kong is depicted wearing a formal gown, royal crown, necklace, and sash insignia decorated with merit badges. A tattoo of an equestrian athlete on her left shoulder makes a visual link to Castiglione's works, pointing to an earlier era of cultural encounter and imperial power. In bringing together the conventions of pageant culture, colonial emblems, and studio portraiture, Lee captures Hong Kong's cultural hybridity, at a time of political uncertainty in the lead-up to the handover.   BW

Holly Lee (born 1953, Hong Kong)
The Great Pageant Show
ca. 1997
Chromogenic print
118.4 × 87.7 cm
2017.415

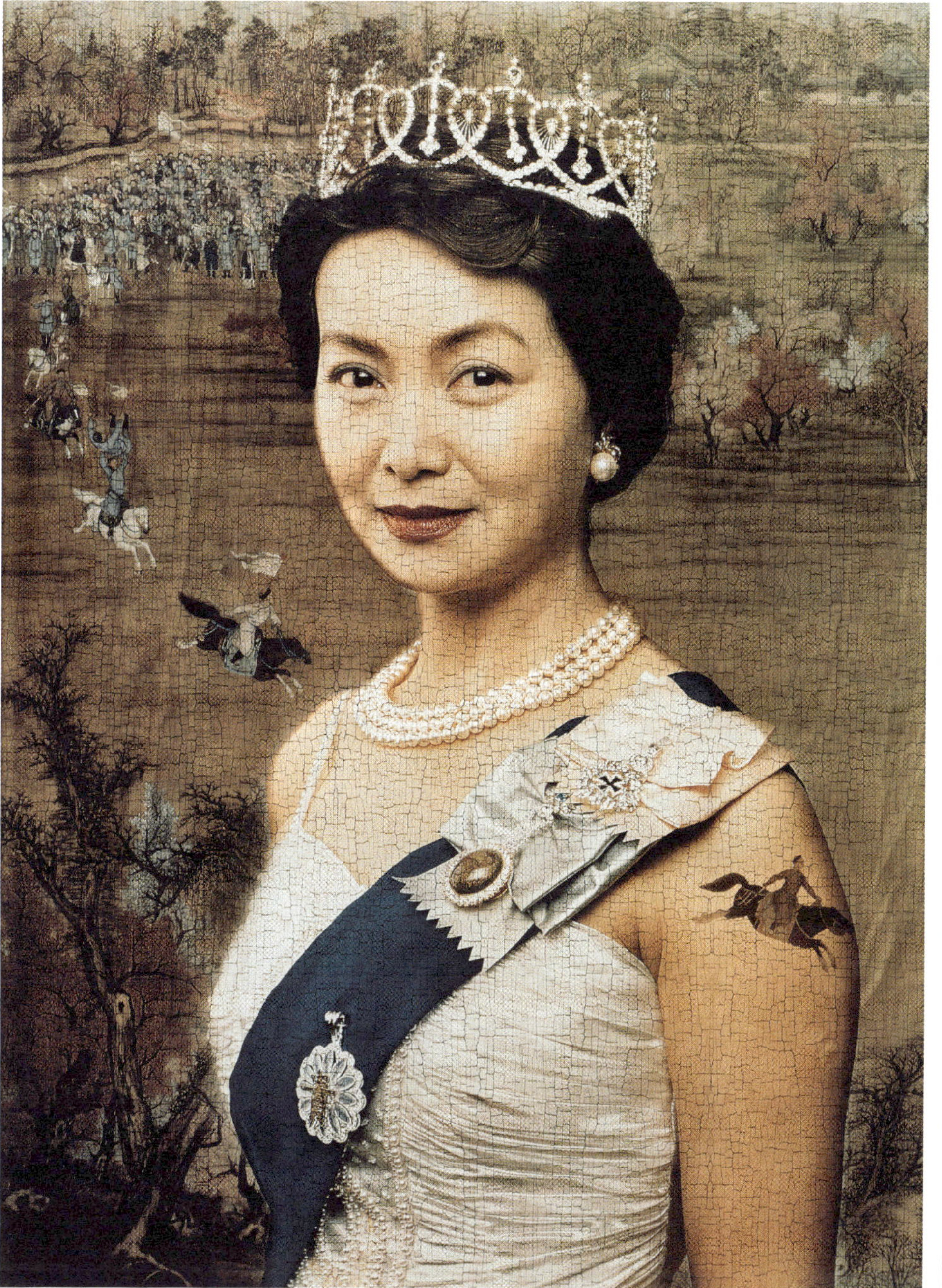

QUIZÁS, QUIZÁS, QUIZÁS

'Perhaps, perhaps, perhaps': an open-ended relationship between art and life in Hong Kong

In this five-panel painting, Lam Tung Pang uses an unconventional approach to engage with traditional ink aesthetics. Choosing plywood as his surface, he depicts a mountainous landscape in charcoal, ink, and pencil. He uses the texture of the wood to approximate the dry-brush style of painting. The flat, naive composition establishes a clear contrast between the classical landscape image—an ideal upheld for its moral resonance and introspective power—and Hong Kong's hyper-dense reality, a condition that influences readings of both the natural and the built environments. Lam extracts elements of landscape painting and recombines them in a new way, producing a work that is a commentary on the individual's changing relationship to the environment as well as a statement on the contemporary potential of a traditional form.   CC

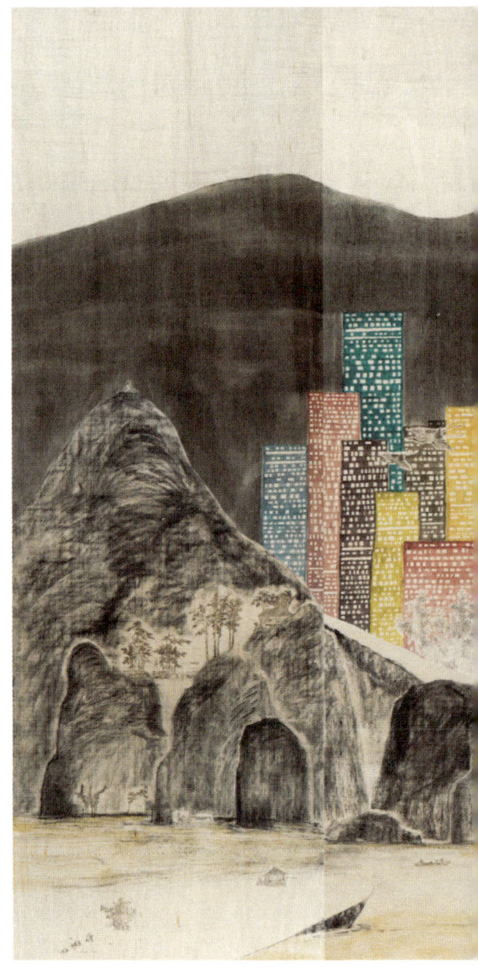

Lam Tung Pang (born 1978, Hong Kong)
The Huge Mountain
2011
Ink, charcoal, pencil, acrylic, and image-transfer on plywood
300 × 500 cm
Gift of William and Lavina Lim, 2020
2020.398

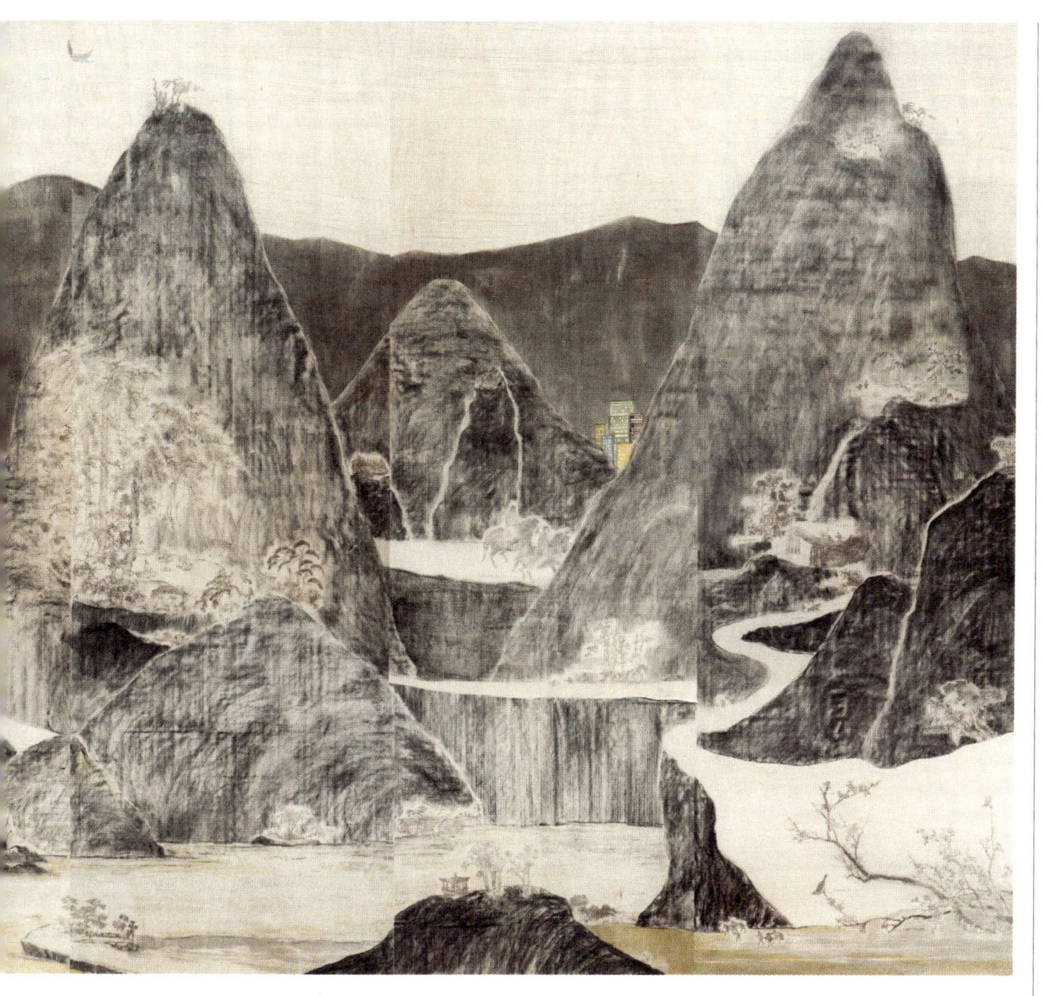

Lee Kit's oeuvre includes readymades, hand-painted cloths, and installations that reproduce settings from everyday life. His works reveal a tension between lightness, understated materials, and the weight of emotions and experiences for which his objects act as ciphers.

In 2006, the Hong Kong Legislative Council passed the Amendments to Smoking Ordinance, banning smoking in all indoor workplaces and public spaces. Around this time, Lee noticed that whenever he was not smoking, he would scratch the surface of a table in his studio. Day after day, over a period of five years, he wore a groove into the tabletop. He photographed the result of his compulsive scratching and sent around three hundred postcards of the image to his friends. The worn-down desk represents the weight of life's meaninglessness. Lee used the postcards, records of years of banality, to document and disseminate a feeling of profound ennui.

As a way to both express and contain his emotions, Lee began painting lines and grids on pieces of cloth early in his career. Since the 2000s, he has introduced these hand-painted cloths into public spaces to project his feelings of anger and helplessness in the face of political and social issues. In 2014, after participating in a protest in Taipei with his friends, Lee organised a picnic using a painted cloth he had made in 2002 as a blanket. The cloth, together with the photographic documentation of the picnic, forms the work *Picnic with Friends at Home on Hand-Painted Cloth, after a Demonstration in a Rainy Day in Taipei*. The cloth is an example of Lee's inquiry into the meaning and limits of painting as a practice, as well as an object that connects friends, art, and society. His painted cloths and installations can be read as records of personal anguish, a yearning for freedom, and a commitment to social responsibility.   CC

Lee Kit (born 1978, Hong Kong)
Scratching the Table Surface
2006–2011
Acrylic on wood and metal
69.3 × 113 × 93.7 cm
2017.274

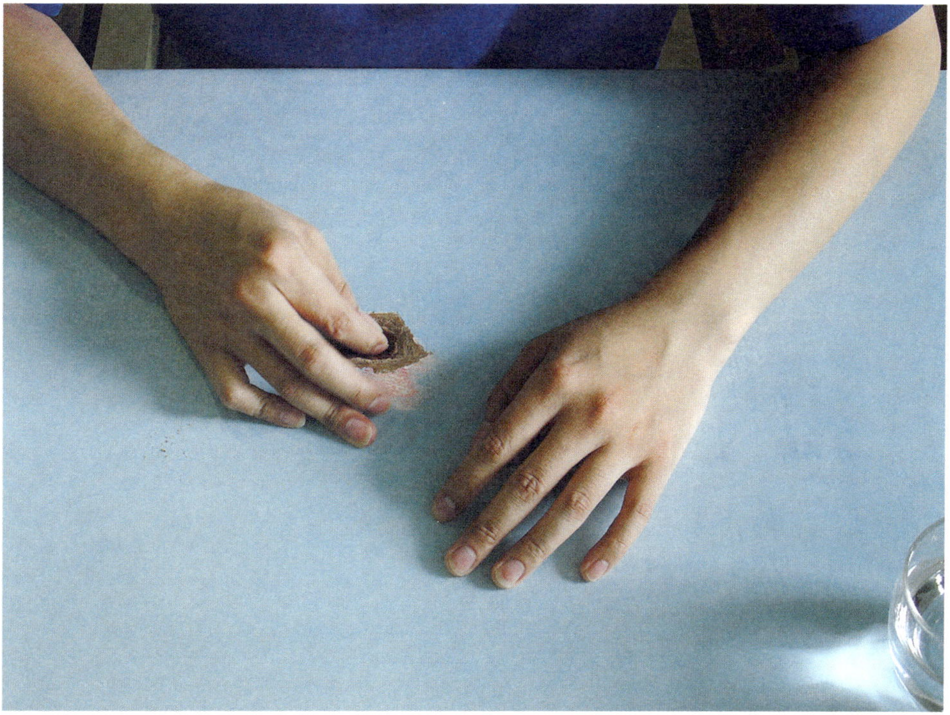

Documentation of the performance

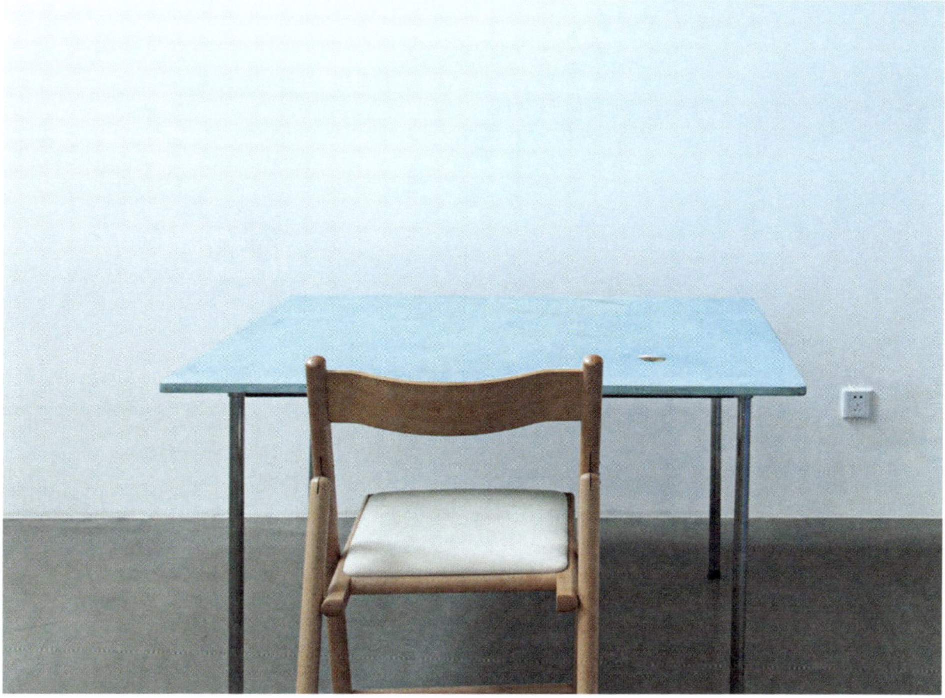

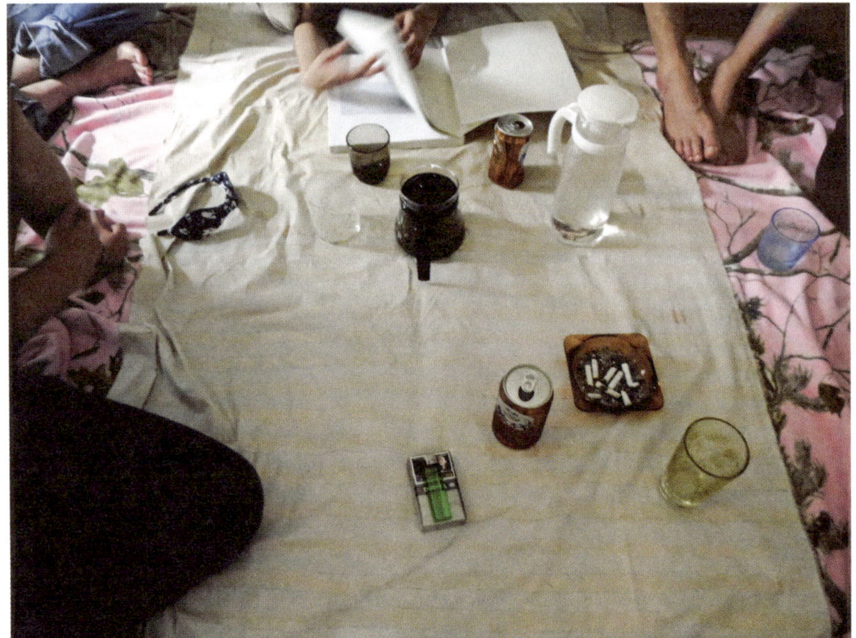

Detail view

Picnic with Friends at Home on Hand-Painted Cloth, after a Demonstration in a Rainy Day in Taipei
2002/2014
Acrylic and ink on fabric, inkjet print
Dimensions variable
2017.272

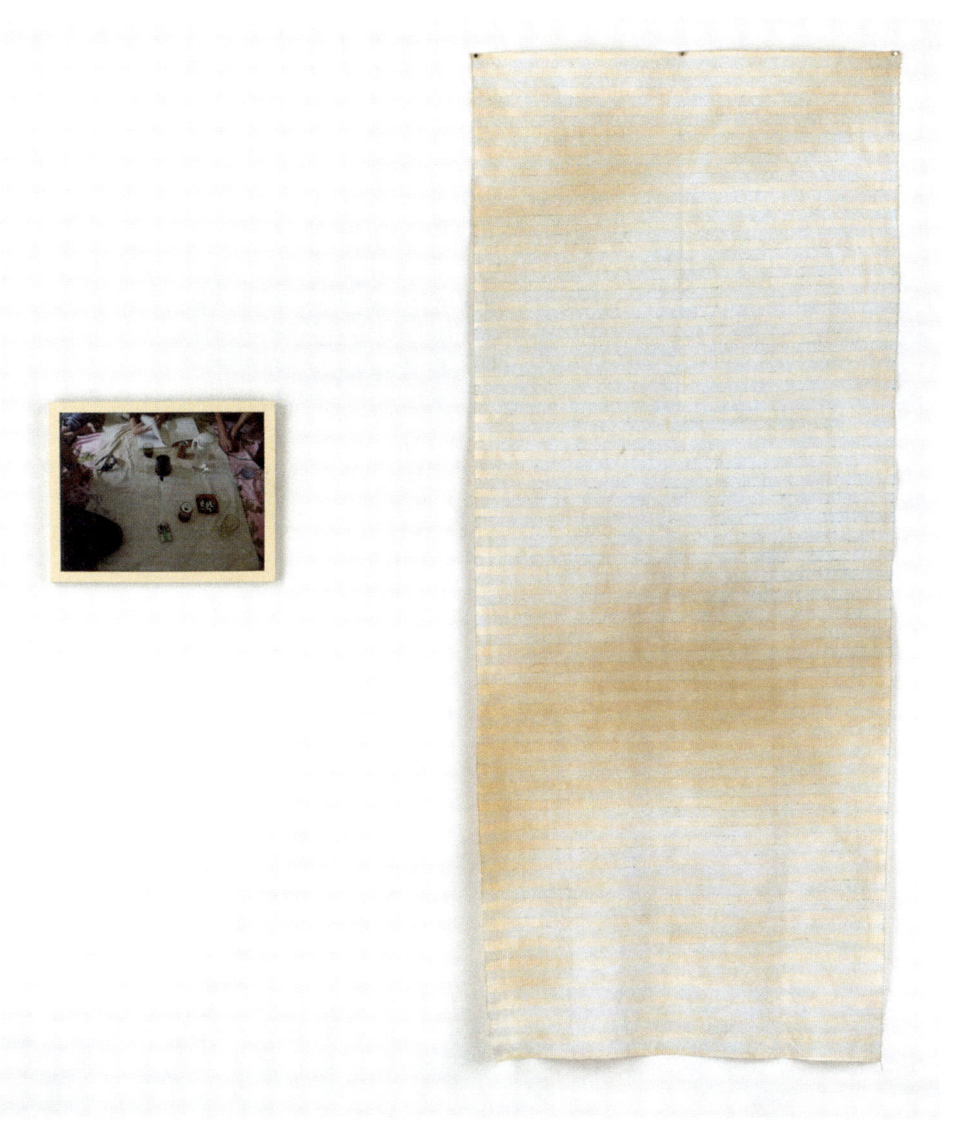

Kwan Sheung Chi's practice spans performance, video, and installation and is distinguished by a quiet resistance to societal and political conventions. *A Shirt I Wore to Work* is an installation consisting of a shirt with a hand-drawn design, and a photograph of the artist wearing the shirt at work. What at first glance appears to be pinstripes on the shirt are in fact the artist's hand-drawn design reading 'I am artist', written in blue ink, repeated across the fabric. Kwan created this pattern with a ballpoint pen, invoking both menial office labour and the focus on penmanship in traditional professional and academic settings. He wore the shirt to his part-time job at an art-leasing company, on a day when his supervisor was out of the office. None of his colleagues commented on it. Kwan's work is a reflection on artistic labour, which is often neglected and undervalued by society.   FT

Kwan Sheung Chi (born 1980, Hong Kong)
A Shirt I Wore to Work
2004
Shirt, metal clothes hanger, and chromogenic print
89 × 65 × 5.8 cm
2012.1665

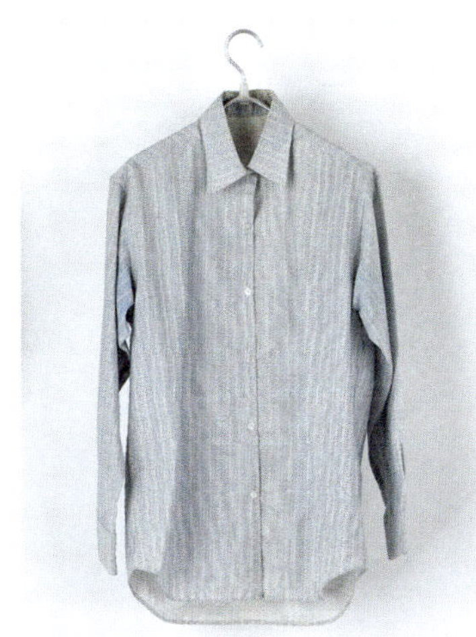

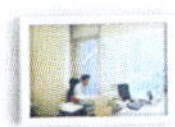

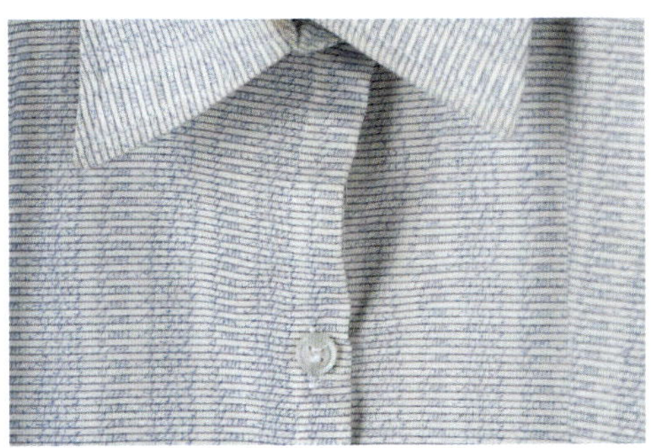

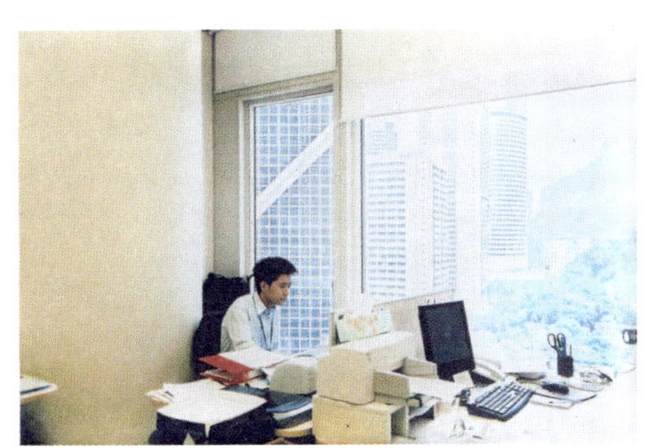

Made as a music video for the Hong Kong indie band No One Remains Virgin, *Under the Lion Crotch* is one of Wong Ping's best-known works. It depicts people under attack by a giant half-mechanical, half-biological lion—a reference to the city's iconic Lion Rock—manipulated by two powerful figures. In Wong's violent, sexually explicit animation, residents confront overwhelming forces beyond their control to fight for their survival and that of their city. The work's title is a reference to the public broadcaster Radio Television Hong Kong's long-running docudrama series *Below the Lion Rock*, which captures the lives of the city's ordinary, working-class citizens and has been lauded for its representation of everyday experience.

A self-taught artist, Wong creates fictional worlds that foreground flat colours and characters constructed of simple geometric forms. His visual style, remarkably free of the influence of any particular school of aesthetics, has a child-like, naive quality that contrasts with the provocative psychosexual themes he often explores.   CC

Wong Ping (born 1984, Hong Kong)
Under the Lion Crotch (stills)
2011
Single-channel digital video (colour, sound)
4 min. 38 sec.
2017.417

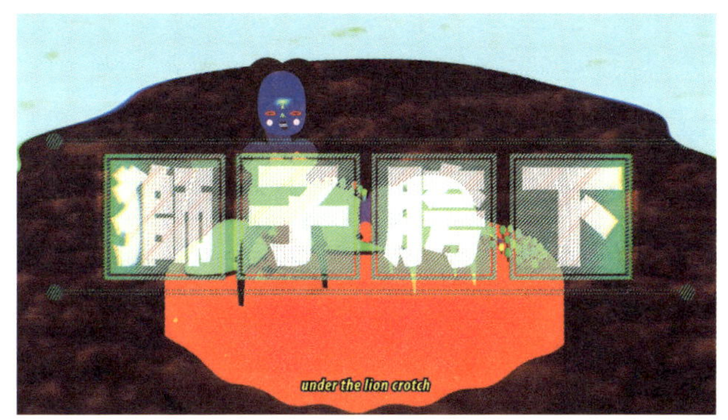
獅子胯下
under the lion crotch

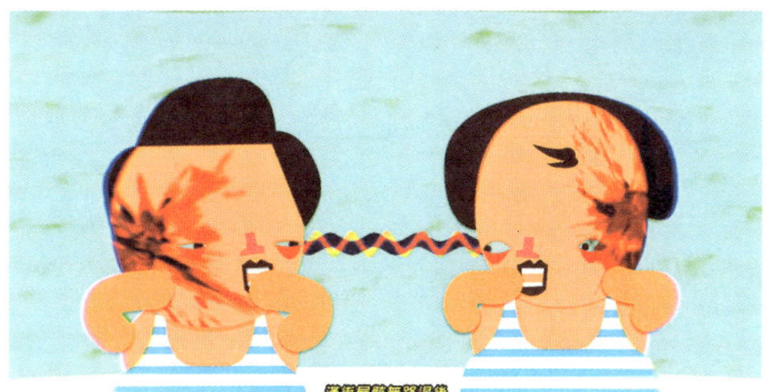
滿街屍骸無路退後
fill the streets with our merry hearses

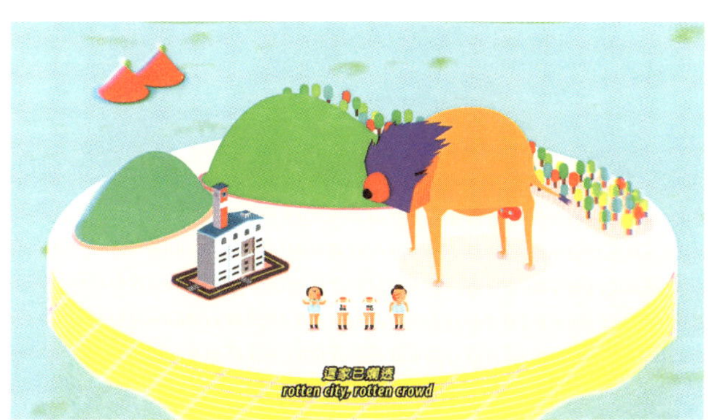
這家已爛透
rotten city, rotten crowd

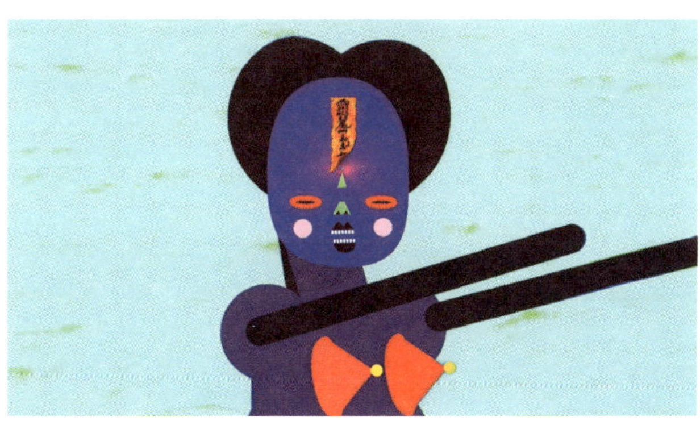

This painting depicts a seated figure using a distorted perspective. The figure stands out in its representation in red, against a subdued background in shades of grey, blue, and brown. The tightly framed composition offers little context for the scene, but the title of the work introduces a possible narrative, within a setting that is central to the practice of traditional Chinese medicine. The connection between the image and the title suggests an implicit contrast between the psychological isolation projected in the figure's posture and the busy urban environment of Hong Kong.

Through her distinctive style of figurative painting, Firenze Lai explores the relationship between the interior and exterior worlds of her subjects. Her sensitive, sympathetic works express the isolation of the individual while alluding to the possibility of connection with others.   CC

Firenze Lai (born 1984, Hong Kong)
The Bone Setting Clinic
2012
Acrylic on canvas
32.7 × 28.6 cm
2012.1620

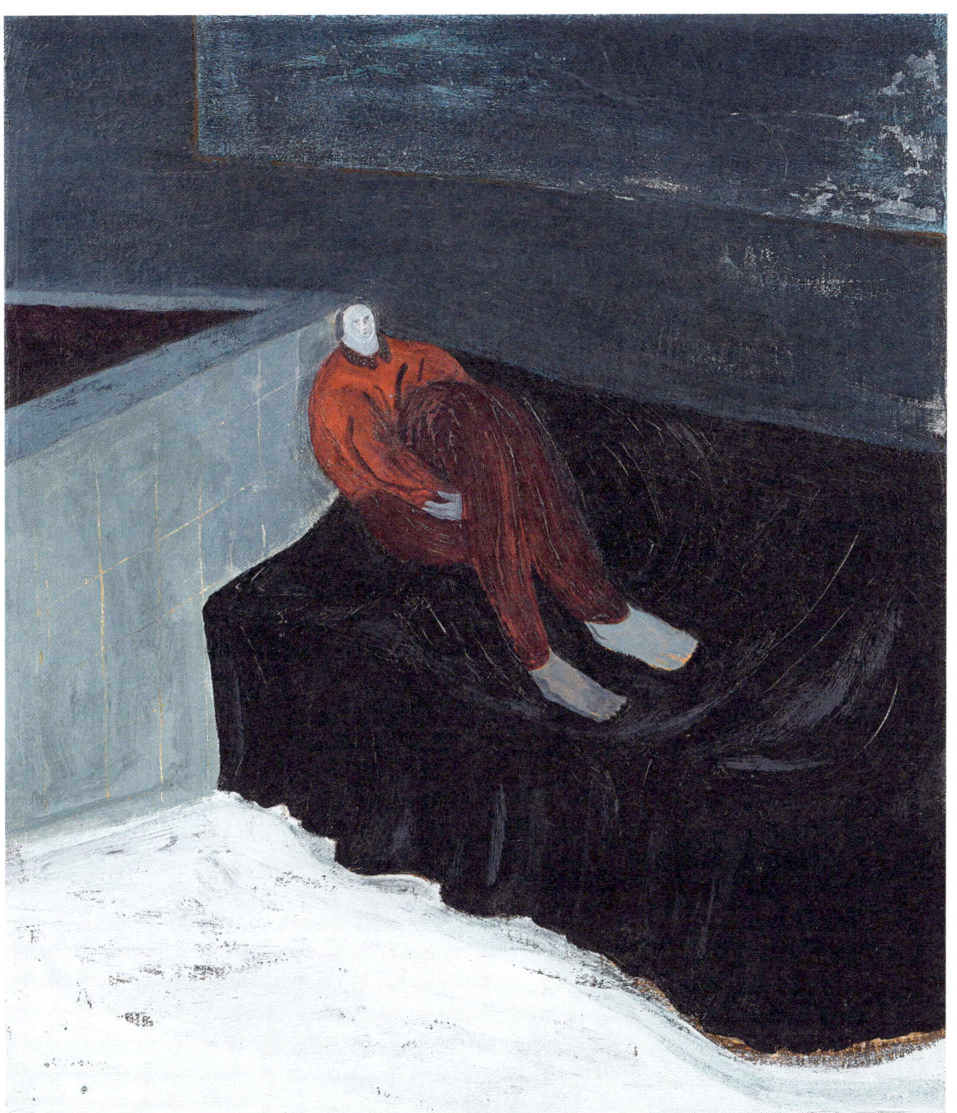

Wilson Shieh subverts expectations of conventional artistic mediums, including meticulous *gongbi* (fine brush) painting, poster design, and paper toys. He mines cultural histories to produce works that have a playful, knowing quality. He often explores his subjects in series, crafting an extended consideration of history, popular culture, and the urban landscape, as well as his own biography.

Eileen Chang and Her Characters is a series of six drawings that offers an interpretation of the renowned writer's life. Shieh directs the viewer's attention to the ways in which elements of Chang's oeuvre mirror her years in Shanghai and Hong Kong. In *Eileen Chang at the University of Hong Kong 1941*, Shieh depicts Chang as a student standing on the verandah of the University of Hong Kong's Main Building. In the background, the roof of the university's historic Great Hall burns. Chang's experiences in wartime Hong Kong left a lasting impression on her. The Japanese occupation of 1941 cut her studies short, and she was forced to return to her native Shanghai. While there, she began to publish her writings and soon established herself as a major literary figure. In other works in this series, Shieh focuses on film adaptations of Chang's novels, including *Father Takes a Bride* (Wong Tin-lam, 1963, with a screenplay by Chang), *Love in a Fallen City* (Ann Hui, 1984), and *Lust, Caution* (Ang Lee, 2007). The final image in this series depicts the writer in Los Angeles, where she died alone in 1995. Drawn in a style that combines narrative detail with comic-book-like simplicity, the works could be part of a storyboard for a film.

Shieh extends his interest in film and popular culture into scenes of his own invention with *Angkor Quartet*. The work is a triptych inspired by Wong Kar-wai's film *In the Mood for Love* (2000), starring Maggie Cheung and Tony Leung. Shieh portrays them with the singer Rebecca Pan—who also appears in the film—and the director in a fictional quartet playing 'Quizás, Quizás, Quizás', Spanish for 'perhaps, perhaps, perhaps'. Nat King Cole's 1958 version of the song is a central musical theme of the film. Set in 1960s Hong Kong, *In the Mood for Love* is the story of two married émigrés whose feelings for each other deepen but remain unrequited. Shieh's whimsical interpretation conveys a longing for Hong Kong's past and refers to the film's final location, Angkor Wat.

Shieh grew up in the last decades of British-administered Hong Kong, and his works reveal a fascination with the history of his city and of modern China. His engagement with biography encompasses prominent political figures. In *Eight Modern China Political Leaders in School*, Shieh presents multilingual first-person statements by Yuan Shikai, Sun Yat-sen, Chiang Kai-shek, Mao Zedong, Zhou Enlai, Deng Xiaoping, Pu Yi, and Chiang Ching-kuo. The humorous, child-like approach brings the viewer into contact with the formative years of these historical figures, offering a subversive yet affectionately humanising reading.   TP

Wilson Shieh (born 1970, Hong Kong)
Eileen Chang and Her Characters – Eileen Chang at the University of Hong Kong 1941
2013
Coloured pencil and collage on paper
55.7 × 40.8 cm
2013.22.3

Angkor Quartet
2004
Ink and colour on silk, triptych
46 × 46 cm (each, average)
Gift of the Yiqingzhai Collection, 2014
2015.114

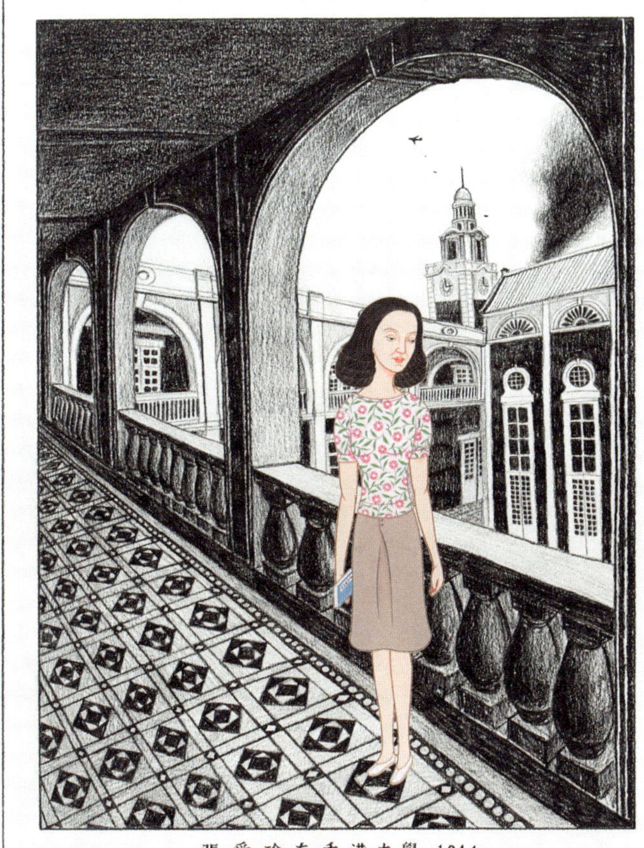

石家豪 Wilson Shieh 2013

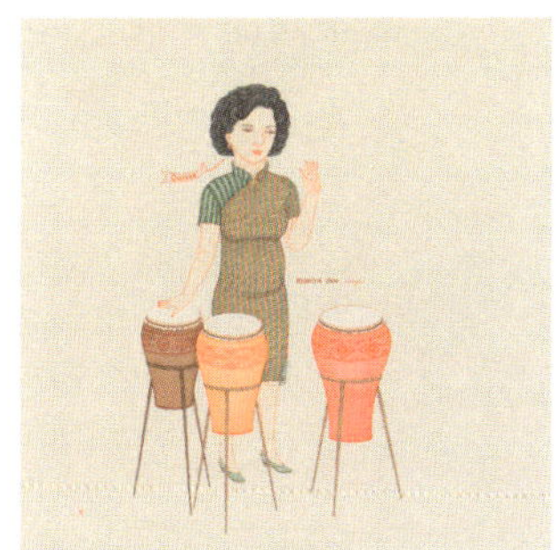

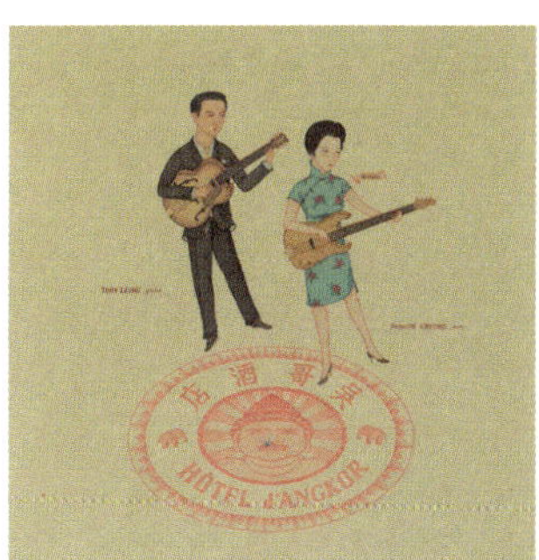

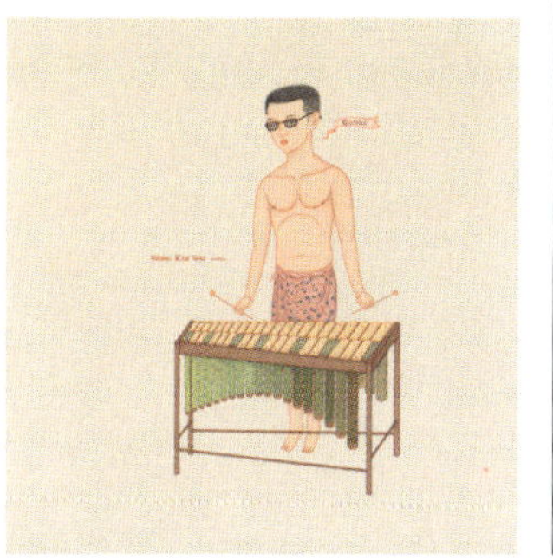

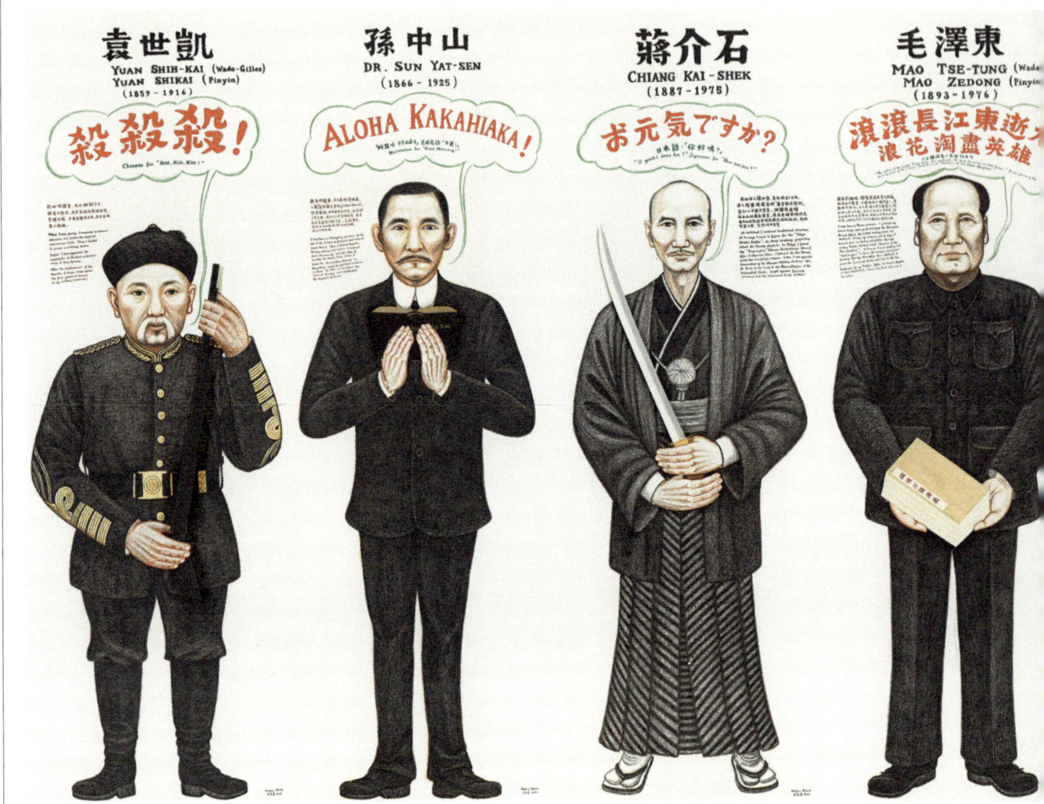

Eight Modern China Political Leaders in School
2012
Coloured pencil, crayon, and collage on paper
75 × 220 cm (each, set of eight)
2013.18

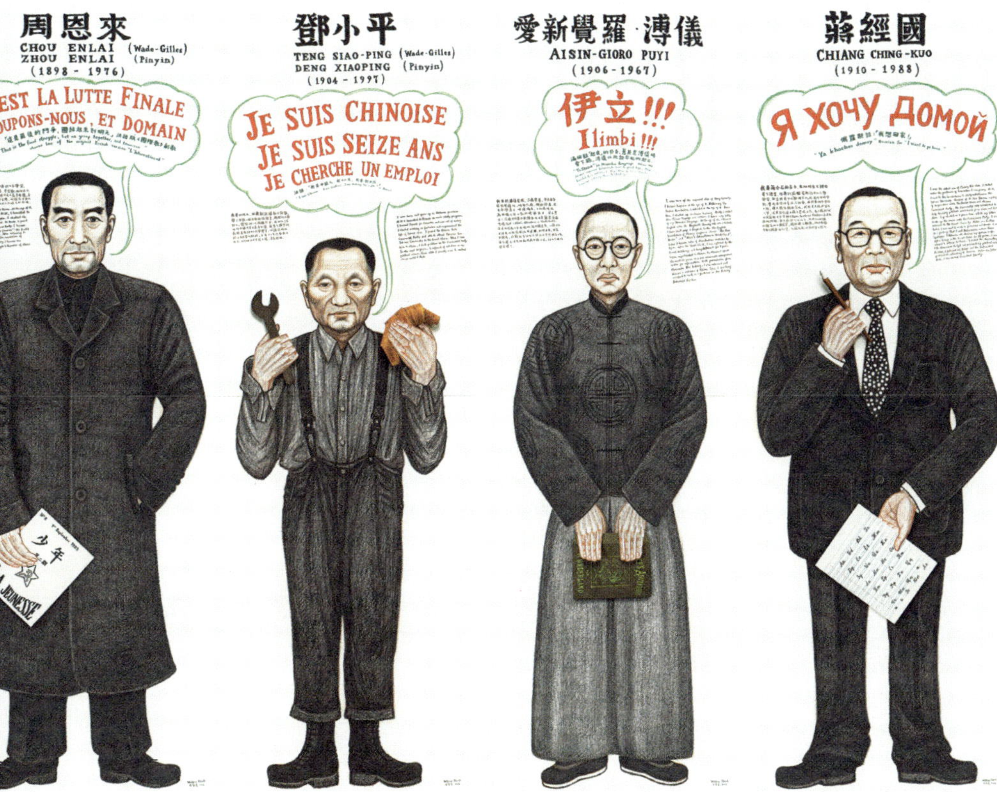
周恩來
CHOU ENLAI (Wade-Gilles)
ZHOU ENLAI (Pinyin)
(1898 - 1976)
EST LA LUTTE FINALE
OUPONS-NOUS, ET DOMAIN

鄧小平
TENG SIAO-PING (Wade-Gilles)
DENG XIAOPING (Pinyin)
(1904 - 1997)
JE SUIS CHINOISE
JE SUIS SEIZE ANS
JE CHERCHE UN EMPLOI

愛新覺羅·溥儀
AISIN-GIORO PUYI
(1906 - 1967)
伊立!!!
Ilimbi !!!

蔣經國
CHIANG CHING-KUO
(1910 - 1988)
Я ХОЧУ ДОМОЙ

In his series *The Prosperous World*, Wong Chung-yu presents a vision of a future Hong Kong. This work, consisting of two drawings and an animation, combines new media and traditional ink art. The perspectival drawings depict pedestrian overpasses, tunnels, and highways in a rugged, mountainous landscape that is distinctive of Hong Kong. The screen at the centre of the composition plays an animation of activities seen through the windows of a residential building. Wong brings the historical language of ink landscapes into a digital present, carving out a new urban space that is simultaneously alien and familiar. The work integrates both utopian and dystopian readings of Hong Kong, a city whose character is defined by contrast and tension between the built and natural environments.   CC

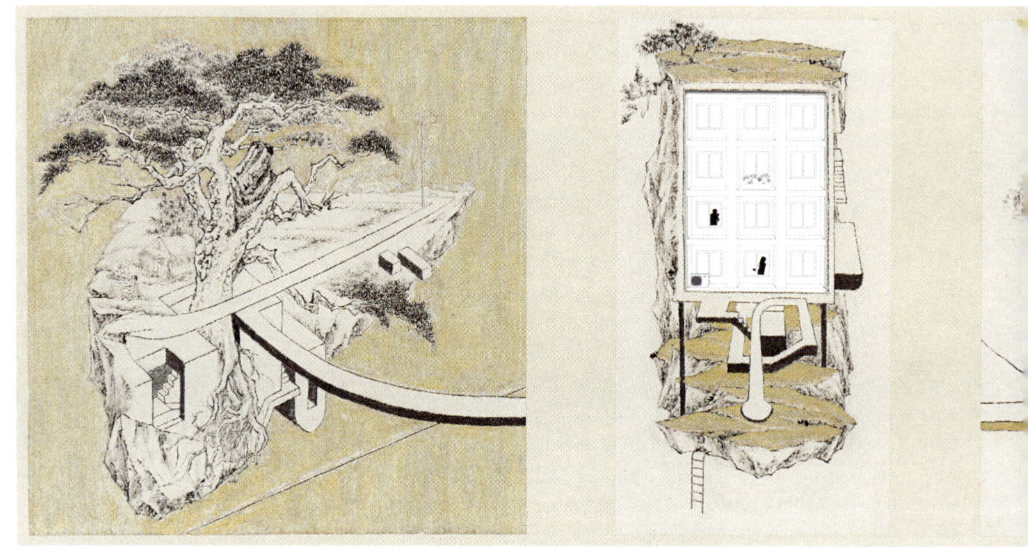

Wong Chung-yu (born 1977, Hong Kong)
The Prosperous World I
2010
Ink and colour on paper and single-channel digital video (colour, sound)
39.1 × 157 × 5.6 cm
8 min.
2017.24

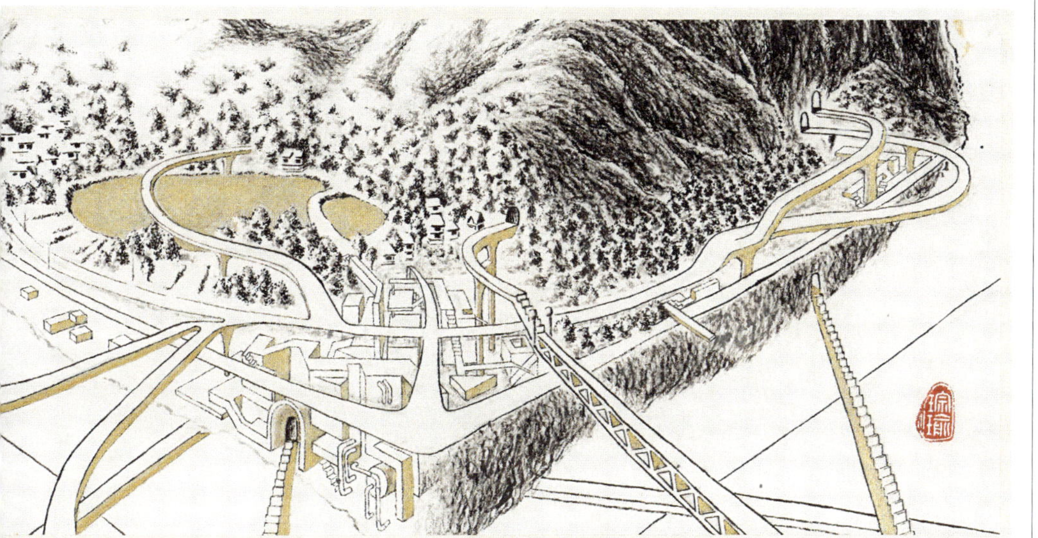

Au Hoi Lam's artistic practice is one of meditative repetition, a process by which she relives and sorts her emotions and memories through the act of painting. *Memento (White Shirt)* is a minimalistic, abstract composition that nevertheless contains rich details related to the artist's relationships and experiences. The work's title proposes a reading of the composition as a souvenir of a moment in the past.

On a dark-grey ground, Au meticulously paints a grid of white lines—over which she applies multiple layers of cyan paint in different shades. Faintly rendered notes and doodles scattered across the surface of the canvas offer fragments related to her memories and thoughts. The delicate ambiguity of these elements invites the viewer to engage in an intimate, subjective relationship with the work.   KW

Au Hoi Lam (born 1978, Hong Kong)
Memento (White Shirt)
2014
Acrylic, pencil, and coloured pencil on linen
122.5 × 122.2 × 5 cm
Brown Family Annual Acquisition Fund, 2014
2014.70

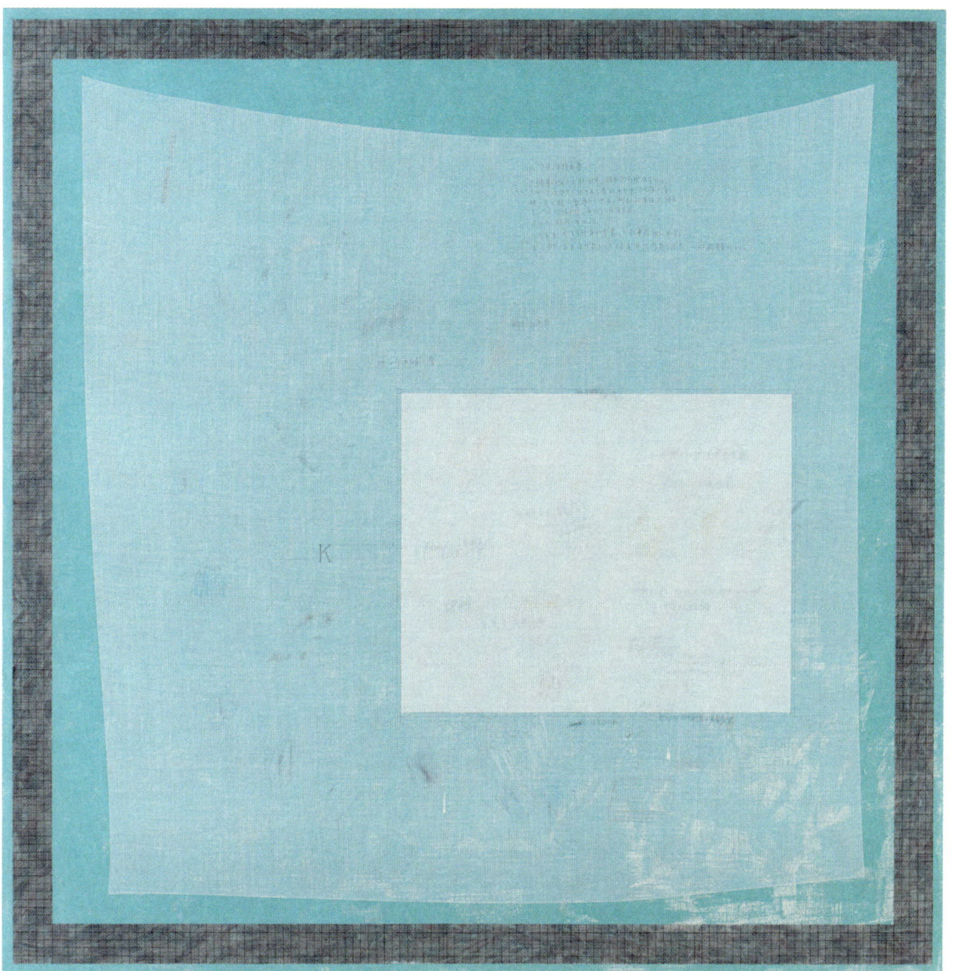

Wong Wai Yin made this work in response to an experience she had in 2007, during a visit to Beijing for the exhibition *Inside Looking Out*. The six artists featured in the exhibition, all of them men, were Wong's artistic contemporaries. While spending time with them on the trip, she was introduced only as a girlfriend, not as an artist in her own right. The video captures a short performance in which Wong strikes the six artists across the head one by one using a folded stool made of cardboard. During the sequence, each of the artists stands against a white background, framed from the chest up, a composition reminiscent of a passport image or even a police record. After a moment, Wong strikes them. Their reactions—pained, stoic, amused—suggest that they are knowing victims in this critique of male privilege, a mocking 'tribute' that overturns typical gender dynamics. The work could be read as a feminist statement, but Wong insists that her oeuvre is anchored entirely in her personal experiences rather than framed in terms of larger questions of gender and society.   FT

Wong Wai Yin (born 1981, Hong Kong)
Tribute to Inside Looking Out – For the male artists along my way (still)
2008
Single-channel digital video (black and white, sound)
2 min. 24 sec.
2016.521

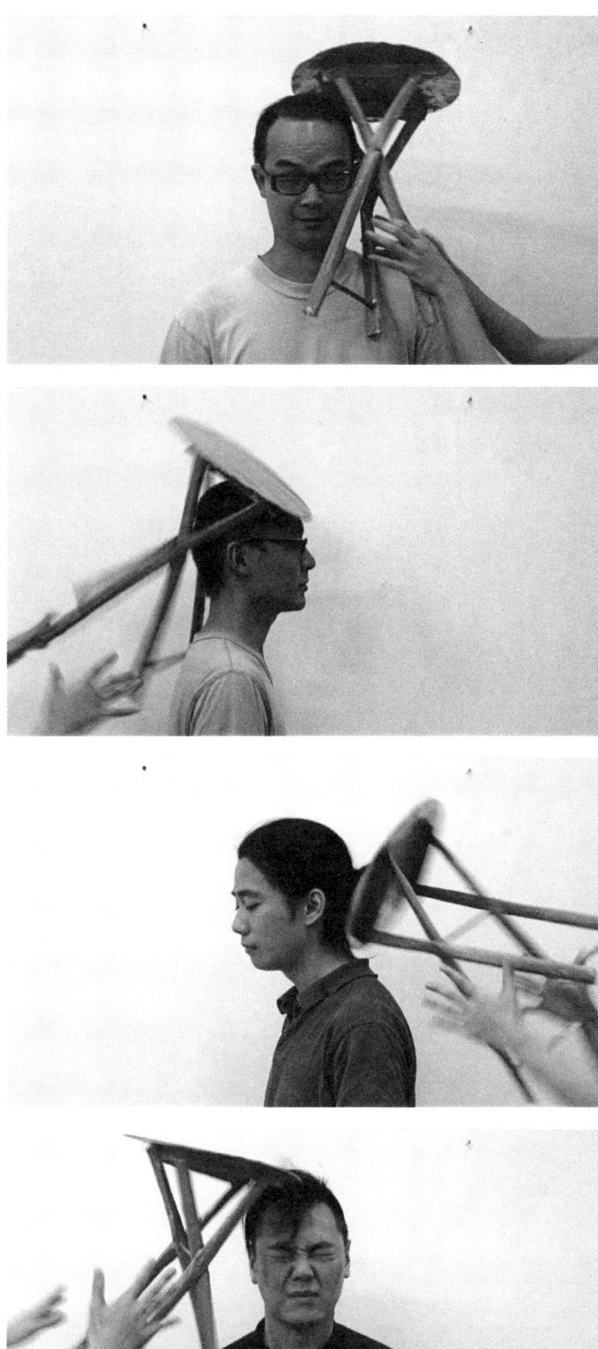

In Kacey Wong's Dragon Garden project, part of his *Drift City* series begun in 2000, the artist is depicted wandering through Dragon Garden in Tuen Mun, performing the role of a solitary intellectual. The project is a love letter to this idyllic location, photographed in the style of a filmic narrative to emphasise the garden's immersive monumentality. It also gestures to the fragile survival of the site. Built between 1949 and 1968, the garden was the vision of the businessman and philanthropist Lee lu-cheung, whose family has continued to maintain it for more than sixty years.

Wong was trained as an architect, and his costume is inspired by the 1931 Beaux-Arts Ball in New York, when some of the city's leading architects dressed as buildings they had designed—among the costumes was William Van Alen's Chrysler Building, which Wong reinterprets for *Drift City*. Wong also cites as an inspiration Madelon Vriesendorp's painting *Flagrant délit* (1975), which depicts the Chrysler Building and the Empire State Building caught in bed together by the Rockefeller Center while skyscrapers with human heads gaze in through the window. As an anthropomorphised building, Wong places himself alongside carefully chosen historical and architectural landmarks around the world. He presents his unspecified quest through photographic portraits, almost always depicting himself alone. These absurd, sometimes haunting images draw attention to history, the environment, and the isolation of the individual.   TP

Kacey Wong (born 1970, Hong Kong)
Drift City (Dragon Garden, Hong Kong 33)
2010
Inkjet print
51 × 33.8 cm
2019.305

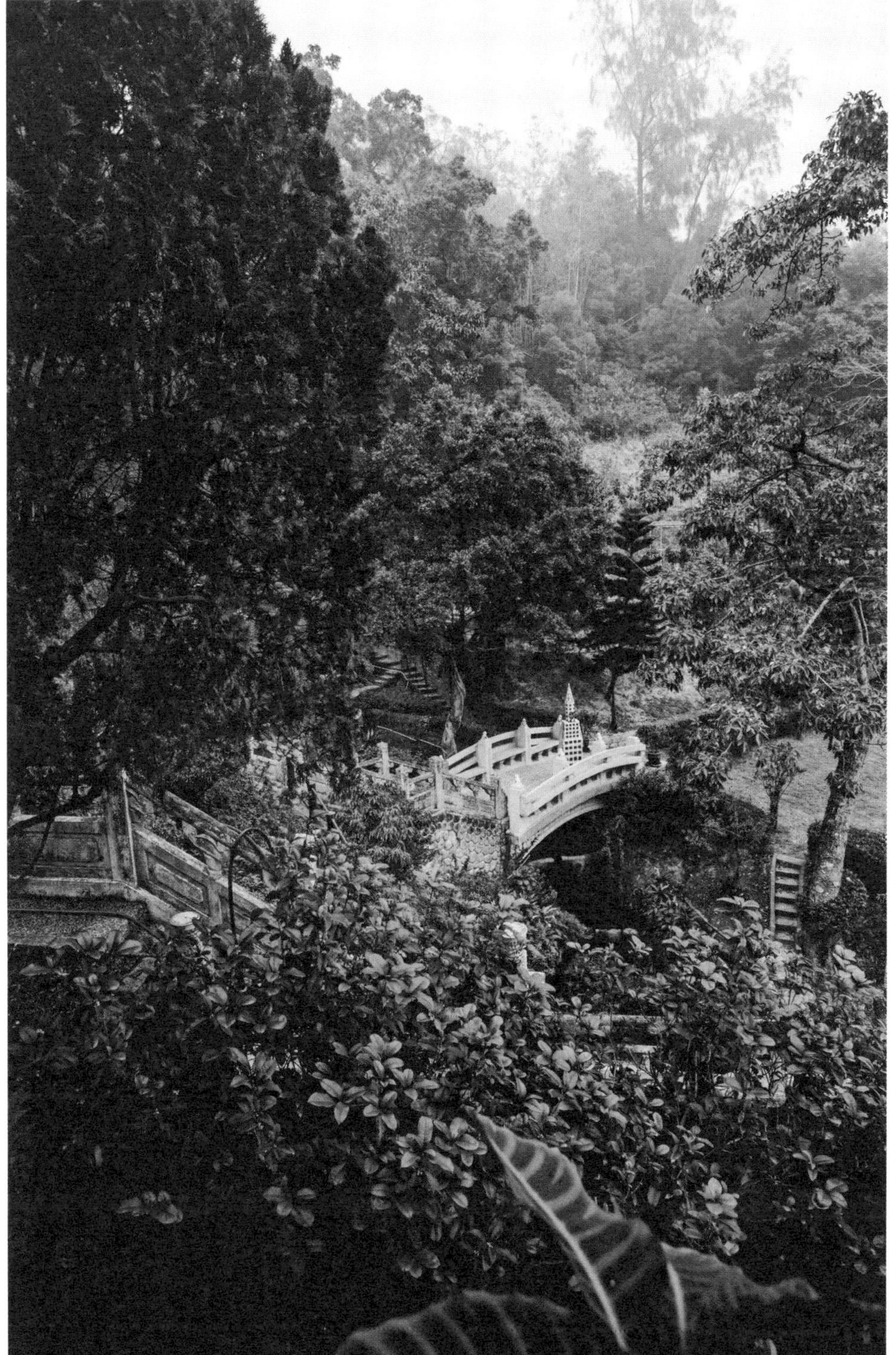

COPYRIGHT AND IMAGE CREDITS

23 © All rights reserved; **24** Courtesy of the collection of Simon Go. © All rights reserved; **27** ©Twemco Industries Ltd.; **30** ©Tai Ping Carpets Ltd.; **31** ©Tai Ping Carpets Ltd.; **33cr** © Kader Industrial Company Limited; **33t, b** © Star Industrial Co., Ltd.; **34tl** © Kader Industrial Company Limited; **34tr, b** © Star Industrial Co., Ltd.; **35** © Star Industrial Co., Ltd. **38** © All rights reserved; **40–41** © Cathay Pacific Airways Limited. Photo: © Milk Design Limited; **43** © Andrew Lee King Fun & Associates Architects Limited; **45** © Sammy's Kitchen Ltd; **46t** © Shair Oi Fong; **46c, bl, br** © M+, Hong Kong. Image courtesy Lam Tung Pang; **47** © All rights reserved; **51** ©Tsang Tsou-choi/King of Kowloon; **53** © Cheung Yee; **54–55** © anothermountainman (Stanley Wong Ping Pui); **57** © anothermountainman (Stanley Wong Ping Pui); **59** Photo: courtesy Lambert Yam & Ruby Yang; **61** © Lo Yuk Ying; **63** © Lo Yuk Ying; **65** © City Magazine, Modern Media; **67** © Capital Artists Ltd.; **68t** © Wing Hang Record Trading Co., Ltd.; **68b** ©Warner Music Hong Kong Ltd.; **69** © Universal Music Ltd.; **71** ©Tommy Li; **73** ©The I Club; **74** © Sharp Leader Ltd. Hong Kong; **75** © Sharp Leader Ltd. Hong Kong; **79** © Pak Sheung Chuen. Image courtesy Pak Sheung Chuen; **81** © Milk Design Ltd. Image Courtesy Milk Design Ltd.; **83** © Michael Young; **85** © Kevin Cheung. Image courtesy Kevin Cheung; **87** ©Vivienne Tam. Image courtesy Vivienne Tam; **88–89** © All rights reserved; **90–91** ©Tsang Kin-Wah. Image courtesy Tsang Kin-Wah; **93** © Alan Kwan; **95** © M+, Hong Kong. Courtesy of Hanart TZ Gallery; **97–99** © Leung Chi Wo & Sara Wong. Courtesy of Blindspot Gallery; **101** © Chow Chun-fai; **110–111** © Chung Wah Nan Architects Limited; **111** © Estate of Alan Fitch; **112** © Estate of Alan Fitch; **113** © All rights reserved; **115t** © John Nye; **115b** © P&T Group; **119** © Penelope Seidler (Creator: Helmut Jacoby; Architect: Harry Seidler and Associates); **121t** © Andrew Lee King Fun & Associates Architects Limited; **121b** © Richmond Surveyors Company. Image courtesy Richard Surveyors Company; **122** © Dennis Lau & Ng Chun Man Architects & Engineers; **123** © Dennis Lau & Ng Chun Man Architects & Engineers; **127** © Simon Kwan & Associates Limited; **129** © Wong & Ouyang (HK) Ltd.; **131t** ©Wong Tung & Partners Ltd. Courtesy of Swire Properties Limited; **131b** ©Wong Tung & Partners Ltd.; **132–133** © Estate of Michael Wolf; **134–135** © Architects Team 3 Pte Ltd, Singapore; **139** © Rocco Design Architects Ltd.; **141t** © Leung, Hing-yee Joan; **141b** © Simon Kwan & Associates Limited; **142** © EDGE Design Institute Ltd. Image courtesy EDGE Design Institute Ltd.; **143** © Gary Chang/EDGE Design Institute Ltd. Image courtesy EDGE Design Institute Ltd.; **144–145** © Zaha Hadid Architects; **146–147** ©Taoho Design; **149** ©Wong & Ouyang (HK) Ltd., Estate of Paul Rudolph/Paul Rudolph Heritage Foundation; **150–151** © Chihoi. Image courtesy Chihoi; **154** © Hong Kong Trade Development Council; **155** © Dong Kingman Junior; **156** © Chung Wah Nan Architects Limited; **157** © Chung Wah Nan Architects Limited; **158** © Hilton; **159** © Hilton; **161t** © Graphic Communication Limited. Courtesy of The Hongkong and Shanghai Banking Corporation Limited; **161c** © Graphic Communication Limited. Reproduced with the permission of Hongkong Land Limited; **161bl** © Graphic Communication

Limited. Special acknowledgement to Dairy Farm Group; **161br** © Hilton; **162** Courtesy of Public Records Office, Government Records Service; **163** © HKSAR Government; **164** © Shinkenchiku-sha. Co. Ltd; **165** © Estate of Alan Fitch; **167** © All rights reserved; **169** © HKSAR Government; **170** © HKSAR Government; **171** © HKSAR Government; **173–175** © Lau Siu Hong Freeman. Image courtesy Lau Siu Hong Freeman; **179** © Helen Ting; **180–181** © Helen Ting; **183** © Photo Pictorial Publishers Ltd.; **185** © Fan Ho; **187** © Ian Lambot; **188** © Suenn Ho; **189** © Greg Girard; **191** ©Tiffany Chung; **193** © Annie Wan. Courtesy of Karin Weber Gallery; **194–195** © Chu Hing Wah. Courtesy of Mr David Pong Chun-Yee; **196–197** © the Artist and Osage Gallery; **199** © Wong Wo Bik; **200–201** ©Trevor Yeung. Image courtesy Trevor Yeung; **202–203** © May Fung; **204–205** © Benny Lam; **207** ©Yau Ching; **209** ©This edition of work is produced and archived in Videotage Media Art Collection (VMAC); **210–211** ©This edition of work is produced and archived in Videotage Media Art Collection (VMAC); **212–213** © Luke Ching Chin Wai; **215** © Anson Mak; **216–217** © Samson Young. Courtesy of Samson Young and Blindspot Gallery; **219** © Estate of Michael Wolf; **220–221** © Martin Parr & Blindspot Gallery. Courtesy of Blindspot Gallery; **222–223** © South Ho Siu Nam; **233** © Andreas Gursky/Courtesy Sprüth Magers/VG Bild-Kunst, Bonn – SACK, Seoul, 2020; **237** © Koon Wai Bong; **238–239** © Grotto Fine Art Limited and Hung Fai; **241** © Leung Kui Ting. Photo: © 2014 Christie's Images Limited; **243** © Kan Tai-keung; **245** © Hon Chi-fun; **248–249** © Leung Mee Ping. Image courtesy Leung Mee Ping. Photo: Dickson Lee; **251–253** © Catherine Yang; **255** © Luis Trust; **256–257** © Gaylord Chan; **260–261** © Estate of Szeto Keung; **263** © Frog King (Kwok Mang-ho); **265t** © Estate of Antonio Mak; **265b** © Chang Chao-Tang; **266–267** © Ho Siu Kee. Image courtesy Ho Siu Kee; **268–269** ©Wong Yankwai; **271** ©Yeung Tong Lung; **272–273** © Lui Chun-kwong. Image courtesy Lui Chun-kwong; **275** © Linda Chiu-han Lai; **277** © courtesy of Angela Su; **279** © Lee Ka-sing; **280** © Lee Ka-sing. Image courtesy Lee Ka-sing; **281t** © Lee Ka-sing; **281b** © Lee Ka-sing. Image courtesy Lee Ka-sing; **283** © Blues Wong; **288–289** © Lam Tung Pang. Image courtesy Lam Tung Pang; **291** © Lee Kit. Image courtesy Lee Kit; **292–293** © Lee Kit; **295** © Kwan Sheung Chi; **297** ©Wong Ping; **299** © Firenze Lai; **301t** ©Wilson Shieh; **301b** ©Wilson Shieh. Courtesy of Mr David Pong Chun-Yee; **302–303** © Wilson Shieh. Courtesy of Wilson Shieh; **304–305** ©Wong Chung Yu; **307** © Au Hoi Lam. Courtesy of Au Hoi Lam; **309** ©Wong Wai Yin; **311** © Kacey Wong.

INDEX

Page numbers in *italic* refer to the illustrations.